Theory of Mind in Middle Childhood and Adolescence

This landmark text integrates diverse perspectives on how humans understand others' minds (or 'theory of mind') beyond early childhood into middle childhood and adolescence. It explores how the neural, cognitive, and social changes of middle childhood and adolescence shape the ongoing development of theory of mind, and how theory of mind helps children navigate their lives.

Drawing on cutting-edge research from leading international experts, this book provides a survey and analysis of the current state and future direction of the field. It is organized around three themes relating to the key issues in contemporary research. The first part focuses on the biological and cognitive bases of theory of mind in middle childhood and adolescence. The second part goes on to explore the social predictors and consequences, considering how theory of mind is shaped by social experiences and, in turn, impacts children's social lives in middle childhood and adolescence. Finally, the third part focuses on theory of mind in the context of neurodiversity, disability, and youth mental health in middle childhood and adolescence.

Offering in-depth understanding for all students and scholars of developmental and cognitive psychology, neuroscience, clinical psychology and psychiatry, and education, this valuable text also identifies an agenda for future scholarship on this exciting topic.

Rory T. Devine is a developmental psychologist at the University of Birmingham, UK, with expertise in children's social and cognitive development, longitudinal research methods, and psychometrics. His research focuses on understanding individual differences in theory of mind and executive function from infancy to adulthood.

Serena Lecce is an associate professor in developmental and educational psychology at the Department of Brain and Behavioral Sciences, University of Pavia, Italy. She directs the Laboratory of Social Cognition – LASC – where she conducts investigations of people's social and emotional functioning and works closely with practitioners and teachers.

Theory of Mind in Middle Childhood and Adolescence

Integrating Multiple Perspectives

Edited by
Rory T. Devine and Serena Lecce

Routledge
Taylor & Francis Group
LONDON AND NEW YORK

First published 2021
by Routledge
2 Park Square, Milton Park, Abingdon, Oxon OX14 4RN

and by Routledge
605 Third Avenue, New York, NY 10158

Routledge is an imprint of the Taylor & Francis Group, an informa business

British Library Cataloguing-in-Publication Data
A catalogue record for this book is available from the British Library

Library of Congress Cataloging-in-Publication Data
Names: Devine, Rory T., author. | Lecce, Serena, author.
Title: Theory of mind in middle childhood and adolescence: integrating multiple perspectives/edited by Rory T. Devine and Serena Lecce.
Description: Abingdon, Oxon; New York, NY: Routledge, [2021] |
Includes bibliographical references and index.
Identifiers: LCCN 2020057101 | ISBN 9780367346188 (pbk) |
ISBN 9780367346171 (hbk) | ISBN 9780429326899 (ebk)
Subjects: LCSH: Philosophy of mind in children. | Cognition in children. |
Child development.
Classification: LCC BF723.P48 D48 2021 | DDC 155.4/13–dc23
LC record available at https://lccn.loc.gov/2020057101

ISBN: 978-0-367-34617-1 (hbk)
ISBN: 978-0-367-34618-8 (pbk)
ISBN: 978-0-429-32689-9 (ebk)

Typeset in Bembo
by Deanta Global Publishing Services Chennai India

Contents

Contributors

Ian A. Apperly is Professor of Cognition and Development and head of research at the School of Psychology, University of Birmingham, UK.

Sander Begeer is Associate Professor in the Faculty of Behavioural and Movement Sciences, Vrije Universiteit Amsterdam, Netherlands.

Sandra Bosacki is a professor in the Department of Educational Studies, Brock University, Canada.

Rory T. Devine is a Assistant Professor in Developmental Psychology in the School of Psychology at the University of Birmingham, UK.

Elian Fink is a Lecturer in Psychology in the School of Psychology at the University of Sussex, UK.

Sarah Foley is a Lecturer in Developmental Psychology at the Moray House School of Education in the University of Edinburgh, UK.

Kristin Hansen Lagattuta is Professor of Psychology at the University of California Davis, USA.

Jessica Hernandez is a research assistant in the Department of Psychology, University of Houston, USA.

Claire Hughes is Professor of Development Psychology at the Centre for Family Research, University of Cambridge, UK.

Hannah J. Kramer is based in the Department of Psychology, University of California Davis, USA.

Serena Lecce is an Associate Professor in developmental and educational psychology at the Department of Brain and Behavioral Sciences, University of Pavia, Italy.

Candida C. Peterson is Professor Emeritus at the School of Psychology, University of Queensland, Australia.

Elizabeth Redcay is Associate Professor in the Department of Psychology, University of Maryland, USA.

Katherine Rice Warnell is Assistant Professor in the Department of Psychology, Texas State University, USA.

Anke M. Scheeren is a Research Associate in the Faculty of Behavioural and Movement Sciences, Vrije Universiteit Amsterdam, Netherlands.

Carla Sharp is Director of the Development Psychopathology Lab and Professor of Psychology at the University of Houston, USA.

Acknowledgments

Rory and Serena wish to thank Helen Pritt for her editorial expertise and all of the authors who contributed to this volume.

Rory and Serena would like to express their continued personal gratitude to Claire Hughes for her guidance and friendship over the years.

Serena extends her thanks to Adriano Pagnin and Tomaso Vecchi for their encouragement since the very beginning of her PhD, to Paola Palladino, and all at the Department of Brain and Behavioral Sciences at the University of Pavia for their support. A special thanks also goes to Federica Bianco, Luca Ronchi, Paola Del Sette, Chiara Basile, Irene Ceccato, Alessia Rosi, Marta Nola, and Marcella Caputi, for their enthusiasm, hard work and commitment to research.

Serena also thanks her colleagues who share similar research interests for the stimulating discussions: Robin Banerjee, Valentina Bambini, Francisco Pons, Marc de Rosnay, Giuliana Pinto, and Floris van Vught.

Serena wishes to give a special thank you to Elena Cavallini, Giancarlo, and her family for their warm and unconditional support, and to her son, Mattia, who is a constant source of inspiration and love.

Rory would like to express his gratitude to Ian Apperly for his mentorship, his colleagues and the excellent graduate students in the School of Psychology at the University of Birmingham, who have been a vital source of inspiration and encouragement.

Finally, Rory would like to express special thanks to his husband, Chris O'Rourke, and his parents Rita and Michael Devine for their love and support.

Introduction

Why study theory of mind in middle childhood and adolescence?

Rory T. Devine and Serena Lecce

For more than four decades, researchers in fields as diverse as psychology, neuroscience, psychiatry, education, literary studies, philosophy, and zoology have sought to understand how humans make sense of others' behavior by inferring their mental states (i.e., thoughts, intentions, emotions, and desires). There are at least two reasons for the enduring fascination with the phenomenon that scholars call 'theory of mind'. First, although it is an everyday occurrence, reading others' minds is complex. It entails understanding that mental states not only exist, but are subjective and underpin others' behavior. Mental states are subjective with respect to the reality to which they refer (e.g., beliefs can be false), the agent that experiences them (e.g., the same reality can give rise to different mental states in different agents), and the time in which they are experienced (e.g., mental states are transitory). Understanding how humans master and use their understanding of others' minds therefore presents an inherently fascinating puzzle. Second, beyond the seeming complexity of this phenomenon, the ability to understand others' thoughts, intentions, emotions, and desires has real-world consequences. Being able to tune in to others' thoughts, feelings, and desires may be crucial for building social relationships and, more generally, for participation in society.

Vast numbers of studies have been published on the development and use of theory of mind over the past 40 years, but the majority of these studies have centered around early childhood, and more specifically, the preschool years. However, the past decade has seen a steady increase in work that extends the developmental scope of research on theory of mind beyond the narrow confines of early childhood into previously neglected developmental territory: Middle childhood and adolescence. The aim of this volume is to understand how the neural, cognitive, psychological, and social changes of middle childhood and adolescence shape the ongoing development of theory of mind and how theory of mind helps children to navigate life during this period of development. Although definitions of developmental stages are contested, middle childhood or juvenility is typically viewed as spanning ages 6 to 12 years and adolescence is viewed as the period commencing in puberty and ending with adult independence (Del Giudice, 2014; Foulkes & Blakemore, 2018). In this volume, we bring together distinct perspectives on theory of mind in middle childhood and adolescence to consolidate emerging knowledge and set the agenda for future research and theory. This introduction provides a context for the chapters to come. We begin by defining what we mean by theory of mind and considering how this capacity is typically measured. Next, we explain why studying theory of mind in middle childhood and adolescence is important. We finish by providing a synoptic overview of the contributions in this volume.

Theory of mind

Researchers from diverse disciplines have studied the capacity to attribute mental states to others using a variety of terms: 'Folk psychology' (e.g., Ratcliffe, 2007), 'common sense psychology' (Morton, 1980), 'mentalizing' (Frith & Frith, 2003), 'social understanding' (Carpendale & Lewis, 2006), 'mindreading' (Apperly, 2010), and, of course, 'theory of mind' (Premack & Woodruff, 1978). Although there may be a degree of overlap between these constructs, there are also some important differences among them. The terms 'folk psychology' and 'social understanding', encompass a wide range of psychological constructs used to explain others' behavior. For example, the ability to attribute emotions and feelings to others is often included under the term 'social understanding' (e.g., Hughes, 2011), while the capacity to appreciate the influence of enduring traits and biographical details on others' behavior is included in 'folk psychology' (e.g., Morton, 1980). The term 'mindreading' mainly refers to the actual use that people make of their mental-state inferences and encompasses the study of biases in mental-state attribution. The term 'theory of mind' stems from the work of Premack and Woodruff (1978) and is classically defined as the ability to attribute mental states to the self and others. Despite this broad definition, research on theory of mind has focused predominantly on preschoolers' understanding of others' (false) beliefs and (different) desires.

Some theorists have questioned the use of the term 'theory of mind' because of its narrow focus, the fact that it connotes possession rather than use, and because it signals loyalty to a particular theoretical viewpoint (Apperly, 2010; Carpendale & Lewis, 2006; Harris, 1991). In choosing the term 'theory of mind' for the title of this volume, we do not wish to constrain the definition of this term, imply that reading minds is an all-or-nothing affair, or endorse a particular theoretical stance. Instead, we seek to position our work alongside the body of research and theory on preschoolers' understanding of mind while expanding the scope of this work to new questions and perspectives. Reflecting the rich diversity of scholarship on theory of mind, the contributions to this volume use different terminology to refer to the act of attributing mental states to others.

Measuring theory of mind

The dominant focus on preschool children in theory of mind research can perhaps be linked to the availability of a brief, inexpensive, and widely-accepted measure: The false belief task. In this task, children are required to predict or explain a character's behavior by inferring the character's mistaken beliefs about the location of an object (moved in the character's absence) (Wimmer & Perner, 1983), the unexpected contents of a standard container (e.g., pencils in a candy box) (Perner et al., 1987), or the misleading identity of an object (e.g., a sponge that looks like a rock) (Gopnik & Astington, 1988). Despite theoretical challenges (e.g., Scott & Baillargeon, 2017; Bloom & German, 2000; Wellman & Liu, 2004), the measure has been widely adopted in the field because it is reliable (e.g., Hughes et al., 2000) and highly sensitive to developmental differences in early childhood (Wellman et al., 2001). Beyond the false belief task, researchers have also charted the early emergence of children's ability to reason about the difference between their own desires and others' desires, their own beliefs and others' beliefs, and their own knowledge and others' knowledge (Wellman & Liu, 2004). Complex false belief tasks have also emerged to measure children's ability to reason about a character's (false) beliefs about another character's beliefs (i.e., second-order false beliefs) (Perner & Wimmer, 1985) and to predict emotions based on false beliefs (Harris et al., 1989). These measures are also sensitive to developmental differences in reasoning about others' minds in early childhood but standard versions of these tasks exhibit marked ceiling effects at the start of middle childhood. The developmental sensitivity of these widely used measures among typically developing children (e.g., Wellman & Liu, 2004) presents a challenge for extending research on theory of mind beyond early childhood.

Consensus has yet to emerge on how best to characterize theory of mind in middle childhood and adolescence. Consequently, the past decade has seen the emergence of a range of different tests. These so-called 'advanced' theory of mind tasks employ a range of stimuli including vignettes (e.g., Banerjee et al., 2011; White et al., 2009), animations (e.g., Austin et al., 2014), film clips (e.g., Devine & Hughes, 2013), still images (e.g., Sebastian et al., 2012), and interactive tasks (e.g., Dumontheil et al., 2010). In addition to using a variety of different stimuli, measures focus on distinct skills including taking others' perspectives (e.g., Dumontheil et al., 2010), attributing intentions (e.g., Leno et al., 2020), and interpreting or explaining behavior (e.g., Banerjee et al., 2011; Devine & Hughes, 2013). Response formats are also varied and include open-ended verbal/written responses (e.g., White et al., 2009), multiple-choice responses (e.g., Osterhaus et al., 2016), and decision-making response times and accuracy (e.g., Apperly et al., 2011). The field has yet to converge upon a universally accepted set of tasks but results from numerous cross-sectional and longitudinal studies point to clear gains in performance on these diverse measures of theory of mind across middle childhood and adolescence (e.g., Apperly et al., 2011; Banerjee et al., 2011; Devine & Hughes, 2013; Dumontheil et al., 2010; Im-Bolter et al., 2016; Lagattuta et al., 2016; Lecce et al., 2017; Osterhaus et al., 2016; Peterson & Wellman, 2019). The diversity of measurement approaches and relative merits and limitations of these measures are considered throughout this volume.

Why middle childhood and adolescence?

Having now defined theory of mind and considered how this construct is measured, we now turn to a more pressing question: Why study theory of mind in middle childhood and adolescence? When asked why he wanted to climb Mount Everest, the British explorer George Mallory quipped 'Because it's there' (*New York Times*, 1923). The relative paucity of research on theory of mind beyond early childhood offers new opportunities for exploration but the absence of research on a topic is not a justification in itself. There are, however, two compelling scientific reasons for extending the developmental reaches of research on theory of mind. First, extending the scope of research on theory of mind into middle childhood and adolescence provides an unrivaled opportunity to test existing theories (which are based largely on data from early childhood) and consider new accounts of theory of mind development (e.g. Apperly, 2010). Second, middle childhood and adolescence are periods characterized by marked biological, cognitive, social, and psychological changes (e.g., Del Giudice, 2014; Foulkes & Blakemore, 2018). Extending research on theory of mind into middle childhood and adolescence raises the possibility of illuminating how theory of mind is shaped by and contributes to these changes.

Theoretical accounts of theory of mind are arguably incomplete in at least three ways (Apperly, 2010; Apperly et al., 2009). First, the emphasis on theory of mind in early childhood has led several theorists to point out that passing a false belief task at age four is not tantamount to possessing a fully-fledged adult understanding of others' minds (e.g., Apperly et al., 2009; Carpendale & Lewis, 2006). Second, alongside this incomplete description of development, prominent theories of theory of mind rely largely on insights gleaned from studies of preschool children (Apperly et al., 2009). Consequently, cognitive (e.g., executive function accounts) and social accounts (e.g., the sibling effect) of theory of mind focus mainly on the emergence of children's understanding of others' desires and beliefs and are relatively silent about the development and use of theory of mind beyond this milestone (e.g., Apperly, 2010; Devine & Hughes, 2014, 2016). Without research on middle childhood and adolescence, it is unclear, for example, if executive function continues to support the ongoing development of theory of mind, or supports the immediate use of theory of mind, or some combination of the two (e.g., Devine et al., 2016). Third, restricting research on theory of mind to early childhood hampers understanding of the naturally occurring and widely documented variation in children's understanding of others' minds (e.g., Hughes & Devine, 2015). By extending research beyond the initial emergence of theory of mind, it is possible to understand whether these apparent differences are temporary or lasting or represent genuine differences in tuning in to others' minds rather than differences in other related capacities (e.g., Apperly, 2012; Hughes & Devine, 2015).

Research on theory of mind in middle childhood and adolescence is likely to provide a fertile ground for future work because the biological, cognitive, psychological, and social transitions associated with middle childhood and adolescence open up new opportunities for research that is not possible in the preschool years. Over the past two decades, researchers have documented marked cognitive and neural changes across middle childhood and adolescence relevant to children's theory of mind. Specifically, cross-sectional and longitudinal studies show that executive functions (a suite of cognitive processes involved in overriding entrenched habits, switching between tasks, and updating information held in mind) show continued growth across middle childhood and adolescence (e.g., Obradovic et al., 2018; Lecce et al., 2017). Moreover, the organization of executive function appears to change across middle childhood and adolescence with models indicating increasing specialization (e.g., Friedman & Miyake, 2017). Large-scale neuroimaging studies highlight that middle childhood and adolescence are times of marked structural change. For example, cortical grey matter volume peaks in middle childhood and declines throughout adolescence, and cerebral white matter volume increases between middle childhood and mid-adolescence before stabilizing in late adolescence (Mills et al., 2016). Evidence for increased functional specialization across middle childhood and adolescence is also emerging: Cross-sectional studies indicate that as children progress through middle childhood and adolescence, neural responses correlate more strongly within specific functional networks (e.g., the 'social brain' network encompassing the bilateral temporo-parietal junction, precuneus, dorso-, middle-, and ventromedial prefrontal cortex) than across functional networks (Richardson et al., 2018). Extending work on theory of mind into middle childhood and adolescence presents new opportunities to examine the cognitive and neural basis of theory of mind.

Middle childhood and adolescence are closely tied with important social milestones. In most 'Western' nations, middle childhood coincides with the period of compulsory primary education and adolescence overlaps with the transition to secondary education and, later on, employment or higher education (e.g., OECD, 2018). Although experiences are likely to differ according to cultural context, participation in formal education requires that children navigate daily interactions with peers and teachers at school. Studies point to increasing time spent with peers and decreasing time spent with family members as children traverse middle childhood and adolescence (Larson & Richards, 1991; Larson et al., 1996). Difficulty managing interactions with peers and teachers cast a long shadow: Poor social interactions with peers and teachers predict later mental health difficulties, poorer academic outcomes, and even difficulties in work (Bornstein et al., 2010; Burt et al., 2008; McCormick & O'Connor, 2015). Alongside the social demands of formal education, middle childhood and adolescence are accompanied by changing family dynamics. Meta-analyses reveal that although parent–child conflict declines in frequency from early (age 10 to 12 years) to late adolescence (age 17 to 22 years), conflict increases in intensity from early to mid-adolescence (age 13 to 16 years) (Laursen et al., 1998). These characteristic changes in children's social lives make middle childhood and adolescence an ideal context for studying the links between theory of mind and children's social lives (e.g., Hughes, 2016).

Finally, alongside these cognitive, neural, and social changes, middle childhood and adolescence are associated with vulnerability for psychological disorders. Data from 27 countries indicate that approximately 12% of children aged between 6 and 11 years and 20% of children aged between 12 and 18 years have a mental health disorder (Polanczyk et al., 2015). Moreover, approximately half of adults with diagnosed mental disorders experienced the onset of their disorder before the age of 15 years (Kim-Cohen et al., 2003). Mental health problems are the leading cause of disability in middle childhood and adolescence and are associated with friendlessness, peer rejection, and poor social adjustment at school (Bornstein et al., 2010; Erskine et al., 2015; Szekely et al., 2016). Emerging evidence from adults suggests that difficulties understanding others' minds cross-cut traditional diagnoses (Cotter et al., 2018). Extending research into middle childhood and adolescence offers a chance to examine whether difficulties tuning into others' minds explain why children with mental health problems experience adverse social outcomes or whether theory of mind acts as a risk or protective factor for mental health problems.

Chapter overview

This volume is organized around three key themes that have emerged from contemporary research on theory of mind in middle childhood and adolescence. The first section focuses on the cognitive and biological bases of theory of mind in middle childhood and adolescence. The second section considers how theory of mind is shaped by social experiences and, in turn, impacts on children's social lives in middle childhood and adolescence. The third section examines theory of mind in the context of neurodiversity, disability, and mental health in middle childhood and adolescence. We now briefly summarize the content of these chapters.

Part I

The four chapters in this section highlight how extending the developmental reaches of theory of mind research beyond early childhood provides new opportunities to gain a more complete understanding of theory of mind. In Chapter 1, Lagattuta and Kramer offer fresh insight on 'what develops' beyond the achievement of false belief understanding in early childhood by examining age-related changes in how children and adolescents make connections between different mental states and life events when predicting and explaining others' behavior. In Chapter 2, Apperly considers how extending the developmental scope of research on 'mindreading' paves the way for reconsidering existing cognitive accounts of theory of mind, including executive function accounts, and generating new theories about the processes underlying the use of mindreading. In Chapter 3, Devine argues that research on theory of mind beyond early childhood provides an opportunity to examine whether individual differences in children's understanding of others' minds are genuine (i.e., stable) and meaningful. In Chapter 4, Rice-Warnell and Redcay examine the neural basis of theory of mind by capitalizing on recent insights on the development of the 'mentalizing network' in middle childhood and adolescence.

Part II

The four contributions to this section investigate how theory of mind is shaped by and contributes to children's social lives in middle childhood and adolescence. Each chapter considers a different facet of children's social lives in middle childhood and adolescence. In Chapter 5, Foley and Hughes interrogate existing evidence about the family correlates of theory of mind in middle childhood and adolescence. In Chapter 6, Fink examines the specificity and potential bidirectionality of the links between theory of mind and close friendships in middle childhood and adolescence. In Chapter 7, Bosacki extends this focus further by considering the complexity of the links between mindreading and children's wider peer relationships in middle childhood and adolescence. In Chapter 8, the concluding chapter of this section, Lecce considers the wider implications of participation in formal education for children's theory of mind and proposes that theory of mind may have consequences for children's academic success.

Part III

The three chapters in the final section examine theory of mind in middle childhood and adolescence in the context of neurodiversity, disability, and youth mental health. In Chapter 9, Begeer and Scheeren highlight how extending research on theory of mind beyond early childhood provides the chance to challenge long-established accounts of autism (e.g., the 'mind blindness' account). In Chapter 10, Peterson demonstrates that studying theory of mind in deaf children can provide new insights about the ongoing development of theory of mind in middle childhood and adolescence, including the importance of interactions with parents, peers, and teachers. In Chapter 11, the final contribution, Sharp and Hernandez propose a dimensional model of mindreading and consider the links between mindreading and psychopathology in middle childhood and adolescence, a developmental period associated with the onset of major psychological disorders.

References

Apperly, I. (2010). *Mindreaders: The Cognitive Basis of Theory of Mind*. London: Psychology Press.

Apperly, I. (2012). What is "theory of mind"? Concepts, cognitive processes and individual differences. *Quarterly Journal of Experimental Psychology, 65*, 825–839. DOI: 10.1080/17470218.2012.676055

Apperly, I.A., Samson, D., & Humphreys, G.W. (2009). Studies of adults can inform accounts of theory of mind development. *Developmental Psychology, 45*, 190–201. DOI: 10.1037/a0014098

Apperly, I.A., Warren, F., Andrews, B.J., Grant, J., & Todd, S. (2011). Developmental continuity in theory of mind: Speed and accuracy of belief-desire reasoning in children and adults. *Child Development, 82*, 1691–1703. DOI: 10.1111/j.1467-8624.2011.01635.x

Austin, G., Groppe, K., & Elsner, B. (2014). The reciprocal relationship between executive function and theory of mind in middle childhood: A 1-year longitudinal perspective. *Frontiers in Psychology, 5*, 655. DOI: 10.3389/fpsyg.2014.00655

Banerjee, R., Watling, D., & Caputi, M. (2011). Peer relations and the understanding of faux pas: Longitudinal evidence for bidirectional associations. *Child Development, 82*, 1887–1905. DOI: 10.1111/j.1467-8624.2011.01669.x

Bloom, P., & German, T.P. (2000). Two reasons to abandon the false belief task as a test of theory of mind. *Cognition*, 77, B25–B31.

Bornstein, M.H., Hahn, C.-S., & Haynes, O.M. (2010). Social competence, externalizing, and internalizing behavioral adjustment from early childhood through early adolescence: Developmental cascades. *Development and Psychopathology, 22*, 717–735. DOI: 10.1017/S0954579410000416

Burt, K., Obradovic, J., Long, J.D., Masten, A. (2008). The interplay of social competence and psychopathology over 20 years: Testing transactional and cascade models. *Child Development, 79*, 359–374.

Carpendale, J.I.M., & Lewis, C. (2006). *How Children Develop Social Understanding*. Oxford: Blackwell Publishing.

Cotter, J., Granger, K., Backx, R., Hobbs, M., Looi, C.Y., & Barnett, J.H. (2018). Social cognitive dysfunction as a clinical marker: A systematic review of meta-analyses across 30 clinical conditions. *Neuroscience and Biobehavioral Reviews, 84*, 92–99. DOI: 10.1016/j.neubiorev.2017.11.014

Del Giudice, M. (2014). Middle childhood: An evolutionary-developmental synthesis. *Child Development Perspectives, 8*, 193–200. DOI: 10.1111/cdep.12084

Devine, R.T., & Hughes, C. (2013). Silent films and strange stories: Theory of mind, gender, and social experiences in middle childhood. *Child Development, 84*, 989–1003. DOI: 10.1111/cdev.12017

Devine, R.T., & Hughes, C. (2014). Relations between false belief understanding and executive function in early childhood: A meta-analysis. *Child Development, 85*, 1777–1794. DOI: 10.1111/cdev.12237

Devine, R.T., & Hughes, C. (2016). Measuring theory of mind across middle childhood: Reliability and validity of the silent films and strange stories tasks. *Journal of Experimental Child Psychology, 149*, 23–40. DOI: 10.1016/j.jecp.2015.07.011

Devine, R.T., White, N., Ensor, R., & Hughes, C. (2016). Theory of mind in middle childhood: Longitudinal associations with executive function and social competence. *Developmental Psychology, 52*, 758–771. DOI: 10.1037/dev0000105

Dumontheil, I., Apperly, I.A., & Blakemore, S. (2010). Online usage of theory of mind continues to develop in late adolescence. *Developmental Science, 13*, 331–338.

Erskine, H.E., Moffitt, T.E., Copeland, W.E., Costello, E.J., Ferrari, A.J., Patton, G., Degenhardt, L., Vos, T., Whiteford, H.A. & Scott, J.G. (2015). A heavy burden on young minds: The global burden of mental and substance use disorders in children and youth. *Psychological Medicine, 2*, 1551–1563. DOI: 10.1017/S0033291714002888

Foulkes, L., & Blakemore, S.-J. (2018). Studying individual differences in human adolescent brain development. *Nature Neuroscience, 21*, 315–323. DOI: 10.1038/s41593-018-0078-4

Friedman, N.P., & Miyake, A. (2017). Unity and diversity of executive functions: Individual differences as a window on cognitive structure. *Cortex, 86*, 186–204. DOI: 10.1016/j.cortex.2016.04.023

Frith, U., & Frith, C.D. (2003). Development and neurophysiology of mentalising. *Philosophical Transactions of the Royal Society of London Series B, 358*, 459–473.

Gopnik, A. & Astington, J.W. (1988). Children's understanding of representational change and its relation to the understanding of false belief and the appearance-reality distinction. *Child Development, 59*, 26–37. Doi: 10.2307/1130386

Harris, P. (1991). The work of the imagination. In A. Whiten (Ed.), *Natural Theories of Mind: Evolution, Development and Simulation of Everyday Mindreading* (pp. 283–304). Oxford: Basil Blackwell.

Harris, P.L., Johnson, C.N., Hutton, D., Andrews, G., & Cooke, T. (1989). Young children's theory of mind and emotion. *Cognition and Emotion, 3*, 379–400.

Hughes, C. (2011). *Social Understanding and Social Lives: From Toddlerhood through to the Transition to School*. London: Psychology Press.

Hughes, C. (2016). Theory of mind grows up: Reflections on new research on theory of mind in middle childhood and adolescence. *Journal of Experimental Child Psychology, 149*, 1–5. DOI: 10.1016/j.jecp.2016.01.017

Hughes, C., Adlam, A., Happé, F., Jackson, J., Taylor, A., & Caspi, A. (2000). Good test-retest reliability for standard and advanced false-belief tasks across a wide range of abilities. *Journal of Child Psychology and Psychiatry, 41*, 483–490.

Hughes, C., & Devine, R.T. (2015). Individual differences in theory of mind from preschool to adolescence: Achievements and directions. *Child Development Perspectives, 9*, 149–153.

Im-Bolter, N., Agostino, A., & Owens-Jaffray, K. (2016). Theory of mind in middle childhood and early adolescence: Different from before? *Journal of Experimental Child Psychology, 149*, 98–115. DOI: 10.1016/j.jecp.2015.12.006

Kim-Cohen, J., Caspi, A., Moffitt, T.E., Harrington, H., Milne, B.J., & Poulton, R. (2003). Prior juvenile diagnoses in adults with mental disorder: Developmental follow-back of a prospective-longitudinal cohort. *Archives of General Psychiatry, 60*, 709–717.

Lagattuta, K.H., Elrod, N.M., & Kramer, H.J. (2016). How do thoughts, emotions, and decisions align? A new way to examine theory of mind during middle childhood and beyond. *Journal of Experimental Child Psychology, 149*, 116–133. DOI: 10.1016/j.jecp.2016.01.013

Larson, R., & Richards, M.H. (1991). Daily companionship in late childhood and early adolescence: Changing developmental contexts. *Child Development, 62*, 284–300.

Larson, R.W., Richards, M.H., Moneta, G., Holmbeck, G., & Duckett, E. (1996). Changes in adolescents' daily interactions with their families from ages 10 to 18: Disengagement and transformation. *Developmental Psychology, 32*, 744–754.

Laursen, B., Coy, K.C., & Collins, W.A. (1998). Reconsidering changes in parent-child conflict across adolescence: A meta-analysis. *Child Development, 69*, 817–832.

Lecce, S., Bianco, F., Devine, R.T., & Hughes, C. (2017). Relations between theory of mind and executive function in middle childhood: A short-term longitudinal study. *Journal of Experimental Child Psychology, 163*, 69–86.

Leno, V.C., Chandler, S., White, P., Yorke, I., Charman, T., Jones, C.R.G., Happé, F., Baird, G., Pickles, A. & Simonoff, E. (2020). Associations between theory of mind and conduct problems in autistic and nonautistic youth. *Autism Research*. DOI: 10.1002/aur.2346

McCormick, M.P., & O'Connor, E.E. (2015). Teacher-child relationship quality and academic achievement in elementary school: Does gender matter? *Journal of Educational Psychology, 107*, 502–516. DOI: 10.1037/a0037457

Mills, K.L., Goddings, A.L., Herting, M.M., Meuwese, R., Blakemore, S.-J., Crone, E.A., Dahl, R.E., Güroglu, B., Raznahan, A., Sowell, E.R. & Tamnes, C.K. (2016). Structural brain development between childhood and adulthood: Convergence across four longitudinal samples. *NeuroImage*, *141*, 273–281.

Morton, A. (1980). *Frames of Mind: Constraints on the Common-Sense Conception of the Mental.* Oxford: Clarendon Press.

New York Times (1923). Climbing Mount Everest is work for supermen. (1923, March 18). *New York Times.*

Obradovic, J., Sulik, M.J., Finch, J.E., & Tirado-Strayer, N. (2018). Assessing students' executive functions in the classroom: Validating a scalable group-based procedure. *Journal of Applied Developmental Psychology*, *55*, 4–13.

OECD (2018). *Education at a Glance: OECD indicators.* Paris: OECD Publishing. DOI: 10.1787/eag-2018-en

Osterhaus, C., Koerber, S., & Sodian, B. (2016). Scaling advanced theory-of-mind tasks. *Child Development*, *87*, 1971–1991. DOI: 10.1111/cdev.12566

Perner, J., Leekam, S.R., & Wimmer, H. (1987). Three-year-olds' difficulty with false belief: The case for a conceptual deficit. *British Journal of Developmental Psychology*, *5*, 125–137. DOI: 10.11111/j.2044-835X.1987.tb01048.x

Perner, J., & Wimmer, H. (1985). "John thinks that Mary thinks that..." Attribution of second-order beliefs by 5-to 10-year old children. *Journal of Experimental Child Psychology*, *39*, 437–471.

Peterson, C.C., & Wellman, H.M. (2019). Longitudinal theory of mind (ToM) development from preschool to adolescence with and without ToM delay. *Child Development*, *90*, 1917–1934. DOI: 10.1111/cdev13064

Polanczyk, G.V., Salum, G.A., Sugaya, L.S., Caye, A., & Rohde, L.A. (2015). Annual research review: A meta-analysis of the worldwide prevalence of mental disorders in children and adolescents. *Journal of Child Psychology and Psychiatry*, *56*, 345–365. DOI: 10.1111/jcpp.12381

Premack, D., & Woodruff, G. (1978). Does the chimpanzee have a theory of mind? *Behavioral and Brain Sciences*, *4*, 515–526.

Ratcliffe, M. (2007). *Rethinking Common-Sense Psychology: A Critique of Folk Psychology, Theory of Mind, and Simulation.* Basingstoke: Palgrave Macmillan.

Richardson, H., Lisandrelli, G., Riobueno-Naylor, A., & Saxe, R. (2018). Development of the social brain from age three to twelve years. *Nature Communications*, *9*, 1027. DOI: 10.1038/s41467-018-03399-2

Sebastian, C.L., Fontaine, N.M.G., Bird, G., Blakemore, S.-J., DeBrito, S.A., McCrory, E.J.P., & Viding, E. (2012). Neural processing associated with cognitive and affective theory of mind in adolescents and adults. *Social Cognitive and Affective Neuroscience*, *7*, 53–63.

Scott, R.M., & Baillargeon, R. (2017). Early false-belief understanding. *Trends in Cognitive Sciences*, *21*, 237–249.

Szekely, E., Pappa, I., Wilson, J.D., Bhamidi, S., Jaddoe, V.W., Verhulst, F.C., Tiemeier, H. & Shaw, P. (2016). Childhood peer network characteristics: Genetic influences and links with early mental health trajectories. *Journal of Child Psychology and Psychiatry*, *57*, 687–694.

Wellman, H.M., Cross, D., & Watson, J. (2001). Meta-analysis of theory-of-mind development: The truth about false belief. *Child Development*, *72*, 655–684.

Wellman, H.M., & Liu, D. (2004). Scaling theory-of-mind tasks. *Child Development*, *75*, 523–541.

White, S., Hill, E., Happe, F., & Frith, U. (2009). Revisiting the strange stories: Revealing mentalising impairments in Autism. *Child Development, 80,* 1097–1117.

Wimmer, H., & Perner, J. (1983). Beliefs about beliefs: Representation and constraining function of wrong beliefs in young children's understanding of deception. *Cognition, 13,* 103–128.

Part I

Cognitive and biological underpinnings

1 Advanced theory of mind in middle childhood and adulthood

Inferring mental states and emotions from life history

Kristin Hansen Lagattuta and Hannah J. Kramer

Children's understanding of their own and others' mental states (e.g., desires, preferences, emotions, beliefs, and thoughts), or 'theory of mind', undergoes significant development from infancy through early childhood. By their fifth birthday, if not earlier, most typically developing children understand quite a lot about minds and connections between minds and the world. For example, they know that people can differ in their desires, preferences, and emotions; they understand that emotions can derive from both situational and mental causes; and they can predict and explain individuals' beliefs, even when those beliefs are false (Kramer & Lagattuta, in press; Wellman, 2014). Despite these remarkable achievements, there is still much to learn. Being a competent interpreter and perspective-taker of the what (e.g., what is someone thinking about?) and why (e.g., why are they having those thoughts?) of mental states, as well as appreciating the interconnectedness among different mental states and life experiences (e.g., how will this past experience bias future mental states? How do thoughts affect emotions?) is no simple feat. There are intriguing setbacks along this developmental path, with even adults committing mindreading errors (Epley et al., 2004; Todd et al., 2011). Indeed, the recognition that children do not 'achieve' a fully mature theory of mind once they pass a basic false belief task has gained increasing momentum in recent years, motivating developmental scientists (many contributing to the current volume) to investigate further progress in theory of mind during middle childhood and beyond (Devine et al., 2016; Lecce et al., 2014; Wang et al., 2016).

In this chapter, we draw primarily from our own research on advanced theory of mind, particularly studies on children's and adults' causal reasoning about how people's life events affect their current and future emotions, thoughts, and decisions, as well as contribute to potential diversity in how individuals interpret the same situation. We also consider children's and adults' beliefs about mental state connections, including desire–emotion, thought–emotion, and expectation–emotion, as well as their inferences about valence cohesion among people's emotions, thoughts, and decisions. Although we emphasize age-related changes, we also discuss sources of individual differences.

We conclude with ideas for future research. Our overall approach has been to delineate developmental progression in explicit mental state reasoning by designing tasks that, although age-appropriate, purposely challenge children's and adults' thinking about the inherent complexity of people's lives and minds (for further reviews, see Kramer & Lagattuta, in press; Lagattuta, 2014, 2018; Lagattuta et al., 2014a, 2015; Lagattuta & Weller, 2014).

The impact of past events on future mental states

Prior life events bias future mental states: What a person has experienced – the good, the bad, and the more mundane – can influence how they feel, think, and make decisions later in time (Karniol & Ross, 1996; Morewedge et al., 2005). Indeed, essential clues as to the what (e.g., what is Mary thinking about? Why is Mary sad?) and why (e.g., why is she having those thoughts and feelings?) of an individual's internal mental states can be gleaned by considering what has happened to them previously. This 'life history theory of mind' (i.e., the knowledge that variations in life events can bias people's future mental states; Lagattuta et al., 2018) follows an extended developmental trajectory. Although there are foundations in early childhood, improvements continue through middle childhood and into adulthood.

Thinking about the past

In initial tests of this knowledge, Lagattuta and colleagues (1997) presented three- to six-year-olds with scenarios featuring characters who experienced a negative event (e.g., Brian feels sad after a yellow car crashes into his parked bicycle), and then a few days later, re-experienced the negative emotion after seeing a reminder of that past event (e.g., the yellow car). Across three studies, results showed significant increases between three and six years in explaining characters' current negative emotions as caused by thinking about the past, with only six-year-olds consistently linking the cause of the thoughts to the visual cue (e.g., 'Brian feels sad because the car reminds him about it'). In contrast, younger children often explained that people remembered the past because 'they wanted to' or 'liked to', failing to recognize that thoughts can be triggered uncontrollably and without intention (see also Davis et al., 2010; Flavell & Green, 1999). Further extensions by Lagattuta and Wellman (2001) clarified that young children first reliably exhibit knowledge about emotions caused by past-oriented thoughts when explaining negative emotions that are atypical or mismatch current events. Not until age six did children consistently explain positive emotions (typical and atypical), typical negative emotions, and behaviors as caused by remembering the past.

Anticipating the future

Past events not only carry weight over time by creating the potential for remembering the past, but they also influence people's anticipations about what will happen next. Indeed, some scientists have proposed that the fundamental purpose of memory is its utility for imagining the future (Schacter et al., 2007; Suddendorf & Corballis, 2007). In Lagattuta (2007), three- to six-year-olds and adults learned about characters who experienced a single negative event (e.g., David feels sad after a red-haired boy stole his toy) and many days later felt worried or made a preventative decision (e.g., hid toys) after seeing that same perpetrator or someone who looked highly similar. Of central interest was the frequency that participants explained characters' current emotions or decisions as caused by thinking a negative event would occur in the future because of the past (e.g., 'Because he thinks the boy will do something bad because he's done bad things before'). Participants age five and older, compared to three- and four-year-olds, more consistently provided these past-to-future explanations. When task difficulty increased (also in Lagattuta, 2007) by requiring participants to first predict and then explain emotions, significant differences emerged between childhood and adulthood. Adults exhibited stronger awareness of the biasing impact of the past on characters' future-oriented mental states as well as the individuated nature of these thoughts and emotions – naïve others would not feel worried due to lack of experience or knowledge about the past. Note that these age differences emerged despite multiple controls in place to verify story comprehension, eliminate memory demands, and scaffold incomplete verbal responses.

Integrating multiple past events

Clearly, a person's life history is far more complex than a single episode. Individuals often have multiple encounters with the same agent, and not all of them are consistent in valence. Thus, we reasoned that further growth in awareness of connections between life experience and mind would likely involve learning how to integrate and weight multiple past events to infer people's mental states. To test this, Lagattuta and Sayfan (2013) presented four- to ten-year-olds and adults with illustrated trials, each featuring a focal character who had two prior experiences with the same perpetrator: Two negative (NN), two positive (PP), a negative followed by a positive (NP), or a positive followed by a negative (PN). Participants predicted how the focal character would feel (happy versus worried, including intensity), think (something good versus bad will happen, including likelihood), and decide (approach versus avoid the perpetrator, including proximity) when re-encountering that agent again. To gain deeper insight into how children and adults prioritized different kinds of past experiences (negative versus positive; initial versus recent past), we used eye-tracking to measure visual attention to past event pictures while participants made mental state judgments. Pilot testing was conducted to equate negative and positive past events in emotional intensity and visual interest, and we included control questions to verify comprehension.

Results showed that children as young as four to five years of age understand that people's past experiences with a particular agent will shape how they later feel, think, and make decisions when seeing that same agent. All age groups attributed significantly more intense positive emotions, thoughts, and decisions for PP > NP > PN > NN pasts. With age, participants inferred a stronger impact of past experience on future mental states (e.g., more intensely negative mental states for NN and PN pasts); thus, differentiation in mental state judgments by past widened during middle childhood and into adulthood. The prioritization of the recent past in mixed-valence trials also appeared in visual attention. PN pasts elicited a recency attention bias (i.e., greater looking to the negative versus positive past event), which magnified with age. Only adults exhibited a recency attention bias for NP pasts. Visual attention also correlated with reasoning: Participants with greater biased attention to the negative event in PN pasts predicted that characters would feel more intensely worried, anticipate a higher likelihood of harm, and make more extreme avoidant decisions; likewise, a greater emphasis on recency in NP pasts correlated with more positive emotion, thought, and decision judgments. Although prior research has shown that children and adults look most at information they find meaningful in a visual scene (Henderson & Hayes, 2017; Lagattuta & Kramer, 2017; Wolfe & Horowitz, 2017), this was the first evidence that researchers can predict semantic judgments based on visual attention. That is, the attention biases appeared to capture aspects of how individuals were actually thinking about the relative importance and future impact of different past events.

Understanding direct connections between past experience and future mental states, however, is conceptually simpler than the awareness that life events can bias how a person feels, thinks, and make decisions across a wide range of future circumstances. That is, humans regularly generalize to new situations that share some similarity to the past (Dunsmoor & Murphy, 2015; Lindquist, 2013; Lerner et al., 2015; Strack & Deutsch, 2004; Wyer et al., 2012). To test children's understanding that past events can influence mental states even when meeting unknown agents, Lagattuta and Kramer (2019) made a critical change to Lagattuta and Sayfan (2013). Instead of the same perpetrator re-appearing in the final scene, it was an agent who looked highly similar to the one from the past. This similar-looking agent was repeatedly marked as 'new' and 'never seen before'. We reasoned that these changes would expose weaknesses or gaps in young children's understanding. Although eye-tracking data confirmed that four- to five-year-olds looked to past events when reasoning about characters' reactions to someone new, this age group discounted the relevance of that information and predicted that characters would have positive emotions, thoughts, and decisions regardless of the past (PP = NP = PN = NN). Adults, in contrast, presumed the same hierarchical judgment pattern (albeit more tempered in intensity) as when the same exact perpetrator returned (i.e., more positive mental state forecasts for PP > NP > PN > NN pasts). Between the ages of six and ten, children moved closer to the adult pattern, with earliest insights about indirect generalization shown for the PP > NN contrast. In a related measure, six- to ten-year-olds also assumed stricter boundaries to the biasing impact of life history on new situations compared to adults.

Conceptually replicating Lagattuta and Sayfan (2013), visual attention biases predicted verbal judgments: Stronger recency biases for PN pasts correlated with more negative emotions, thoughts, and decisions; stronger recency biases in NP pasts correlated with more positive mental state forecasts.

Interim summary and individual differences

Children develop the initial understanding that prior life experiences can impact future mental states by three to five years of age, with the strongest insights revealed when asked to explain negative emotions that mismatch current events. During middle childhood and into adulthood, children better integrate and weight multiple pieces of past event evidence to infer how those life experiences will bias future mental states in both direct and generalized ways. Indeed, adults anticipate minds to generalize far beyond initial episodes to shape how individuals respond to a wide range of new situations. Given the significant relation between theory of mind and executive function (higher-order, self-regulatory cognitive abilities; see Diamond, 2013) in three- to five-year-olds (Carlson & Moses, 2001; Devine & Hughes, 2014; Sabbagh et al., 2006), as well as in older children and adults (Apperly et al., 2009; Hughes & Devine, 2015; Lecce et al., 2017; Wang et al., 2016), we have investigated connections between four- to ten-year-olds' and adults' life history theory of mind and individual variability in executive function. Lagattuta et al. (2018) found that both age and verbal working memory independently predicted stronger knowledge that past experiences bias a person's future mental states (inhibitory control did not contribute beyond age and verbal working memory). These data suggest that executive function skills may support social meaning-making; that is, discerning how individuals draw from the past to construct their truth about the social world. Still, age explained significant variance outside of executive function. Consistent with a positivity bias in three- to seven-year-olds (Bamford & Lagattuta, 2019; Boseovski, 2010; Giles & Heyman, 2003), younger children's lower differentiation by past type is also reflective of a more positive worldview, one that downplays the diagnostic value of people's anti-social, negative behavior. Thus, age-related differences in understanding the biasing impact of mental states over time may also stem in part from learning how to use behaviors to infer their psychological traits and future actions (Liu et al., 2007; Miller & Aloise-Young, 2018; Rholes & Ruble, 1986).

Mental diversity versus common ground

So far in this chapter, we have emphasized age-related improvements in children's understanding that people's individual life experiences can bias how they feel, think, and make decisions in future situations. The underlying assumption is that growth in theory of mind from early through middle childhood and into adulthood involves increasing recognition of mental diversity – that people vary in their mental states and these differences derive in part from their person-specific life experiences. Indeed, children's developing knowledge about the 'subjectivity' of the mind – that individuals can experience different emotions, desires, preferences, beliefs, thoughts, and other mental states – has been a major emphasis in research on the development of theory of mind since its inception in the 1980s (see Wellman & Lagattuta, 2000). Importantly, however, people do not always experience vastly different mental states: There often can be substantial common ground, or mutual agreement, in how individuals interpret and respond to situations. Thus, we set out to investigate children's developing awareness about when and how past experience does and does not shape mental states.

As a first test, we created new variants of tasks used in prior research showing that children develop an interpretive theory of mind, or knowledge that a single situation can be open to multiple legitimate interpretations, by six to seven years of age (Carpendale & Chandler, 1996; Pillow & Mash, 1999; Taylor, 1988). Lagattuta et al. (2010b) showed participants two characters – Sam and Alex – who lived in different houses. For relevant-past and irrelevant-past trials, one character came outside of their house, saw and labeled a full picture, and then went back inside. The picture was then covered aside from a small window. Participants predicted and explained what picture the knowledgeable and the naïve character would think is hiding underneath the occluded picture as well as what a second naïve character would think (all open-ended questions). For relevant-past trials (closest to a standard interpretive theory of mind task), past experience should affect interpretation because prior access was needed to identify the picture from the ambiguous part (e.g., the curve of the elephant's back; the knowledgeable character should have true belief; both naïve characters should have unshared false beliefs). For irrelevant-past trials, past experience was unnecessary because the visible part clearly identified the picture (e.g., flowers in a picture of flowers; all characters should have true beliefs that share common ground). A third trial type, distinct-pasts trials, was structurally identical, except that Sam and Alex each saw a different full picture (e.g., a snake for one, a snail for the other) that could match the visible part in the occluded drawing; thus, Sam's and Alex's interpretations should be biased by their specific past experiences (e.g., one should think 'snake' and the other should think 'snail'; the second naïve person should have a unique false belief).

Analyses revealed that from four to nine years of age and between childhood and adulthood individuals develop a stronger awareness of both mental diversity and common ground. Most fascinating was evidence for a U-shaped developmental curve, appearing at both the group and individual level. At six to seven years of age, when children first consistently passed relevant-past trials (showing a strong understanding of mental diversity) they made more mistakes than older and younger participants on irrelevant-past trials. They erred by failing to infer common ground and by unnecessarily explaining mental states as caused by person-specific past experiences. Indeed, six- to seven-year-olds found it more difficult to predict that people would share common ground than to predict that a naïve character would hold a false belief. Another error most common in six- to seven-year-olds occurred on the distinct-past trials. Here, this age group overapplied the general rule that people who differ in past experience will have different thoughts by failing to also consider that 'incorrect' characters would hold specific false beliefs biased by their past (e.g., think 'snail' instead of a random false belief). Even from eight to nine years to adulthood, there was improvement in knowing the precise ways characters would be wrong on the distinct-past trials. This is not to say that adults exhibited perfect performance. Where adults erred frequently, and intriguingly more often than all other child age groups, was to predict that two naïve characters would hold the same false belief on the relevant-past trials (e.g., both think 'apple' when seeing the ambiguous curve). This error of over-assuming common ground fits with the false consensus effect found in young adults who tend to believe erroneously that others share their same attitudes and beliefs (Dunning & Hayes, 1996; Krueger & Clement, 1994).

To investigate further aspects of developmental change and continuity in mindreading abilities across a wide age range, Lagattuta et al. (2014b) presented four- to ten-year-olds and adults with a new interpretive theory-of-mind probability task in which participants first predicted a naïve person's interpretation of an occluded drawing and then judged the likelihood that this naïve person would have several different interpretations. During the testing procedure, participants viewed a full picture before it was occluded aside from a small window. The experimenter showed a photograph of a gender-matched person (Tom or Tina) and told participants that they would be trying to guess what picture Tom/Tina would think is hiding underneath. Hidden pictures included a castle (right angle revealed through window), a cloud (curve revealed through window), and a panda (panda face appeared through window). Thus, both the castle and cloud pictures required prior access to the full picture to identify accurately (akin to relevant-past trials from Lagattuta et al., 2010b), whereas the panda did not (akin to the irrelevant-past trials from Lagattuta et al., 2010b). With the picture now mostly occluded, the experimenter asked the participant to predict what picture Tom/Tina would think is hiding underneath (open-ended question). Next, the experimenter laid out a series of pictures in random order on the table. For the cloud and castle trials, options included the actual picture, the prototypical shape associated with the visible portion (e.g., 'square' for the right angle visible on the castle), improbable thoughts (picture is possible given the visible part, but an unlikely thought; e.g., 'robot' and 'cabin' for castle), and impossible thoughts (no part matched the visible portion; e.g., 'tent' and 'bicycle' for castle). For the panda, aside from the picture of the panda, all options were impossible. Participants used a graduated-peg probability scale (they received pretraining) to rate from 0 to 10 how likely Tom/Tina would have that specific thought.

Consistent with Lagattuta et al. (2010b), there was significant age-related improvement from four to ten years in the ability to suggest a unique, false interpretation for the naïve person (cloud and castle trials). Yet, this explicit understanding was not sufficient to simulate accurately that naïve perspective.

Across age, participants inflated the probability that the naïve person would guess the actual picture compared with (1) the other equally improbable pictures and (2) the thought probability ratings of a separate group of uninformed participants. These quantitative errors when trying to create another's naïve perspective fit with results from hindsight bias tasks where participants try to reconstruct their former naïve stance (Bernstein et al., 2011; Pohl et al., 2010). More generally, studies have found that even adults have difficulty setting aside an egocentric bias, or 'curse of knowledge', to track and identify others' mental states (Birch & Bloom, 2007; Epley et al., 2004; Royzman et al., 2003; Todd et al., 2011), or even to forecast their own future mental states (Kramer et al., 2017). Finally, results from the identifiable panda trial replicated the age-specific over-interpretive mind bias discovered by Lagattuta et al. (2010b): Compared with older and younger age groups, six- to ten-year-olds provided higher probability ratings for non-panda images despite these alternatives being impossible. That is, they overextended their knowledge that different past experiences yield mental diversity to clear-cut situations where there should be common ground.

Interim summary and individual differences

From four to ten years of age and between childhood and adulthood, children gain a deeper understanding of whether and how differences in prior experience lead to between-person diversity in interpretation versus common ground. At six to seven years (and continuing to age ten), when children show consistent understanding that a single situation could be open to multiple legitimate interpretations, they overextend this knowledge to unambiguous situations where individuals should share common ground. Persistent mindreading errors occur even into adulthood in the ability to take the perspective of a naïve person (i.e., they exhibit an egocentric bias) as well as to appreciate that two naïve people are unlikely to share the same thoughts (i.e., they over-presume consensus). Thus, knowing that minds can actively construct varying interpretations (i.e., having an interpretive theory of mind) is not always sufficient for accurately predicting if, when, or in what ways people's mental states will differ.

One way that we have addressed sources of individual variability in interpretive theory of mind is to include measures of executive function in the testing procedures. In Lagattuta et al. (2010b), contributions of age, working memory, and inhibitory control varied by the specific trial type: For irrelevant-past trials, age was the only predictor; for relevant-past trials, the connection between age and performance was mediated by inhibitory control; and for the distinct-pasts trials working memory and inhibitory control partially mediated the relation between age and performance. Lagattuta et al. (2014b) found that children and adults higher in verbal working memory and inhibitory control could better quarantine their privileged knowledge and take a naïve perspective on reality. Thus, similar to findings from Lagattuta et al. (2018), it appears that competencies in executive function not only contribute to the emergence of early theory of mind abilities but are also recruited for more advanced types of mental state reasoning. As a further exploration, we have also discovered that even after accounting for age and executive function, family structure matters. Paralleling research on early theory of mind showing that three- to six-year-olds with older siblings are more likely to pass false belief tasks (e.g., Lewis et al., 1996; Ruffman et al., 1998), we found that four- to ten-year-olds with more older siblings or more same-sex siblings demonstrated stronger understanding of mental diversity in both their predictions (i.e., inferring how knowledgeable and naïve characters would think) and explanations (i.e., explaining mental states in relation to differences in past experience) on Lagattuta et al.'s (2010b) relevant-past and distinct-past trials (Kennedy et al., 2015). Thus, the benefits of siblings for fostering advances in social cognition appears to last beyond early childhood.

Understanding interconnections among different mental states

A further way that we have investigated the development of a more advanced theory of mind is to assess children's and adults' beliefs about connections between and among different kinds of mental states. That is, although children acquire knowledge that people can have desires, emotions, beliefs, and thoughts by three to five years of age, there is still much to learn during middle childhood and into adulthood about how these varying mental states interact. We acknowledge that this topic intersects quite closely with our previous sections. We will not repeat those findings here, but instead highlight additional methods we have created for studying age-related improvements in theory of mind, organized by type of mental state connection.

Desire and emotion

By two to three years of age, children know that desires shape emotions – getting what one wants feels good and not getting what one wants feels bad (e.g., Wellman & Woolley, 1990). In real life, however, people cannot always get what they want – there are rules and norms that discourage or forbid such behaviors. In Lagattuta (2005), four- to seven-year-olds and adults predicted and explained how characters would feel exhibiting willpower or transgressing in situations where desires conflicted with rules. With age, children increasingly predicted inverse relations between desires and emotions: Desire fulfillment (transgression) can feel bad and desire inhibition (willpower) can feel good. These changes in predictions were accompanied by increasing mention of rules and future consequences in emotion explanations and decreasing emphasis on desire fulfillment. To explore further, Lagattuta (2008) told and showed three- to six-year-olds and adults (using pictorial thought bubbles) what characters were thinking most about (rules, future consequences, desires) after deciding to transgress or comply with rules. When primed to consider rules and future consequences, even four- to five-year-olds judged that desire fulfillment (transgression) would feel bad and desire inhibition (willpower) would feel good. Still, because not all rules are equivalent (see Killen & Smetana, 2006), we reasoned that children may be less apt to recognize the emotional benefits of desire inhibition in situations where rules infringed on the personal domain (e.g., friendship or clothing choice) versus moral rules. Lagattuta et al. (2010a) found that although there were age-related increases between four and seven in predicting that people will comply with moral rules and feel good (despite desire inhibition), all age groups most often judged that people would disobey rules that violated the personal domain and that this non-compliance would feel emotionally satisfying.

As further extensions, we investigated five- to thirteen-year-olds' reasoning about the emotional consequences of inhibiting versus fulfilling desires in situations where characters' personal desires conflicted with the welfare of others. In these scenarios, inhibiting desires would prevent harm to others (e.g., refrain from stealing a desired object that belonged to someone else) or would allow time to assist someone in need (e.g., forgo a party to help someone). In Weller and Lagattuta (2013) characters encountered another person who was either from their racial ingroup or outgroup, and in Weller and Lagattuta (2014) the target of help or harm was from the gender ingroup or outgroup. With increasing age, children expected more intensely positive emotions following self-sacrificial helping decisions. They further judged that individuals would feel better inhibiting desires to help others versus to refrain from harming them. Conversely, they inferred that characters would feel worse fulfilling desires by harming others versus not helping. Whereas children expected people to feel happier helping the racial ingroup versus outgroup and happier ignoring the needs of the racial outgroup versus ingroup (Weller & Lagattuta, 2013), only females showed an in-group bias in emotion ratings (Weller & Lagattuta, 2014). Although we emphasize the findings on emotion here, these paradigms also included judgments about whether or not characters would help as well as their beliefs about obligation and permissibility.

Thought and emotion

Two effective strategies for coping with negative emotions and events include cognitive distraction (thinking about something else) and cognitive reappraisal (changing how you think about a situation; Gross & Thompson, 2007; Lyubomirsky et al., 2015). Lagattuta et al. (1997) presented four- to six-year-olds with character pairs who either ruminated on a negative event (e.g., were thinking most about their dead pet fish) or engaged in cognitive distraction (e.g., were thinking most about what to play on the piano). Children predicted and explained how each character felt, including whether their emotions changed when they shifted their thought focus (e.g., first ruminated then tried cognitive distraction and vice versa). Although all age groups competently predicted emotions in line with thought focus, there was significant growth between ages four and six in explaining these emotions as explicitly caused by changes in mental activity (e.g., 'He feels OK because playing the piano is pretty fun and it might take his mind off the [dead] fish'). In contrast, younger children more often focused on the situation itself (e.g., 'My mom says that food makes you feel a little better'). Relatedly, Bamford and Lagattuta (2012) showed five- to ten-year-olds with scenarios featuring two characters who experienced the same negative, positive, or ambiguous events. One character mentally framed the outcome positively whereas the other thought negatively. Children predicted and explained how each character felt. With increasing age, children expected larger between-person differences in emotions, with ten-year-olds also more frequently explaining emotions as caused by thinking compared to younger age groups (e.g., 'Because she is thinking on the good side of things'). Younger age groups, in comparison, emphasized the situation (e.g., 'She has a cast').

We have also examined age-related changes in children's understanding of mental causes of fear and cognitive strategies for lessening fear. Sayfan and Lagattuta (2008) showed three-, five-, and seven-year-olds and adults scenarios involving two different-aged characters (e.g., infant and child, child and grownup) encountering something that looks like an imaginary (e.g., ghost) or real (e.g., spider) fear-inducing entity. Participants predicted and explained how each character felt. Results showed significant age-related increases from three to seven and between seven and adulthood in expecting characters to differ in fear intensity and to explain these emotions in relation to cognitive mental states (e.g., 'The baby's not afraid because it doesn't know that snakes are dangerous'; 'She thinks ghosts are real') as opposed to external characteristics of the person (e.g., 'She's not really big') or object ('Because the alligator has teeth'). Although all child age groups expected adult characters to feel least afraid, it was not until adulthood that babies were expected to experience lower fear than children. In a further extension, Sayfan and Lagattuta (2009) documented significant improvement between four and seven years in knowledge about mental sources of fear as well as in understanding how mental strategies, such as cognitive reappraisal and cognitive distraction, can lessen fear intensity (see also Bamford & Lagattuta, 2010 for similar developmental findings on children's reasoning about the emotional effects of prayer).

Although we have focused on children's reasoning about how the mind affects emotions, we have also considered the reverse relation – their awareness that emotional states can affect performance on cognitively demanding tasks. What makes this topic particularly fascinating is that young children are often told by teachers and parents to 'get a good night's rest' or 'eat a healthy breakfast' to maximize their school performance, but they are rarely informed to 'not feel sad' prior to taking a test. In Amsterlaw et al. (2009), five- and seven-year-olds and adults predicted and explained how characters who experienced a variety of emotional (mad, sad, happy, proud) and physiological (hungry, tired, satiated, wide awake) states would perform on challenging school work (e.g., a math or spelling test). Results showed that children developed knowledge about the impairing effects of negative internal states earliest: All age groups expected negative physiological states and emotions to disrupt cognitive performance, but there was an increase between four and seven years in endorsing the benefits of positive physiological states and emotions. In addition, there was improvement from four to seven and between childhood and adulthood in explaining the underlying cognitive mechanisms by which internal states could affect performance (e.g., 'He's mad, so he won't be able to concentrate'), with children exhibiting the strongest understanding when explaining reasons for declines in cognitive performance.

Expectation and emotion

Managing expectations, including knowing when to lower and raise expectations, has also been shown to be an effective strategy for emotional wellbeing (Sweeny & Shepperd, 2010). We tested growth in children's and adults' beliefs about how expectations carry forward through time to shape later emotional responses (Lara et al., 2019). Four- to ten-year-olds and adults responded to scenarios featuring sets of three characters who had varying expectations about a future outcome. For example, in one scenario about a raffle, one child expected to win the big teddy bear, one child expected to win nothing at all, and the third child decided to just think about something in the present scene. Participants predicted and explained how each character would feel following a positive outcome (e.g., all kids win the big teddy bear), a negative outcome (e.g., all kids lose and get nothing), and an attenuated outcome (e.g., all kids win a small consolation prize). Children as young as four to five years exhibited a strong understanding that thoughts impact emotions in the here and now (replicating Bamford & Lagattuta, 2012; Lagattuta et al., 1997). What changed significantly from four to ten years and between childhood and adulthood, however, was children's awareness that this direct relation between thoughts and emotions inverses over time: High expectations carry a future emotional cost (e.g., disappointment when outcomes are worse than expected) and low expectations can be emotionally beneficial (e.g., delight from an unexpected gain). There was also significant improvement during childhood and between childhood and adulthood in explaining post-outcome emotions in relation to prior expectations (e.g., 'He expected to have his favorite dessert but ended up not getting it'). Notably, children demonstrated the earliest knowledge about the costs of high expectations in negative outcomes, with only adults judging that prior low expectations can provide an emotional boost for positive outcomes.

Interconnections among emotions, thoughts, and decisions. Scientific theories of emotion, decision making, and psychological wellbeing emphasize interrelations among emotions, thoughts, and decisions – how individuals think affects how they feel, and their feelings and thoughts shape their actions (Baumeister et al., 2007; Ellis, 1991; Wood et al., 2002). In Lagattuta et al. (2016), we examined four- to ten-year-olds' and adults' predictions for whether mental state dyads (emotion–thought, thought–decision, emotion–decision) and triads (emotion–thought–decision) would cohere in valence – that is, thinking positively leads to happiness and approach behaviors whereas negative thoughts elicit worry and avoidance. To do this, participants predicted how characters would feel (worried versus happy), think (anticipate positive versus negative future), and decide (approach versus avoid) re-encountering perpetrators who had helped them, harmed them, or both helped and harmed them in the past. Findings indicated significant increases between four and ten years in predicting that mental state dyads and triads would cohere in valence. Across age, children and adults more frequently predicted coherent emotion–thought connections compared with emotion–decision or thought–decision dyads. The most common break in connecting mental states was inferring that a person could feel happy and anticipate good but still make an avoidant decision.

Interim summary and individual differences

Although children understand straightforward connections between desires and emotions (e.g., desire fulfillment feels good), thoughts and emotions (e.g., thinking positive thoughts feels good), and expectations and emotions (e.g., expecting a positive future outcome feels good) by four to five years of age, there is improvement during middle childhood into adulthood in identifying and explaining inverse relations (e.g., desire fulfillment can feel bad; prior high expectations can have a future cost) as well as in reasoning about interrelations among emotions, thoughts, and decisions. Between the ages of four and ten and between childhood and adulthood, children also develop a deeper understanding of the impact of thinking on emotions, including how and why cognitive strategies can improve emotions, as well as how emotions can impact thinking and problem-solving.

We have explored some sources of individual differences in knowledge about mental state connections. For example, in Lagattuta et al. (2016) we documented that both age and executive function (verbal working memory and inhibitory control) independently predicted the frequency that participants formed valence-matched mental state triads (e.g., predict feel worried + anticipate negative future + avoid). Bamford and Lagattuta (2012) found that parent self-reported optimism (but not parent reports of child optimism) correlated with several aspects of children's reasoning about the benefits of positive thinking: Children with parents higher (versus lower) in optimism predicted that characters would gain a greater emotional boost from positive thinking in negative situations, judged a greater difference between positive versus negative thinkers in negative situations, and more often explained emotions as caused by how characters were thinking about events. Thus, parent worldviews and coping strategies likely also help shape how children learn about and understand connections between and among mental states.

Future directions

We view theory of mind as a diverse construct involving multiple aspects of mental state reasoning that vary in developmental timetables. Thus, we encourage researchers to continue creating measures that incorporate the complex, yet everyday ways that people navigate their social worlds. This section provides suggestions for expanding experimental paradigms, identifying individual differences and potential developmental mechanisms, as well as exploring connections to social competence and wellbeing.[1]

Expanding experimental paradigms

One major limitation of current assessments is that they rarely require children and adults to consider the mental states of several people simultaneously. Outside of the lab, however, it is common that people need to interpret and integrate multiple perspectives in group settings; for example, deciding where to go to lunch with friends, playing team sports, and making decisions in a business meeting. Thus, measures that require reasoning about multiple minds (not just singletons or dyads) would augment scientific knowledge about developmental changes in how children and adults think about conflicting and overlapping vantage points among several people. The more these paradigms can incorporate individuals of differing social identities (e.g., diverse races, genders, wealth statuses), the more they would reflect the world in which people increasingly live (Kennedy et al., 2017).

Relatedly, we are intrigued by measuring beliefs about perspectives that are often neglected. For example, research on the understanding of emotions, including our own, has emphasized children's and adults' reasoning about how the target of another person's actions will feel, think, and make decisions. It would be important to examine more comprehensively beliefs about the mental states of the person doing the negative and positive actions. Although we have investigated how actors would feel and make decisions in some contexts (Lagattuta, 2005, 2008; Lagattuta et al., 2010a; Weller & Lagattuta, 2013, 2014; see also Arsenio, 2014), this provides a limited window into how children and adults reason about what is going through an actor's mind (e.g., beliefs, motivations, expectations; e.g., Killen et al., 2011) before, during, and after engaging in certain actions. It would also be informative to examine children's and adults' reasoning about the cognitions and emotions of observers of interpersonal events, including how an observer's relation (e.g., parent, friend, stranger) to the actor and to the target influences how they interpret, learn from, and emotionally respond to these episodes.

More research is also needed to explore how children and adults incorporate aspects of time into their mental state reasoning. For example, one shortcoming of the standard location-change false-belief task is that the assessment ends before Sally finds her missing marble (Wimmer & Perner, 1983). In reality, if a person does not find what they are looking for, they continue searching. This premature end to the task leaves open an interesting question: How long do children and adults think it would take for a person to resolve ignorance? In other words, would individuals think Sally will immediately search in the true location (exhibiting a curse of knowledge; Birch & Bloom, 2007), or would they recognize that it would likely take her a while to find the lost object, especially if there were multiple places it could be? More generally, there needs to be broader inquiry about children's and adults' beliefs about how long different cognitive and emotional mental states last, including what needs to be done to change them (Kramer et al., 2019; Magid et al., 2018). For example, how do children and adults determine whether it is worthwhile to try to change someone's mind? How do they consider and weight facets such as the person's motivation for holding the belief (e.g., political, family), the source of their belief (e.g., science, religion), how long the believer has held the belief (e.g., for a long time versus just came to it), and the 'convincer's' relative social status to the 'believer'?

Individual variability and developmental mechanisms

We have found that connections between executive function and advanced theory of mind appear whether tasks have higher (e.g., having to disregard privileged knowledge; Lagattuta et al., 2010b, 2014b) or lower (e.g., no information needs to be inhibited; Lagattuta et al., 2016, 2018) executive demands. Devising additional theory-of-mind tasks that carry varying executive burdens would clarify relations among age, executive function, and theory of mind in these older age groups (see also Hughes & Devine, 2015; Lecce & Bianco, 2018; Lecce et al., 2017; Wang et al., 2016). We have further documented some family correlates of advanced theory of mind, including relations between sibling composition and children's reasoning about mental diversity (Kennedy et al., 2015), and an association between parental optimism and children's knowledge about the impact of positive thinking on emotions (Bamford & Lagattuta, 2012). These data suggest that interpersonal experiences with close family members, including the conversations and behaviors that sustain these increasingly complex relationships as children mature, may foster more advanced mental state reasoning. Improvements in understanding the impact of life history on current and future mental states may further be catalyzed by children's expanding social interactions with individuals from a range of backgrounds who express varying alignment or misalignment in their thoughts and emotions. More generally, although individual differences in theory of mind have been extensively studied in early childhood, it would be important to test the extent to which these predictors endure, or new factors emerge, in older age groups (see Devine & Hughes, 2015; Lagattuta et al., 2014a, 2015).

Connections to social competence and wellbeing

Beyond understanding mechanisms of change in children's and adults' ability to reason about minds, it will also be important to explore how these advanced mind-reading abilities may translate into more competent social behaviors as well as improved emotional wellbeing. For example, the ability to appreciate non-obvious causes of emotions (e.g., knowledge that past events shape future mental states and emotions; see Lagattuta, 2007; Lagattuta & Kramer, 2019; Lagattuta & Sayfan, 2013) could lead individuals to be more sensitive to others' idiosyncratic emotional reactions, as well as more attuned to the sources of their own emotions, including biased generalizations from past experience. Awareness of when others are likely versus unlikely to share perspectives, as well as skill in setting aside privileged knowledge to take a naïve perspective (Lagattuta et al., 2010a, 2014), could help people be more effective parents, teachers, managers, and leaders. Recognizing that getting what you want can feel bad and that a blocked desire can feel good (Lagattuta, 2005, 2008; Lagattuta et al., 2010a) could not only promote greater compliance with social and moral norms but also give individuals space to better consider how their own actions impact the future wellbeing of others. Awareness of expectation–emotion connections (Bamford & Lagattuta, 2019; Lagattuta & Sayfan, 2011; Lara et al., 2019) may bolster people's ability to cope with negative outcomes, support others facing disappointment, and better appreciate the ways in which they, themselves, may cause negative reactions in others (e.g., not living up to others' expectations). Future research is needed to explore these possibilities; longitudinal studies would be especially revealing about potential causal directions.

Conclusion

It is an incredibly challenging cognitive task to interpret, anticipate, regulate, and reason about the causes and consequences of mental states. Although children meet several remarkable milestones between the ages of three and five, these initial understandings further develop in complexity, depth, and scope during middle childhood and into adulthood. Indeed, even seemingly small methodological changes can reveal significant gaps in children's and adults' explicit knowledge about mental states as well as their mindreading abilities (e.g., Lagattuta et al., 2010b, 2014b; Lagattuta & Kramer, 2019). We look forward to continuing to be part of a growing international research effort to create innovative new paradigms to investigate developmental changes and continuities in theory of mind across a wide age range.

Acknowledgments

We thank the thousands of children and families who participated in the research we review in this chapter, the outstanding undergraduate and graduate students who contributed to the success of these studies, and the National Science Foundation, the National Institute of Mental Health, and the Amini Foundation for the Study of Affects for funding.

Note

1 Although our focus has been on typically developing children and adults, it would be informative to widen participant samples for the below suggestions (and the paradigms we have summarized in this chapter) to individuals with developmental disorders.

References

Amsterlaw, J., Lagattuta, K.H., & Meltzoff, A.N. (2009). Young children's reasoning about the effects of emotional and physiological states on academic performance. *Child Development, 80*, 115–133. doi: 10.1111/j.1467-8624.2008.01249.x

Apperly, I.A., Samson, D., & Humphreys, G.W. (2009). Studies of adults can inform accounts of theory of mind development. *Developmental Psychology, 45*, 190–201. doi: 10.1037/a0014098

Arsenio, W.F. (2014). Moral emotion attributions and aggression. In M. Killen & J.G. Smetana (Eds.), *The Handbook of Moral Development* (pp. 235–255). New York: Psychology Press.

Bamford, C., & Lagattuta, K.H. (2010). A new look at children's understanding of mind and emotion: The case of prayer. *Developmental Psychology, 46*, 78–92. doi: 10.1037/a0016694

Bamford, C., & Lagattuta, K.H. (2012). Looking on the bright side: Children's knowledge about the benefits of positive versus negative thinking. *Child Development, 83*, 667–682. doi: 10.1111/j.1467-8624.2011.01706.x

Bamford, C., & Lagattuta, K.H. (2019). Optimism and wishful thinking: Consistency across populations in children's expectations for the future. *Child Development* [advanced online]. doi: 10.1111/cdev.13293

Baumeister, R.F., Vohs, K.D., DeWall, C.N., & Zhang, L. (2007). How emotion shapes behavior: Feedback, anticipation, and reflection, rather than direct causation. *Personality and Social Psychology Review, 11*, 167–203. doi: 10.1177/1088868307301033

Bernstein, D.M., Erdfelder, E., Meltzoff, A.N., Peria, W., & Loftus, G.R. (2011). Hindsight bias from 3 to 95 years. *Journal of Experimental Psychology – Learning Memory and Cognition, 37*, 378–391. doi: 10.1037/a0021971

Birch, S.A.J., & Bloom, P. (2007). The curse of knowledge in reasoning about false beliefs. *Psychology Science, 18*, 382–386. doi: 10.1111/j.1467-9280.2009.01909.x

Boseovski, J.J. (2010). Evidence for "rose-colored glasses": An examination of the positivity bias in young children's personality judgments. *Child Development Perspectives, 4*, 212–218. doi: 10.1111/j.1750-8606.2010.00149.x

Carlson, S.M., & Moses, L.J. (2001). Individual differences in inhibitory control and children's theory of mind. *Child Development, 72*, 1032–1053. doi: 10.1111/1467-8624.00333

Carpendale, J.I., & Chandler, M.J. (1996). On the distinction between false belief and understanding and subscribing to an interpretive theory of mind. *Child Development, 67*, 1686–1706. doi: 10.1111/j.1467-8624.1996.tb0181.x

Davis, E.L., Levine, L.J., Lench, H.C., & Quas, J.A. (2010). Metacognitive emotion regulation: Children's awareness that changing thoughts and goals can alleviate negative emotions. *Emotion, 10*, 498–510. doi: 10.1037/a0018428

Devine, R.T., & Hughes, C. (2014). Relations between false belief understanding and executive function in early childhood: A meta-analysis. *Child Development, 85*, 1777–1794. doi: 10.1111/cdev.12237

Devine, R.T., White, N., Ensor, R., & Hughes, C. (2016). Theory of mind in middle childhood: Longitudinal associations with executive function and social competence. *Developmental Psychology, 52*, 758–771. doi: 10.1037/dev0000105

Diamond, A. (2013). Executive functions. *Annual Review of Psychology, 64*, 135–168. doi: 10.1146/annurev-psych-113011-143750

Dunning, D., & Hayes, A.F. (1996). Evidence for egocentric comparison in social judgment. *Journal of Personality and Social Psychology, 71*, 213–229. doi: 10.1037/0022-3514.71.2.213

Dunsmoor, J.E., & Murphy, G.L. (2015). Categories, concepts, and conditioning: How humans generalize fear. *Trends in Cognitive Sciences, 19*, 73–77. doi: 10.1016/j.tics.2014.12.003

Ellis, A. (1991). The revised ABC's of the rational-emotive therapy (RET). *Journal of Rational-Emotive and Cognitive-Behavior Therapy, 9*, 139–172.

Epley, N., Keysar, B., Van Boven, L., & Gilovich, T. (2004). Perspective taking as egocentric anchoring and adjustment. *Journal of Personality and Social Psychology, 87*, 327–339. doi: 10.1037/0022-3514.87.3.327

Flavell, J.H. & Green, F.L. (1999). Development of intuitions about the controllability of different mental states. *Cognitive Development, 14*, 133–146. doi: 10.1016/S0885-2014(99)80021-5

Giles, J.W., & Heyman, G.D. (2003). Preschoolers' beliefs about the stability of antisocial behavior: Implications for navigating social challenges. *Social Development, 12*, 182–197. doi: 10.1111/1467-9507.00228

Gross, J.J. & Thompson, R.A. (2007). Emotion regulation: Conceptual foundations. In J.J. Gross (Ed.), *Handbook of Emotion Regulation* (pp. 3–24). New York: Guilford Press.

Henderson, J.M., & Hayes, T.R. (2017). Meaning-based guidance of attention in scenes as revealed by meaning maps. *Nature Human Behaviour, 1*, 743–747. doi: 10.1038/s41562-017-0208-0

Hughes, D., & Devine, R.T. (2015). Individual differences in theory of mind from preschool to adolescence: Achievements and directions. *Child Development Perspectives, 9*, 149–153. doi: 10.1111/cdep.12124.

Karniol, R., & Ross, M. (1996). The motivational impact of temporal focus: Thinking about the future and the past. *Annual Review of Psychology, 47*, 593–620. doi: 10.1146/annurev.psych.47.1.593

Kennedy, K., Lagattuta, K.H., Kramer, H.J., & Hjortsvang, K.H. (April, 2017). Thinking about a party of five: Children's and adults' reasoning about mental diversity in a group of minds. Presented at the Biennial Meeting of the Society for Research in Child Development, Austin, TX.

Kennedy, K., Lagattuta, K.H., & Sayfan, L. (2015). Sibling composition, executive function, and children's thinking about mental diversity. *Journal of Experimental Child Psychology, 132*, 121–139. doi: 10.1016/j.jecp.2014.11.007

Killen, M., Mulvey, K.L., Richardson, C., & Jampol, N. (2011). The accidental transgressor: Morally relevant theory of mind. *Cognition, 119*, 192–215. doi: 10.1016/j.cognition.2011.01.006

Killen, M., & Smetana, J.G. (2006). Social-cognitive domain theory: Consistencies and variations in children's moral and social judgments. In M. Killen & J.G. Smetana (Eds.), *Handbook of Moral Development* (pp. 137–172). New York: Psychology Press.

Kramer, H.J., Goldfarb, D., Tashjian, S.M., & Lagattuta, K.H. (2017). "These pretzels are making me thirsty": Older children and adults struggle with induced-state episodic foresight. *Child Development, 88*, 1554–1562. doi: 10.1111/cdev.12700

Kramer, H.J., & Lagattuta, K.H. (in press). Developmental changes in emotion understanding during middle childhood. In D.D. Dukes, E. Walle, & A.C. Samson, (Eds.), *Oxford Handbook on Emotional Development* (pp. XX–XX). Oxford: Oxford University Press.

Kramer, H.J., Lagattuta, K.H., Gweon, H., & Zaki, J. (2019). This too shall pass…but when? Children's and adults' beliefs about the time course of mental experiences. Presented at the Biennial Meeting of the Society for Research in Child Development, Baltimore, MD.

Krueger, J., & Clement, R.W. (1994). The truly false consensus effect: An ineradicable and egocentric bias in social perception. *Journal of Personality and Social Psychology, 67*, 596–610. doi: 10.1037/0022-3514.67.4.596

Lagattuta, K.H. (2005). When you shouldn't do what you want to do: Young children's understanding of desires, rules, and emotions. *Child Development, 76*, 713–733. doi: 10.1111/j.1467-8624.2005.00873.x

Lagattuta, K.H. (2007). Thinking about the future because of the past: Young children's knowledge about the causes of worry and preventative decisions. *Child Development, 78*, 1492–1509. doi: 10.1111/j.1467-8624.2007.01079.x

Lagattuta, K.H. (2008). Young children's knowledge about the influence of thoughts on emotions in rule situations. *Developmental Science, 11*, 809–818. doi: 10.1111/j.1467-7687.2008.00727.x

Lagattuta, K.H. (2014). Linking past, present, and future: Children's ability to connect mental states and emotions across time. *Child Development Perspectives, 8*, 90–95. doi: 10.1111/cdep.12065

Lagattuta, K.H. (2018). Where does it come from, where does it go? The benefits of examining moral judgments across a wide age range. *Human Development, 60*, 350–356. doi: 10.1159/000485575

Lagattuta, K.H., Elrod, N., & Kramer, H.J. (2016). How do thoughts, emotions, and decisions align? A new way to examine theory of mind during middle childhood and beyond. *Journal of Experimental Child Psychology, 149*, 116–133. doi: 10.1016/j.jecp.2016.01.013

Lagattuta, K.H., Hjortsvang, K., & Kennedy, K. (2014). Theory of mind and academic competence during early childhood: Emotion understanding, relationships, and learning from others. In O.N. Saracho (Ed.), *Contemporary Perspectives in Early Childhood Education* (pp. 245–267). Charlotte, NC: Information Age Publishing.

Lagattuta, K.H., & Kramer, H.J. (2017). Try to look on the bright side: Children and adults can (sometimes) override their tendency to prioritize negative faces. *Journal of Experimental Psychology: General, 146*, 89–101. doi: 10.1037/xge0000247

Lagattuta, K.H. & Kramer, H.J. (2019). Advanced emotion understanding: Children's and adults' knowledge that minds generalize from prior emotional events. *Emotion* [advanced online]. doi: 10.1037/emo0000694

Lagattuta, K.H., Kramer, H.J., Kennedy, K., Hjortsvang, K., Goldfarb., D., & Tashjian, S.M. (2015). Beyond Sally's missing marble: Further development in children's understanding of mind and emotion during middle childhood. *Advances in Child Development and Behavior, 48*, 185–217. doi: 10.1016/bs.acdb.2014.11.005

Lagattuta, K.H., Nucci, L., & Bosacki, S.L. (2010b). Bridging theory of mind and personal domain: Children's reasoning about resistance to parental control. *Child Development, 81*, 616–635. doi: 10.1111/j.1467-8624.2009.01419.x

Lagattuta, K.H. & Sayfan, L. (2011). Developmental changes in children's understanding of future likelihood and uncertainty. *Cognitive Development, 26*, 315-330. DOI: 10.1016/j.cogdev.2011.09.004

Lagattuta, K.H. & Sayfan, L. (2013). Not all past events are equal: Biased attention and emerging heuristics in children's past-to-future forecasting. *Child Development, 84*, 2094–2111. doi: 10.1111/cdev.12082

Lagattuta, K.H., Sayfan, L., & Blattman, A.J. (2010a). Forgetting common ground: Six- to seven-year-olds have an overinterpretive theory of mind. *Developmental Psychology, 46*, 1417–1432. doi: 10.1037/a0021062

Lagattuta, K.H., Sayfan, L., & Harvey, C. (2014). Beliefs about thought probability: Evidence for persistent errors in mindreading and links to executive control. *Child Development, 85*, 659–674. doi: 10.1111/cdev.12154

Lagattuta, K.H., Tashjian, S.M., & Kramer, H.J. (2018). Does the past shape anticipation for the future? Contributions of age and executive function to advanced theory of mind. *Zeitschrift für Psychologie, 226*, 122–133. doi: 10.1027/2151-2604/a000328

Lagattuta, K.H., & Weller, D. (2014). Interrelations between theory of mind and morality: A developmental perspective. In M. Killen & J.G. Smetana (Eds.), *The Handbook of Moral Development* (pp. 385–407). New York: Psychology Press.

Lagattuta, K.H., & Wellman, H.M. (2001). Thinking about the past: Early knowledge about the links between prior experience, thinking, and emotion. *Child Development, 72*, 82–102. doi: 10.1111/1467-8624.00267

Lagattuta, H.M., Wellman, H.M., & Favell, J.H. (1997). Preschoolers understanding of the link between thinking and feeling: Cognitive cuing and emotional change. *Child Development, 68*, 1081–1104. doi: 10.1111/j.1467-8624.1997.tb01986.x

Lara, K.H., Lagattuta, K.H., & Kramer, H.J. (2019). Is there a downside to anticipating the upside? Children's and adults' reasoning about how prior expectations shape future emotions. *Child Development, 90*, 1170–1184. doi: 10.1111/cdev.12994

Lecce, S., & Bianco, F. (2018). Working memory predicts changes in children's theory of mind during middle childhood: A training study. *Cognitive Development, 47*, 71–81. doi: 10.1016/j.cogdev.2018.04.002

Lecce, S., Bianco, F., Devine, R.T., & Hughes, C. (2017). Relations between theory of mind and executive function in middle childhood: A short-term longitudinal study. *Journal of Experimental Child Psychology, 163*, 69–86. doi: 10.1016/j.jecp.2017.06.011

Lecce, S., Bianco, F., Devine, R.T., Hughes, C., & Banerjee, R. (2014). Promoting theory of mind during middle childhood: A training program. *Journal of Experimental Child Psychology, 126*, 52–67. doi: 10.1016/j.jecp.2014.03.002

Lerner, J.S., Li, Y., Valdesolo, P. & Kassam, K.S. (2015). Emotion and decision making. *Annual Review of Psychology, 66*, 799–823. doi: 10.1146/annurev-psych-010213-115043

Lewis, C., Freeman, N.H., Kyriakidou, C., Maridaki-Kassotaki, K., & Berridge, D.M. (1996). Social influences on false belief access: Specific sibling influences or general apprenticeship? *Child Development, 67*, 2930–2947. doi: 10.1111/j.1467-8624.1996.tb01896.x

Lindquist, K.A. (2013). Emotions emerge from more basic psychological ingredients: A modern psychological constructionist model. *Emotion Review, 5*, 356–368. doi: 10.1177/1754073913489750

Liu, D., Gelman, S.A., & Wellman, H.M. (2007). Components of young children's trait understanding: Behavior-to-trait inferences and trait-to-behavior predictions. *Child Development, 78*, 1543–1558. doi: 10.1111/j.1467-8624.2007.01082.x

Lyubomirsky, S., Layous, K., Chancellor, J., & Nelson, S.K. (2015). Thinking about rumination: The scholarly contributions and intellectual legacy of Susan Nolen-Hoeksema. *Annual Review of Clinical Psychology, 11*, 1–22. doi: 10.1146/annurev-clinpsy-032814-112733

Magid, R.W., Yan, P., Siegel, M.H., Tenenbaum, J.B., & Schulz, L.E. (2018). Changing minds: Children's inferences about third party belief revision. *Developmental Science, 21*, e12553. doi: 10.1111/desc.12553

Miller, P.H., & Aloise-Young, P.A. (2018). Revisiting young children's understanding of the psychological causes of behavior. *Child Development, 89*, 1441–1461. doi: 10.1111/cdev.12891

Morewedge, C.K., Gilbert, D.T., & Wilson, T.D. (2005). The least likely of times: How remembering the past biases forecasts of the future. *Psychology Science, 16*, 626–630. doi: 10.111/j.1467-9280.2005.01585.x

Pillow, B.H., & Mash, C. (1999). Young children's understanding of interpretation, expectation and direct perception as sources of false belief. *British Journal of Developmental Psychology, 17*, 263–276. doi: 10.1348/026151099165267

Pohl, R.F., Bayen, U.J., & Martin, C. (2010). A multiprocess account of hindsight bias in children. *Developmental Psychology, 46*, 1268–1282. doi: 10.1037/a0020209

Rholes, W.S., & Ruble, D.N. (1986). Children's impressions of other persons: The effects of temporal separation of behavioral information. *Child Development, 57*, 872–878. doi: 10.2307/11303064

Royzman, E.B., Cassidy, K.W., & Baron, J. (2003). "I know, you know": Epistemic egocentrism in children and adults. *Review of General Psychology, 7*, 38–65. doi: 10.1037/1089-2680.7.1.38

Ruffman, T., Perner, J., Naito, M., Parkin, L., & Clements, W. (1998). Older (but not younger) siblings facilitate false belief understanding. *Developmental Psychology, 34*, 161–174.

Sabbagh, M.A., Xu, F., Carlson, S.M., Moses, L.J., & Lee, K. (2006). The development of executive functioning and theory of mind: A comparison of Chinese and U.S. preschoolers. *Psychology Science, 17*, 74–81. doi: 10.1111/j.1467-9280.2005.01667.x

Sayfan, L., & Lagattuta, K.H. (2008). Grownups are not afraid of the scary stuff, but kids are: Young children's and adults' reasoning about children's, infants', and adults' fears. *Child Development, 79*, 821–835. doi: 10.1111/j.1467-8624.2008.01161.x

Sayfan, L., & Lagattuta, K.H. (2009). Scaring the monster away: What children know about managing fears of real and imaginary creatures. *Child Development, 80*, 1756–1774. doi: 10.1111/j.1467-8624.2009.01366.x

Schacter, D.L., Addis, D.R., & Buckner, R.L. (2007). Remembering the past to imagine the future: The prospective brain. *Nature Reviews Neuroscience, 8*, 657–661. doi: 10.1038/nrn2213

Strack, F., & Deutsch, R. (2004). Reflective and impulsive determinants of social behavior. *Personality and Social Psychology Review, 8*, 220–247. doi: 10.1207/s15327957pspr0803_1

Suddendorf, T., & Corballis, M.C. (2007). The evolution of forecast: What is mental time travel, and is it unique to humans? *Behavioral and Brain Sciences, 30*, 299–313. doi: 10.1017/S0140525X07001975

Sweeny, K., & Shepperd, J.A. (2010). The costs of optimism and the benefits of pessimism. *Emotion, 10*, 750–753. doi: 10.1037/a0019016

Taylor, M. (1988). Conceptual perspective taking: Children's ability to distinguish what they know from what they see. *Child Development, 59*, 703–718. doi: 10.2307/1130570

Todd, A.R., Hanko, K., Galinsky, A.D., & Mussweiler, T. (2011). When focusing on differences leads to similar perspectives. *Psychology Science, 22*, 134–141. doi: 10.1177/0956797610392929

Wang, Z., Devine, R.T., Wong, K.K., & Hughes, C. (2016). Theory of mind and executive function during middle childhood across cultures. *Journal of Experimental Child Psychology, 149*, 6–22. doi: 10.1016/j.jecp.2015.09.028

Weller, D., & Lagattuta, K.H. (2013). Helping the in-group feels better: Children's judgments and emotion attributions in response to prosocial dilemmas. *Child Development*, *84*, 253–268. doi: 10.1111/j.1467-8624.2012.01837.x

Weller, D., & Lagattuta, K.H. (2014). Children's judgments about prosocial decisions and emotions: Gender of the helper and recipient matters. *Child Development*, *85*, 2011–2028. doi: 10.1111/cdev.12238

Wellman, H.M. (2014). *Making Minds: How Theory of Mind Develops*. Oxford: Oxford University Press.

Wellman, H.M., & Lagattuta, K.H. (2000). Developing understandings of mind. In S. Baron-Cohen, H. Tager-Flusberg, & D.J. Cohen (Eds.), *Understanding Others Minds: Perspectives From Developmental Cognitive Neuroscience* (pp. 21–49). Oxford University Press.

Wellman, H.M., & Woolley, J.D. (1990). From simple desires to ordinary beliefs: The early development of everyday psychology. *Cognition*, *35*, 245–275. doi: 10.1016/0010-0277(90)00024-E

Wimmer, H., & Perner, J. (1983). Beliefs about beliefs: Representation and constraining function of wrong beliefs in young children's understanding of deception. *Cognition*, *13*, 103–128. doi: 10.1016/0010-0277(83)90004-5

Wolfe, J.M., & Horowtiz, T.S. (2017). Five factors that guide attention in visual search. *Nature Human Behaviour*, *1*. doi: 10.1038/s41562-017-0058

Wood, W., Quinn, J.M., & Kashy, D.A. (2002). Habits in everyday life: Thought, emotion, and action. *Journal of Personality and Social Psychology*, *83*, 1281–1297. doi: 10.1037/0022-3514.83.6.1281

Wyer, R.S., Xu, A.J., & Shen, H. (2012). The effects of past behavior on future goal-directed activity. *Advances in Experimental Social Psychology*, *47*, 237–283. doi: 10.1016/B978-0-12-394281-4.00014-3

2 Cognitive basis of mindreading in middle childhood and adolescence

Ian A. Apperly

Since seminal work in the 1980s (e.g., Wellman, 2014), research on mindreading has been dominated by questions about when and how infants and young children develop the ability to think about other people's mental states. This work has produced many valuable insights, as well as ongoing controversies. However, its success has tended to obscure the lack of any account of how children develop into adults after they first show signs of thinking about the minds of others. The past 15 years have seen an increasing number of studies of mindreading in adults, providing the basis for models of the cognitive and neural basis of mature mindreading that are the terminus of development (e.g., Apperly, 2011; Schaafsma et al., 2015). A full account of the development of mindreading must not only address the relatively poor description we currently have of the abilities of children beyond early childhood. This work must also explain the processes by which children develop from their first successes in simple mindreading tasks under the most favorable conditions into the flexible abilities of adults. These abilities enable relevant and sophisticated mindreading inferences about a variety of people in a wide range of contexts, and the use of these inferences to guide communication and other forms of coordinated social behavior. Therefore, while I will review some of the growing literature on mindreading in middle childhood and adolescence as I go, my focus will be on the broader questions of how to think about these developmental changes.

I will start with a summary of a cognitive model of mindreading in adults. The focus on adults is deliberate because while research from younger children tells us a great deal about the cognitive requirements of mindreading in this age group, it is often fundamentally ambiguous about whether a cognitive process that appears necessary in young children is necessary because it is part of the mature system that is being constructed or because it is necessary for the process of construction itself (Apperly et al., 2009). Findings from adults tell us about the mature system.

A cognitive model

I will summarize a model of the cognitive basis of mindreading that brings together a wide range of work in the field. It is at once quite detailed and also a great simplification, not least because it focuses on 'epistemic' mental states such as beliefs, knowledge, and visual perspectives. Nonetheless, it provides a way of thinking about the component processes of mindreading that ought to be extensible to other cases.

Working horizontally, Figure 2.1 distinguishes processes involved in inference, storage, and use of mindreading information. While these are often all involved in a given instance of mindreading (and confounded in the majority of mindreading tasks), they are clearly separable. For example, if you tell me what you think, I do not need to infer this information from your behavior or my knowledge of your other beliefs, but I can store this information and use it to predict what you will do or interpret what you say in light of what you think. Equally, in another situation, I might succeed in inferring and storing what you think, but neglect to use this information when I predict your behavior or interpret your message. And if I am interacting with multiple people, this might raise the demands on storing what they each think independently from any difficulties associated with inferring or using this information. It is possible to devise experimental tasks that selectively target inference (Hartwright et al., 2014), storage (Apperly et al., 2008), and use (e.g., Apperly et al., 2011; Barr, 2008; Keysar et al., 2000). For example, Apperly et al. (2008) targeted storage by presenting participants with short sentences describing what someone thought (e.g., 'He thinks the object on the table is blue') and what was the case in reality (e.g., 'Really, the object on the table is red'). These were followed by a picture that probed for one or the other piece of information. Participants did not have to infer what someone thought and did not have to use this information to predict action, interpret a message, or make subsequent inferences;

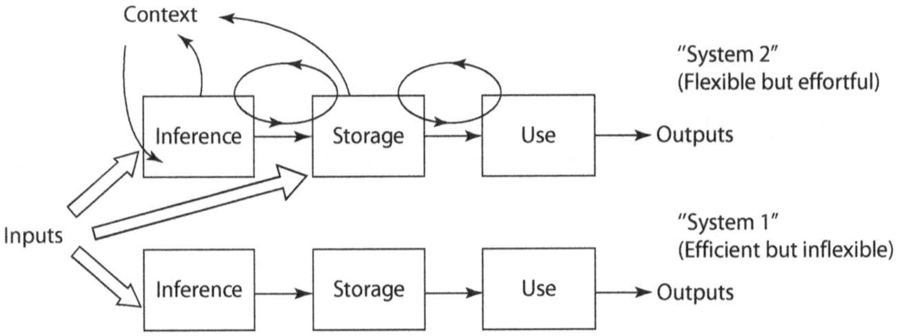

Figure 2.1 A cognitive model of mindreading (simplified from Apperly, 2010). The model distinguishes processes involved in inference, storage and use of information about others' mental states. "System 2" makes flexible, context-sensitive mindreading inferences by drawing richly upon background knowledge, in processes represented by the grey arrows. Oval arrows indicate that System 2 mindreading will often involve repeated cycles of reasoning. System 1 processes manage to be more cognitively efficient by limiting their interaction with background information and limiting their processing over inputs. For clarity, only one System 1 process is depicted, but there are likely to be multiple processes, for example to enable mindreading of belief-like states, goals, and emotions.

they simply had to hold the presented information briefly in mind and report it back. This task can be extended to require both storage and use of mindreading information to predict behavior. In Apperly et al. (2011), participants read sentences about where an agent thought an object was hidden (in one of two boxes), where it was really hidden, and whether the agent wished to obtain or avoid the object. Participants then had to predict whether the agent would open the box they thought contained the object (if they wanted it), or the empty box (if they wished to avoid it). Hartwright et al. (2014) extended the task further to include trials that required a mindreading inference. In this version of the task, the sentence describing the target's wish to obtain or avoid the object was replaced with a photograph of their face (with different targets from trial to trial). Happy and sad faces indicated desires to obtain or avoid the object and made low demands for mindreading inferences. Neutral faces required participants to consider whether that particular person would want to obtain or avoid that particular object, and so we anticipated that they would make higher demands on mindreading inferences. Of course, no one task can perfectly isolate mindreading inference or use from at least some demands upon storage. However, it is possible to draw conclusions from systematic comparisons between tasks or within the conditions of a given task.

Perhaps the best current evidence that these component processes have some psychological reality comes from variation in the patterns of neural activity across different tasks. For example, the great majority of studies find that mindreading recruits activity in the medial prefrontal cortex (mPFC) and bilateral temporoparietal junction (TPJ) (Molenberghs et al., 2016). However, using tasks that can vary these component processes independently, we have found evidence that TPJ is recruited whenever participants store or use mindreading information, while mPFC may not be recruited unless participants need to make a novel mindreading inference that goes beyond the information given about the target person (Hartwright et al., 2014). Interestingly, across a variety of tasks targeting these different component processes, behavioral evidence of 'egocentric bias' is almost universally observed, whether in slower judgments of another's perspective when it differs from one's own (Samson et al., 2010), or in errors of interpreting another's message in terms of one's own privileged knowledge rather than their limited perspective or false belief (Keysar et al., 2003). Neuroimaging and neuropsychology suggest that resisting egocentric interference is correlated with activity in the inferior frontal gyrus (McCleery et al., 2011; Hartwright et al., 2012; Ramsey et al., 2013) and is impaired by damage to this brain region (Samson et al., 2005, 2015), even though this region is not part of the standard 'social brain network' (Molenberghs et al., 2016).

Working vertically, Figure 2.1 distinguishes between mindreading processes that are flexible, relatively effortful, and controlled and those that are less effortful and more automatic, corresponding to a distinction often made in cognitive psychology between 'System 2' and 'System 1' processes (e.g., Evans & Stanovich, 2013). Prototypical mindreading needs to be highly flexible: I need to be able to ascribe mental states concerning just about anything, to just about anybody, and to do so in a way that is sensitive to that particular person and the context that they are in. Highly flexible cognitive processes tend to be cognitively effortful, and indeed there is much evidence to suggest that such mindreading in adults is cognitively effortful. Merely viewing stimuli that afford mindreading does not guarantee that mindreading inferences will be made (Apperly et al., 2006; Back & Apperly, 2010). When mindreading inferences are made, adults show a pervasive tendency for egocentric biases (Royzman et al., 2003), and resisting egocentric interference appears to be effortful (Epley et al., 2004). Mindreading can be disrupted by the concurrent performance of an executive task (Bull et al., 2008) and by brain lesions that affect executive control (Samson et al., 2005, 2015). Individual differences in adults' mindreading performance are often correlated with individual differences in executive control and working memory (e.g., Bradford et al., 2018; German & Hehman, 2006; Mckinnon & Moskovich, 2007; Qureshi et al., 2019). These characteristics are what would be expected if we think of mindreading as a flexible set of reasoning processes enabling the ascription of mental states to a wide range of people in a diverse set of situations.

However, other evidence indicates that some mindreading may be more cognitively efficient and automatic, but also limited in the kinds of mindreading they can perform. Several paradigms provide converging evidence that task-irrelevant information about what someone else sees and has seen (i.e. their belief) can influence participants' own expectations, judgments, and actions (a phenomenon known as 'altercentric interference'; e.g., Kovács et al., 2010; Samson et al., 2010), that these effects may not be disrupted by concurrent tasks (e.g., Qureshi et al., 2010), and that participants may have limited awareness or control over them (e.g., Schneider et al., 2012). As with other 'System 1' processes, the efficiency of these processes comes at the expense of limitations on the kinds of problems they can tackle. While altercentric interference is consistently observed for Level 1 visual perspective-taking (about what someone sees) it is only observed for Level 2 perspective-taking (about precisely how they see it from their own perspective) when participants are instructed or motivated for perspective-taking (e.g., Elekes et al., 2016; Surtees et al., 2016). Similarly, altercentric interference is observed when the other person has a false belief about the presence or absence of an object, but not about the object's identity (Edwards & Low, 2017). Interpretation of these findings in terms of two distinct sets of mindreading processes is contested (e.g., Apperly & Butterfill, 2009; Butterfill & Apperly, 2013; Carruthers, 2017; Heyes, 2014). What is uncontroversial, I think, is that there is a tension between demands that mindreading be highly flexible and context-sensitive on the one hand, and efficient enough to keep up with fast-moving social interactions on the other hand. In the model here, that tension is resolved by proposing different systems that make different trade-offs between these requirements.

This short summary provides an overview of key phenomena observed in adults' mindreading and a model for thinking about the underlying cognitive processes. I hope it is clear that there is a substantial gap between the well-studied abilities of children to pass the most sensitive possible tests of mindreading concepts (e.g., Wellman, 2014) and the abilities of adults to deploy those concepts in ways that are both sophisticated and flexible in some circumstances, and efficient and automatic in others. This requires us to conceive how can children become better at mindreading, once they've acquired basic mindreading concepts. In what follows, I shall use this model of the adult terminus of development as a basis for highlighting some important questions about the changes taking place during later childhood and adolescence.

Increasing capacity for effortful mindreading

One possibility is that, in contrast to qualitative changes in mindreading concepts in younger children, mindreading in middle childhood and beyond undergoes quantitative changes in capacity. The challenge here is that current theories have little to say about what it could mean to have a greater or a lesser capacity for mindreading per se. Therefore the best candidates for drivers of such changes are developments in executive control. Executive control processes have a close relationship with the development of mindreading in young children (e.g., Devine & Hughes, 2014), and, on the evidence above, appear to be necessary for mindreading in adults. The possibility is made even more compelling when coupled with evidence that executive control processes continue to improve across middle childhood and adolescence (Anderson et al., 2001; Davidson et al., 2006; Huizinga et al., 2006; Luciana et al., 2005).

Mindreading performance across later development

There is evidence, from tasks very similar to those used with adults, to support the possibility that mindreading continues to be effortful and that performance improves across later childhood and adolescence. Surtees et al. (2012) tested children aged six to ten on a task that required simple (Level 1) inferences about the visual perspective-taking task of a cartoon character (Samson et al., 2010). As with adults, all age groups showed egocentric effects, giving slower responses when their perspective was different from that of the avatar. However, older children made faster judgments of the avatar's perspective and made fewer errors than younger children. Apperly et al. (2011) tested six- to eleven-year-olds on a task where they were told a character's belief (true or false) about an object's location and his desire to obtain or avoid the object (so it was unnecessary to infer these mental states) and tested for how quickly children could use this information to predict the character's search behavior. All age groups responded more slowly when the character had a false belief and when he had a desire to avoid the object, but older children were faster and more accurate on all judgments. Dumontheil et al. (2010) tested 7- to 17-year-olds on the 'director task' (Keysar et al., 2000) that requires an inference about the director's visual perspective and, critically, the use of this perspective to interpret her instructions to move objects. All age groups made egocentric errors, whereby they moved an object that the director could not see and so could not be talking about, but older participants made many fewer such errors.

The studies just described help establish continuity between some key phenomena seen in adults' mindreading and improvements in the abilities seen in middle childhood and adolescence. Two further studies have sought to relate this evidence of improving performance to specific challenges that might face children when attempting to use their mindreading abilities. Research with adult participants by Barr (2008) suggests that, when using a speaker's perspective to interpret their utterance, the main source of egocentric effects is not with perspective-taking per se but with the subsequent step of integrating perspective and language. This led Wang, Frisson et al. (2016) to hypothesize that children might make fewer egocentric errors on the director task when the director's instruction was simpler (e.g., 'nudge the small ball') compared with when it was more complex (e.g., 'nudge the small ball one slot up'). They found that this was indeed the case: Not only did ten-year-olds make fewer egocentric errors than eight-year-olds, but both age groups made far fewer (approximately half) errors when the director's instruction was simpler. Note that children's difficulty here was not with understanding the instructions themselves: Performance was close to ceiling on control trials with the same instructions but no need for perspective-taking. Rather, children found it more difficult to take account of the speaker's perspective while simultaneously working to comprehend a more complex sentence. It seems plausible that this integration of information draws upon children's working memory capacity. These results highlight a realistic constraint on children's capacity to put their mindreading abilities to practical use.

A second plausible challenge for using mindreading abilities is to keep in mind the perspective of the other person until it needs to be used. The standard form of the director task minimizes this requirement because it is always possible to see which items the director can and cannot see, and so to verify whether she could be referring to a particular object after she has delivered her instruction. Moreover, the number of items that the director cannot see is held constant. Zhao et al. (2018) adapted the task so that participants actually had to remember the director's perspective. Following a brief study period when the director's partial access to the array of objects could be encoded, all of the objects were blocked from the director's view, meaning that the director's perspective had to be held in mind for the remaining duration of the trial. Moreover, Zhao et al. (2018) varied the number of objects that were in the director's perspective from three to nine. As in Wang, Frisson et al. (2016), eight-year-olds made more egocentric errors than ten-year-olds. Importantly, both age groups made more egocentric errors when the size of the director's perspective was larger, and when the director's perspective actually had to be remembered. Of course, we probably should not be surprised that mindreading is more difficult when it places higher memory demands. What is, perhaps, surprising is that these studies are unusual in seeking to identify and manipulate factors that affect capacity for mindreading.

What drives developmental changes?

The previous paragraphs present the glass-half-full perspective on developmental change in mindreading capacity. But I think there is an alternative perspective that is equally important and perhaps more challenging. The challenge is that the evidence just described provides a surprisingly thin story about developmental change. For example, perhaps the most ubiquitous phenomenon in research on mindreading is the tendency for errors and biases to be systematically egocentric, rather than random. Moreover, this accords with folk wisdom about the development of social abilities, which views children as more egocentric than adults. It is striking, therefore, that while the studies by Apperly et al. (2011), Dumontheil et al. (2010), and Surtees & Apperly (2012) provide clear evidence of improving response times and error rates, they provide almost no evidence of reduction in egocentrism. More precisely, if we operationalize egocentrism as the difference between a test condition that involves a conflict between self and other perspectives and a control condition that does not, then age-related change in egocentrism should be observed in an interaction between effects of condition and age. Only Dumontheil et al. (2010) observed such an interaction, and this was entirely due to the adult age group showing proportionately lower egocentrism than the four younger age groups. Of course, we should not underestimate the value of improvements in the speed of mindreading for success in fast-moving social interactions (Apperly, 2011, p. 163). If we assume that the default under time pressure is to respond according to one's own perspective, then an improvement in speed alone may account for a valuable reduction in egocentric errors. But it is important to recognize that this is not due to a reduction in conflict between self and other perspectives, and perhaps not, therefore, due to improvements in inhibitory control.

There is an analogous limitation in the findings of Wang, Frisson et al. (2016) and Zhao et al. (2018). In both studies, older children performed better than younger children, and performance in low-load conditions was better than in high-load conditions, but if older children performed better overall because they had greater capacity to deal with the load placed on perspective-taking, we might have expected an interaction between age and condition. Wang et al. (2016) found no interaction, and Zhao et al. (2018) only found weak evidence for interactions.

Convergence between experimental and individual differences approaches?

I have focussed primarily on experimental evidence from children because these studies make the most direct links with research on adults, on which the cognitive model is based. Interestingly, I think there are similarities between the picture described here and emerging evidence from studies of individual differences and longitudinal development. These studies use different mindreading tasks, such as the strange stories task (White et al., 2009), the silent films task (Devine & Hughes, 2013), and the animated triangles task (Castelli et al., 2000). In comparison with the experimental tasks described above, these tasks trade greater face validity and superior measurement characteristics with reduced insight into the underlying cognitive processes. Performance on these tasks shows clear improvement over middle to late childhood (e.g., Devine & Hughes, 2016) and concurrent correlations with working memory and executive function (Devine et al., 2016). However, once concurrent relationships are accounted for, there is little evidence that earlier executive function (including inhibitory control) predicts later mindreading, and there is evidence that earlier working memory predicts later mindreading when the lag between earlier and later testing is short (Lecce et al., 2017) but not when it is long (Devine et al., 2016). Moreover, in a cross-cultural study, Wang, Devine et al. (2016) found a double-dissociation between higher mindreading and lower executive function in a UK sample and lower mindreading and higher executive function in a Hong Kong sample, despite concurrent correlations between these variables in both samples. I think it is important to note that the challenge here is not that the key findings are inconsistent across studies – the evidence from both experimental and individual differences approaches is surprisingly consistent. The challenge is that both approaches provide clear evidence that capacity for memory and executive control is relevant for mindreading across later childhood and adolescence, and much weaker evidence that increasing capacity for memory and executive control is a driver of developmental change in mindreading. I am not sure a full response to these challenges is currently possible, but I think the following observations may cast some light.

Scaffolding or bricks?

In Apperly et al. (2009) we used the metaphor of building a house to distinguish between distinctive roles that might be played by language or executive function in mindreading. On the one hand, such a function may resemble scaffolding during housebuilding: It plays a critical role in the construction of mindreading but has no enduring role in the finished structure. On the other, it may resemble bricks, which serve a role in construction because they are part of the finished structure. Evidence from adults can help distinguish between these roles by providing evidence of the finished structure, and work on adults provides clear evidence that mature mindreading continues to depend upon working memory and executive function. Let us imagine that in later childhood, working memory and executive function are only serving the role of bricks, and not scaffolding; that is to say, they are necessary throughout development but are not serving a unique role in the process of construction. In that case, we could observe concurrent relationships between mindreading, working memory, and executive function at every age, but there is no reason to think that earlier memory and executive abilities should predict later mindreading once concurrent relationships are controlled for. Note that this proposal for later development of mindreading contrasts with evidence that executive function serves a scaffolding role in early mindreading (Devine & Hughes, 2014), but fits with recent evidence from middle childhood (Devine et al., 2016) suggesting that executive abilities could be serving different roles (as scaffolding and as bricks respectively) in earlier and later development. At the risk of stretching the analogy, it is also relevant to observe that an over-supply of bricks without appropriate scaffolding does not result in faster building of the house. If, as Wang, Devine et al. (2016) suggest, the scaffolding for later mindreading is social in origin, this may explain why high executive control does not guarantee high mindreading performance.

Limiting steps

Evidence from adults with severe executive impairment following brain injury suggests that executive function remains necessary for adults' success on some of the simplest mindreading tasks, such as first-order false belief tasks (Samson et al., 2005, 2015). However, in neurologically healthy adults we observe near-perfect accuracy on false belief tasks despite continuing individual differences in executive function. This does not mean that simple false belief tasks pose no executive requirement for healthy adults – indeed, neuroimaging studies suggest that they do – but rather all healthy adults can muster the necessary executive capacity: Executive processes are not a limiting step for healthy adults' success. The concept of limiting steps is useful because it can help explain why performance on a mindreading task may not correlate with performance on an executive task even when we believe the executive process is necessary for mindreading. Conversely, it may help explain why Wang et al. (2015) and Zhao et al. (2018) found little evidence of interaction between children's age and the effect of memory load manipulations on mindreading. We should observe an interaction with age only if memory capacity ceased to be a limiting factor in older children. In contrast, if memory capacity continues to be a limiting factor irrespective of whether memory load is low or high, then we should see effects of memory load and effects of age, but no interaction.

It is relatively early days for studies of this kind in later childhood and adolescence, and the conclusions I am suggesting here are certainly tentative. However, I hope this discussion illustrates the value of careful task analysis of the contributions that processes such as memory and executive function might make to mindreading, and how these may change over developmental time.

Automatization and efficiency

The last section addressed developmental changes in cognitively effortful mindreading. As described in the introduction and Figure 2.1, there is also evidence that not all adults' mindreading is so effortful. Let us assume that adults do indeed have some capacities for mindreading that are relatively automatic in their operation. How do adults end up with these capacities? There are two broad categories of answer.[1] Firstly, some capacity for automatic processes could be an original feature of the architecture for mindreading that develops in infancy or early childhood. Secondly, children's initial mindreading might all be relatively effortful, but some aspects may become automatized with repeated practice. (Thirdly, both might be true.) The idea of original automaticity gains some credibility from evidence that infants may be capable of simple mindreading (e.g., Scott & Baillargeon, 2017). Since infants have relatively limited resources for effortful cognitive processing, it is plausible that their mindreading abilities are efficient and relatively automatic. Perhaps, as appears to be the case for some other domains, such as number cognition, the abilities seen in infants remain intact as efficient, automatic, but inflexible components of the adult system (Apperly & Butterfill, 2009). The idea of automatization is surely plausible given clear examples of other abilities, such as word-reading, that are clearly effortful as they first develop, but become highly automatized over time (Stroop, 1935; Norton & Wolf, 2012).

Studying automatic processes in development

Distinguishing between these possibilities requires us to study changes in automaticity over developmental time. That is difficult in infants and young children as we currently lack tasks for this age range that provide direct evidence of automaticity. Tasks used with adults, which have provided more direct evidence of automaticity, usually require a substantial number of trials and measurement of response times (e.g., Kovacs et al., 2010; Samson et al., 2010), fixation durations (e.g., Schneider et al., 2012), or movement trajectories (van der Wel et al., 2014). By adapting one such task, we were able to test whether simple (Level 1) visual perspective-taking became more automatic between six and ten years of age (Surtees & Apperly, 2012).

In the 'dot-perspective' task, participants judge the number of discs that can be seen on the walls of a cartoon room, on some trials from the perspective of an avatar, and on other trials from their own 'self' perspective (Samson et al., 2010). Sometimes the avatar saw the same number of discs as the participant (consistent trials) and sometimes they saw fewer (inconsistent trials). The critical phenomenon for current purposes is 'altercentric interference', which is when adult participants respond more slowly on self trials when their perspective is inconsistent with the avatar's compared with when it is consistent. We interpret this interference as evidence that participants are automatically processing the avatar's perspective. The critical inferential step in adapting this to study development is to interpret the size of this 'altercentric interference' as an index of automatization. And this leads to the prediction that if altercentric interference is the result of an initially effortful perspective-taking process becoming automatized over developmental time, then younger children should show a smaller altercentric effect than older children.

In this study, we found no evidence to support automatization. Older children were certainly faster at responding than younger children, but the altercentric effect (i.e., the difference between consistent and inconsistent trials) changed in proportion to these overall changes and was not proportionately greater in older children. Of course, we only tested six- to ten-year-old children, so this study does not rule out the possibility that automatization has already reached asymptote by six years of age. Considering that Level 1 visual perspective-taking is first observed at 24 months (Flavell et al., 1981) or younger (Sodian et al., 2007), this is clearly a possibility. Equally, it is possible that such simple perspective-taking is cognitively efficient and relatively automatic from its earliest development. Distinguishing between these possibilities requires testing of younger children which is challenging with tasks that rely upon measuring response times. Future studies may succeed in identifying automatic processes with passively acquired measures, such as evoked brain responses. For current purposes, this study serves to illustrate how it is possible to conduct multi-trial response time studies with children older than those typically tested in studies of mindreading, and use this approach to seek evidence of automatization.

Practice makes…

While Surtees and Apperly (2012) found no evidence of automatization in one study, it remains highly plausible that some mindreading processes do become automatized. Equally, it is very important to realize that automatization is almost certainly going to be limited to special cases and that we should take care to distinguish automatization from other developmental improvements that result from experience and practice.

Automatization is possible when there are reliable correlations between the input to a cognitive process and the output of that process so that these inputs and outputs can become directly associated for more efficient processing. The development of reading provides clear contrasting cases of where this does and does not occur (e.g., Hoover & Gough, 1990). Children learn to decompose the visual form of words into graphemes, which must in turn be mapped to phonological representations that are then used to generate the sound of the word. Anyone who has seen a young child read will recognize that these processes are effortful. Nonetheless, the mappings between the visual form and phonological representations of words are sufficiently regular that repeated experience can lead to automatization. While this benefits fluent reading, it also leads to interference when the word's meaning is not the intended object of attention (e.g., Stroop, 1935).

The case of single-word reading contrasts with the problem of deriving the meaning of a written sentence. In contrast with single words, we often read sentences that we have never seen before, so there is much less potential for automatically mapping form to meaning. Moreover, the meaning of a sentence is often richly dependent upon the broader textual context in which it features (think of Macbeth's question: 'Is this a dagger which I see before me?'), and the same sentence can have quite different meanings across different contexts. While sentence reading does benefit from statistical regularities in language (Arciuli & Simpson, 2012), these regularities are sufficiently limited that sentence reading is a poor candidate for automatization, and indeed sentence comprehension is an effortful, attention-demanding process, even for adults (Rayner et al., 2012). Nonetheless, practice with sentence reading (and comprehension of the broader text) does result in significant improvements, not least because readers gain skill in selecting information from the textual context that is necessary for comprehending the sentence currently being read (Rayner et al., 2012).

The case of text reading provides a useful basis for framing expectations about mindreading. Simple visual perspective-taking – whether it is originally automatic, or automatized – is a good candidate for an automatic mindreading process because clear regularities exist between the input of observing an agent oriented toward an object and the output of registering that the agent sees the object. Such abilities may be important enablers of fast-moving social interaction. However, consider what Macbeth might be thinking as he contemplates the imaginary dagger, or an adolescent trying to interpret whether a peer's ambiguous behavior is an invitation to closer friendship or an attempt to humiliate. Such cases are perhaps more representative of the majority of mindreading inferences than simple visual perspective-taking. Moreover, they are notably more like sentence reading than single-word reading, insofar as they likely concern a unique combination of circumstances, where it is necessary to go beyond the information that is immediately available in order to make an interpretation, and where there are only vague criteria for selecting relevant information from that background. Based on the example of sentence reading, we should expect that such mindreading is a skill that can be developed and honed through social experience, but a skill that nonetheless remains relatively effortful and attention-demanding.

Flexible mindreading and children's changing social worlds

It seems plausible that changes in children's social environments are at least as important for continuing developments in mindreading as increasing cognitive capacities and opportunities for practice-based automatization.

Through later childhood and adolescence the social world of children expands to include more people, a greater range of contexts, and the increasing importance of friendships and romantic relationships with peers (e.g., Brown, 1990; Steinberg & Morris, 2001). Whereas social concepts such as reciprocity, loyalty, trust, and commitment can often be taken for granted in a close family context, expansion of children's social worlds brings a greater requirement to evaluate relationships in these terms, which will often require mindreading (e.g., Bigelow & LaGaipa, 1980; Youniss, 1982). However, limitations on how we most often study mindreading mean that it is not at all clear how these social changes could have an effect on older children. In this final, and most speculative, section, I hope to provide some pointers.

Of course, the idea that social experience contributes to mindreading has been widely discussed (e.g., Carpendale & Lewis, 2006; Wellman, 2014). The literature's emphasis on the mindreading milestones of early childhood has led researchers' main focus to be on how social experience might influence the acquisition of basic mindreading concepts, indexed by success on the simplest possible mindreading tasks (Apperly, 2012). Katherine Nelson indicates a deeper and more enduring influence of socialization when she suggests that mindreading requires children to become members of 'a community of minds' (Nelson, 2005, 1996; see also Fernyhough, 2008), though she gives limited detail on the benefits conferred by membership. Related ideas are developed by Hutto (e.g., 2007), who argues that mindreading is fundamentally grounded in socially constructed narrative abilities, an idea that receives some empirical support from evidence that narrative fiction can promote mindreading (Kidd & Castano, 2013). Zawidzki (2013) brings this line of thinking full-circle by suggesting that socialization also shapes us to be interpretable by mindreaders; that is to say, in becoming a mindreader we also learn to think and act in ways that are reasonable in terms of mental states that could be ascribed to us.

While Nelson, Hutto, and Zawidzki come from rather different theoretical traditions from the cognitive approach of this chapter, there is a striking convergence in concerns here. In particular, there is a recognition that we need to face up to the problem of how mindreaders 'flesh out' (Hutto, 2007, p. 55) the limited information that is often directly available about someone's thoughts and feelings; and that understanding how we form coherent mindreading explanations may tell us something fundamental about what mindreading is and how it develops. However, while they cast light on the phenomena we may be seeking to explain, these approaches do not take us very far in advancing a cognitive approach to mindreading. This is because they seek to ground one poorly-understood ability (mindreading) in another ability (narrative comprehension, or abductive inferences) that is poorly-understood, at least in terms of cognitive processes. How, then, might we gain further insight into these processes?

Children's changing social worlds as changes in culture

A series of recent studies has shown intriguing cultural effects on mindreading judgments in children and adults. Perez-Zapata et al. (2016) tested Australian and Chilean participants using the 'strange stories' task (e.g., White et al., 2009), which requires relatively subtle and contextualized inferences about the mental states of story characters. By adapting the surface form (e.g., names of characters and places) but not the underlying inferential structure, the authors created story variants situated in an Australian or Chilean context. Australian and Chilean adults completed both variants of the task, and each showed more accurate (and, if anything, faster) mindreading judgments for stories situated in their own culture. No such pattern was observed on control stories that did not require mindreading. Subsequent studies with older children and adults suggest that such effects are not solely due to prejudice against out-group members or to variation in participants' perception of similarity between themselves and 'own-country' versus 'foreign' social targets (Ekerim-Akbulut et al., 2019; Gönültaş et al., 2019). It is important to emphasize that there is no suggestion here of cultural differences in basic mindreading concepts, nor in overall mindreading ability. Nor do these studies examine exotic or unusual cases of mindreading. Instead, for perfectly ordinary mindreading these studies highlight the role of culturally acquired knowledge in 'fleshing out' the directly-available information in order to make appropriate mindreading inferences. This complexity is imperfectly captured in the top left part of Figure 2.1, where mindreading inferences are part of a processing loop that includes background knowledge. While these studies perhaps resonate most clearly with the challenges of mindreading in a 'foreign country', I would like to suggest that they provide a potent analogy for the challenge of mindreading anyone in an unfamiliar context, whether that is a different age, environment (e.g., home versus school versus work) or social group: Each has the potential to be like another country, where people do things differently.

From this observation we might think it important to ensure that our tests of mindreading are 'culture-fair'; to ensure that the abilities of participants are not underestimated by testing their mindreading of targets from a different group from their own (whether the group difference was due to nationality, age, or other variables). This is a valid point if one's objective is to test the mindreading ability of a group independently from the effects of familiarity with context and culture (Devine & Hughes, 2016). But I hope it is clear that the ability to use context to make appropriate mindreading inferences is an essential component of mindreading and not a mere confound to be controlled. With this in mind, it is equally valid to evaluate the ability of an individual or a group to mindread across a wide range of people and situations. I think this may be one way to operationalize what Nelson (1996) meant when she wrote of children becoming members of the 'community of minds'. It seems plausible that the ability to make relevant mindreading inferences across different contexts is a significant developmental challenge for children as they extend their social range, and also a substantial and enduring source of individual variability in mindreading ability.

Conclusion

It will be apparent by this point that even our understanding of mindreading in adults is very much a work in progress. Nonetheless, I think it provides a valuable lens through which to view questions about development, not least because it describes the mature system that children are building. This perspective shifts the emphasis from children's acquisition of mindreading concepts towards the processes that enable such concepts to be deployed in the face of competing demands for flexibility and efficiency. Significant challenges remain for conceptualizing these abilities, to understand what underwrites the intuition that children in middle childhood and adolescence are better mindreaders than younger children, and that within the same age group some individuals are better mindreaders than others. There is an acute need, I think, for conceptualizing and measuring how context-sensitive mindreading inferences are made, and how this might change over development. Likewise, challenges remain in the development of mindreading tasks that are appropriate for older children or adults. There is clearly a tension between the desire to have tasks – and task analyses – that makes the component processes of mindreading transparent, and the desire to have tasks that do justice to the complexity of mindreading in realistic contexts. However, tackling these challenges is exciting, and I think we are poised to view mindreading not merely as a set of milestones in preschool children, but as a much more extended development throughout childhood, and indeed across adulthood as well.

Note

1 These ideas are discussed in more detail in Apperly (2010).

References

Anderson, V.A., Anderson, P., Northam, E., Jacobs, R., & Catroppa, C. (2001). Development of executive functions through late childhood and adolescence in an Australian sample. *Developmental Neuropsychology, 20*(1), 385–406.

Apperly, I. (2011). *Mindreaders: The Cognitive Basis of "Theory of Mind"*. Hove, UK: Psychology Press.

Apperly, I.A., Back, E., Samson, D., & France, L. (2008). The cost of thinking about false beliefs: Evidence from adult performance on a non-inferential theory of mind task. *Cognition, 106*, 1093–1108.

Apperly, I.A. & Butterfill, S.A. (2009). Do humans have two systems to track beliefs and belief-like states? *Psychological Review*, 116, 953–970. DOI: 10.1037/a10016923

Apperly, I.A., Riggs, K.J., Simpson, A., Chiavarino, C. & Samson, D. (2006). Is belief reasoning automatic? *Psychology Science, 17*(10), 841–844.

Apperly, I.A., Samson, D., & Humphreys, G.W. (2009). Studies of adults can inform accounts of theory of mind development. *Developmental Psychology, 45*(1), 190–201.

Apperly, I.A., Warren, F., Andrews, B.J., Grant, J. & Todd, S. (2011). Error patterns in the belief-desire reasoning of 3- to 5-year-olds recur in reaction times from 6 years to adulthood: Evidence for developmental continuity in theory of mind. *Child Development. 82*(5), 1691–703.

Arciuli, J., & Simpson, I.C. (2012). Statistical learning is related to reading ability in children and adults. *Cognitive Science, 36*(2), 286–304.

Back, E., & Apperly, I.A. (2010). Two sources of evidence on the non-automaticity of true and false belief ascription. *Cognition, 115*(1), 54–70.

Barr, D.J. (2008). Pragmatic expectations and linguistic evidence: Listeners anticipate but do not integrate common ground. *Cognition, 109*(1), 18–40.

Bigelow, B.J., & LaGaipa, J.J. (1980). The development of friendship values and choice. In H.C. Foot, A.J. Chapman & J.R. Smith (Eds.), *Friendship and Social Relations in Children* (pp. 15–44). Transaction Publishing. London, UK.

Bradford, E.E., Jentzsch, I., Gomez, J.C., Chen, Y., Zhang, D., & Su, Y. (2018). Cross-cultural differences in adult theory of mind abilities: A comparison of native-English speakers and native-Chinese speakers on the self/other differentiation task. *Quarterly Journal of Experimental Psychology, 71*(12), 2665–2676.

Brown, B.B. (1990). Peer groups and peer cultures. In S.S. Feldman and G.R. Elliott (Eds.), *At the Threshold: The Developing Adolescent* (pp. 171–196). Cambridge, MA: Harvard University Press.

Bull, R., Phillips, L.H. & Conway, C.A. (2008). The role of control functions in mentalizing: Dual-task studies of Theory of Mind and executive function. *Cognition, 107*, 663–672.

Butterfill, S. & Apperly, I.A. (2013). How to construct a minimal theory of mind. *Mind & Language, 28*(2), 606–637.

Carpendale, J., & Lewis, C. (2006). *How Children Develop Social Understanding*. Blackwell Publishing. Oxford, UK.

Carruthers, P. (2017). Mindreading in adults: Evaluating two-systems views. *Synthese, 194*(3), 673–688.

Castelli, F., Happé, F., Frith, U., & Frith, C. (2000). Movement and mind: A functional imaging study of perception and interpretation of complex intentional movement patterns. *Neuroimage, 12*(3), 314–325.

Davidson, M.C., Amso, D., Anderson, L.C., & Diamond, A. (2006). Development of cognitive control and executive functions from 4 to 13 years: Evidence from manipulations of memory, inhibition and task switching. *Neuropsychologia, 44*, 2037 –2078.

Devine, R.T., & Hughes, C. (2013). Silent films and strange stories: Theory of mind, gender, and social experiences in middle childhood. *Child Development, 84*(3), 989–1003.

Devine, R.T., & Hughes, C. (2014). Relations between false belief understanding and executive function in early childhood: A meta-analysis. *Child Development, 85*(5), 1777–1794.

Devine, R.T., & Hughes, C. (2016). Measuring theory of mind across middle childhood: Reliability and validity of the silent films and strange stories tasks. *Journal of Experimental Child Psychology, 149*, 23–40.

Devine, R.T., White, N., Ensor, R., & Hughes, C. (2016). Theory of mind in middle childhood: Longitudinal associations with executive function and social competence. *Developmental Psychology, 52*(5), 758.

Dumontheil, I., Apperly, I.A., & Blakemore, S.J. (2010). Online use of mental state inferences continues to develop in late adolescence. *Developmental Science, 13*(2), 331–8.

Edwards, K., & Low, J. (2017). Reaction time profiles of adults' action prediction reveal two mindreading systems. *Cognition, 160*, 1–16.

Ekerim-Akbulut, M., Selçuk, B., Slaughter, V., Hunter, J.A., & Ruffman, T. (2019). In two minds: Similarity, threat, and prejudice contribute to worse mindreading of outgroups compared with an ingroup. *Journal of Cross-Cultural Psychology, 51*(1). doi:10.1177/0022022119883699.

Elekes, F., Varga, M., & Király, I. (2016). Evidence for spontaneous level-2 perspective taking in adults. *Consciousness and Cognition, 41*, 93–103.

Epley, N., Keysar, B., Van Boven, L., & Gilovich, T. (2004). Perspective taking as egocentric anchoring and adjustment. *Journal of Personality and Social Psychology, 87*(3), 327.

Evans, J.S.B., & Stanovich, K.E. (2013). Dual-process theories of higher cognition: Advancing the debate. *Perspectives on Psychological Science, 8*(3), 223–241.

Fernyhough, C. (2008). Getting Vygotskian about theory of mind: Mediation, dialogue, and the development of social understanding. *Developmental Review 28*, 225–262.

Flavell, J.H., Everett, B.A., Croft, K., & Flavell, E.R. (1981). Young children's knowledge about visual-perception – further evidence for the level 1-level 2 distinction. *Developmental Psychology, 17*, 99–103.

German, T.P., & Hehman, J.A. (2006). Representational and executive selection resources in 'theory of mind': Evidence from compromised belief-desire reasoning in old age. *Cognition, 101*(1), 129–152.

Gönültaş, S., Selçuk, B., Slaughter, V., Hunter, J.A., & Ruffman, T. (2019). The capricious nature of theory of mind: Does mental state understanding depend on the characteristics of the target?. *Child Development, 91*(2), e280–e298.

Hartwright, C., Apperly, I.A., & Hansen, P.C. (2012). Multiple roles for executive control in belief-desire reasoning: Distinct neural networks are recruited for self perspective inhibition and complexity of reasoning. *Neuroimage*, 61(4), 921–930.

Hartwright, C., Apperly, I.A., & Hansen, P.C. (2014). Representation, control or reasoning? distinct functions for theory of mind within the medial prefrontal cortex. *Journal of Cognitive Neuroscience, 26*(4), 683–698.

Heyes, C. (2014). Submentalizing I am not really reading your mind. *Perspectives on Psychological Science, 9*(2), 131–143.

Hoover, W.A., & Gough, P.B. (1990). The simple view of reading. *Reading and Writing, 2*(2), 127–160.

Huizinga, M., Dolan, C.V., & Van Der Molen, M.W. (2006). Age-related change in executive function: Developmental trends and a latent variable analysis. *Neuropsychologia, 44*, 2017–2036.

Hutto, D.D. (2007). The narrative practice hypothesis: Origins and applications of folk psychology. *Royal Institute of Philosophy Supplements, 60*, 43–68.

Keysar, B., Barr, D.J., Balin, J.A., & Brauner, J.S. (2000). Taking perspective in conversation: The role of mutual knowledge in comprehension. *Psychology Science, 11*(1), 32–38.

Keysar, B., Lin, S., & Barr, D.J. (2003). Limits on theory of mind use in adults. *Cognition, 89*(1), 25–41.

Kidd, D., & Castano, E. (2019). Reading literary fiction and theory of mind: Three preregistered replications and extensions of Kidd and Castano (2013). *Social Psychological and Personality Science, 10*(4), 522–531.

Kovács, Á.M., Téglás, E., & Endress, A.D. (2010). The social sense: Susceptibility to others' beliefs in human infants and adults. *Science, 330*, 1830–1834.

Lecce, S., Bianco, F., Devine, R.T., & Hughes, C. (2017). Relations between theory of mind and executive function in middle childhood: A short-term longitudinal study. *Journal of Experimental Child Psychology, 163*, 69–86.

Luciana, M., Conklin, H.M., Hooper, C.J., & Yarger, R.S. (2005). The development of nonverbal working memory and executive control processes in adolescents. *Child Development, 76*(3), 697–712.

McCleery, J.P., Surtees, A.D., Graham, K.A., Richards, J.E., & Apperly, I.A. (2011). The neural and cognitive time course of theory of mind. *Journal of Neuroscience, 31*(36), 12849e12854.

McKinnon, M.C. & Moscovitch, M. (2007). Domain-general contributions to social reasoning: Theory of mind and deontic reasoning re-explored. *Cognition, 102*, 179–218.

Molenberghs, P., Johnson, H., Henry, J.D., & Mattingley, J.B. (2016). Understanding the minds of others: A neuroimaging meta-analysis. *Neuroscience & Biobehavioral Reviews, 65*, 276–291.

Nelson, K.A. (1996). *Language in Cognitive Development: The Emergence of the Mediated Mind*. Cambridge: Cambridge University Press.

Nelson, K.A. (2005). Language pathways into the community of minds. In J.W. Astington & J.A. Baird (Eds.), *Why Language Matters for Theory of Mind* (pp. 26–49). Oxford: Oxford University Press.

Norton, E.S., & Wolf, M. (2012). Rapid automatized naming (RAN) and reading fluency: Implications for understanding and treatment of reading disabilities. *Annual Review of Psychology, 63*, 427–452.

Perez-Zapata, D., Slaughter, V., & Henry, J.D. (2016). Cultural effects on mindreading. *Cognition, 146*, 410–414.

Qureshi, A., Apperly, I.A. & Samson, D. (2010). Executive function is necessary for perspective-selection, not Level-1 visual perspective-calculation: Evidence from a dual-task study of adults. *Cognition, 117*(2), 230–236.

Qureshi, A.W., Monk, R.L., Samson, D. & Apperly, I.A. (2019). Does interference between self and other perspectives in theory of mind tasks reflect a common underlying process? Evidence from individual differences in theory of mind and inhibitory control. *Psychonomic Bulletin and Review, 27*, 178–190.

Ramsey, R., Hansen, P., Apperly, I. & Samson, D. (2013). Seeing it my way or your way: Frontopareital brain areas sustain viewpoint-independent perspective. *Journal of Cognitive Neuroscience*, 25, 670–684 DOI: 10.1162/jocn_a_00345

Rayner, K., Pollatsek, A., Ashby, J., & Clifton Jr, C. (2012). *Psychology of Reading*. Hove, UK: Psychology Press.

Royzman, E.B., Cassidy, K.W. & Baron, J. (2003). "I know, you know": Epistemic egocentrism in children and adults. *Review of General Psychology*, 7(1), 38–65.

Samson, D., Apperly, I.A., Braithwaite, J.J., Andrews, B.J., & Bodley Scott, S.E. (2010). Seeing it their way: Evidence for rapid and involuntary computation of what other people. *Journal of Experimental Psychology – Human Perception and Performance, 36*(5), 1255.

Samson, D., Apperly, I.A., Kathirgamanathan, U. & Humphreys, G.W. (2005). Seeing it my way: A case of selective deficit in inhibiting self-perspective. *Brain, 128*, 1102–1111.

Samson, D., Houthuys, S., & Humphreys, G.W. (2015). Self-perspective inhibition deficits cannot be explained by general executive control difficulties. *Cortex, 70*, 189e201.

Schaafsma, S.M., Pfaff, D.W., Spunt, R.P., & Adolphs, R. (2015). Deconstructing and reconstructing theory of mind. *Trends in Cognitive Sciences, 19*(2), 65–72.

Schneider, D., Bayliss, A.P., Becker, S.I., & Dux, P.E. (2012). Eye movements reveal sustained implicit processing of others' mental states. *Journal of Experimental Psychology: General, 141*(3), 433.

Scott, R.M., & Baillargeon, R. (2017). Early false-belief understanding. *Trends in Cognitive Sciences, 21*(4), 237–249.

Sodian, B., Thoermer, C., & Metz, U. (2007). Now I see it but you don't: 14-month-olds can represent another person's visual perspective. *Developmental Science, 10*(2), 199–204.

Steinberg, L., & Morris, A.S. (2001). Adolescent development. *Journal of Cognitive Education and Psychology, 2*(1), 55–87.

Stroop, J.R. (1935). Studies of interference in serial verbal reactions. *Journal of Experimental Psychology, 18*(6), 643.

Surtees, A. & Apperly, I.A. (2012). Egocentrism and automatic perspective-taking in children and adults. *Child Development, 83*(2), 452–460.

Surtees, A. Samson, D. & Apperly, I.A. (2016). Unintentional perspective-taking calculates whether something is seen, but not how it is seen. *Cognition, 146*, 97–105.

van der Wel, R.P., Sebanz, N., & Knoblich, G. (2014). Do people automatically track others' beliefs? Evidence from a continuous measure. *Cognition, 130*(1), 128–133.

Wang, J.J., Frisson, S., Ali, M. & Apperly, I.A. (2016). Language complexity modulates 8- and 10-year-olds' success at using their theory of mind abilities in a communication task. *Journal of Experimental Child Psychology, 149*, 62–71.

Wang, Z., Devine, R.T., Wong, K.K., & Hughes, C. (2016). Theory of mind and executive function during middle childhood across cultures. *Journal of Experimental Child Psychology, 149*, 6–22.

Wellman, H.M. (2014). *Making Minds: How Theory of Mind Develops*. Oxford: Oxford University Press.

White, S., Hill, E., Happé, F., & Frith, U. (2009). Revisiting the strange stories: Revealing mentalizing impairments in autism. *Child Development, 80*(4), 1097–1117.

Youniss, J. (1982). *Parents and Peers in Social Development: A Sullivan-Piaget Perspective*. Chicago: University of Chicago Press.

Zawidzki, T.W. (2013). *Mindshaping: A New Framework for Understanding Human Social Cognition*. Cambridge, MA: MIT Press.

Zhao, L., Wang, J.J. & Apperly, I.A. (2018). The cognitive demands of remembering a speaker's perspective and managing common ground size modulate 8- and 10-year-olds' perspective-taking abilities. *Journal of Experimental Child Psychology, 174*, 130–149.

3 Individual differences in theory of mind in middle childhood and adolescence

Rory T. Devine

In writing about historical novelists, Hilary Mantel argued that they work 'at the point where what is enacted meets what is dreamed, where politics meets psychology, where private and public meet' (Mantel, 2017). Mantel's (2017) argument highlights the distinction between recording a person's actions and interpreting a person's mental states, what some consider a dividing line between the historian and the novelist. Mantel (2017) acknowledges that historians and novelists do not fall into neat categories, the former focused on events and actions, the latter focused on thoughts and motives. Instead, historians and novelists differ from each other in the degree to which they attempt to explain and interpret others' behavior with reference to thoughts, intentions, and emotions. Mantel (2017) highlights two features of humans' ability to infer the contents of others' minds. The first is that all people (not just historians and novelists) vary in the degree to which they reason about others' thoughts, feelings, and desires. Indeed, for more than two decades researchers have consistently shown that children vary in their performance on a range of measures of theory of mind (e.g., Hughes & Devine, 2015). The second is that individual differences in mindreading are not trivial but instead have real-world significance. After all, greater flexibility, ease, and/or interest in mindreading may be essential attributes for award-winning historical novelists. This chapter evaluates the claim that there are genuine and meaningful individual differences in theory of mind (ToM) in childhood and adolescence.

Individual differences in ToM task performance in early childhood (typically measured using the false belief task) can arise because children have a shaky grasp of mental-state concepts (e.g., Gopnik & Wellman, 1992), lack the necessary executive function to shift focus to another person's point of view (e.g., Devine & Hughes, 2014), possess insufficient linguistic ability to articulate thoughts about others' minds (e.g., Milligan et al., 2007), or some combination of all three (Apperly, 2012). Consequently, it is not clear if observed individual differences in early childhood are genuine, that is, whether variation in ToM task performance reflects stable differences in the sensitivity, ease, and fluency with which children enter into the minds of others, or if they are meaningful, that is, whether differences in ToM have consequences for children's social lives (Hughes & Devine, 2015). After all, observed individual differences can arise for many reasons (e.g., measurement error) and may not capture differences in the underlying construct of interest. The extension of ToM research into middle childhood and adolescence provides an opportunity to test whether variation in ToM task performance reflects genuine individual differences in mindreading use because children should possess a basic understanding of mental concepts (or 'theory of mind competence'), such as beliefs, knowledge, and desires, and the linguistic and executive capacities to complete standard false belief tasks (e.g., Apperly, 2012).

The first aim of this chapter is to examine the degree to which individual differences in ToM are genuine, that is, whether variation in ToM task performance reflects stable differences in the sensitivity, ease, and fluency with which children enter into the minds of others (or 'theory of mind use') (Hughes & Devine, 2015). The chapter begins by scrutinizing the extent to which a single latent ability (i.e., ToM) underpins performance on a range of tasks purported to measure ToM. The chapter then examines the degree to which individual differences in ToM are stable over time in early and middle childhood. To this end, I report the results of a meta-analysis of longitudinal data on the rank-order stability of ToM. The second aim of this chapter is to ascertain whether individual differences in ToM are meaningful, that is, whether variation in ToM matters for children's social lives. The chapter considers evidence from a longitudinal study examining the social consequences of individual differences in ToM task performance.

Are there genuine individual differences in theory of mind?

There are at least two ways to determine whether individual differences in children's ToM task performance are genuine, that is, if variation in performance reflects stable underlying differences in children's flexibility, ease, and/or interest in reading others' minds rather than transient or inconsequential fluctuations in performance. First, according to the common factor model, if variation in performance on a set of measures (or 'indicators') is influenced by individual differences in an underlying latent ability or propensity (in this case, children's ToM use), then a latent factor will explain, in part, the correlations between each observed measure (e.g., Brown, 2015). Examining the relations between measures in a ToM battery can therefore shed light on the underlying latent variable (Finch & French, 2015). Second, if individual differences in ToM task performance capture a stable dimension of difference between children, then longitudinal studies, where children complete ToM tests on two or more occasions, will reveal rank-order consistency (stability) in ToM test performance even if children exhibit mean level changes over time (discontinuity) (Bornstein et al., 2017). This model can be tested by examining longitudinal correlations between earlier and later measures of ToM (Boogert et al., 2018).

Evidence for coherence among theory of mind tasks

Researchers have examined the relations between tasks designed to measure ToM in early childhood for two decades. In one study, Hughes et al. (2000) reported high levels of internal consistency (capturing the strength of inter-item correlations) across a battery of tasks measuring five-year-old children's first- and second-order false belief understanding and ability to predict emotions based on false beliefs. Each test item in the battery included control questions to ensure that children understood the task and could recall story events. The test battery comprised tasks focusing on children's understanding of beliefs but each task used different scenarios and materials (e.g., puppets, pictures, deceptive objects). It is therefore unlikely that the observed correlations can be attributed to common demands placed on children's working memory or to shared task variance arising from the use of similar questions and materials.

Further evidence for the claim that genuine individual differences in ToM explain task performance in early childhood comes from innovative work using latent variable modeling (e.g., Hughes et al., 2011). Latent variable modeling approaches, such as confirmatory factor analysis (CFA), permit researchers to test how well a hypothesized measurement model fits a given set of observed test scores (Brown, 2015). Crucially, CFA permits researchers to tackle the so-called task impurity problem (Miyake et al., 2000) by distinguishing between different sources of variance in observed test scores. For example, Figure 3.1 shows a hypothetical model in which the observed variance in a battery of ToM tasks measured on one occasion can be partitioned using CFA. In this

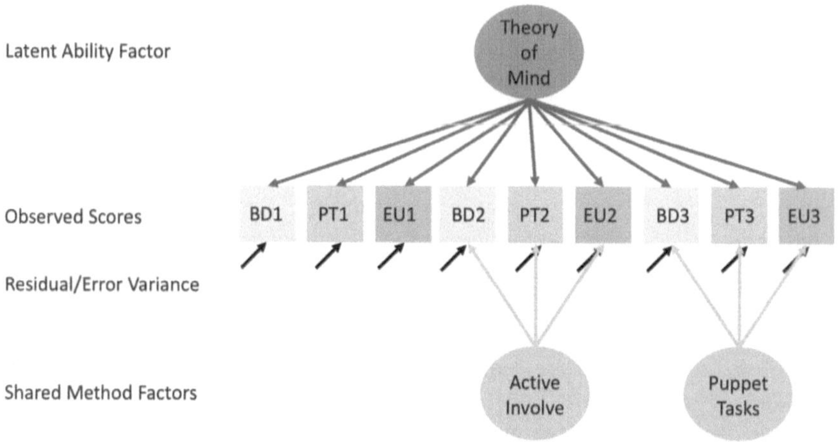

Figure 3.1 Hypothetical latent factor model. Note: Covariance between nine tasks measuring belief-desire reasoning (BD), perspective-taking (PT), and emotion understanding (EU) is explained by one latent ability factor (i.e., theory of mind), two latent method factors (i.e., items requiring active involvement in the test scenario and items involving puppet scenarios), and measurement error.

hypothetical example, children completed nine tasks differing in content (i.e., three involved belief-desire reasoning, three involved perspective-taking, and three involved emotion understanding) and method of administration (i.e., three used picture book stimuli, three used active participant involvement, and three used puppet scenarios). Variance in observed test scores was explained by one latent ability factor of interest (i.e., individual differences in ToM), two latent factors accounting for shared-method effects (e.g., items involving puppet scenarios correlate more strongly with other items that use puppet scenarios than with items based on active involvement in the test scenario), and measurement error (Brown, 2015; Geiser & Lockhart, 2012). This approach allows researchers to obtain 'error-free' estimates when studying individual differences in the latent ability factor of interest and sheds light on the organization of individual differences in a given domain (Friedman & Miyake, 2017).

In a study of 241 preschool children, Hughes et al. (2018) used CFA to test a single latent factor model on a battery of diverse false belief tasks (including change-of-location stories and misleading identity objects). Each false belief task loaded onto the single latent factor when shared method variance (i.e., task similarity between two measures) was accounted for in the model. Furthermore, each of the task indicators loaded onto the single latent factor when simultaneously regressed onto a measure of verbal ability. Even though false belief tasks differed in terms of the stimuli used (e.g., puppets, deceptive objects, picture books) and response requirements (e.g., predicting or explaining a false belief, attributing an emotion based on a false belief), a substantial amount of variance in each task was accounted for by a single latent factor. Coherence between tasks strengthens the view that performance differences within early childhood (even in narrow age ranges) may represent genuine variation in children's ToM.

Other researchers have applied modern psychometric methods (e.g., item response theory) to examine the measurement properties of ToM test batteries (e.g., Wellman & Liu, 2004). However, it is important to distinguish between measures designed to detect developmental differences and those designed to capture individual differences. Wellman and Liu (2004) created a short scale aimed at measuring developmental progression in children's understanding of different mental concepts (e.g., desires, beliefs, ignorance, false beliefs) using carefully matched methods and materials for each task. The ToM scale items are highly sensitive to age-related differences between three-, four-, and five-year-old children such that children of a given age are likely to pass a specific set of items in a predictable sequence (Wellman & Liu, 2004; Wellman et al., 2006). By design, the ToM scale is not sensitive to differences in performance within specific age groups but is exquisitely attuned to identifying 'early' and 'late' mastery of specific concepts. For example, data from Wellman and Liu (2004) showed pronounced skew among five-year-old children, with the majority of these children (21/25) scoring at or near ceiling performance. The ToM scale is therefore not suitable for studying individual differences in ToM with children aged five and over. In contrast with the false belief task batteries described earlier (e.g., Hughes et al., 2000), which focus on measuring one mental concept (i.e., false beliefs) across multiple task settings, the ToM scale measures multiple mental concepts across closely matched task settings. The false belief task battery yields within-age-group individual differences in performance in five-year-old children (Hughes et al., 2005) and the ToM scale yields developmental differences between three-, four-, and five-year-old children (Wellman & Liu, 2004). To enhance within-age variance on the ToM scale, each specific mental concept (e.g., two individuals can have different desires) could be tested using a range of task settings with different characters and materials.

The past decade has witnessed concerted efforts to examine the relations between tasks purported to measure individual differences in ToM in middle childhood and adolescence. One challenge is that standard false belief tasks, relying on simple behavioral responses, are inadequate indicators of individual differences in ToM after age six (e.g., Wellman et al., 2001). However, the presence of ceiling effects in middle childhood and adolescence in false belief task performance (as well as measures of desire understanding and second-order false belief understanding) should not be interpreted as signaling an absence of individual differences in ToM beyond early childhood. Psychometricians interested in general intelligence have long challenged similarly erroneous conclusions by pointing out that when children complete intelligence tests designed for adults, there is little variation in test performance but this does not mean there are no individual differences in intelligence in childhood (Anastasi, 1948). This further underscores the importance of distinguishing a latent ability (or propensity) from the tasks used to measure that ability.

The limited developmental scope of classic false belief tasks has stimulated the proliferation of novel tasks designed to measure ToM beyond early childhood. Complex or 'advanced' ToM tasks used in middle childhood and adolescence employ a range of stimuli including vignettes (e.g., Bosacki & Astington, 1999; White et al., 2009), animations (e.g., Castelli et al., 2000), film clips (e.g., Devine & Hughes, 2013), and still images (e.g., Baron-Cohen et al., 2001). These tasks measure distinct skills including but not limited to decoding facial expressions (e.g., Baron-Cohen et al., 2001), perspective-taking (e.g., Dumontheil et al., 2010), intention attribution (e.g., Castelli et al., 2000), and interpreting or explaining behavior (e.g., Banerjee et al., 2011; Devine & Hughes, 2013). Advanced ToM tasks also employ different response formats including open-ended verbal/written responses (e.g., White et al., 2009), multiple-choice responses (e.g., Baron-Cohen et al., 2001), and decision-making response times and accuracy (e.g., Apperly et al., 2011; Dumontheil et al., 2010). Many tasks were created to detect between-group (mean) differences to compare children with autism and typically developing children (e.g., White et al., 2009; Baron-Cohen et al., 2001) or to study developmental differences in performance between children in different age groups (e.g., Apperly et al., 2011; Dumontheil et al., 2010). Unlike experimental research (including studies focused on differences between age groups), research on individual differences requires tasks that capture substantial within-group variance (Goodhew & Edwards, 2019). This quality is undesirable in experimental research where between-group differences are the focus of interest. Consequently, not all measures of ToM are suited to studying individual differences.

Several studies have examined the relations between advanced ToM measures in middle childhood and adolescence to determine whether test performance can be explained by a single latent ToM factor. Large studies using task batteries in more than 400 eight- to ten-year-old children have reported low levels of internal consistency between the Strange Stories task (White et al., 2009), the Faux Pas task (Banerjee et al., 2011), the Reading the Mind in the Eyes task (Baron-Cohen et al., 2001), and second-order false belief tasks (Osterhaus et al., 2016). Smaller studies using similar task batteries involving 193 4- to 12-year-old children (Rice-Warnell & Redcay, 2019) and 112 7- to 13-year-old children (Hayward & Homer, 2017) have also reported weak correlations between advanced ToM tests. At first glance, these studies suggest a lack of coherence between measures of ToM in middle childhood.

In contrast with these results, studies of children aged between 7 and 13 years have shown consistent associations between children's performance on the Strange Stories (Happé, 1994) and Silent Film tasks (Devine & Hughes, 2013). The Strange Stories and Silent Film tasks require participants to explain a character's behavior with reference to mental states (e.g., beliefs, desires, emotions) based on either a text vignette (Strange Stories task) or a short film clip (Silent Film task). Data from 230 children aged between 8 and 13 indicated that both tasks captured variation in performance in middle childhood and early adolescence as indicated by low levels of ceiling performance (Devine & Hughes, 2013). Items from both tasks loaded onto a single latent factor and associations between these tasks could not be explained by either verbal ability or differences in age (Devine & Hughes, 2013). Further studies using different samples have replicated these findings (Wang et al., 2016) and shown consistent correlations between performance on the Silent Film and Strange Stories tasks (Lecce et al., 2017). A large-scale study of 460 children aged 7 to 13 years revealed marked individual differences in performance on each task (indicated by low levels of ceiling performance) and that items from each task loaded onto a single latent factor (Devine & Hughes, 2016). Latent variable models showed that the association between the Strange Stories and Silent Film tasks was not accounted for by differences in verbal ability, age, or narrative comprehension (as measured by control items on the Strange Stories task). Extending this work, Devine et al. (2016) administered the Strange Stories, Silent Film, and Triangles Animation (Castelli et al., 2000) tasks to 137 ten-year-old children participating in an ongoing longitudinal study. Like the Strange Stories and Silent Film tasks, the Triangles Animation task required children to describe behavior with reference to mental states. These three tasks were moderately correlated with each other and loaded onto a single latent factor. These results indicate that tasks targeting similar aspects of ToM (i.e., explaining behavior with reference to mental states) and using a similar response format (i.e., open-ended verbal response) capture variation in performance and correlate with each other despite using different stimuli.

Contrasting findings about the coherence of measures of advanced ToM in middle childhood and adolescence can be interpreted through both a statistical and a substantive lens (Rouder & Haaf, 2019). From a statistical perspective, inconsistent results across studies may reflect the use of tests with varying degrees of discriminating power, that is, the extent to which a test captures between-participant variance at different ages (Cooper et al., 2019). Existing studies indicate that second-order false belief tasks, while sensitive to age-related differences up to age six, exhibit ceiling effects in middle childhood (e.g., Osterhaus et al., 2016) and may therefore be unsuitable for studying individual differences in ToM in this developmental period. The Silent Film and Strange Stories tasks, in contrast, exhibit substantial variance in middle childhood and early adolescence, with few participants performing at floor or ceiling. Crucially, children's performance on these measures varies considerably within each age group studied. Children's raw scores on the Silent Film task range from 0 to 10 (out of 12) in children aged seven, eight, and nine years and from 2 to 12 in children aged 10, 11, and 12 years (Devine & Hughes, 2016). While this feature of the test is undesirable for studying differences between age groups, it indicates that the Silent Film task captures differences in performance that are not entirely due to age. This property means that performance is not easily categorized as 'early' or 'late' mastery but instead may be better viewed as individual differences in ToM use. Such differences in the discriminating power of ToM tests may explain contrasting results about the coherence of ToM measures.

A second statistical source of inconsistency is sample size and composition. The majority of studies have adopted large samples but these samples span a wide age range across middle childhood and early adolescence with relatively few cases within any one age group. This approach is suitable for studying developmental differences between children in different age groups but limits conclusions about individual differences within a particular age group. Samples should be large enough to capture variation in task performance within a specific age group. For example, the Strange Stories, Silent Film, and Triangle Animations tasks exhibited marked variation even within narrow age ranges (Devine et al., 2016; Lecce et al., 2017). Such variation is essential for studying individual differences in ToM and for examining the relations between tasks (Cooper et al., 2019).

There are also substantive reasons why studies show inconsistent patterns of results regarding the coherence of ToM tasks. The task impurity problem is a perennial challenge in research on individual differences in cognition (e.g., Hedge et al., 2018). Advanced ToM tests vary in the stimuli employed, the specific skills assessed, and the response format used. Even if task performance across different advanced measures were underpinned by a single latent variable, correlations between scores on different ToM tests, like other measures of cognition (e.g., Miyake et al., 2000), would be attenuated (and sometimes inflated) by unique task demands. Unique task demands are those aspects of task performance that are unrelated to the underlying construct of interest. It is not unusual for executive function tasks to show weak to moderate correlations despite measuring related constructs (e.g., Miyake et al., 2000). This pattern holds among measures of ToM in middle childhood and early adolescence, with correlations ranging from weak to moderate in strength (e.g., Devine et al., 2016; Lecce et al., 2017). Task demand differences might therefore mask genuine relations between these tasks.

Another substantive reason for inconsistent results about the coherence of ToM tasks is that variation in task performance on an experimental measure may not reflect individual differences in the construct of interest (Hedge et al., 2018). Devine et al. (2016) reported that scores on the Director task (Dumontheil et al., 2010), which is typically used to study age-related differences in perspective-taking, did not load onto a ToM latent factor in a sample of ten-year-old children. This does not mean that the Director task does not measure perspective-taking or ToM. The Director task might capture developmental differences in ToM between children, adolescents, and adults (Dumontheil et al., 2010) but may not be sensitive to individual differences in perspective-taking within these age groups. Here, lessons can be learned from early childhood research on ToM and the distinction between developmental differences and individual differences. False belief task batteries that measure a single mental concept using different characters, materials, and response formats yield striking individual differences in task performance among five-year-old children (e.g., Hughes et al., 2000). In contrast, the ToM scale (e.g., Wellman & Liu, 2004) measures multiple mental concepts (i.e., desires, knowledge, beliefs) using closely matched scenarios and exhibits ceiling effects among five-year-old children. False belief task batteries and the ToM scale both measure ToM but, arguably, the former is more sensitive to individual differences in five-year-old children and the latter is more sensitive to developmental differences between three- and five-year-old children. Note that extension of the ToM Scale through the addition of a new item has revealed further developmental differences between early and middle childhood in recognizing sarcasm, but variation in task performance in middle childhood was confined to the advanced item, meaning that this task battery may not be ideally suited to studying individual differences in middle childhood and adolescence (Peterson et al., 2012). Hedge et al. (2018) caution that experimental tasks used in cognitive psychology are designed to maximize between-group differences and may not be suited to studying individual differences within a particular group. Measures yielding less reliable between-group differences in experimental research may be suitable for studying individual differences (Goodhew & Edwards, 2019). Even when tasks capture within-group variation in performance, it cannot be assumed that the measure in question taps meaningful individual differences in the construct of interest (Mollon et al., 2017). Within age-group variance in task performance might be enhanced by broadening the range of scenarios in which children must apply their understanding of different mental concepts. In contrast, between-age group variance might be enhanced by testing different mental concepts using similar task settings.

A final substantive reason for inconsistent results across studies examining coherence is that tasks purporting to measure a single unitary ability (in this case ToM), may capture distinct components of that ability. Researchers have capitalized on latent variable modeling to study the functional organization of individual differences in executive function (e.g., Friedman & Miyake, 2017). Studies of the underlying structure of individual differences in ToM in middle childhood and adolescence require discriminating tasks and large samples. Bifactor models (see Figure 3.1), where each test item loads onto a single general latent factor (e.g., reflecting individual differences in ToM) and additional common latent factors (e.g., reflecting differences in a specific domain of mindreading and/or variance due to specific task demands), will allow researchers to determine the extent to which individual differences in ToM task performance reflect variation in children's flexibility, ease, and/or interest in reading others' minds rather than task-specific factors or more general cognitive abilities (e.g., Clark et al., 2016).

In summary, there is growing evidence that individual differences in ToM task performance are explained in part by variation in an underlying latent construct in early childhood. Although results are less consistent in middle childhood and adolescence, when studies adopt discriminating measures (such as the Strange Stories and Silent Film tasks) and large samples, performance across different measures of advanced ToM is explained by individual differences in an underlying latent factor. Since the overlap between measures is not accounted for by verbal ability, individual differences in this latent factor in early and middle childhood arguably reflect genuine differences in children's ToM.

Evidence for stability of individual differences in theory of mind

In addition to cross-sectional consistency, the presence of rank-order or temporal stability in test performance helps distinguish random variation in task performance from genuine individual differences (e.g., Mollon et al., 2017; Steyer et al., 1999). The widening of the developmental limits of research on theory of mind provides an opportunity to examine rank-order stability over extended periods of time, providing new insights about the nature of early emerging individual differences. Homotypic stability occurs when there is rank-order consistency in the same construct (e.g., ToM) measured using the same task (e.g., the false belief task) over time (Bornstein et al., 2017). Although it is possible to examine homotypic stability in children's false belief understanding in early childhood, the limited variance in false belief tasks beyond early childhood precludes investigations of homotypic stability in ToM from early to middle childhood. Researchers interested in individual differences in a wide range of domains (e.g., intelligence, temperament, attachment) typically conceptualize stability as heterotypic. Heterotypic stability occurs when children's rank-order position on an earlier task predicts their rank-order position on a later task that is assumed to measure the same underlying construct (e.g., ToM) (Bornstein et al., 2017). For example, researchers have examined how individual differences in performance on age-appropriate batteries of false belief understanding at age three predict performance on batteries including second-order false belief tasks at age six (Hughes et al., 2011). If variation in ToM task performance signals the presence of stable trait-like individual differences in ToM use, then longitudinal studies should reveal rank-order consistency (stability) in ToM test performance even if children exhibit mean level changes over time (discontinuity) (Bornstein et al., 2017).

Figure 3.2 describes the search strategy, screening, and inclusion criteria used to capture data for a meta-analysis of published literature on the rank-order stability of individual differences in ToM across childhood. Of the 76 longitudinal studies identified, stability coefficients were available for 58 studies representing 7,185 children aged between 24 and 176.5 months at baseline (*Mdn* = 48.74 months) and between 39 and 188.46 months at the final wave (*Mdn* = 66.25 months). Sample sizes ranged from 21 to 1,567 (*Mdn* = 75 children) and participants were drawn from 14 different countries. Studies

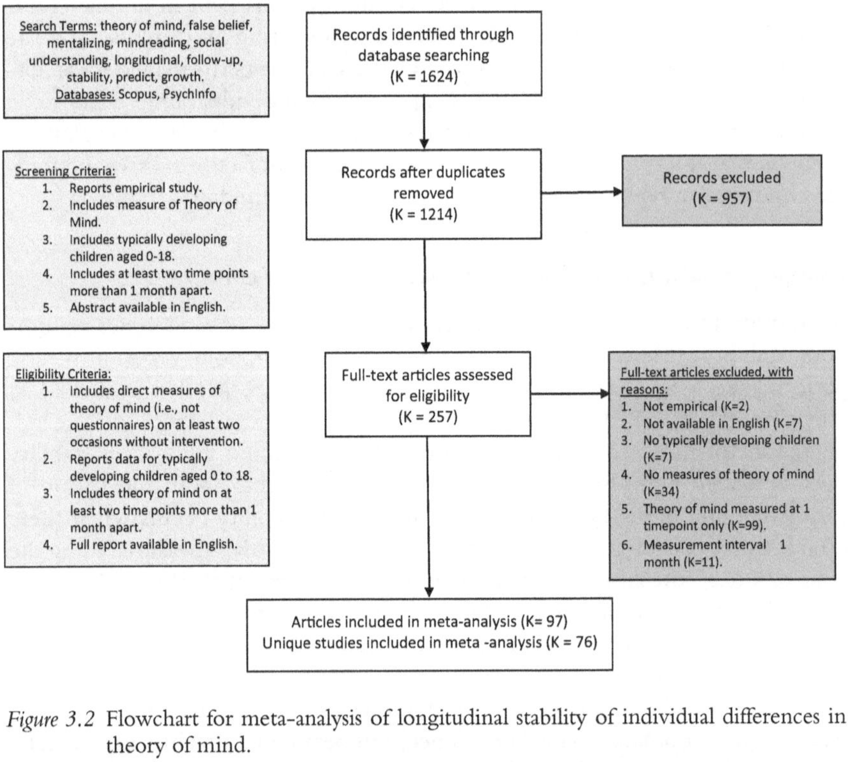

Figure 3.2 Flowchart for meta-analysis of longitudinal stability of individual differences in theory of mind.

included between 2 and 6 measurement occasions (*Mdn* = 2) and the longest testing intervals ranged from 3 to 81 months (*Mdn* = 12 months). The majority of studies (82.8%) had a testing interval of under 24 months. Thirty-seven studies focused on early childhood (i.e., 24–71 months), 12 studies focused on middle childhood and early adolescence (i.e., ≥ 72 months at baseline), and 9 studies spanned early to middle childhood. Thirty-five studies used the same ToM measures on more than one occasion and 23 studies used different ToM measures on each occasion. Effect sizes for rank-order stability (the average longitudinal correlation between ToM measures in studies with more than two testing occasions) are presented in Figure 3.3.

A random-effects model using a restricted maximum likelihood estimator revealed that individual differences in ToM exhibited moderate longitudinal rank-order stability, $r = .40$, 95%CI [.35, .44], $Z = 17.47$, $p < .001$. Longitudinal stability coefficients ranged from .11 to .77, indicating heterogeneity across studies, $I^2 = 78.79\%$, $Q\ (57) = 316.88$, $p < .001$. The symmetry of the funnel plot (Figure 3.4) indicated no evidence of publication bias, $Z = -1.23$, $p = 0.218$. An inverse variance weighted random intercept, fixed-slopes model using a restricted maximum likelihood estimator was used to investigate the moderating effects of developmental period, longest testing interval, and whether or not the same test battery was used throughout the longitudinal study. The model accounted for 6.4% of the variance in longitudinal stability coefficients, $Q\ (4,53) = 3.43$, $p = 0.488$. There was no significant difference in longitudinal stability estimates between studies focused on early childhood and studies extending from early to middle childhood, B = 0.025, SE = 0.089, β = .04, Z = 0.278, $p = 0.781$, between studies focused on early childhood and studies focused on middle childhood and adolescence, B = −0.016, SE = 0.079, β = −.03, Z = −0.199, $p = 0.842$, or between studies extending from early to middle childhood and studies focused on middle childhood and adolescence, B = −0.041, SE = 0.104, β = −.08, Z = −0.392, $p = 0.695$. The stability coefficient was unrelated to the duration of the longest testing interval, B = −0.004, SE = 0.003, β = −.23, Z = −1.424, $p = 0.154$. There was no difference in stability between studies using the same measures of ToM and studies using different measures of ToM, B = 0.027, SE = 0.066, β = .07, Z = 0.410, $p = 0.682$. These results show that there is moderate rank-order stability in individual differences in ToM in early and middle childhood even when studies adopt different measures of individual differences in ToM performance.

Although limited in developmental scope, the meta-analysis provides insights about the nature of individual differences in ToM. In a meta-analysis of longitudinal twin studies, Tucker-Drob and Briley (2014) reported that the stability of general intelligence was moderate in early childhood ($r = .30$) but strong in middle childhood ($r = .60$) and adolescence ($r > .70$) (Tucker-Drob & Briley, 2014). Although not as stable as intelligence, individual differences in ToM appear to be as stable as ratings of temperament and personality in children. Meta-analysis indicates that individual differences in temperament/personality

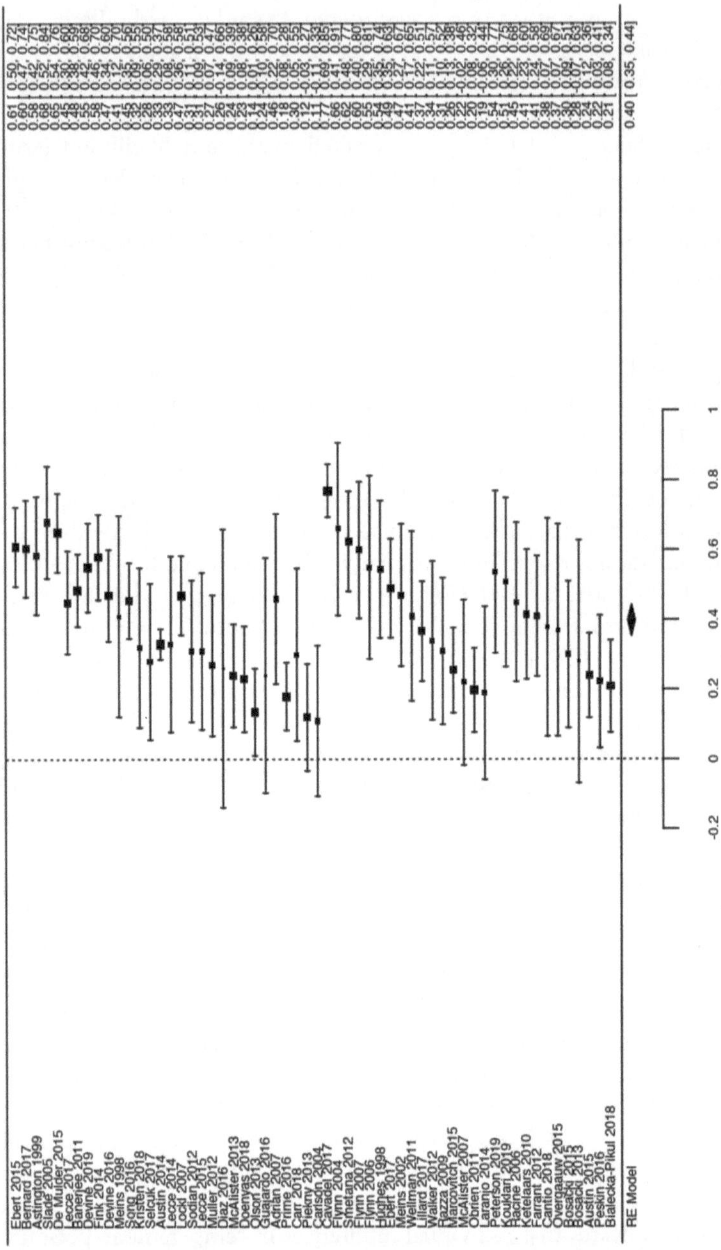

Figure 3.3 Forest plot showing longitudinal correlations and mean correlation.

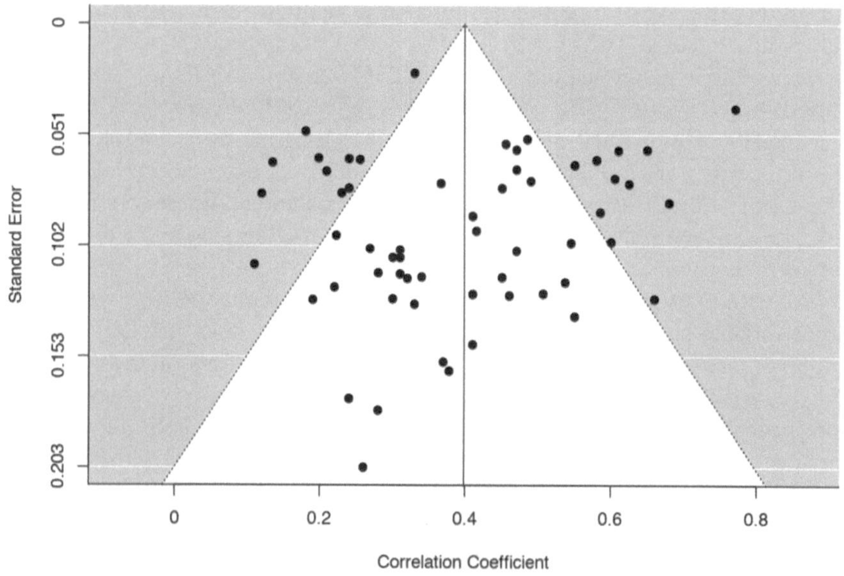

Figure 3.4 Funnel plot of longitudinal correlations.

show moderate stability in early (r = .52) and middle (r = .45) childhood and in adolescence (r = .47) (Roberts & Del Vecchio, 2000). Moreover, individual differences in ToM also appear to be as stable as meta-analytic estimates for the stability of attachment security (r = .43) (Fraley, 2002).

Intelligence and personality are typically viewed as *genuine* dimensions of individual differences (Rust & Golombok, 2008). Like individual differences in ToM, these phenomena exhibit moderate longitudinal stability in early and middle childhood. Claims about the relative stability of individual differences in intelligence, personality, and attachment security typically assume heterotypic stability because researchers assume that individual differences in the underlying latent construct in question can be distinguished from the tasks used to measure that construct at a given age (e.g., Bayley, 1949). Viewed in light of research on intelligence, personality, and attachment security, the moderate stability of individual differences in ToM task performance supports the claim that there are genuine individual differences in ToM. Rank-order stability challenges the view that individual differences in ToM are temporary or trivial differences between children. This meta-analysis raises the possibility that early-emerging individual differences in false belief task performance may act as a marker of more enduring differences in ToM use with prognostic importance (Dunn et al., 1991).

The rank-order stability of intelligence, personality, and attachment security also highlights how other factors (e.g., intelligence, temperament) might confound estimates of the stability of individual differences in ToM. It is worth noting that the partial longitudinal correlation between earlier and later individual differences in ToM controlling for verbal ability using 30 separate studies showed that individual differences in ToM remained relatively stable over time, $r = .30$, 95%CI [.25, .36], $Z = 10.57$, $p < .001$. Future work tracking the stability of individual differences in ToM alongside other domains (e.g., executive function, intelligence, personality) and over extended developmental periods will elucidate the extent to which individual differences in ToM task performance reflect a genuine, distinct trait-like dimension of difference between children.

Contemporary measurement theory provides a framework to integrate latent variable studies of within-time coherence across tasks and longitudinal studies of rank-order stability in task performance to shed light on the nature of individual differences in ToM. Latent state-trait (LST) theory was devised by personality theorists in an effort to understand temporary and lasting sources of variance in observed test scores (Geiser & Lockhart, 2012; Steyer et al., 1999). According to LST theory, longitudinal data are needed to ascertain the degree to which variation in task performance measured on a single occasion reflects trait-like individual differences or state-like fluctuations (Hamaker et al., 2017). Figure 3.5 shows a hypothetical LST model of three repeatedly administered

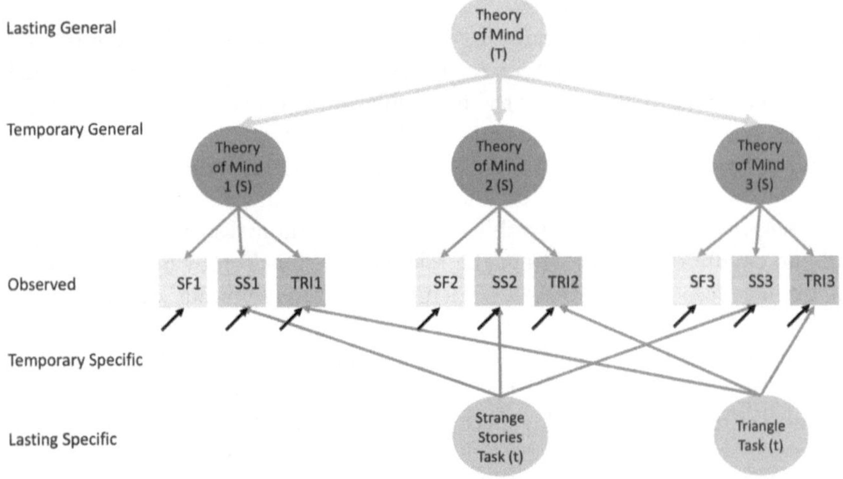

Figure 3.5 Hypothetical latent state trait model of theory of mind measured on three occasions. Note: SF = Silent Film task. SS = Strange Stories task. TRI = Triangle Animation task. 1 = time 1. 2 = time 2. 3 = time 3. T = lasting general factor or 'trait'. S = temporary general factor or 'state'. t = lasting specific factor or 'method' factors. The Silent Film task is used as a referent method in this model (Geiser & Lockhart, 2012). Diagonal black arrows indicate residual (temporary task specific) variance.

tests of ToM. This model distinguishes between lasting general variance (i.e., trait-like variance in ToM) and temporary general variance (i.e., state-like variance in ToM) in the focal latent ability (Hamaker et al., 2017). Observed score variance can be further partitioned into lasting specific variance (i.e., variance related to a specific method used on multiple occasions) and temporary specific variance (i.e., random error) (Hamaker et al., 2017). Longitudinal LST models present new possibilities for studying the correlates and consequences of individual differences in lasting latent traits and temporary latent states (Steyer et al., 2015).

Are there meaningful individual differences in Theory of Mind?

This chapter has shown that (1) there is growing evidence that an underlying latent factor accounts for variance in batteries of tasks purported to measure ToM in early and middle childhood and (2) individual differences in performance on ToM tasks show moderate rank-order stability over time in early and middle childhood. Although these results suggest that there are genuine, stable individual differences in mindreading performance in early and middle childhood, it is not clear whether these differences are meaningful (Hughes & Devine, 2015). Although there may be disadvantages to being highly attuned to the minds of others (e.g., children with high levels of ToM show greater sensitivity to criticism – Lecce et al., 2014), if genuine individual differences in ToM exist in early and middle childhood, then relatively high levels of mindreading are likely to confer benefits for survival (more specifically social adjustment) over and above differences in related abilities such as language and executive function (Dunn et al., 1991; Hughes, 2011; Thornton & Lukas, 2012; Waytz et al., 2010). There is considerable evidence linking individual differences in ToM and a range of real-world social outcomes in early childhood (Lecce & Devine, 2021). For example, individual differences in false belief task performance are associated with peer popularity (e.g., Slaughter et al., 2015), having reciprocated friendships (Fink et al., 2015), and ratings of prosocial behavior (Imuta et al., 2016) in early childhood. The growing evidence linking individual differences in ToM and a range of social outcomes in middle childhood and adolescence is discussed in Chapters 6, 7, and 8 of this book and will not be examined in detail here. Instead, this section highlights one study examining the claim that individual differences in ToM in middle childhood are socially meaningful.

There are at least three ways to interpret the observed correlation between individual differences in ToM and children's social competence. The *social consequences account* (e.g., Hughes & Devine, 2015) predicts that individual differences in ToM are a basis for successful social interactions. In contrast, the *training ground hypothesis* (e.g., Jenkins & Astington, 2000) suggests that mastery of social interactions allows children to hone their ToM. Alternatively, the *common correlate account* proposes that apparent associations between ToM and social competence are better explained by domain-general abilities such as language and executive function (Astington, 2003).

Devine et al. (2016) examined the relations between individual differences in ToM and social competence in middle childhood in a sample of 137 children seen in the first (age six) and final years of primary school (age ten) in an effort to test these competing theoretical accounts. Children completed an age-appropriate battery of tasks designed to measure individual differences in ToM, executive function, and language ability at both time points. Children's teachers provided ratings of social competence (i.e., the degree to which children manage social interactions at school effectively). Controlling for variation in verbal ability and executive function, individual differences in ToM were uniquely associated with teacher-rated social competence at both time points in the study. Crucially, cross-lagged longitudinal analyses revealed a unidirectional association between ToM at age six and teacher-rated social competence at age ten (but not vice versa). These results are noteworthy for two reasons. First, these results indicate that the relations between ToM and social competence in middle childhood cannot be explained away by language ability or executive function. Second, the longitudinal design provides compelling evidence for a developmental association between individual differences in ToM and children's social competence. Together these results challenge the training ground account and the common correlate account. Although further consideration about precisely what aspects of social competence might benefit from skilled mindreading (Lecce & Devine, 2021) is called for, this study provides support for the claim that individual differences in ToM are meaningful in that variation in ToM task performance is related to children's social competence in early and middle childhood.

Conclusions and future directions

This chapter has examined the claim that individual differences in ToM are genuine and meaningful by drawing on three strands of evidence. First, studies adopting batteries of ToM tasks indicate that performance across a range of different tasks purported to measure ToM can be explained by a single underlying latent factor in early and middle childhood. Second, meta-analysis of longitudinal data indicates that individual differences in ToM task performance exhibit moderate rank-order stability over time. Third, individual differences in ToM exhibit unique developmental associations with aspects of social competence over and above potentially confounding influences of executive function and language ability.

This chapter highlights three implications for future research on individual differences in ToM in middle childhood and beyond. First, psychometricians have emphasized the importance of decoupling tasks from the latent constructs these tasks purport to measure (Anastasi, 1948). The absence of measures suited to studying changes in ToM performance over a wide age range creates challenges for research on developmental differences, but studies of the (heterotypic) stability of individual differences are not precluded by the availability of such measures because the focus is on rank-order stability rather than mean-level differences (discontinuity) (Bornstein et al., 2017). It is not controversial to suggest that the false belief task, despite its many strengths, should not be conflated with the underlying ability or propensity to reason about others' minds (e.g., Bloom & German, 2000). The meta-analysis of longitudinal data in this chapter indicates that the false belief task may provide an early marker of lasting individual differences in ToM (albeit within a narrow developmental window between the ages of three and five). This view challenges the idea that individual differences in performance on the false belief task simply capture *temporary* differences in children's mastery of mental concepts or differences arising from task performance factors (Hughes & Devine, 2015). Instead, early-emerging individual differences in false belief task performance signal lasting variation in mindreading that persists after children reach ceiling performance on false belief tasks.

Second, limited variation in performance on false belief tasks (and second-order false belief tasks) beyond age six does not signal the absence of individual differences in ToM beyond early childhood. Likewise, weak correlations between tasks purporting to measure ToM do not automatically support the view that task performance does not rely on an underlying latent ability. Numerous tasks attempting to measure different aspects of ToM beyond early childhood have emerged in recent years but not all of these measures are suited to studying individual differences in ToM. Tasks with high discriminating power, or the ability to capture between-participant variance within specific age groups (Cooper et al., 2019), are most suitable for studying individual differences in ToM use. Measures designed to index developmental differences in ToM may not be suited to studying individual differences in ToM. Here it is important to emphasize that a focus on individual differences in ToM use does not preclude the possibility that there are further conceptual developments (or new 'competencies') in mindreading in middle childhood and adolescence. The key point is that research on developmental differences can be distinguished from research on individual differences. There may be quantitative differences in qualitative shifts in understanding others' minds (Miller, 2010). Careful consideration of whether a measure captures variation in performance within a particular age group is warranted before conclusions about the structure of individual differences in ToM can be drawn.

Third, modern psychometric approaches such as latent variable modeling offer powerful tools for studying individual differences in cognition (e.g., Devine & Hughes, 2016; Willougby & Blair, 2011). Confirmatory factor analysis (CFA) can be used to distinguish between a latent ToM factor, task-specific variance (e.g., particular response formats or stimuli), and random error (Brown, 2015). Bifactor modeling can shed light on whether test performance is underpinned by a general latent factor (e.g., ToM) alongside more specific skills (e.g., reasoning about beliefs, reasoning about emotions) and methodological factors (Clark et al., 2016). Latent variable modeling of carefully selected batteries of discriminating tasks tapping distinct domains of

ToM, using different stimuli and response formats, will elucidate the organization of individual differences in mindreading in middle childhood and beyond.

Theory of mind is not an all-or-nothing achievement. Instead, there are genuine individual differences in mindreading. Researchers have capitalized on the presence of individual differences in ToM task performance to test theoretical accounts of ToM over the past two decades but there has been remarkably little consideration of how individual differences in ToM should be construed (e.g., Apperly, 2012; Conway & Bird, 2018; Hughes & Devine, 2015). The extension of the developmental scope of ToM research into middle childhood and adolescence provides new opportunities for investigating the nature and consequences of individual differences in ToM. Undoubtedly, cognitive processes, such as executive function and language, contribute to the flexibility and ease with which children reason about others' minds in complex social situations. However, based on the evidence presented in this chapter, individual differences in theory of mind task performance cannot be explained entirely by differences arising from executive function or language (or indeed other 'performance' factors) (Devine et al., 2016). Instead, individual differences in mindreading may reflect differences in fluency (e.g., mastery over a repertoire of mental states and how these relate to various social contexts) or propensity (e.g., sensitivity to others' minds or motivation to reason about others' minds) or some combination of these. The aim of this chapter was to evaluate the claim that there are genuine and meaningful individual differences in ToM in early and middle childhood. The evidence discussed in this chapter provides further support for the view that, like historians and novelists, children vary in the degree to which they reason about others' thoughts, feelings, and desires and that these stable differences between children have real-world significance.

Acknowledgment

I would like to thank Ian Apperly, Serena Lecce, and Christina Pomareda Gillesen for their helpful comments and insightful feedback on this chapter.

References

Anastasi, A. (1948). *Differential Psychology* (3rd ed.). New York: Macmillan, Ltd.

Apperly, I. (2012). What is "theory of mind"? concepts, cognitive processes and individual differences. *Quarterly Journal of Experimental Psychology, 65*, 825–839. doi:10.1080/17470218.2012.676055

Apperly, I.A., Warren, F., Andrews, B.J., Grant, J., & Todd, S. (2011). Developmental continuity in theory of mind: Speed and accuracy of belief-desire reasoning in children and adults. *Child Development, 82*, 1691–1703. doi:10.1111/j.1467-8624.2011.01635.x

Astington, J.W. (2003). Sometimes necessary, never sufficient: False-belief understanding and social competence. In B. Repacholi & V. Slaughter (Eds.), *Individual Differences in Theory of Mind* (pp. 13–38). Hove, East Sussex: Psychology Press.

Banerjee, R., Watling, D., & Caputi, M. (2011). Peer relations and the understanding of faux pas: Longitudinal evidence for bidirectional associations. *Child Development, 82*, 1887–1905. doi:10.1111/j.1467-8624.2011.01669.x

Baron-Cohen, S., Wheelwright, S., Hill, J., Raste, Y., & Plumb, I. (2001). The "reading the mind in the eyes" test revised version: A study with normal adults, and adults with Asperger syndrome or high-functioning Autism. *Journal of Child Psychology and Psychiatry, 42*, 241–251.

Bayley, N. (1949). Consistency and variability in the growth of intelligence from birth to eighteen years. *Journal of Genetic Psychology, 75*, 165–196.

Bloom, P., & German, T.P. (2000). Two reasons to abandon the false belief task as a test of theory of mind. *Cognition, 77*, B25–B31.

Boogert, N.J., Madden, J.R., Morand-Ferron, J., & Thornton, A. (2018). Measuring and understanding individual differences in cognition. *Philosophical Transactions of the Royal Society of London Series B Biological Sciences, 373*, 20170280.

Bornstein, M.H., Putnick, D.L., & Esposito, G. (2017). Continuity and stability in development. *Child Development Perspectives, 11*, 113–119.

Bosacki, S.L., & Astington, J.W. (1999). Theory of mind in preadolescence: Relations between social understanding and social competence. *Social Development, 8*, 237–255.

Brown, T.A. (2015). *Confirmatory Factor Analysis for Applied Research* (2nd ed.). London: Guilford Press.

Castelli, F., Happé, F., Frith, U., & Frith, C. (2000). Movement and mind: A functional imaging study of perception and interpretation of complex intentional movement patterns. *NeuroImage, 12*, 314–325. doi:10.1006/nimg.2000.0612

Clark, C.A.C., Chevalier, N., Nelson, J.M., James, T.D., Garza, J.P., Choi, H., & Espy, K.A. (2016). Executive control in early childhood. *Monographs of the Society for Research in Child Development, 81*, 7–29.

Conway, J.R., & Bird, G. (2018). Conceptualizing degrees of theory of mind. *Proceedings of the National Academy of Sciences of the United States of America, 115*, 1408–1410.

Cooper, S.R., Jackson, J.J., Barch, D.M., & Braver, T.S. (2019). Neuroimaging of individual differences: A latent variable modeling perspective. *Neuroscience and Biobehavioral Reviews, 98*, 29–46.

Devine, R.T., & Hughes, C. (2013). Silent films and strange stories: Theory of mind, gender, and social experiences in middle childhood. *Child Development, 84*, 989–1003. doi:10.1111/cdev.12017

Devine, R.T., & Hughes, C. (2014). Relations between false belief understanding and executive function in early childhood: A meta-analysis. *Child Development, 85*, 1777–1794. doi:10.1111/cdev.12237

Devine, R.T., & Hughes, C. (2016). Measuring theory of mind across middle childhood: Reliability and validity of the silent films and strange stories tasks. *Journal of Experimental Child Psychology, 149*, 23–40. doi:10.1016/j.jecp.2015.07.011

Devine, R.T., White, N., Ensor, R., & Hughes, C. (2016). Theory of mind in middle childhood: Longitudinal associations with executive function and social competence. *Developmental Psychology, 52*, 758–771. doi:10.1037/dev0000105

Dumontheil, I., Apperly, I.A., & Blakemore, S. (2010). Online usage of theory of mind continues to develop in late adolescence. *Developmental Science, 13*, 331–338.

Dunn, J., Brown, J., Slomkowski, C., Tesla, C., & Youngblade, L. (1991). Young children's understanding of other people's feelings and beliefs: Individual differences and their antecedents. *Child Development, 62*, 1352–1366.

Finch, W.H. & French, B.F. (2015). *Latent variable modelling with* R. London. Taylor and Francis.

Fink, E., Begeer, S., Peterson, C.C., Slaughter, V. & De Rosnay, M. (2015). Friends, friendlessness, and the social consequences of gaining a theory of mind. *British Journal of Developmental Psychology, 33*, 27–30. DOI 10.1111/bjdp.12080

Fraley, R.C. (2002). Attachment stability from infancy to adulthood: Meta-analysis and dynamic modeling of developmental mechanisms. *Personality and Social Psychology Review, 6*, 123–151.

Friedman, N.P., & Miyake, A. (2017). Unity and diversity of executive functions: Individual differences as a window on cognitive structure. *Cortex, 86*, 186–204. doi:10.1016/j.cortex.2016.04.023

Geiser, C. & Lockhart, G. (2012). A comparison of four approaches to account for method effects in latent state-trait analyses. *Psychological Methods, 17*, 255–283.

Goodhew, S.C., & Edwards, M. (2019). Translating experimental paradigms into individual-differences research: Contributions, challenges, and practical recommendations. *Consciousness and Cognition, 69*, 14–25.

Gopnik, A., & Wellman, H.M. (1992). Why the child's theory of mind really is a theory. *Mind & Language*, 7, 145–171.

Hamaker, E.L., Schuurman, N.K., Zijlmans, E. (2017). Using a few snapshots to distinguish mountains from waves: weak factorial invariance in the context of trait-state research. *Multivariate behavioural research, 52*, 47–60.

Happé, F.G.E. (1994). An advanced test of theory of mind: Understanding of story characters' thoughts and feelings by able autistic, mentally handicapped, and normal children and adults. *Journal of Autism and Developmental Disorders, 24*, 129–154.

Hayward, E.O., & Homer, B.D. (2017). Reliability and validity of advanced theory-of-mind measures in middle childhood and adolescence. *British Journal of Developmental Psychology, 35*, 454–462.

Hedge, C., Powell, G., & Sumner, P. (2018). The reliability paradox: Why robust cognitive tasks do not produce reliable individual differences. *Behavior Research Methods, 50*, 1166–1186.

Hughes, C. (2011). *Social Understanding and Social Lives: From Toddlerhood through to the Transition to School.* London: Psychology Press.

Hughes, C., Adlam, A., Happe, F., Jackson, J., Taylor, A., & Caspi, A. (2000). Good test-retest reliability for standard and advanced false-belief tasks across a wide range of abilities. *Journal of Child Psychology and Psychiatry, 41*, 483–490.

Hughes, C., & Devine, R.T. (2015). Individual differences in theory of mind from preschool to adolescence: Achievements and directions. *Child Development Perspectives, 9*, 149–153.

Hughes, C., Devine, R.T., & Wang, Z. (2018). Does parental mind-mindedness account for cross-cultural differences in preschoolers' theory of mind? *Child Development, 89*, 1296–1310.

Hughes, C., Ensor, R., & Marks, A. (2011). Individual differences in false belief understanding are stable from 3 to 6 years of age and predict children's mental state talk with school friends. *Journal of Experimental Child Psychology, 108*, 96–112. doi:10.1016/j.jecp.2010.07.012

Hughes, C., Jaffee, S., Happe, F., Taylor, A., Caspi, A., & Moffitt, T.E. (2005). Origins of individual differences in theory of mind: From nature to nurture? *Child Development, 76*, 356–370.

Imuta, K., Henry, J.D., Slaughter, V., Selcuk, B., & Ruffman, T. (2016). Theory of mind and prosocial behavior in childhood: A meta-analytic review. *Developmental Psychology, 52*, 1192–1205. doi:10.1037/dev0000140

Jenkins, J.M., & Astington, J.W. (2000). Theory of mind and social behavior: Causal models tested in a longitudinal study. *Merrill-Palmer Quarterly, 46*, 203–220.

Lecce, S., Bianco, F., Devine, R.T., & Hughes, C. (2017). Relations between theory of mind and executive function in middle childhood: A short-term longitudinal study. *Journal of Experimental Child Psychology, 163*, 69–86. doi:10.1016/j.jecp.2017.06.011

Lecce, S., Caputi, M. & Hughes, C. (2011). Does sensitivity to criticism mediate the relationship between theory of mind and academic achievement? *Journal of Experimental Child Psychology, 110*, 313–331.

Lecce, S., & Devine, R.T. (2021). Social interaction in early and middle childhood: The role of theory of mind. In H.J. Ferguson & E.E.F. Bradford (Eds.), *The Cognitive Basis of Social Interaction Across the Lifespan* (pp. 46–68). Oxford, UK: Oxford University Press.

Mantel, H. (2017, June 3). Why I became a historical novelist. *The Guardian*.

Miller, P.H. (2010). Piaget's Theory: Past, present and future. In U. Goswami (Ed.), *The Wiley-Blackwell Handbook of Childhood Cognitive Development* (2nd ed., p. 649-672). Oxford, UK: Wiley Blackwell.

Milligan, K., Astington, J.W., & Dack, L.A. (2007). Language and theory of mind: Meta-analysis of the relation between language ability and false-belief understanding. *Child Development, 78*, 622–646.

Miyake, A., Friedman, N.P., Emerson, M.J., Witzki, A.H., & Howerter, A. (2000). The unity and diversity of executive functions and their contributions to complex "frontal lobe" tasks: A latent variable analysis. *Cognitive Psychology, 41*, 49–100. doi:10.1006/cogp.1999.0734

Mollon, J.D., Bosten, J.M., Peterzell, D.H., & Webster, M.A. (2017). Individual differences in visual science: What can be learned and what is good experimental practice? *Vision Research, 141*, 4–15.

Osterhaus, C., Koerber, S., & Sodian, B. (2016). Scaling of advanced theory of mind tasks. *Child Development, 87*, 1971–1991.

Peterson, C.C., Wellman, H.M. & Slaughter, V. (2012). The mind behind the message: Advancing theory-of-mind scales for typically developing children, and hose with deafness, autism, or Asperger syndrome. *Child Development, 83*, 469–485.

Rice Warnell, K., & Redcay, E. (2019). Minimal coherence among varied theory of mind measures in childhood and adulthood. *Cognition, 191*, 103997.

Roberts, B.W., & DelVecchio, W.F. (2000). The rank-order consistency of personality traits from childhood to old age: A quantitative review of longitudinal studies. *Psychological Bulletin, 126*, 3–25.

Rouder, J.N., & Haaf, J.M. (2019). A psychometrics of individual differences in experimental tasks. *Psychonomic Bulletin & Review, 26*, 452–467.

Rust, J., & Golombok, S. (2008). *Modern Psychometrics: The Science of Psychological Assessment*. London: Routledge.

Slaughter, V., Imuta, K., Peterson, C.C., & Henry, J.D. (2015). Meta-analysis of theory of mind and peer popularity in the preschool and early school years. *Child Development, 86*, 1159–1174.

Steyer, R., Mayer, A., Geiser, C. & Cole, D.A. (2015). A theory of states and traits – revised. *Annual Review of Clinical Psychology, 11*, 71–98.

Steyer, R., Schmitt, M., Eid, M. (1999). Latent state-trait theory and research in personality and individual differences. *European Journal of Personality, 13*, 389–408.

Thornton, A., & Lukas, D. (2012). Individual variation in cognitive performance: Developmental and evolutionary perspectives. *Philosophical Transactions of the Royal Society of London Series B Biological Sciences, 367*, 2773–2783.

Tucker-Drob, E., & Briley, D.A. (2014). Continuity of genetic and environmental influences on cognition across the life span: A meta-analysis of longitudinal twin and adoption studies. *Psychological Bulletin, 140*, 949–979.

Wang, Z., Devine, R.T., Wong, K.K., & Hughes, C. (2016). Theory of mind and executive function during middle childhood across cultures. *Journal of Experimental Child Psychology, 149*, 6–22.

Waytz, A., Gray, K., Epley, N. & Wegner, D.M. (2010). Causes and consequences of mind perception. *Trends in Cognitive Sciences, 14*, 383–388.

Wellman, H.M., Cross, D., & Watson, J. (2001). Meta-analysis of theory-of-mind development: The truth about false belief. *Child Development, 72*, 655–684.

Wellman, H.M. Fang, F., Liu, D., Zhu, L. & Liu, G. (2006). Scaling theory of mind understandings in Chinese children. *Psychological Science, 17*, 1075–1081.

Wellman, H.M., & Liu, D. (2004). Scaling theory-of-mind tasks. *Child Development, 75*(2), 523–541.

White, S., Hill, E., Happé, F., & Frith, U. (2009). Revisiting the Strange Stories: Revealing mentalising impairments in Autism. *Child Development, 80*, 1097–1117.

Willoughby, M., & Blair, C. (2011). Test-retest reliability of a new executive function battery for use in early childhood. *Child Neuropsychology, 17*, 564–579. doi:10.1080/09297049.2011.554390

4 Neural bases of theory of mind in middle childhood and adolescence

Katherine Rice Warnell and Elizabeth Redcay

A critical human social skill is the ability to infer others' mental states (i.e., thoughts, beliefs, and desires) and use this information to predict that person's behavior, an ability known as theory of mind (ToM). While the vast majority of behavioral work on ToM has examined childhood, the study of its neural underpinnings has been dominated by work in adults. This adult research has identified a 'mentalizing network' that is consistently engaged across diverse ToM tasks (Molenberghs et al., 2016; Schurz et al., 2014). However, the focus on adults has left a significant gap in our understanding of how the brain supports the development of ToM abilities and how social development influences functional brain development. Middle childhood and adolescence offer a particularly ripe opportunity to address these questions because of the significant changes in both social-cognitive abilities and social environments that are associated with these developmental periods. In the current chapter, we discuss the extant literature examining functional development of the mentalizing network. Much of this work is motivated by the need to understand the neural computations that support different aspects of ToM reasoning at different ages. Another body of work addresses how theory of mind and the mentalizing network are used within social contexts. In reviewing the current literature, we also highlight important areas for future study, including innovative new approaches to address these questions.

Social development in middle childhood and adolescence

Middle childhood and adolescence are characterized by significant social change. In middle childhood, children spend increasingly more time with peers (Parker et al., 2006) and social networks expand (Feiring & Lewis, 1991). Adolescence marks another critical time in social and emotional development (for review see Guyer et al., 2016; Picci & Scherf, 2016). The shift toward greater time spent with peers that begins in middle childhood continues to increase dramatically (Hartup & Stevens, 1997; Lam et al., 2014). Correspondingly, the salience of peers and peer acceptance peaks in importance (Nelson et al., 2005). Puberty brings with it a host of biological changes that influence brain development (Herting & Sowell, 2017) and may provide a second sensitive period (Furhmann et al., 2015) in which the brain reshapes itself towards the increasing focus on peers (e.g., Picci & Scherf, 2016; Nelson et al., 2005). Middle childhood and adolescence are also marked by developmental changes in social cognition (for review see Hughes & Devine, 2015; Lagattuta et al., 2015; Kilford et al., 2016). While our understanding of social-cognitive change in middle childhood is still limited, even fewer studies have examined how these changes are supported by changes in the developing brain.

Two decades of neuroimaging of ToM in adults have yielded a remarkably consistent set of regions that engage more when making judgments about mental states compared with a control condition, which often requires making a non-mental judgment about a person (e.g., tall or short) or physical aspect of the environment (e.g., the wind shut the window). These regions include bilateral anterior and posterior temporal cortices (i.e., temporoparietal junction [TPJ]; superior temporal sulcus [STS]; anterior temporal lobe [ATL]) and anterior and posterior midline regions (i.e., ventral and dorsal medial prefrontal cortex [vMPFC, dMPFC]; precuneus and posterior cingulate cortex [PCC]; see Mahy et al., 2014 for review; see Figure 4.1). While these regions, particularly the TPJ, pSTS, and dMPFC are consistent across diverse tasks and thus may constitute a 'core' ToM (or mentalizing) network, other regions show some variability depending on the specific process elicited by the task (see Molenberghs et al., 2016 and Schurz et al., 2014 for meta-analyses).

Research examining the structural and functional maturation of the mentalizing network suggests middle childhood and adolescence are periods of change. Much of this work has focused on the development of the default mode network (DMN), which is a network that overlaps with the mentalizing network (Schilbach et al., 2012; Spreng et al., 2009). This network can be identified during a resting state (i.e., when participants are not engaged in a specific task). Regions within this network become more functionally integrated from childhood into adulthood (Fair et al., 2008), though the pattern is complex (Sherman et al., 2014), affected by gender and pubertal status (Ernst et

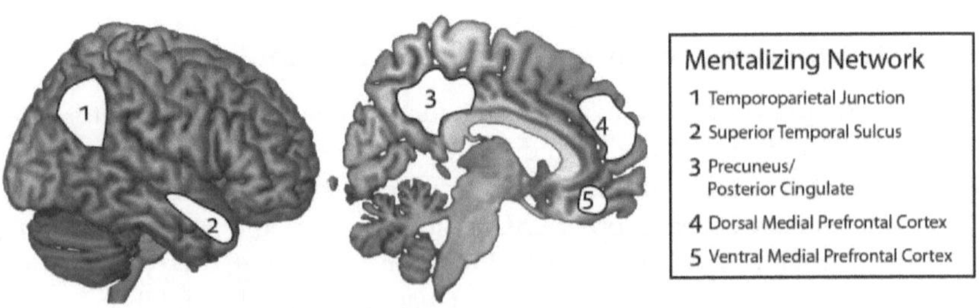

Figure 4.1 The mentalizing network. Key regions associated with the mentalizing network are marked white. Only the medial and right lateral surfaces are shown but both right and left temporoparietal junction and superior temporal sulcus are part of this network.

al., 2019), and sensitive to head motion artifact (Power et al., 2012), which is often also related to age. Further, mentalizing regions show a protracted period of structural development with cortical thinning continuing into adulthood, with the exception of the anterior temporal lobe which shows a quadratic curve peaking in cortical thickness in late adolescence (Mills et al., 2014). The focus of the current chapter is how the development of the mentalizing network is related to social and social-cognitive abilities and age.

Neural bases of theory of mind computations and changes with age

Middle childhood

Neural selectivity

Despite evidence for early neural selectivity for ToM reasoning (i.e., brain responses specific to ToM versus control conditions) in preschool (Sabbagh et al., 2009) and even infancy (Hyde et al., 2018), research from later childhood continues to indicate developmental change in neural sensitivity and selectivity, though the specific pattern of change is not yet clear due to limited studies and small samples. In the first study to examine the neural bases of ToM reasoning in children, Kobayashi et al. (2007) demonstrated greater activation of bilateral TPJ for ToM reasoning (predictions based on second-order beliefs) compared to non-ToM reasoning (predictions based on social and physical, but not mental-state, information) in both children (aged 8 to 11 years) and adults. Compared with adults, children demonstrated greater activation within the superior temporal gyrus, temporal pole, and vMPFC, suggesting potentially greater demand on language and ToM-related regions to perform the task. Subsequent studies found a different pattern of age-related differences. Specifically, bilateral TPJ showed greater neural selectivity for stories with mental states, as compared with physical descriptions of people (Saxe et al., 2009; Gweon et al., 2012). In other words, during middle childhood, a region within the TPJ transitions from one that represents social information in general to one that selectively represents mental states. This finding does not mean that the TPJ only represents mental state information, as evidence shows this heterogeneous portion of the cortex is associated with attention reorienting and memory processes (e.g., Dugué et al., 2018). Rather, the region within the TPJ that is relevant for ToM increases in its selectivity during middle childhood. Children additionally completed a behavioral ToM task in which they read two stories and answered questions that assessed understanding of different components of ToM, including desire, emotion, and false belief (Gweon et al., 2012). Composite scores on this ToM battery were related to right TPJ selectivity, suggesting that this change in selectivity may be functionally relevant for developmental change in ToM abilities.

However, this finding of increasing selectivity for mental compared with non-mental social information in middle childhood was not found in two recent studies (Alkire et al., 2018; Mukerji et al., 2019). Mukerji and colleagues (2019) used a standard ToM localizer from the adult literature in which children listened to stories where a character had a false belief and stories in which a non-social representation, such as painting or a book, was no longer an accurate depiction of the world (e.g., because the person in the painting had aged). They found greater engagement of the mentalizing network for reasoning about false beliefs compared with false non-social representations in children aged 9 to 13 years but activation was not related to age or task performance. In a novel task, Alkire et al. (2018) asked children (aged 8 to 12 years) to make predictions about what a character would choose based on mental (e.g., 'I am bored') or non-mental (e.g., 'I have a kite') state information (Alkire et al., 2018). Although regions of the mentalizing network were engaged for the mental versus non-mental contrast, no age-related differences were seen.

One reason for the lack of age-related differences in these two recent studies may be that the age range was too narrow and/or old to capture the shift in neural selectivity reported previously. For example, other studies included preschoolers in their sample, and if increased selectivity is predominately happening earlier in development, these changes may be missed in studies that only examine middle childhood. Across all the studies reviewed in this section, inconsistencies may also be due to cross-sectional designs and small sample sizes, as none of these studies had more than 32 child participants and three had 20 or fewer. Such small samples make it difficult to determine exactly when in development increased neural selectivity may be occurring.

Using a novel naturalistic imaging approach, Richardson et al. (2018) overcame the prior sample size limitations by collecting functional neuroimaging data during movie viewing from over 120 children aged three to twelve years. Children watched a commercially available animated movie that contained mental state events (e.g., a character being embarrassed) and physical events (e.g., a character being bitten). They found evidence for continuous age-related increases in response magnitude within the ToM network for events requiring more advanced representation of mental states such as considering the relevance of prior mental states and emotions in relation to current events. These findings support prior work demonstrating increasing selectivity of mentalizing regions with age during ToM processing. Nonetheless, given the limited and inconsistent findings, further research is needed to determine how neural selectivity for ToM reasoning changes over middle childhood. Future work would benefit from the use of large samples and longitudinal designs to best capture developmental change.

The studies discussed above generally examined one single type (e.g., second-order belief) or multiple types of ToM reasoning (e.g., beliefs and desires), but did not include a specific comparison of these different facets of ToM. However, behaviorally, different types of ToM show differential rates of development (Wellman & Liu, 2004). Further, data suggest that performance on different types of ToM tasks show very little to no relation to each other (Warnell & Redcay, 2019). One area where this has been addressed in middle childhood is by comparing beliefs and desire. In adults, the RTPJ demonstrates robust selectivity for beliefs when compared with other social characteristics about a person whereas the MPFC responds to social information more generally (Saxe & Powell, 2006). Bowman et al. (2012) extended this question to children (aged seven to eight years) and found similar selectivity for beliefs over the posterior-temporal cortex and sensitivity to both beliefs and desires over midfrontal components. In a follow-up study, Bowman et al. (2015) found selectivity for beliefs compared with desires within the RTPJ in 21 children aged six to ten years. No age-related differences were found. The lack of age-related findings may, again, be due either to sample size limitations or due to the fact that a larger age range is necessary to capture a gradual change in neural selectivity found within the TPJ (e.g., Gweon et al., 2012; Richardson et al., 2018). These two explanations may also intersect, such that individual differences in the trajectory of increased neural selectivity would necessitate large samples and wide age ranges in order to capture age-related changes. Outside of beliefs and desires, another distinction made in the ToM literature is cognitive versus affective ToM, which has predominantly been addressed in adolescence (discussed below).

Functional connectivity

While neural selectivity indexes how sensitive a region is to a specific type of stimulus, functional connectivity gives information on how regions within a network work together. Functional connectivity in neuroimaging is measured by looking at the correlation (or coherence) in brain response over time between two regions. Connectivity can be examined during a task designed to examine a specific process (e.g., false belief reasoning), during movie viewing (in which multiple cognitive processes are engaged to process an external stimulus), or during a resting state (e.g., passively viewing shapes, which invites inward processing). Unlike during tasks, functional connectivity during rest is thought to reflect the intrinsic organization of the brain, shaped by a history of co-activation between regions.

Only a handful of studies have examined how functional connectivity within the mentalizing network is related to ToM abilities in childhood. In a large sample of over 120 children aged 4 to 8 years, Xiao et al. (2019) demonstrated no age-related differences in functional connectivity while watching abstract shapes. However, functional connectivity between RTPJ and other regions of the mentalizing network (LTPJ and PC) was related to parent-reported ToM as measured by the Theory of Mind Inventory (Hutchins et al., 2012), which asks questions about children's understanding of ToM-related concepts, including sarcasm, presented versus real emotion, and using mental states to predict behaviors. These correlations remained even when controlling for age, IQ, gender, head motion, and memory ability (Xiao et al., 2019). With a wider age range (ages 3 to 12 years) and using a movie selected to elicit mental state reasoning, age-related differences were found in connectivity within the mentalizing network. Specifically, connectivity within the mentalizing network increased while connectivity between the mentalizing network and pain network (identified when viewing others in pain) decreased with age (Richardson et al., 2018). In other words, the networks became more integrated within each network and more segregated from each other – a pattern that indicates functional specialization. Connectivity within the mentalizing network while watching a movie was also related to performance on a battery of ToM tasks outside of the scanner but this relation was no longer significant when controlling for age and head motion, and there was no systematic difference between children who passed versus failed a canonical false belief task (Richardson et al., 2018). In slightly older children (aged 9 to 13 years), connectivity between mentalizing regions was greater during a false belief reasoning task than control (false photo reasoning). However, connectivity was not related to age (Mukerji et al., 2019). Thus, both individual differences in ToM ability and age may drive increasing integration within the mentalizing network; however, age-related differences may occur more gradually over a wider age window. These findings suggest that gradual, continuous change between connections within the mentalizing network may underlie ToM development.

Current methodological innovations offer promising ways forward when studying neurodevelopmental trajectories in ToM. Many prior studies are limited in their age range and sample size, given the difficulties that young children have staying still, particularly when completing tasks. These difficulties are accentuated by the fact that rather than motion simply introducing noise, motion can systematically bias neuroimaging data (e.g., Power et al., 2012). Researchers have come up with a variety of solutions in order to decrease children's motion, including offering real-time feedback, providing training sessions, acquiring imaging data over multiple sessions, and using movies as in-scanner stimuli (e.g., Greene et al., 2018; Meissner et al., preprint; Raschle et al., 2009; Vanderwal et al., 2015). For example, in two of the papers reviewed in this section (Richardson et al., 2018; Xiao et al., 2019), researchers had children or parents complete ToM measures outside of the scanner so that children in the scanner only had to watch videos. Although such videos can simply be of abstract shapes, they can also contain naturalistic social stimuli, allowing for greater insight into real-world social processing (Redcay & Moraczewski, 2020). Including larger samples and a variety of targeted naturalistic social stimuli will help illuminate neurodevelopmental trajectories of mental state understanding, and we further elaborate on how new techniques and approaches can inform our understanding of ToM at the end of this chapter. Although naturalistic social videos are informative stimuli for a variety of ages, as children age into adolescence, they can begin to complete more complicated neuroimaging tasks that allow for more precise comparisons with similar task-based adult research.

Adolescence

While research in middle childhood has focused on examining neural specificity for belief reasoning, research in adolescence has addressed understanding intentions more generally and has also considered affective ToM, or reasoning about others' affective states. For both intention understanding and affective theory of mind, the TPJ figures less prominently. Rather, the STS and MPFC are key players.

Intentions

Blakemore et al. (2007) had participants read scenarios where they either imagined themselves (e.g., 'you are at a cinema and have trouble seeing the screen') or a natural occurrence ('a huge tree suddenly comes crashing down in the forest') and answered a question about the likelihood of an action or consequence. Both adolescents and adults engaged regions of the mentalizing network for making intentional versus physical judgments. However, adolescents relied more on MPFC to make intentional judgments while adults relied more on pSTS, suggesting a possible anterior to posterior shift in processing intentions.

Affective theory of mind

This finding of greater MPFC activity in adolescents than adults has been found consistently across ToM studies in adolescents, though the majority of those have examined affective ToM processing. While both affective and cognitive ToM vignettes engage core ToM regions (e.g., TPJ and MPFC), only affective ToM stories engaged vMPFC, and this vMPFC engagement was greater for adolescents than adults (Sebastian et al., 2012). Similarly, Gunther Moor and colleagues (2012) presented black and white photographs of the eye region and asked participants to either infer the mental state or, as a control condition, determine the age and gender. Compared with the control, reading mental states from pictures of eyes engaged the STS in early and late adolescents and adults, but only early adolescents showed engagement of MPFC (Gunther Moor et al., 2012). Further, functional connectivity between the MPFC and STS was greater in adolescents than adults when reading emotional scenarios (Burnett et al., 2009). Finally, early and late adolescents (aged 9 to 14 years) engaged greater MPFC than adults when listening to ironic compared with sincere statements (Wang et al., 2006a). While studies examining specific types of ToM computations (e.g., cognitive or affective) are more limited, more research in adolescence has examined how ToM or the mentalizing network are used in social contexts such as peer evaluation and social interaction. These studies on ToM use are discussed in the next section.

Neural bases of theory of mind use and changes with age

Beyond traditional ToM paradigms (e.g., false belief reasoning), the mentalizing network has also been developmentally implicated in a broad array of social-interactive tasks, including those which do not appear to involve explicit mentalizing demands. In this section, we review the neural bases of ToM use in school-aged children and adolescents, with a focus on how the mentalizing network may support real-world social interaction. We do not intend for this section to be a fully exhaustive meta-analysis, but rather to illustrate the range of domains in which ToM processes may be developmentally relevant and to highlight those domains that seem to correspond to the greatest age-related changes from middle childhood through adolescence.

Social perspective-taking

Mentalizing regions are often implicated in neuroeconomic games, such as those that involve cooperation, trust, or reciprocity, potentially due to the demands of seeing another's perspective (see Cutler & Campbell-Meiklejohn, 2019 for review). Although the bulk of neuroeconomic studies have been done in adults, extending such paradigms to adolescents offers important insight into the development of these brain networks (Van Duijvenvoorde & Crone, 2013). For example, van den Bos and colleagues (2011) examined neural activity in individuals aged 12 to 22 in a dyadic, turn-taking trust-based game in which players have the opportunity to reciprocate prosocially or act selfishly. Older adolescents showed increased activity in left TPJ, potentially suggesting increased deliberation about others' perspectives. In contrast, younger adolescents showed more invariant activity in MPFC, regardless of their partner's actions, which the authors interpreted as reflecting more self-based processing. Other neuroeconomic studies have also found evidence for age-based increases in mentalizing network activity from childhood and early adolescence through adulthood (Fett et al., 2014; Steinmann et al., 2014). Future research should continue to investigate potential modulators of the relation between age and mentalizing network activation during interactive games.

Another frequently studied measure of social perspective-taking is the director's task (Keysar et al., 2000). In this task, an array of objects is set up such that the participant on one side of the array can see all the objects, but for the person on the other side (the director), some of the objects are occluded. The director instructs the participant to move objects (e.g., the 'smallest ball') and the participant must take into account the director's perspective (e.g., that the smallest ball from the participant's perspective might not be the smallest ball from the director's). In contrast to many canonical ToM tasks, performance on this task shows protracted improvement over adolescence (Dumontheil et al., 2010; Tamnes et al., 2018). An fMRI study of the director's task found differences in dMPFC recruitment between adolescents and adults, such that adolescents engaged the region even on trials in which they did not need to consider the director's viewpoint (Dumontheil et al., 2012). This finding is potentially in contrast to findings from neuroeconomic games that indicate more linear increases in mentalizing network activity from adolescence to adulthood, suggesting that age and social context may interact in predicting when and how the ToM network is engaged.

Self- and other-appraisal

Adolescence is often considered to be a time of increased social sensitivity, particularly with regard to concerns about others' opinions about oneself (e.g., Buhrmester, 1996). Neuroimaging research examining the neural bases of self- and other-evaluation also suggests developmental changes, including in regions linked to mentalizing, such as MPFC (see Pfeifer & Peake, 2012 for review). For example, children aged nine to ten recruited dMPFC more than adults when evaluating statements about themselves (Pfeifer et al., 2007), with longitudinal research suggesting that between ages 10 and 13, vMPFC activity specifically may increase in response to self-evaluation in social, but not academic domains (Pfeifer et al., 2013). Although adults do not appear to activate the mentalizing network when engaging in self-reflection (Pfeifer & Peak, 2012), a study of adolescents aged 11 to 14 showed elevated recruitment of mentalizing regions (TPJ, dMPFC, STS) when reflecting on their own traits (Pfeifer et al., 2009), consistent with other research showing increased TPJ activation for self- versus other-judgments in adolescence (Romund et al., 2017). A complementary line of work has compared the neural bases of thinking about one's own traits and thinking about what others think of one's traits, finding reduced differences between the two conditions in adolescents compared to young adults (Pfeifer et al., 2009). Thus, it is possible that early adolescence is a time of increased perspective-taking, even in contexts where such perspective-taking is not explicitly demanded. A caveat, however, is that one study with a slightly different design failed to replicate these age effects in mentalizing regions (Jankowski et al., 2014), underscoring the importance of continued replication efforts.

Outside of explicit trait judgments, there is evidence that adolescents recruit the mentalizing network even in social contexts that contain no explicit social appraisal. Specifically, Somerville and colleagues (2013) designed a paradigm in which individuals aged 8 to 22 believed they were being observed via video feed while at rest in the scanner. Even though these participants received no feedback and could not see who was ostensibly observing them, dMPFC activity and self-reported levels of embarrassment peaked in adolescence. Such findings indicate that adolescence may be a time of heightened recruitment of mentalizing network activity, although more research is needed to determine the exact function of this region during such tasks.

Social interaction

Even in contexts without explicit mentalizing demands, evidence from middle childhood and adolescence suggests that social interaction engages the ToM network (see Redcay & Warnell, 2018 for review). For example, children aged 7 to 13 years showed increased activity in the mentalizing network, including TPJ and precuneus, when listening to live versus recorded speech that contained no reference to mental state content (Rice et al., 2016). Similarly, during simulated, text-based peer interaction, children aged 8 to 12 years demonstrated increased activity in similar regions of the mentalizing network when interacting with a peer versus computer (Warnell et al., 2018). Suggestively, increased activity in TPJ and STS was present even on trials where the child received a message that the peer was unavailable, potentially indicating a general engagement during the possibility of real-time social interaction or that children were anticipating or mentally simulating the peer's response on subsequent trials. A follow-up study in the same age range found that many of the same regions that were activated when making mental-state judgments about story characters were also activated when making non-mental-state judgments about interactive partners (Alkire et al., 2018). Further, no regions were recruited more when making mental-state versus non-mental-state judgments about interactive partners, also attesting to the developmental sensitivity of the mentalizing network to social interaction more broadly. In a separate modality, an interactive joint attention paradigm also found evidence for developmental activation in the mentalizing network (Oberwelland et al., 2016).

Age-related findings from the social interaction literature are more mixed, with middle childhood samples finding both increased (Warnell et al., 2018) and decreased (Alkire et al., 2018) ToM network response to interactive (i.e., chatting in real-time with peers) versus non-interactive conditions with age, potentially due to the non-interactive control conditions employed (i.e., messaging with a computer versus answering questions about characters in stories). In an interactive joint attention context, adolescents showed greater specialization than children in the mentalizing network, with TPJ and precuneus activated more specifically by self-initiated joint attention as opposed to other trial types (e.g., response to joint attention). Ultimately, studies with larger samples and a variety of tasks are necessary to isolate developmental changes in how the mentalizing network supports social interaction.

Relations to real-world behaviors

Beyond the specific experimental contexts discussed in the previous sections, engagement of the mentalizing network may be related to real-world outcomes. For example, Peake and colleagues (2013) put adolescents in a simulated driving game in which their performance was ostensibly being watched by real peers. Participants played the game twice, once before and once after social exclusion from these peers. Researchers found increased activity in the mentalizing network for safe decisions after exclusion versus before exclusion, suggesting potentially increased reflection on the peer's mental state. Interestingly, however, adolescents who reported themselves as more susceptible to peer influence showed relatively greater activity in social-cognitive regions when making risky choices. The specific risk-taking scenario may influence mentalizing activity, as, during a different risk-taking paradigm, McCormick and colleagues (2018) found adolescents showed decreased activity in the mentalizing network compared with younger children when presented with social information extraneous to the task goal.

Developmental activity in the mentalizing network has also been linked to prosocial behaviors (see Do et al., 2017 for review). In a paradigm in which adolescents aged 12 to 16 years believed they were donating money while alone and while being observed by peers, peer presence increased donation amounts and activity in the mentalizing network (Van Hoorn et al., 2016). Further, TPJ activity when being observed positively correlated with the amount donated, and this mentalizing network activity peaked in young adolescents (aged 12 to 13 years). In another cross-sectional study, participants aged 8 to 25 years played a game where they could win prizes for friends, disliked peers, or themselves (Braams et al., 2014). Overall, ToM activity was higher when playing on behalf of another, with quadratic relations between age and vMPFC activity when winning prizes for a disliked peer. A similar quadratic pattern was found by Do and colleagues (2019), such that early adolescents showed increased pSTS, temporal pole, and IFG activation when engaging in costly prosocial actions. Thus, as in other ToM-relevant domains, adolescence, and potentially early adolescence in particular, may represent a time of peak mentalizing network activity.

Titrating the influence of the mentalizing network

Although the regions of the mentalizing network have been extensively characterized across dozens of studies – at least in adulthood – core regions of this network are also involved in a variety of other processes. For example, TPJ is involved in attentional reorienting, even in tasks with no social components (e.g., Dugué et al., 2018). Even if these networks are distinguishable in highly controlled studies when participants are presented with multiple types of stimuli, individual variability in spatial patterns of neural activation makes it difficult to extrapolate ToM processing to a new sample of individuals simply because, for example, TPJ activity is observed during peer interaction or self-appraisal (i.e., the reverse inference problem; Poldrack, 2006).

There are two key ways to tackle the question of reverse inference in developmental ToM research. First, large-scale databases of activation patterns across a variety of paradigms (e.g., Neurosynth; Yarkoni et al., 2011) are tools to help increase the precision of mapping coordinates to function. Additionally, these databases should be paired with more sophisticated types of data analysis, such as multivoxel pattern analysis (MVPA), which allow for better correspondence between neural activity and mental function (Poldrack, 2011). Another way forward is to develop paradigms or use localizers (e.g., Dodell-Feder et al., 2011) that more precisely highlight the role of the mentalizing network. For example, Alkire and colleagues (2018) developed an interactive paradigm in which children made mental- and non-mental-state predictions about story characters and about peers ostensibly completing the task in another laboratory. Crucially, this method produced a 2 (Peer, Character) x 2 (Mental, Non-mental) design in order to titrate the relative influence of social interaction and mental state reasoning on ToM network activation. Developing targeted hypotheses and paradigms will help clarify how and when the ToM network is activated across middle childhood and adolescence.

Summary and future directions

Overall, the mentalizing network shows developmental continuity, with similar regions involved from early childhood onward when engaging in mental state computations. Developmental changes from the preschool years through adolescence appear to be gradual and continuous both in neural selectivity and functional connectivity, with some research linking these changes to improved ToM abilities. Preliminary evidence suggests that there may be increased specialization for particular types of ToM tasks, but more work needs to be done. Many of the most striking findings from middle childhood and adolescence relate to ToM network activation across a variety of social contexts, with evidence that adolescents may show increased mentalizing network activity as compared with both children and adults. Although ToM neural development is a growing area of research, there are several important and unexplored avenues that will help illuminate how brain and behavioral changes co-occur during this developmental period.

Combining multimethod neural and behavioral approaches

Although the last two decades have had a rapid increase in neuroimaging data collection and analysis techniques, the majority of developmental ToM neuroimaging studies are task-based, comparing activation when processing mental states to a control condition. Further, such paradigms typically examine only a single ToM task in each sample. Such research has yielded impressive insight into the development of ToM in childhood and adolescence, but future research should incorporate multiple behavioral and neuroimaging measures.

Given mounting evidence for the multifaceted nature of ToM (Warnell & Redcay, 2019; Schaafsma et al., 2015), some meta-analytical adult research has compared neural correlates across ToM tasks, finding evidence for commonalities and differences (Mohlenbergs et al., 2016; Schurz et al., 2014). In children and adolescents, however, such systematic, quantitative comparisons have not been done. Meta-analyses are an important direction for future developmental ToM research, especially as the body of literature spanning a variety of paradigms continues to grow.

Although such a meta-analysis would be useful, it is also important to examine multiple tasks – both implicit and explicit – in single samples. So far, this has only begun to be examined, for example, in comparisons of affective versus cognitive ToM (Sebastian et al., 2012) and belief versus desire reasoning (Bowman et al., 2012, 2015). However, a more comprehensive examination is warranted. Such studies would also benefit from larger sample sizes and more nuanced consideration of effect sizes and power analyses in neuroimaging (Cremers et al., 2017; Reddan et al., 2017), which will also increase confidence in the replicability of brain-behavior relations (e.g., Yarkoni, 2009).

Ideally, research spanning diverse measures of ToM performance should be conducted longitudinally. Existing cross-sectional work has been useful for beginning to understanding developmental changes in ToM computation and use (e.g., Gweon et al., 2012; Richardson, 2018; Sommerville et al., 2013), but individual-level growth curves would allow for finer mapping of the relations between brain and behavior. To date, work by Bowman and colleagues (2019) found longitudinal associations between task-independent EEG patterns in mentalizing regions, specifically MPFC, at age four and both age seven ToM ability and age seven fMRI activation in the same region during false belief tasks. Additionally, Overgaauw and colleagues (2015) followed adolescents aged 12 to 19 over a two-year period, collecting fMRI data while they inferred mental states from photographs of the eyes. Broadly, activation patterns were stable across time points, but dMPFC activity and right IFG activity showed evidence of developmental change. Outside of these studies, however, longitudinal examinations are limited. Such research is complicated by the fact that most of the ToM measures used with young children (e.g., false belief tasks) do not produce variability at older ages. Examining brain activity during naturalistic viewing paradigms (e.g., of social movie clips) may provide one method for needed longitudinal research (e.g., Richardson et al., 2018; see Redcay & Moraczewski, 2020 for discussion of these methods), and such methods should be paired with ToM tasks that capture variability across ages. Future developmental ToM research should also consider how changes in the mentalizing network connect with changes in other domains and use multimodal neuroimaging techniques, as fully probing the spatial and temporal neural correlates of ToM development will require involving multiple methods at multiple ages.

Moving from the laboratory to the real world

Recent years have seen an increased call for socially interactive neuroscience, also called 'second-person neuroscience' (e.g., Redcay & Schilbach, 2019; Schilbach et al., 2013). As opposed to paradigms in which participants merely observe social stimuli (e.g., view photographs, listen to audio clips), socially interactive neuroscience involves the participant in a dynamic social context with one or more partners. As discussed in the previous section, across such paradigms, the mentalizing network is frequently implicated in both children (Redcay & Warnell, 2018) and adults (Redcay & Schilbach, 2019), and future ToM research ought to include a focus on interactive paradigms.

Such interactive research also should consider the identity of the child or adolescent's social partner. For example, research on adolescent risk-taking using a driving stimulator has found evidence that although sitting next to a peer increases activation in reward regions during risk-taking (Chein et al., 2011), sitting next to one's mother decreases activation in the same regions

(Telzer et al., 2015). Interactive joint attention paradigms have also found increased neural activation in children and adolescents when initiating gaze shifts with familiar versus unfamiliar partners (Oberwelland et al., 2016). Very little neural research on ToM development, however, has compared activity when reasoning about the mental states of different social partners. One possibility is that mental state reasoning about close social partners is less taxing than more distant partners, given that such states are more frequently experienced. In contrast, we may engage in increased cognitive elaboration when engaging with close others, and future research should test these hypotheses.

Considering typical and atypical development

A move to more naturalistic paradigms should also incorporate atypical development, especially as social difficulties in conditions such as autism and social anxiety disorder are often most acute in real-world contexts (e.g., Klin et al., 2003; Schilbach, 2016). Although there is behavioral evidence for ToM impairments in a variety of clinical disorders (Chapter 9; Chapter 11 this volume), research on the corresponding neural correlates has been less extensive and is often inconclusive, especially in developmental populations. For example, even though the neural bases of ToM in ASD are relatively well-studied compared with other clinical conditions, results are mixed. Some studies of children and adolescents have found reduced neural responsivity in the ToM network (Carter et al., 2012; O'Nions et al., 2014), whereas others have found increased mentalizing network activity (Wang et al., 2006b; White et al., 2014), and still others have found different patterns depending on the specific ToM regions (Yuk et al., 2018). Recent studies using multivariate pattern analysis suggest the representations of mentalizing may differ between ASD and TD participants (Richardson et al., 2020). Given inconsistent findings, future research on mentalizing in atypical development should compare across different task types and more extensively consider symptomatic heterogeneity (Muller & Fishman, 2018), including cases of comorbid conditions and of subclinical or trait-level disorders. Longitudinal studies would also help inform the developmental cascades that may lead from early social difficulties to ToM-specific impairments, or, conversely, to the compensatory mechanisms that allow for success on specific tasks.

Conclusions

Overall, middle childhood and adolescence represent important times to study the brain bases of ToM in typical and atypical development. These time periods represent continued advancement and refinement of our ability to understand the minds of others, but much is still unknown about how exactly neural development reflects and supports these changes. Further, the cascading processes linking neural and behavioral ToM development likely have social-cognitive implications throughout the lifespan. To date, existing literature indicates broad similarity in the regions involved in mental state processing throughout development, with gradually increasing neural selectivity from early childhood through adolescence. Outside of explicit mental state processing, the ToM network is developmentally recruited for a variety of social tasks, with potential peaks in adolescence. Ultimately, large-scale, longitudinal studies examining atypical and typical development are essential to comprehend the form and function of the developing ToM network. Such research will help us better understand how the developing brain unfolds in the social world.

References

Alkire, D., Levitas, D., Warnell, K.R., & Redcay, E. (2018). Social interaction recruits mentalizing and reward systems in middle childhood. *Human Brain Mapping, 39*(10), 3928–3942. https://doi.org/10.1002/hbm.24221

Blakemore, S.J., den Ouden, H., Choudhury, S., & Frith, C. (2007). Adolescent development of the neural circuitry for thinking about intentions. *Social Cognitive and Affective Neuroscience, 2*(2), 130–139. https://doi.org/10.1093/scan/nsm009

Bowman, L.C., Dodell-Feder, D., Saxe, R., & Sabbagh, M.A. (2019). Continuity in the neural system supporting children's theory of mind development: longitudinal links between task-independent EEG and task-dependent fMRI. *Developmental Cognitive Neuroscience, 40*, 100705. https://doi.org/10.1016/j.dcn.2019.100705

Bowman, L.C., Kovelman, I., Hu, X., & Wellman, H.M. (2015). Children's belief- and desire-reasoning in the temporoparietal junction: evidence for specialization from functional near-infrared spectroscopy. *Frontiers in Human Neuroscience, 9*, 560. https://doi.org/10.3389/fnhum.2015.00560

Bowman, L.C., Liu, D., Meltzoff, A.N., & Wellman, H.M. (2012). Neural correlates of belief- and desire-reasoning in 7- and 8-year-old children: an event-related potential study. *Developmental Science, 15*(5), 618–632. https://doi.org/10.1111/j.1467-7687.2012.01158.x

Braams, B.R., Peters, S., Peper, J.S., Güroğlu, B., & Crone, E.A. (2014). Gambling for self, friends, and antagonists: differential contributions of affective and social brain regions on adolescent reward processing. *NeuroImage, 100*, 281–289. https://doi.org/10.1016/j.neuroimage.2014.06.020

Buhrmester, D. (1996). Need fulfillment, interpersonal competence, and the developmental contexts of early adolescent friendship. In W.M. Bukowski, A.F. Newcomb & W.W. Hartup (Eds), *The Company They Keep: Friendship in Childhood and Adolescence* (pp. 158–185). New York: Cambridge University Press.

Burnett, S., Bird, G., Moll, J., Frith, C., & Blakemore, S-J. (2009). Development during adolescence of the neural processing of social emotion. *Journal of Cognitive Neuroscience, 21*(9), 1736–1750. https://doi.org/10.1162/jocn.2009.21121

Carter, E.J., Williams, D.L., Minshew, N.J., & Lehman, J.F. (2012). Is he being bad? Social and language brain networks during social judgment in children with autism. *PLoS One*, 7(10). https://doi.org/10.1371/journal.pone.0047241

Chein, J., Albert, D., O'Brien, L., Uckert, K., & Steinberg, L. (2011). Peers increase adolescent risk taking by enhancing activity in the brain's reward circuitry. *Developmental Science, 14*(2), F1–F10. https://doi.org/10.1111/j.1467-7687.2010.01035.x

Cremers, H.R., Wager, T.D., & Yarkoni, T. (2017). The relation between statistical power and inference in fMRI. *PloS one, 12*(11). https://doi.org/10.1371/journal.pone.0184923

Cutler, J., & Campbell-Meiklejohn, D. (2019). A comparative fMRI meta-analysis of altruistic and strategic decisions to give. *NeuroImage*, *184*, 227–241. https://doi.org/10.1016/j.neuroimage.2018.09.009

Do, K.T., McCormick, E.M., & Telzer, E.H. (2019). The neural development of prosocial behavior from childhood to adolescence. *Social Cognitive and Affective Neuroscience*, *14*(2), 129–139. https://doi.org/10.1093/scan/nsy117

Do, K.T., Moreira, J.F.G., & Telzer, E.H. (2017). But is helping you worth the risk? Defining prosocial risk taking in adolescence. *Developmental Cognitive Neuroscience*, *25*, 260–271. https://doi.org/10.1016/j.dcn.2016.11.008

Dodell-Feder, D., Koster-Hale, J., Bedny, M., & Saxe, R. (2011). fMRI item analysis in a theory of mind task. *NeuroImage*, *55*(2), 705–712. https://doi.org/10.1016/j.neuroimage.2010.12.040

Dugué, L., Merriam, E.P., Heeger, D.J., & Carrasco, M. (2018). Specific visual subregions of TPJ mediate reorienting of spatial attention. *Cerebral Cortex*, *28*(7), 2375–2390. https://doi.org/10.1093/cercor/bhx140

Dumontheil, I., Apperly, I.A., & Blakemore, S.J. (2010). Online usage of theory of mind continues to develop in late adolescence. *Developmental Science*, *13*(2), 331–338. https://doi.org/10.1111/j.1467-7687.2009.00888.x

Dumontheil, I., Hillebrandt, H., Apperly, I.A., & Blakemore, S.J. (2012). Developmental differences in the control of action selection by social information. *Journal of Cognitive Neuroscience*, *24*(10), 2080–2095. https://doi.org/10.1162/jocn_a_00268

Ernst, M., Benson, B., Artiges, E., Gorka, A.X., Lemaitre, H., Lago, T., … & Martinot, J-L. (2019). Pubertal maturation and sex effects on the default-mode network connectivity implicated in mood dysregulation. *Translational Psychiatry*, *9*(1), 1–14. https://doi.org/10.1038/s41398-019-0433-6

Fair, D.A., Cohen, A.L., Dosenbach, N.U., Church, J.A., Miezin, F.M., Barch, D.M., … & Schlaggar, B.L. (2008). The maturing architecture of the brain's default network. *Proceedings of the National Academy of Sciences of the United States of America*, *105*(10), 4028–4032. https://doi.org/10.1073/pnas.0800376105

Feiring, C., & Lewis, M. (1991). The transition from middle childhood to early adolescence: sex differences in the social network and perceived self-competence. *Sex Roles*, *24*, 489–509. https://doi.org/10.1007/BF00289335

Fett, A.K.J., Gromann, P.M., Giampietro, V., Shergill, S.S., & Krabbendam, L. (2014). Default distrust? An fMRI investigation of the neural development of trust and cooperation. *Social Cognitive and Affective Neuroscience*, *9*(4), 395–402. https://doi.org/10.1093/scan/nss144

Fuhrmann, D., Knoll, L.J., & Blakemore, S.J. (2015). Adolescence as a sensitive period of brain development. *Trends in Cognitive Sciences*, *19*(10), 558–566. https://doi.org/10.1016/j.tics.2015.07.008

Greene, D.J., Koller, J.M., Hampton, J.M., Wesevich, V., Van, A.N., Nguyen, A.L., … & Shimony, J.S. (2018). Behavioral interventions for reducing head motion during MRI scans in children. *NeuroImage*, *171*, 234–245. https://doi.org/10.1016/j.neuroimage.2018.01.023

Gunther Moor, B., Op de Macks, Z.A., Güroğlu, B., Rombouts, S.A., Van der Molen, M.W., & Crone, E.A. (2012). Neurodevelopmental changes of reading the mind in the eyes. *Social Cognitive and Affective Neuroscience*, 7(1), 44–52. https://doi.org/10.1093/scan/nsr020

Guyer, A.E., Silk, J.S., & Nelson, E.E. (2016). The neurobiology of the emotional adolescent: from the inside out. *Neuroscience & Biobehavioral Reviews*, *70*, 74–85. https://doi.org/10.1016/j.neubiorev.2016.07.037

Gweon, H., Dodell-Feder, D., Bedny, M., & Saxe, R. (2012). Theory of mind performance in children correlates with functional specialization of a brain region for thinking about thoughts. *Child Development*, *83*(6), 1853–1868. https://doi.org/10.1111/j.1467-8624.2012.01829.x

Hartup, W.W., & Stevens, N. (1997). Friendships and adaptation in the life course. *Psychological Bulletin*, *121*(3), 355. https://doi.org/10.1037/0033-2909.121.3.355

Herting, M.M., & Sowell, E.R. (2017). Puberty and structural brain development in humans. *Frontiers in Neuroendocrinology*, *44*, 122–137. https://doi.org/10.1016/j.yfrne.2016.12.003

Hughes, C., & Devine, R.T. (2015). Individual differences in theory of mind from preschool to adolescence: achievements and directions. *Child Development Perspectives*, *9*(3), 149–153. https://doi.org/10.1111/cdep.12124

Hutchins, T.L., Prelock, P.A., & Bonazinga, L. (2012). Psychometric evaluation of the Theory of Mind Inventory (ToMI): a study of typically developing children and children with autism spectrum disorder. *Journal of Autism and Developmental Disorders*, *42*(3), 327–341. https://doi.org/10.1007/s10803-011-1244-7

Hyde, D.C., Simon, C.E., Ting, F., & Nikolaeva, J.I. (2018). Functional organization of the temporal-parietal junction for theory of mind in preverbal infants: a near-infrared spectroscopy study. *Journal of Neuroscience*, *38*(18), 4264–4274. https://doi.org/10.1523/JNEUROSCI.0264-17.2018

Jankowski, K.F., Moore, W.E., Merchant, J.S., Kahn, L.E., & Pfeifer, J.H. (2014). But do you think I'm cool?: developmental differences in striatal recruitment during direct and reflected social self-evaluations. *Developmental Cognitive Neuroscience*, *8*, 40–54. https://doi.org/10.1016/j.dcn.2014.01.003

Keysar, B., Barr, D.J., Balin, J.A., & Brauner, J.S. (2000). Taking perspective in conversation: the role of mutual knowledge in comprehension. *Psychology Science*, *11*(1), 32–38. https://doi.org/10.1111/1467-9280.00211

Kilford, E.J., Garrett, E., & Blakemore, S.J. (2016). The development of social cognition in adolescence: an integrated perspective. *Neuroscience & Biobehavioral Reviews*, *70*, 106–120. https://doi.org/10.1016/j.neubiorev.2016.08.016

Klin, A., Jones, W., Schultz, R., & Volkmar, F. (2003). The enactive mind, or from actions to cognition: lessons from autism. *Philosophical Transactions of the Royal Society of London Series B Biological Sciences*, *358*(1430), 345 360. https://doi.org/10.1098/rstb.2002.1202

Kobayashi, C., Glover, G.H., & Temple, E. (2007). Children's and adults' neural bases of verbal and nonverbal 'theory of mind'. *Neuropsychologia*, *45*(7), 1522–1532. https://doi.org/10.1016/j.neuropsychologia.2006.11.017

Lagattuta, K.H., Kramer, H.J., Kennedy, K., Hjortsvang, K., Goldfarb, D., & Tashjian, S. (2015). Beyond Sally's missing marble: further development in children's understanding of mind and emotion in middle childhood. *Advances in Child Development and Behavior*, *48*, 185–217. https://doi.org/10.1016/bs.acdb.2014.11.005

Lam, C.B., McHale, S.M., & Crouter, A.C. (2014). Time with peers from middle childhood to late adolescence: developmental course and adjustment correlates. *Child Development*, *85*(4), 1677–1693. https://doi.org/10.1111/cdev.12235

Mahy, C.E., Moses, L.J., & Pfeifer, J.H. (2014). How and where: theory-of-mind in the brain. *Developmental Cognitive Neuroscience*, *9*, 68–81. https://doi.org/10.1016/j.dcn.2014.01.002

McCormick, E.M., Perino, M.T., & Telzer, E.H. (2018). Not just social sensitivity: adolescent neural suppression of social feedback during risk taking. *Developmental Cognitive Neuroscience*, *30*, 134–141. https://doi.org/10.1016/j.dcn.2018.01.012

Meissner, T.W., Walbrin, J., Nordt, M., Koldewyn, K., & Weigelt, S. (preprint). Head motion during fMRI tasks is reduced in children and adults if participants take breaks. *bioRxiv*, 816116. https://doi.org/10.1101/816116

Mills, K.L., Lalonde, F., Clasen, L.S., Giedd, J.N., & Blakemore, S.J. (2014). Developmental changes in the structure of the social brain in late childhood and adolescence. *Social Cognitive and Affective Neuroscience, 9*(1), 123–131. https://doi.org/10.1093/scan/nss113

Molenberghs, P., Johnson, H., Henry, J.D., & Mattingley, J.B. (2016). Understanding the minds of others: a neuroimaging meta-analysis. *Neuroscience & Biobehavioral Reviews, 65*, 276–291. https://doi.org/10.1016/j.neubiorev.2016.03.020

Mukerji, C.E., Lincoln, S.H., Dodell-Feder, D., Nelson, C.A., & Hooker, C.I. (2019). Neural correlates of theory-of-mind are associated with variation in children's everyday social cognition. *Social Cognitive and Affective Neuroscience, 14*(6), 579–589. https://doi.org/10.1093/scan/nsz040

Müller, R.A., & Fishman, I. (2018). Brain connectivity and neuroimaging of social networks in autism. *Trends in Cognitive Sciences, 22*(12), 1103–1116. https://doi.org/10.1016/j.tics.2018.09.008

Nelson, E.E., Leibenluft, E., McClure, E.B., & Pine, D.S. (2005). The social re-orientation of adolescence: a neuroscience perspective on the process and its relation to psychopathology. *Psychological Medicine, 35*(2), 163–174. https://doi.org/10.1017/S0033291704003915

Oberwelland, E., Schilbach, L., Barisic, I., Krall, S.C., Vogeley, K., Fink, G.R., … & Schulte-Rüther, M. (2016). Look into my eyes: investigating joint attention using interactive eye-tracking and fMRI in a developmental sample. *NeuroImage, 130*, 248–260. https://doi.org/10.1016/j.neuroimage.2016.02.026

O'Nions, E., Sebastian, C.L., McCrory, E., Chantiluke, K., Happe, F., & Viding, E. (2014). Neural bases of Theory of Mind in children with autism spectrum disorders and children with conduct problems and callous-unemotional traits. *Developmental Science, 17*(5), 786–796. https://doi.org/10.1111/desc.12167

Overgaauw, S., van Duijvenvoorde, A.C., Gunther Moor, B., & Crone, E.A. (2015). A longitudinal analysis of neural regions involved in reading the mind in the eyes. *Social Cognitive and Affective Neuroscience, 10*(5), 619–627. https://doi.org/10.1093/scan/nsu095

Parker, J.G., Rubin, K.H., Erath, S.A., Wojslawowicz, J.C., & Buskirk, A.A. (2006). Peer relationships, child development, and adjustment: a developmental psychopathology perspective. In D. Cicchetti & D.J. Cohen (Eds.), *Developmental psychopathology: Theory and method* (pp. 419–493). New Jersey: John Wiley & Sons Inc.

Peake, S.J., Dishion, T.J., Stormshak, E.A., Moore, W.E., & Pfeifer, J.H. (2013). Risk-taking and social exclusion in adolescence: neural mechanisms underlying peer influences on decision-making. *NeuroImage, 82*, 23–34. https://doi.org/10.1016/j.neuroimage.2013.05.061

Pfeifer, J.H., Kahn, L.E., Merchant, J.S., Peake, S.J., Veroude, K., Masten, C.L., … & Dapretto, M. (2013). Longitudinal change in the neural bases of adolescent social self-evaluations: effects of age and pubertal development. *Journal of Neuroscience, 33*(17), 7415–7419. https://doi.org/10.1523/JNEUROSCI.4074-12.2013

Pfeifer, J.H., Lieberman, M.D., & Dapretto, M. (2007). "I know you are but what am I?!": neural bases of self-and social knowledge retrieval in children and adults. *Journal of Cognitive Neuroscience, 19*(8), 1323–1337. https://doi.org/10.1162/jocn.2007.19.8.1323

Pfeifer, J.H., Masten, C.L., Borofsky, L.A., Dapretto, M., Fuligni, A.J., & Lieberman, M.D. (2009). Neural correlates of direct and reflected self-appraisals in adolescents and adults: when social perspective-taking informs self-perception. *Child Development, 80*(4), 1016–1038. https://doi.org/10.1111/j.1467-8624.2009.01314.x

Pfeifer, J.H., & Peake, S.J. (2012). Self-development: integrating cognitive, socioemotional, and neuroimaging perspectives. *Developmental Cognitive Neuroscience, 2*(1), 55–69. https://doi.org/10.1016/j.dcn.2011.07.012

Picci, G., & Scherf, K.S. (2016). From caregivers to peers: puberty shapes human face perception. *Psychology Science, 27*(11), 1461–1473. https://doi.org/10.1177/0956797616663142

Poldrack, R.A. (2006). Can cognitive processes be inferred from neuroimaging data?. *Trends in Cognitive Sciences, 10*(2), 59–63. https://doi.org/10.1016/j.tics.2005.12.004

Poldrack, R.A. (2011). Inferring mental states from neuroimaging data: from reverse inference to large-scale decoding. *Neuron, 72*(5), 692–697. https://doi.org/10.1016/j.neuron.2011.11.001

Power, J.D., Barnes, K.A., Snyder, A.Z., Schlaggar, B.L., & Petersen, S.E. (2012). Spurious but systematic correlations in functional connectivity MRI networks arise from subject motion. *NeuroImage, 59*(3), 2142–2154. https://doi.org/10.1016/j.neuroimage.2011.10.018

Raschle, N.M., Lee, M., Buechler, R., Christodoulou, J.A., Chang, M., Vakil, M., ... & Gaab, N. (2009). Making MR imaging child's play-pediatric neuroimaging protocol, guidelines and procedure. *Journal of Visualized Experiments, 29*, e1309. doi:10.3791/1309

Redcay, E., & Moraczewski, D. (2020). Social cognition in context: a naturalistic imaging approach. *NeuroImage, 216*, 116392. doi:10.1016/j.neuroimage.2019.116392

Redcay, E., & Schilbach, L. (2019). Using second-person neuroscience to elucidate the mechanisms of social interaction. *Nature Reviews. Neuroscience, 20*(8), 495–505. https://doi.org/10.1038/s41583-019-0179-4

Redcay, E., & Warnell, K.R. (2018). A social-interactive neuroscience approach to understanding the developing brain. *Advances in Child Development and Behavior, 54*, 1–44. https://doi.org/10.1016/bs.acdb.2017.10.001

Reddan, M.C., Lindquist, M.A., & Wager, T.D. (2017). Effect size estimation in neuroimaging. *JAMA Psychiatry, 74*(3), 207–208. doi:10.1001/jamapsychiatry.2016.3356

Rice, K., Moraczewski, D., & Redcay, E. (2016). Perceived live interaction modulates the developing social brain. *Social Cognitive and Affective Neuroscience, 11*, 1354–1362. https://doi.org/10.1093/scan/nsw060

Richardson, H. (2019). Development of brain networks for social functions: confirmatory analyses in a large open source dataset. *Developmental Cognitive Neuroscience, 37*, 100598. https://doi.org/10.1016/j.dcn.2018.11.002

Richardson, H., Gweon, H., Dodell-Feder, D., Malloy, C., Pelton, H., Keil, B., Kanwisher, N. & Saxe, R. (2020). Response patterns in the developing social brain are organized by social and emotion features and disrupted in children diagnosed with autism spectrum disorder. *Cortex, 125*, 12–29. https://doi.org/10.1016/j.cortex.2019.11.021

Richardson, H., Lisandrelli, G., Riobueno-Naylor, A., & Saxe, R. (2018). Development of the social brain from age three to twelve years. *Nature Communications, 9*(1), 1–12. https://doi.org/10.1038/s41467-018-03399-2

Romund, L., Golde, S., Lorenz, R.C., Raufelder, D., Pelz, P., Gleich, T., Heinz, A. & Beck, A. (2017). Neural correlates of the self-concept in adolescence: a focus on the significance of friends. *Human Brain Mapping, 38*(2), 987–996. https://doi.org/10.1002/hbm.23433

Sabbagh, M.A., Bowman, L.C., Evraire, L.E., & Ito, J.M. (2009). Neurodevelopmental correlates of theory of mind in preschool children. *Child Development, 80*(4), 1147–1162. https://doi.org/10.1111/j.1467-8624.2009.01322.x

Saxe, R., & Powell, L.J. (2006). It's the thought that counts: specific brain regions for one component of theory of mind. *Psychology Science, 17*(8), 692–699. https://doi.org/10.1111/j.1467-9280.2006.01768.x

Saxe, R.R., Whitfield-Gabrieli, S., Scholz, J., & Pelphrey, K.A. (2009). Brain regions for perceiving and reasoning about other people in school-aged children. *Child Development, 80*(4), 1197–1209. https://doi.org/10.1111/j.1467-8624.2009.01325.x

Schaafsma, S.M., Pfaff, D.W., Spunt, R.P., & Adolphs, R. (2015). Deconstructing and reconstructing theory of mind. *Trends in Cognitive Sciences, 19*(2), 65–72. https://doi.org/10.1016/j.tics.2014.11.007

Schilbach, L. (2016). Towards a second-person neuropsychiatry. *Philosophical Transactions of the Royal Society of London series B Biological Sciences, 371*(1686), 20150081. https://doi.org/10.1098/rstb.2015.0081

Schilbach, L., Bzdok, D., Timmermans, B., Fox, P.T., Laird, A.R., Vogeley, K., & Eickhoff, S.B. (2012). Introspective minds: using ALE meta-analyses to study commonalities in the neural correlates of emotional processing, social & unconstrained cognition. *PloS One*, 7(2). https://doi.org/10.1371/journal.pone.0030920

Schilbach, L., Timmermans, B., Reddy, V., Costall, A., Bente, G., Schlicht, T., & Vogeley, K. (2013). Toward a second-person neuroscience. *Behavioral and Brain Sciences, 36*(4), 393–414. https://doi.org/10.1017/S0140525X12000660

Schurz, M., Radua, J., Aichhorn, M., Richlan, F., & Perner, J. (2014). Fractionating theory of mind: a meta-analysis of functional brain imaging studies. *Neuroscience & Biobehavioral Reviews, 42*, 9–34. https://doi.org/10.1016/j.neubiorev.2014.01.009

Sebastian, C.L., Fontaine, N.M., Bird, G., Blakemore, S.J., De Brito, S.A., McCrory, E.J., & Viding, E. (2012). Neural processing associated with cognitive and affective Theory of Mind in adolescents and adults. *Social Cognitive and Affective Neuroscience*, 7(1), 53–63. https://doi.org/10.1093/scan/nsr023

Sherman, L.E., Rudie, J.D., Pfeifer, J.H., Masten, C.L., McNealy, K., & Dapretto, M. (2014). Development of the default mode and central executive networks across early adolescence: a longitudinal study. *Developmental Cognitive Neuroscience, 10*, 148–159. https://doi.org/10.1016/j.dcn.2014.08.002

Somerville, L.H., Jones, R.M., Ruberry, E.J., Dyke, J.P., Glover, G., & Casey, B.J. (2013). The medial prefrontal cortex and the emergence of self-conscious emotion in adolescence. *Psychology Science, 24*(8), 1554–1562. https://doi.org/10.1177/0956797613475633

Spreng, R.N., Mar, R.A., & Kim, A.S. (2009). The common neural basis of autobiographical memory, prospection, navigation, theory of mind, and the default mode: a quantitative meta-analysis. *Journal of Cognitive Neuroscience, 21*(3), 489–510. https://doi.org/10.1162/jocn.2008.21029

Steinmann, E., Schmalor, A., Prehn-Kristensen, A., Wolff, S., Galka, A., Mohring, J., Gerber, W., Petermann, F., Stephani, U. & Siniatchkin, M. (2014). Developmental changes of neuronal networks associated with strategic social decision-making. *Neuropsychologia, 56*, 37–46. https://doi.org/10.1016/j.neuropsychologia.2013.12.025

Tamnes, C.K., Overbye, K., Ferschmann, L., Fjell, A.M., Walhovd, K.B., Blakemore, S.J., & Dumontheil, I. (2018). Social perspective taking is associated with self-reported prosocial behavior and regional cortical thickness across adolescence. *Developmental Psychology, 54*(9), 1745. https://doi.org/10.1037/dev0000541

Telzer, E.H., Ichien, N.T., & Qu, Y. (2015). Mothers know best: redirecting adolescent reward sensitivity toward safe behavior during risk taking. *Social Cognitive and Affective Neuroscience, 10*(10), 1383–1391. https://doi.org/10.1093/scan/nsv026

van den Bos, W., van Dijk, E., Westenberg, M., Rombouts, S.A., & Crone, E.A. (2011). Changing brains, changing perspectives: the neurocognitive development of reciprocity. *Psychology Science, 22*(1), 60–70. https://doi.org/10.1177/0956797610391102

Van Duijvenvoorde, A.C., & Crone, E.A. (2013). The teenage brain: a neuroeconomic approach to adolescent decision making. *Current Directions in Psychological Science, 22*(2), 108–113. https://doi.org/10.1177/0963721413475446

Van Hoorn, J., Van Dijk, E., Güroğlu, B., & Crone, E.A. (2016). Neural correlates of prosocial peer influence on public goods game donations during adolescence. *Social Cognitive and Affective Neuroscience, 11*(6), 923–933. https://doi.org/10.1093/scan/nsw013

Vanderwal, T., Kelly, C., Eilbott, J., Mayes, L.C., & Castellanos, F.X. (2015). Inscapes: a movie paradigm to improve compliance in functional magnetic resonance imaging. *NeuroImage, 122*, 222–232. https://doi.org/10.1016/j.neuroimage.2015.07.069

Wang, A.T., Lee, S.S., Sigman, M., & Dapretto, M. (2006a). Developmental changes in the neural basis of interpreting communicative intent. *Social Cognitive and Affective Neuroscience, 1*(2), 107–121. https://doi.org/10.1093/scan/nsl018

Wang, A.T., Lee, S.S., Sigman, M., & Dapretto, M. (2006b). Neural basis of irony comprehension in children with autism: the role of prosody and context. *Brain, 129*(4), 932–943. https://doi.org/10.1093/brain/awl032

Warnell, K.R., & Redcay, E. (2019). Minimal coherence among varied theory of mind measures in childhood and adulthood. *Cognition, 191*, 103997. https://doi.org/10.1016/j.cognition.2019.06.009

Warnell, K.R., Sadikova, E., & Redcay, E. (2018). Let's chat: developmental neural bases of social motivation during real-time peer interaction. *Developmental Science, 21*, e12581. https://doi.org/10.1111/desc.12581

Wellman, H.M., & Liu, D. (2004). Scaling of theory-of-mind tasks. *Child Development, 75*(2), 523–541. https://doi.org/10.1111/j.1467-8624.2004.00691.x

White, S.J., Frith, U., Rellecke, J., Al-Noor, Z., & Gilbert, S.J. (2014). Autistic adolescents show atypical activation of the brain's mentalizing system even without a prior history of mentalizing problems. *Neuropsychologia, 56*, 17–25. https://doi.org/10.1016/j.neuropsychologia.2013.12.013

Xiao, Y., Geng, F., Riggins, T., Chen, G., & Redcay, E. (2019). Neural correlates of developing theory of mind competence in early childhood. *NeuroImage, 184*, 707–716. https://doi.org/10.1016/j.neuroimage.2018.09.079

Yarkoni, T. (2009). Big correlations in little studies: inflated fMRI correlations reflect low statistical power—Commentary on Vul et al.(2009). *Perspectives on Psychological Science, 4*(3), 294–298. https://doi.org/10.1111/j.1745-6924.2009.01127.x

Yarkoni, T., Poldrack, R.A., Nichols, T.E., Van Essen, D.C., & Wager, T.D. (2011). Large-scale automated synthesis of human functional neuroimaging data. *Nature Methods, 8*(8), 665. https://doi.org/10.1038/nmeth.1635

Yuk, V., Urbain, C., Pang, E.W., Anagnostou, E., Buchsbaum, D., & Taylor, M.J. (2018). Do you know what I'm thinking? Temporal and spatial brain activity during a theory-of-mind task in children with autism. *Developmental Cognitive Neuroscience, 34*, 139–147. https://doi.org/10.1016/j.dcn.2018.08.001

Part II

Social correlates and consequences

5 Family influences on theory of mind in middle childhood

Sarah Foley and Claire Hughes

Despite impressive literature on family influences upon preschool children's acquisition of a 'theory of mind' (ToM) (Devine & Hughes, 2018), much less is known about how families influence ToM in middle childhood. This is a significant gap because several distinct theoretical perspectives highlight the potential importance of social interactions in shaping children's understanding of mental states. Examples of theoretical approaches that have already proven valuable in the literature include Bowlby's (1969) attachment theory, social constructivist accounts (e.g., Heyes & Frith, 2014) based on Vygotsky's (1978) socio-cultural theory, and 'theory-theory' models of children's mentalizing (e.g., Wellman & Gopnik, 2012) that are based on the work of Piaget (e.g., Piaget & Inhelder, 1969). In addition, theoretical models of the links between variation in family socioeconomic status (SES) and child outcomes hinge on three key mechanisms: Investment, stress, and social selection effects. This chapter, therefore, begins with a brief outline of the common and distinct predictions offered by each theoretical account. Next, we summarize research findings regarding links between individual differences in ToM in the primary school years and variations in salient family characteristics and relationships. The most notable of these include socio-economic status (SES), presence and/or quality of sibling relationships, quality of parent–child relationships, and frequency of parental mental state talk (MST). While the findings support the sustained importance of family SES for children's ToM in the school years, our understanding of the mechanisms underpinning this association remains patchy. By contrast, research findings regarding sibling influences indicate both a sustained influence and a developmental contrast in the nature of sibling influences, which can be characterized as a shift from siblings as playmates in the preschool years to siblings as tutors in middle childhood. Studies focusing on the parent–child relationship yield a more mixed picture, with significant effects only emerging in the context of adversity (i.e. children exposed to maltreatment or neglect). Finally, we discuss results that suggest that in middle childhood, children's ToM benefits from exposure to advanced rather than simple MST. Overall, it is clear that more longitudinal research with larger and more diverse samples is needed to elucidate if and how normative variation in parents' attitudes and behaviors influence children's ToM in the school years.

Theoretical perspectives

Building upon Bowlby's (e.g., 1969) attachment theory, Ainsworth and colleagues (1978) noted that different styles of caregiving have distinct effects upon attachment security. Specifically, caregivers who consistently provide prompt and appropriate responses typically have securely attached infants. In contrast, low caregiver sensitivity predisposes infants to avoidant behaviors, while inconsistent parenting predisposes infants to display resistant behaviors (Ainsworth et al., 1978) and, more worryingly, neglectful or abusive parenting is associated with disorganized attachment (Main & Solomon, 1986). Fonagy and colleagues (1991) and Meins et al. (2001) have identified dimensions of caregivers' cognitions that contribute to individual differences in caregivers' sensitivity. For Fonagy et al. (1991), caregivers' reflective function, defined as the capacity to recognize mental states in both oneself and others, shapes the quality of caregiver–child interactions. For Meins et al. (2001) what matters most is variation in caregivers' mind-mindedness (namely, the propensity to view the infant as an agent, with individual thoughts, feelings, and interests). Each of these models highlights the importance of caregivers for children's own emerging mentalizing skills. Specifically, when caregivers are consistently attentive to children's thoughts and feelings, social interactions become more rewarding and plentiful, thus accelerating the rate at which children acquire the ability to attribute mental states to themselves and others.

Insights from Vygotskian (1978) sociocultural theory have enabled researchers to posit mechanisms that underpin this process of learning from interactions with caregivers that go beyond simple effects of quantity and consistency. Specifically, drawing on the construct of a 'zone of proximal development' sociocultural accounts highlight the importance of caregivers' responses that are finely tuned to the child's current focus of attention or level of understanding. For example, Ebert et al. (2017) have shown that links between family talk and preschoolers' ToM vary by family SES, such that the benefits of elaborative mental state talk are restricted to high SES families. Whilst most research in this field has focused on the first few years of life, this sociocultural perspective suggests that the nature of social influences upon children's mentalizing may also shift across developmental periods.

At this point, it is worth noting that children are active social partners, such that the sensitivity of interactions is unlikely to depend solely upon caregiver characteristics. In addition, although often overlooked, children's close relationships with other children (e.g., siblings, friends, peers) are likely to have a powerful influence on children's mentalizing skills. Each of these points demonstrates the potential utility of Piagetian (1959) theoretical perspectives – in particular, the insight that development comes from discussion and discussion is only possible between equals. Note also that siblings and peers become especially important as social partners as children enter middle childhood and adolescence (see Chapter 6 of this volume).

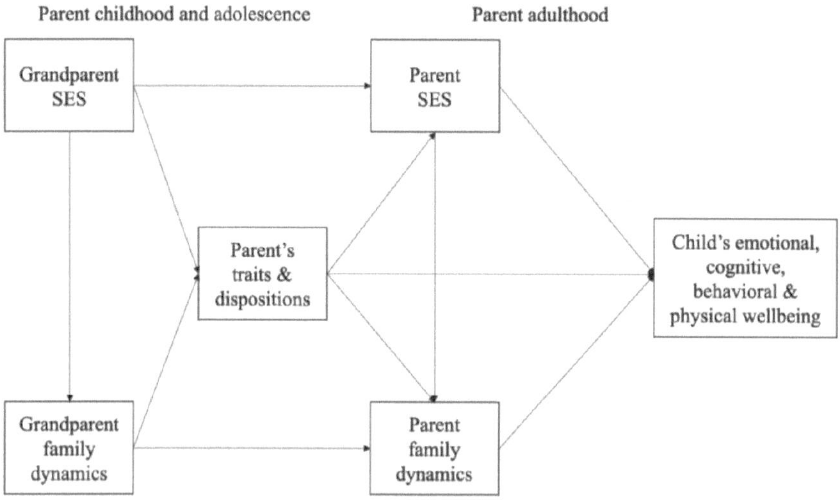

Figure 5.1 Interactionist model of SES, family interaction processes, and child development (adapted with permission from Conger et al., 2010).

Last but not least, it should be noted that variation in family SES is likely to affect child outcomes through multiple processes. Empirical reviews (e.g., Conger et al., 2010) demonstrate robust support for two contrasting theoretical models that highlight either positive investment effects (e.g., cognitive stimulation, neighborhood resources) or negative effects of family stress (i.e., financial stress can lead to problems of parental wellbeing that compromise the quality of parent–child interactions). In general, investment models appear particularly useful in explaining SES effects on children's cognitive development, while family stress effects are more useful in explaining SES effects on children's socioemotional adjustment. Note also that associations between SES and child outcomes are not necessarily causal, in that characteristics that make an individual a valued employee may also underpin positive parenting. Integrating this 'social selection' effect with the family stress model, Conger et al. (2010) have proposed an interactionist model in which parents' individual and demographic characteristics each contribute to child outcomes (see Figure 5.1).

Overview of existing evidence

While preschoolers' acquisition of ToM has been intensively studied, advances in children's ToM across the school-age years have received much less attention (see the Introduction to this volume). Moreover, within this limited pool of research into ToM in middle childhood, studies typically focus on either the cognitive underpinnings of ToM (most notably executive function) or the social consequences of ToM. Arguably, then, researchers are guilty of double neglect of social influences upon ToM in middle childhood. Addressing this gap, in this section, we provide an overview of research findings regarding the nature and strength of associations between individual differences in school-aged children's ToM performance and variation in salient family characteristics and relationships.

With regard to the current chapter's focus on social influences in ToM, several developmental changes point to the possibility of contrasting mechanisms between the preschool years and middle childhood. In particular, as children's social horizons widen, family influences on ToM may become less salient. Alternatively, one could argue that as children become more autonomous and independent, the challenges for parents do not simply disappear but rather shift in nature, such that variation in parental discipline and monitoring may become more significant. Equally, as children's language skills improve, variation in their conversational exposure to mental states is likely to increase in significance, perhaps eclipsing the influence of pretend play, which provides an important forum for reflecting on different perspectives in the preschool years (Schwebel et al., 1999; Lillard et al., 2013; Dore et al., 2015; Semeijn, 2019). In addition, research on sibling relationships confirms that siblings remain an important source of learning in middle childhood (Howe & Recchia, 2009). Thus, the apprenticeship model of sibling influences cited by theorists working with preschoolers (e.g., Lewis et al., 1996) may extend to middle childhood. There are therefore multiple reasons for evaluating the magnitude and nature of family influences on ToM in middle childhood.

The starting point for this review comes from Devine and Hughes' (2018) meta-analysis of family influences on false belief understanding in children aged three to seven years of age. This meta-analysis revealed that four distinct family variables (i.e., socioeconomic status [SES], number of siblings, maternal mind-mindedness, and maternal use of mental state talk [MST]) all show small but consistent positive associations with young children's false belief understanding. Table 5.1 provides a summary of measures of family influence adopted within studies of ToM in middle childhood (defined here as spanning ages 6 to 12 years). Note that these measures include ratings and interview responses provided by the children themselves as well as their parents. As a result, studies of sibling influence on ToM in middle childhood have been able to go beyond the typical reliance upon simple indicators of sibling presence or number of siblings to include qualitative features of sibling relationships. As described elsewhere in this volume, assessments of ToM encompass a variety of forms (see Chapter 3). Alongside the specifier of at least one family variable (e.g., SES, number of siblings, mental state talk, parental style), our review included all English-language empirical studies that adopted at least one of the following ToM measures: A test of first or second-order false belief comprehension, the Strange Stories task, the interpretive theory of mind task, the Director task, the Triangles task, the Eyes task, the Faux Pas task, and the Silent Film task.

Even with these relatively broad criteria, our search revealed just 30 studies, including several that we do not discuss in this chapter because the use of

Table 5.1 Family influence measures used in middle childhood

Family influence	*Description of measure*	*Focus*	*Example study/measure*
Socioeconomic status	Single items	Education, income, or occupation.	Clemmensen et al. (2016)
	Family Affluence Scale (completed by child)	Family affluence.	Currie et al. (2008)
	Risk scale	Multi-factor index of maternal SES risk: 19 years or younger at birth, not married, not in stable relationship, basic education (fewer than 5 GCSEs), and working-class occupation.	Paine et al. (2018)
Siblings	Single items	Number/presence of siblings, timing of sibling arrival.	Paine et al. (2018)
	Sibling Relationship Questionnaire	Child asked to rate the warmth and conflict within their sibling relationship.	Furman & Buhrmester (1985)
Parent–child relationship	Family separation anxiety test with six pictures of separation	Child asked to describe their feelings and justify and foresee future.	Klagsbrun & Bowlby (1976)
	Parenting Attitudes Inventory	Parents rate their focus on conformity and autonomy.	Vinden (2001)
	Parental authority questionnaire	Parents rate their authoritativeness, authoritarianism, and permissiveness.	Buri (1991)
	Official records and interviews	Parental responses coded for severity, onset, and duration of maltreatment.	Cicchetti et al. (2003)
Mental state talk	Observed mother–child interactions using 10–13 photos of everyday situations involving people with children	Mental state talk coded, including cognitions/desires/emotions.	Ruffman et al. (2002)
	Observed mother–child picture-book interaction	Frequency of mental state talk coded.	Adapted: Turnbull et al. (2008); Brown & Dunn (1991); Ruffman et al. (2002)
	Observed mother and child talk about four social dilemmas	Proportional mental state talk scores – distinguishing between basic and advanced mental state talk (e.g., contrastives, talk about contrasting perspectives, recursion, and relationship between mental states and advanced emotions).	Bosacki & Astington (1999); Ruffman et al. (2002)

small samples (e.g., fewer than 30 families) was a significant methodological limitation. For ease, we have organized the sections of this chapter according to each type of family influence on ToM considered. Specifically, we first outline the evidence for associations between ToM and variation in distal family influences (e.g., SES, siblings). Next, we consider associations between ToM and variation in more proximal influences (e.g., parent–child relationships). Within each section, we highlight key methodological features and summarise the findings from the main studies identified by our systematic review.

Socioeconomic status

Given that SES was one of the four family predictors of preschool ToM identified by Devine & Hughes (2018), we begin our review by summarizing ToM studies involving school-aged children, acknowledging at the outset that all of these studies treated SES as a background measure rather than as a primary variable of interest. In total, our systematic review identified 13 studies, with the SES indicator being maternal education for eight studies, family income for three studies, and a combined measure for five studies. Of these 13 studies, seven included samples of more than 100 families, within which two studies measured SES by maternal education, one by family affluence, and four by a composite measure – these nine studies are the focus of our summary review.

We begin by considering the findings from the two studies noted above that included maternal education as an index of family SES. Within this group, just one study (Devine et al., 2016) included prior ToM scores as a control variable for a British sample of ten-year-olds and their families, such that the significant association, $r = .40$, between maternal education and a latent factor for ToM is particularly noteworthy. A second study, notable for its large sample size (1,630 Danish 11-year-olds) was designed to examine 'hyper-ToM' (defined as below-median ToM scores coupled with above-median frequencies of reference to mental states in a series of 24 questions about a storybook character) (Clemmensen et al., 2016). As a result, only a categorical ToM measure (below/above median) was available and this was unrelated to mothers' educational level, $r = -.03$.

The remaining studies assessed SES via either family affluence or a composite index. These investigations included a large nine-year-old twin sample in the UK (N = 695 twin pairs) who completed three vignettes from the Strange Stories task (Happé, 1994), with performance (0–6-point scale) examined in relation to a composite measure of SES that included both parents' education and occupational status (Ronald et al., 2006). These two measures were significantly associated ($r = .24$). In addition, a path model showed that SES explained a significant 6% of the variance in ToM. More recently, Paine et al. (2018) gave 221 seven-year-olds a task adapted from second-order false belief paradigms. Performance (indexed by a 0–2-point scale) was examined in relation to a multi-factor index of maternal SES risk: 19 years or younger at birth, not married, not in a stable relationship, basic education (fewer than 5 GCSEs), and a working-class occupation. As expected, this risk measure was inversely related to ToM scores, $r = -.18$. Three further studies, reported in two papers (Devine & Hughes, 2013; Wang et al., 2016) included latent variable measures of ToM that each included the Family Affluence Scale (Currie et al., 2008) as a measure of SES as well as the Triangles task (Castelli et al., 2000) and the Silent Film task (Devine & Hughes, 2016) to assess ToM. In addition, Wang et al.'s (2016) cross-cultural study of 216 11- to 12-year-olds from the UK and Hong Kong also included the Strange Stories task (Happé, 1994). Each of these studies showed a modest but significant association between family SES and latent ToM scores (Standardized β ranged from .16 to .21).

Taking into consideration the methodological limitations of three of the four studies to index SES via maternal education, the overall picture from these nine studies is that the association between SES and ToM reported in Devine & Hughes' (2018) meta-analytic review of family influences on preschool false belief understanding persists into middle childhood. That said, few of these studies examined the extent to which this association remained significant once other child characteristics (e.g., verbal ability) were taken into account, such that the uniqueness of this association remains to be established.

Sibling relationships

Beyond SES, family size (i.e., number of siblings) is another readily measured family characteristic that, in preschool samples, has been shown to display small but significant associations with ToM performance (mean $r = .16$, Devine & Hughes, 2018). Sibling relationships shift in quality (i.e., closeness/intimacy) as children grow up, become more independent, and forge increasingly important relationships with peers (for a review, see White & Hughes, 2017). As a result, it is difficult to extrapolate findings across age groups. Moreover, the majority of ToM studies of school-aged children to include information about siblings are likely to be under-powered. Our summary review shall therefore focus on just two studies, which either included both relatively large samples (N > 100) and/or went beyond the simple presence or absence of siblings to include more detailed measures of the quality of sibling relationships.

In the first of these studies, Kennedy et al. (2015) included an affluent sample of 191 American children aged from 4 to 12 years (mean age = 7 years) to test whether the association between ToM performance and siblings differed by age group, sibling gender composition, and age gap. Supporting an apprenticeship model of sibling influences (e.g., Lewis et al., 1996), their analyses showed that once effects of child age and executive function were taken into account, the number of older siblings and same-sex siblings each predicted variance in children's performance on ToM prediction and explanation tasks.

More recently, Paine and colleagues (2018) reported on sibling effects for the demographically diverse sample of 229 first-born seven-year-old children taking part in the prospective longitudinal Cardiff Child Development Study. Using a task adapted from second-order false belief paradigms (Coull et al., 2006; Perner

& Wimmer, 1985), this study showed that children with a younger sibling were more likely to succeed fully on a second-order false belief task, and this contrast remained significant even when effects of children's verbal IQ were taken into account. To examine this sibling advantage in more detail, Paine and colleagues (2018) constructed four groups that differed according to the timing of sibling birth: No sibling, or small, medium, or large age gap. This analysis showed that, compared with the no sibling group, only the medium and large gap between sibling births was associated with superior ToM performance.

Together, the findings from these two studies indicate that siblings have an enduring influence as children grow up. Positive findings include:

(1) the across-age consistency of findings for a positive association between number of older/same-sex siblings and ToM performance reported by Kennedy and colleagues (2015);
(2) the superior second-order false belief understanding shown by seven-year-old children with younger siblings, reported by Paine and colleagues (2018).

Note that Kennedy and colleagues (2015) found that having a same-sex sibling was particularly beneficial; this contrasts with the literature with younger children. Thus, while there is a stable beneficial effect of siblings on ToM performance across school-age as well as preschool years, the factors underpinning this benefit may be age-specific, perhaps reflecting the above-noted age-related shifts in siblings' relationship quality. Paine and colleagues' (2018) finding that first-born children did not show any ToM advantage if their younger siblings were relatively close in age suggests that the benefits of having a sibling may be relatively indirect. For example, a possible mediator of this benefit may be an increase in parent–child internal state talk following the arrival of a baby sibling (for a review of the literature on the transition to siblinghood, see Volling, 2012).

Parent–child relationships

As noted above, sibling influences on ToM in middle childhood appear likely to include both direct apprenticeship effects and indirect effects. Potential mediators include features of the parent–child relationship (e.g., increased reference to others' points of view following the arrival of a baby). This point provides a natural lead into how parent–child relationships may contribute to variation in ToM among school-aged children. Our systematic review of the field revealed two key strands of work, one focused on normative variation in family experiences and the other focused on children exposed to maltreatment or neglect. For ease of presentation, we consider these two strands separately below.

Attachment and parenting style

To our knowledge, just one study has examined links between school-aged children's attachment to caregivers and their understanding of ToM (Marchetti et al., 2014). In this Italian study of 91 six- to ten-year-old children, participants completed the family separation anxiety test (F-SAT; Klagsbrun & Bowlby, 1976), which includes six pictures of separations. For each picture, children described and justified their feelings as well as predicting the character's future. Children's responses, coded on a 0–4-point attachment scale, were then examined in relation to their performance on a test of metacognitive vocabulary (METVOC; Astington & Pelletier, 1998) and tests of first- and second-order false belief tasks. Children's attachment scores showed significant associations with metacognitive vocabulary, $r = .33$, and first-order ToM, $r = .25$, but not with second-order ToM, $r = .08$ (Marchetti, personal communication, 2019).

Two smaller studies have examined school-aged children's ToM performance in relation to mothers' self-reported parenting style. The first of these included 30 well-educated Australian mothers, who completed the conformity and autonomy subscales of Vinden's (2001) Parenting Attitudes Inventory (modified), and their eight-year-old children, who completed both first and second-order false belief tasks as well as the five tasks in Wellman and Liu's (2004) ToM scale. This study showed that, when the effects of child vocabulary scores were controlled, children's first- and second-order false belief understanding showed no significant association with the parental measures (O'Reilly & Peterson, 2014). In contrast, children's ToM scale scores displayed a positive association with parental emphasis on autonomy ($r = .39$), coupled with a negative association with parental emphasis on conformity ($r = -.50$). Interestingly, a brief glance at the items included in these scales highlights the likelihood that these associations may reflect variation in parents' propensity to mentalize about their child. For example, items from the autonomy scale include 'I like my child to stand up for his/her own opinions even if it means disagreeing with me' and 'Children should think for themselves and not be afraid to speak their minds'. Conversely, items from the conformity scale include 'I don't think my child needs to know why I'm asking him to do something' and 'I think my child is too young to make decisions for himself about things like what clothes to wear'.

In another small-scale study, Tafreshi & Racine (2016) reported non-significant associations between scores for interpretive ToM in a Canadian sample of 38 seven-year-old children's and their mothers' self-reported scores on Buri's (1991) Parental Authority Questionnaire for authoritativeness ($r = .11$) or authoritarianism ($r = -.16$) or permissiveness ($r = -.02$). However, note that the small sample size limited the study's power to detect significant effects. That said, children's ToM scores were associated with scores on an interview-based measure of mothers' views on knowledge and learning. We discuss this association later in the chapter, in the section on mental state talk.

In summary, studies of normative variation in parent–child relationships and ToM performance in middle childhood yield relatively mixed findings, with individual studies reporting significant associations for some measures of ToM but not others (and no consistent pattern across studies). In part, these mixed results may reflect the relatively small samples involved in each study. In addition, the cross-sectional nature of the studies constrains causal conclusions. For example, parents may be more likely to grant autonomy to children who display better mentalizing skills.

Parental neglect or maltreatment

Within ToM research on children facing extreme levels of family adversity, two separate studies deserve mention. The first of these included 217 adoptees in the UK, including 52 within-UK adoptees and 144 infants adopted before 43 months of age from deprived institutional settings in Romania (Long et al., 2008). Assessments conducted at ages 6 and 11 showed that, compared with the within-UK adoptees, the adoptees from Romania demonstrated poor ToM (and executive function). This contrast was particularly clear for children who had experienced more than six months of institutional care.

The second, more recent study involved 105 Australian nine-year-olds, half of whom had experienced maltreatment but had yet to receive therapy (O'Reilly & Peterson, 2014). The type and severity of maltreatment as well as the onset and duration were coded using a procedure created by Cicchetti and colleagues (2003) and the two groups were matched in terms of child age, gender balance, family composition, and parent education. All children completed a battery of ToM tasks that included false belief tasks (Baron-Cohen et al., 1985; Wellman & Liu, 2004); a Belief-Emotion task (Wellman & Liu, 2004); a second-order false belief task (Perner & Wimmer, 1985), and Wellman and Liu's (2004) ToM scale. This study showed a significant group difference in false belief understanding, but no group difference in total cognitive verbs used in the second-order false belief explanations or for the ToM scale. Within the maltreated group, child age and severity of child's past maltreatment emerged as significant predictors of variation in children's scores for both standard and advanced false belief tasks; in addition, the education level for custodial parent also independently predicted standard false belief scores.

Together, the findings from these two studies suggest a negative association between children's second-order false belief understanding and their experience of family adversity. For example, in the context of maltreatment, it may be especially adaptive to be good at reading parents' facial expressions, but the stressful nature of living with abusive parents may make it harder to predict others' emotions. Once again, the cross-sectional design of these studies limits conclusions regarding the independence and direction of effects. For example, ToM skills appear to play a buffering role in mitigating the impact of harsh parenting on preschoolers' behavioral problems (Hughes & Ensor, 2006), indicating that children with poor mentalizing skills may be more likely to find themselves in coercive cycles of violence. Likewise, children with autism, who typically show marked delays in their acquisition of ToM (Baron-Cohen, 2000) have been reported to be at increased risk of abuse (Jones et al., 2012).

Mental state talk

As noted above, contrasts in parent–child talk may mediate sibling effects. This argument builds upon meta-analytic findings of a consistent positive association between parents' use of mental state talk and preschoolers' false belief understanding. We will now consider whether there is evidence that parental mental state talk continues to show an association with ToM performance across the school-age years. Here, our systematic review of the field yielded three eligible studies.

The first study, conducted by Tafreshi and Racine (2016) involved a relatively small and affluent Canadian sample of 38 mother–child dyads, who coded for mental state talk (MST) during a wordless picture-book task. The seven-year-old children's interpretative ToM was assessed via a puppet task (Carpendale & Chandler, 1996), alongside a semi-structured maternal interview designed to assess mothers' personal epistemology (i.e., views on knowledge and knowing; Hutchins et al., 2009). While child interpretive ToM scores showed a positive but non-significant association with mothers' MST ($r = .18$), interpretive ToM scores were robustly associated with mothers' personal epistemology scores ($r = .56$). Moreover, a regression analysis showed that over and beyond the 32% of variance in interpretive ToM scores accounted for by child age and household income, mothers' personal epistemology scores explained an additional 19% in interpretive ToM scores. In discussing this finding, the authors note that parents' beliefs about emotions are likely to impact their emotional socialization goals and strategies.

In the second study, conducted in North America by Pearson and Pillow (2016), 38 children aged between five and ten years of age completed second-order false belief tasks and were filmed with their mothers discussing four stories involving social dilemmas (used to assess both MST and children's mentalizing skills). As expected, there were age-related improvements in children's task performance and use of both basic MST (i.e., reference to beliefs, desires, emotions, personality traits) and advanced MST (i.e., talk about contrasting perspectives, reference to recursive mental states and complex emotions). Of particular interest to this chapter is the positive association between mothers' and children's advanced MST ($r = .56$), as well as between maternal advanced MST and children's success on the social dilemmas task ($r = .47$).

The final study reports on the latest (age 11 wave) of a longitudinal study of 53 children growing up in middle-upper SES families in New Zealand. At this wave, Carr et al. (2018) used the Strange Stories task to assess ToM, and a picture task, 10–13 photos of everyday situations involving people (Ruffman et al., 2002) to assess maternal MST. While this study showed no significant concurrent association between maternal MST and child ToM ($r = .13$), early MST did predict later ToM.

Together, the findings from these three studies demonstrate only limited evidence for an association between parental MST and child ToM in school-aged children. The inconsistency of results across studies is open to several interpretations, of which the first is power. Specifically, in their meta-analytic review of MST and ToM in preschoolers, Devine and Hughes (2018) reported a mean association of just r = .21, suggesting that a sample of more than 200 families would be needed to achieve 80% power.

Alternatively, the exceptional positive findings from Pearson and Pillow (2016) suggest that while simple reference to MST is sufficient to foster early emerging ToM skills, more advanced forms of conversation about mental states (e.g., explanations, reference to contrasting thoughts or feelings) are necessary to foster more advanced ToM skills.

Discussion

In their meta-analytic review of family influences on false belief understanding for children aged between three and seven years, Devine and Hughes (2018) reported modest correlations with four different markers. Specifically, false belief understanding was associated with maternal MST (r = .21, CI = .14 to .27), SES (r = .18, CI=.14 to .22), number of siblings (r = .14, CI = .08 to .20), and maternal mind-mindedness (r = .16, CI = .09 to .23). Together, the studies of family influences on ToM in middle childhood reviewed in this chapter suggest that families do continue to matter, but it is clear that several methodological issues require attention before reaching strong conclusions. Note also that while the overarching emphasis on middle childhood within this volume shaped our focus on this period, family influences are likely to be relatively long-range and so straddle distinct developmental periods. Support for this view comes from two longitudinal studies that demonstrate unique predictive effects of maternal MST in early childhood upon ToM in middle childhood (Carr et al., 2018; Ensor et al., 2014).

In the first of these studies, Ensor and colleagues (2014) tracked 105 families from ages two to six years to demonstrate stability in mothers' use of cognitive talk across this four-year period. Importantly, Ensor and colleagues (2014) were able to follow up with 77 of these families across a further four-year period to show that both age-two and age-six measures of maternal cognitive talk predicted children's success on the Strange Stories task at age ten. Interestingly, these associations were independent and were each comparable in magnitude to the stability of ToM from ages six to ten (r = .18 to .20). This eight-year design is notable in that it allowed this research team to demonstrate a specific independent effect of mother–toddler cognitive talk upon ToM at age ten, even controlling for effects of mother–child cognitive talk at age six. At a theoretical level, this finding supports the idea that toddlerhood is a sensitive period for family influences on children's cognitive development.

That said, the second longitudinal study (Carr et al., 2018) involved a similar temporal reach but did not show any specific independent association between maternal mental state talk at the first time-point (age three) and ToM at the final (age ten) time-point. Here, two between-study differences in methodology deserve note. First, the 53 families in Carr et al.'s (2018) study were better educated than the families followed by Ensor et al. (2014). Second, in contrast with the focus on cognitive talk adopted by Ensor et al. (2014), Carr et al. (2018) combined references to cognitive states with references to other mental states to create an aggregate measure of maternal talk. Theoretically, these contrasts are interesting in that they suggest that links between family talk and child ToM may: (1) Vary by SES (i.e., stronger for less educated families); and (2) show specificity (i.e., stronger effects for cognitive terms than for other mental state terms).

At a practical level, these findings are also important in that they indicate long-term benefits for early interventions focused on improving the quality of parent–child talk. An obvious avenue for future research is therefore to track children over longer periods, in order to identify the temporal reach of early family experiences. Echoing the need to examine similar processes across extended developmental periods, three of the four factors considered by Devine and Hughes' (2018) review of the preschool literature were also evident in the studies of ToM in middle childhood reviewed in this chapter. We consider these separately below.

Socioeconomic status

Compared with the findings reported by Devine and Hughes (2018) in their review of 50 studies of children aged three to seven years, the findings from the nine studies reviewed in this chapter suggest a similar magnitude for associations between ToM and family SES in the preschool years and in middle childhood. This similarity indicates that schooling does little to narrow the gap in ToM between children from affluent versus disadvantaged families. Importantly, however, none of the studies included in this review investigated the mechanisms underpinning SES contrasts in ToM. Addressing this gap is an important avenue for future research. For example, other reviews have demonstrated robust associations between SES and variation in children's performance on tests of executive function and language (e.g., Last et al., 2018; Noble et al., 2007). As each of these cognitive domains shows links with ToM (e.g., Devine & Hughes, 2014; Milligan et al., 2007), an obvious question for future studies is therefore to identify the relative overlap or independence in the SES-related factors that contribute to variation in these three key aspects of children's cognition. As noted earlier, theoretical accounts have identified three distinct mechanisms that deserve greater attention in future research: Family stress (which may matter most in the first few years of parenthood), investment (which may grow in importance as children's social horizons widen), and social selection, whereby common parental traits (e.g., persistence) may underpin positive changes in both SES and child outcomes. Studies with genetically informative designs will help to identify the extent to which we can attribute SES-related contrasts in ToM to direct environmental influences.

Sibling relationships

In contrast to the apparent stability of SES-related effects on ToM in preschoolers and in middle childhood, the findings reviewed in this chapter suggest a shift in the nature of sibling influences between the preschool years and middle childhood. Specifically, while the analyses conducted by Devine and Hughes (2018) showed no moderation effect of birth order (i.e., presence of older versus younger siblings), it showed a significant moderation effect of sibling age, such that it was only the presence of child-age siblings that was associated with better false belief understanding. This conclusion makes an interesting contrast with the conclusions from two of the middle childhood studies reviewed in this chapter (Kennedy et al., 2015; Paine et al., 2018). Specifically, these studies showed that: (1) Among 4- to 12-year-olds, the sibling advantage was restricted to the presence of older siblings; and (2) among first-born seven-year-olds, the sibling advantage was only evident in the context of an average or large age gap. Together, these findings suggest that while play may be a key mediator of sibling benefits in the preschool years, teaching or apprenticeship plays a stronger role in the sibling advantage in middle childhood.

Consistent with Dunn et al.'s (1991) landmark study that reported a developmental association between cooperative sibling play at 33 months and false belief understanding at 40 months, findings from two of the sibling studies highlight the importance of sibling relationship *quality* for individual differences in ToM in middle childhood. Specifically, Howe and colleagues (2001) found that children who reported warmth in the sibling relationship showed elevated levels of internal state language. Less directly, Kennedy and colleagues (2015) reported that alongside birth order, sibling gender composition also moderated the association between sibling presence and ToM, such that children with same-sex siblings were particularly likely to do well, a finding that they attribute to the importance of intimacy in the sibling relationship. Future cross-cultural studies may provide a valuable test of theoretical models that highlight distinct aspects of sibling relationships (e.g., intimacy versus opportunities for teaching). With this in mind, studies of this age group typically draw on self-report measures (e.g., the Sibling Relationship Questionnaire; Furman & Burhmester, 1985). For example, in a meta-analytic review of sibling relationship quality and psychopathology, only four of 34 studies included observational methods (Buist et al., 2013). Nonetheless, there are a few interesting paradigms available. Three of these come from a study of 30 teenage sibling pairs, specifically observations of (1) a 'hot topics' discussion about a disagreement, (2) an abstract-puzzle activity, and (3) planning a weekend of family activities (Kramer & Kowal, 2005). These paradigms can provide rich measures of sibling conflict, cooperation, competition, and pro-social behavior, which in turn can provide a more nuanced understanding of the association between the quality of sibling relationships and children's developing understanding of mind.

Parent–child relationships

Our review included studies that adopted a variety of different measures of parent–child interactions or relationships. These included both parent and child ratings and, in the absence of extreme forms of neglect or maltreatment, yielded rather mixed findings that highlight the need for larger sample sizes in future studies. For the studies that included children who had experienced either neglect or maltreatment, the findings were somewhat more robust and in the expected direction. Together, these results support theoretical models that indicate threshold effects (or 'good enough' parenting).

Beyond the need for increased sample sizes, the studies reviewed in this chapter showed a conspicuous lack of attention to fathers' influences on children's ToM. This gap is especially striking given that fathers are more likely to become involved in childcare once their children reach school age (Raley et al., 2012). Underscoring the potential importance of including paternal measures, findings from a longitudinal study of 106 families demonstrated that fathers' references to desires and emotions during a picture-book task when their child was three years old predicted individual differences in children's ToM scores at five years old, whilst mothers' earlier use did not (LaBounty et al., 2008). At a theoretical level, the growth of studies that include fathers has shifted in emphasis from identifying contrasts between maternal and paternal influences to exploring cumulative influences of different family members on child outcomes.

Mental state talk

Interestingly, while Devine and Hughes (2018) were able to identify 14 studies that examined maternal mind-mindedness as a predictor of preschoolers' false belief understanding, our systematic review did not reveal any study of ToM in school-aged children that included a measure of parental mind-mindedness. That said, recent findings indicate that maternal mind-mindedness reduces the impact of social disadvantage on children's disruptive behavior in the preschool years (Meins et al., 2013) and in pre-adolescence (Hughes et al., 2017). Unfortunately, neither study assessed children's ToM, such that the exact mechanism underpinning this buffering effect remains to be examined in future studies. Returning to our initial summary of how attachment theory might inform analyses of parental influences on children's ToM, future directions for further research include examining links between maternal characteristics (e.g., mind-mindedness, reflective function, autonomy support), relationship characteristics (e.g., quantity, quality, and content of interactions), and child characteristics (e.g., academic achievement, behavioral adjustment, and psychological wellbeing).

Importantly, findings from the first study to examine preschoolers' false belief understanding in relation to both maternal mind-mindedness *and* maternal MST are reassuring regarding the absence of measures for mind-mindedness in the current studies. Specifically, Devine and Hughes (2019) found that preschoolers' false belief understanding showed similarly robust concurrent associations with both maternal mind-mindedness and mental state talk, but longitudinally, only maternal MST showed significant associations with children's false belief understanding. These findings have both theoretical and practical implications. Theoretically, the asymmetry in longitudinal associations coupled with similar concurrent associations may suggest that mind-mindedness may affect children's false belief understanding through multiple pathways (e.g., genetic effects, indirect effects of autonomy support as well as mental state talk). At a practical level, however, the findings indicate that interventions to foster family support for children's ToM should focus on encouraging parents to use mental states in their family conversations, rather than simply holding mentalistic representations of their children.

At least four separate investigations reviewed in this chapter included measures of mental state talk. An emerging theme from these studies was that ToM in middle childhood is likely to show particularly close associations with parents' use of advanced forms of mental state talk (e.g., contrastive phrases, reference to mixed emotions). Paradigms such as the 'revealed differences task' (similar to the method to assess sibling relationship quality reported by Kramer & Kowal, 2005), have been successfully used to examine parents' relationships with older adolescents (e.g., Allen et al., 1994) and may provide a means through which to capture naturally occurring variation in parents' and children's use of more sophisticated mental state talk. Indirect support for the importance of exposure to more complex references to mental states comes from a recent meta-analysis of 14 studies, in which Dodell-Feder and Tamir (2018) reported that adult social-cognition was improved by reading fiction that is typically rich in complex mental state reference.

Conclusion

Our review of the literature on family influences upon ToM in middle childhood suggests three main conclusions. The first of these concerns the need to increase methodological rigor (e.g., larger samples, greater attention to the psychometric properties of measures, adoption of longitudinal designs) in order to achieve greater reliability in study conclusions. The second is that, notwithstanding this criticism, social influences upon ToM in middle childhood appear comparable in magnitude to those reported in the preschool period, suggesting that family influences continue to help children refine their use of ToM beyond early childhood. Our third conclusion is that this similarity in magnitude may mask a qualitative shift in the nature of these influences, with respect to both child outcomes (e.g., from understanding false belief in the preschool years to understanding complex emotions in middle childhood) and specific mechanisms of family influence. For example, with respect to associations with SES, one plausible developmental contrast concerns the relative salience of family stress and investment models. Based on recent analyses of data collected across seven waves in the NICHD study (Raffington et al.,

2018), we predict that family stress is especially damaging in the early years of life, while variations in parental investment may be particularly salient in middle childhood. As we noted earlier in this chapter, SES is typically only included as a control measure. An obvious avenue for future work is to devote more theoretical attention to potential interactions between effects of family interaction and family background on children's growing understanding of others' minds.

References

Ainsworth, M., Blehar, M., Waters, E., & Wall, S. (1978). *Patterns of Attachment: A Psychological Study of the Strange Situation*. Hillsdale, NJ: Erlbaum.

Allen, J.P., Hauser, S.T., Bell, K.L., & O'Connor, T.G. (1994). Longitudinal assessment of autonomy and relatedness in adolescent-family interactions as predictors of adolescent ego development and self-esteem. *Child Development, 65*, 179–194. DOI: 10.1111/j.1467-8624.1994.tb00743.x

Astington, J.W., & Pelletier, J. (1998). *Metacognitive Vocabulary test*. Institute of Child Study, University of Toronto, Unpublished.

Baron-Cohen, S. (2000). Theory of mind and autism: A fifteen-year review. In S. Baron-Cohen, H. Tager-Flusberg, & D. Cohen (Eds.), *Understanding Other Minds: Perspectives from Developmental Cognitive Neuroscience* (2nd ed.). Oxford: Oxford University Press.

Baron-Cohen, S., Leslie, A., & Frith, U. (1985). Does the autistic child have a "theory of mind"? *Cognition, 21*, 37–46. doi:10.1016/0010-0277(85)90022-8

Bosacki, S., & Astington, J. (1999). Theory of mind in preadolescence: Relations between social understanding and social competence. *Social Development, 8*, 237–255.

Bowlby, J. (1969). *Attachment and Loss, Vol. 1: Attachment. Attachment and Loss*. New York: Basic Books.

Brown, J., & Dunn, J. (1991). "You can cry, mum": The social and developmental implications of talk about internal states. Special issue: Perspectives on the child's theory of mind: II. *British Journal of Developmental Psychology, 9*, 237–256.

Buist, K.L., Deković, M., & Prinzie, P. (2013). Sibling relationship quality and psychopathology of children and adolescents: A meta-analysis. *Clinical Psychology Review, 33*, 97–106. DOI: 10.1016/j.cpr.2012.10.007

Buri, J.R. (1991). Parental authority questionnaire. *Journal of Personality Assessment, 57*, 110–119. doi:10.1207/s15327752jpa5701_13

Carpendale, J., & Chandler, M. (1996). On the distinction between false belief understanding and subscribing to an interpretive theory of mind. *Child Development, 67*, 1686–1706. doi:10.2307/1131725

Carr, A., Slade, L., Yuill, N., Sullivan, S., & Ruffman, T. (2018). Minding the children: A longitudinal study of mental state talk, theory of mind, and behavioral adjustment from the age of 3 to 10. *Social Development, 27*, 826–840. doi:10.1111/sode.12315

Castelli, F., Happe, F., Frith, U., & Frith, C. (2000). Movement and mind: A functional imaging study of perception and interpretation of complex intentional movement patterns. *NeuroImage, 12*, 314–325. doi:10.1006/nimg.2000.0612

Cicchetti, D., Rogosch, F., Maughan, A., Toth, S., & Bruce, J. (2003). False belief understanding in maltreated children. *Development and Psychopathology, 15*, 1067–1091. doi:10.1017/S0954579403000440

Clemmensen, L., Van Os, J., Drukker, M., Munkholm, A., Rimvall, M., Væver, M., Rask, C.U., Bartels-Velthuis, A.A., Skovgaard, A.M. Jeppesen, P. (2016). Psychotic experiences and hyper-theory-of-mind in preadolescence—A birth cohort study. *Psychological Medicine, 46*, 87–101. doi:10.1017/S0033291715001567

Conger, R., Conger, K., & Martin, M. (2010). Socioeconomic status, family processes, and individual development. *Journal of Marriage and Family, 72*, 685–704. doi:10.1111/j.1741-3737.2010.00725.x

Coull, G., Leekam, S., & Bennett, M. (2006). Simplifying second-order belief attribution: What facilitates children's performance on measures of conceptual understanding?. *Social Development, 15*, 260–275. doi:10.1111/j.1467-9507.2006.00340.x

Currie, C., Molcho, M., Boyce, W., Holstein, B., Torsheim, T., & Richter, M. (2008). Researching health inequalities in adolescents: The development of the Health Behavior in School-Aged Children (HBSC) family affluence scale. *Social Science & Medicine, 66*, 1429–1436. doi:10.1016/j.puhe.2019.03.001

Devine, R., & Hughes, C. (2013). Silent films and strange stories: Theory of mind, gender, and social experiences in middle childhood. *Child Development, 84* 989–1003. doi:10.1111/cdev.12017

Devine, R., & Hughes, C. (2014). Relations between false-belief understanding and executive function in early childhood: A meta-analysis. *Child Development, 85*, 1777–1794. doi:10.1111/cdev.12237

Devine, R., & Hughes, C. (2016). Measuring theory of mind across middle childhood: Reliability and validity of the silent films and strange stories tasks. *Journal of Experimental Child Psychology, 149*, 23–40. doi:10.1016/j.jecp.2015.07.011

Devine, R., & Hughes, C. (2018). Family correlates of false belief understanding in early childhood: A meta-analysis. *Child Development, 89*, 971–987. doi:10.1111/cdev.12682

Devine, R.T., & Hughes, C.(2019). Let's talk: Parents' mental talk (not mind-mindedness or mindreading capacity) predicts children's false belief understanding. *Child Development, 90*, 1236–1253. DOI: 10.1111/cdev.12990

Devine, R.T., White, N., Ensor, R., & Hughes, C. (2016). Theory of mind in middle childhood: Longitudinal associations with executive function and social competence. *Developmental Psychology, 52*, 758–771. DOI: 10.1037/dev0000105

Dodell-Feder, D., & Tamir, D. (2018). Fiction reading has a small positive impact on social cognition: A meta-analysis. *Journal of Experimental Psychology: General, 147*, 1713–1727. doi:10.1037/xge0000395

Dore, R.A., Smith, E.D., & Lillard, A.S. (2015). How is theory of mind useful? Perhaps to enable social pretend play. *Frontiers in Psychology, 6*, 1559. doi: 10.3389/fpsyg.2015.01559

Dunn, J., Brown, J., Slomkowski, C., Tesla, C., & Youngblade, L. (1991). Young children's understanding of other people's feelings and beliefs: Individual differences and their antecedents. *Child Development, 62*, 1352–1366. doi:10.2307/1130811

Ebert, S., Peterson, C., Slaughter, V., & Weinert, S. (2017). Links among parents' mental state language, family socioeconomic status, and preschoolers' theory of mind development. *Cognitive Development, 44*, 32–48. doi:10.1016/j.cogdev.2017.08.005

Ensor, R., Devine, R., Marks, A., & Hughes, C. (2014). Mothers' cognitive references to 2-year-olds predict theory of mind at ages 6 and 10. *Child Development, 85*, 1222–1235. doi:10.1111/cdev.12186

Fonagy, P., Steele, M., Steele, H., Moran, G., & Higgitt, A. (1991). The capacity for understanding mental states: The reflective self in parent and child and its significance for security of attachment. *Infant Mental Health Journal, 12*, 201–218. doi:10.1002/1097-0355(199123)12:3&lt

Furman, W., & Buhrmester, D. (1985). Children's perceptions of the personal relationships in their social networks. *Developmental Psychology, 21* 1016–1024. doi:10.1037/0012-1649.21.6.1016

Gopnik, A. & Wellman, H.M. (2012). Reconstructing constructivism: causal models, Bayesian learning mechanisms, and the theory theory. *Psychological Bulletin, 138,* 1085–1108.

Happé, F. (1994). An advanced test of theory of mind: Understanding of story characters' thoughts and feelings by able autistic, mentally handicapped, and normal children and adults. *Journal of Autism and Development Disorders, 24,* 129–154. doi:10.1007/BF02172093

Heyes, C., & Frith, C. (2014). The cultural evolution of mindreading. *Science, 344,* 1357.

Howe, N., & Recchia, H. (2009). Individual differences in sibling teaching in early and middle childhood. *Early Education and Development, 20,* 174–197. doi:10.1080/10409280802206627

Howe, N., Aquan-Assee, J., Bukowski, W.M., Lehoux, P.M., & Rinaldi, C.M. Siblings as confidants: Emotional understanding, relationship warmth, and sibling self-disclosure. *Social Development, 10,* 439–454.

Hughes, C., Aldercotte, A., & Foley, S. (2017). Maternal mind-mindedness provides a buffer for pre-adolescents at risk for disruptive behavior. *Journal of Abnormal Child Psychology, 45,* 225–235. doi:10.1007/s10802-016-0165-5

Hughes, C., & Ensor, R. (2006). Behavioral problems in two-year-olds: Links with individual differences in theory of mind, executive function and negative parenting. *Journal of Child Psychology & Psychiatry & Allied Disciplines, 47,* 488–497. doi:10.1111/j.1469-7610.2005.01519.x

Hutchins, T., Bond, L., Silliman, E., & Bryant, J. (2009). Maternal epistemological perspectives and variations in mental state talk. *Journal of Speech, Language, and Hearing Research, 52,* 61–80. doi:10.1044/1092-4388(2008/07-0161)

Jones, L., Bellis, M., Wood, S., Hughes, K., McCoy, E., Eckley, L., Bates, G., Mikton, C. Shakespeare, T. & Officer, A. (2012). Prevalence and risk of violence against children with disabilities: A systematic review and meta-analysis of observational studies. *The Lancet, 380,* 899–907. doi:DOI: 10.1016/S0140-6736(12)60692-8

Kennedy, K., Lagattuta, K., & Sayfan, L. (2015). Sibling composition, executive function, and children's thinking about mental diversity. *Journal of Experimental Child Psychology, 132,* 121–139. doi:10.1016/j.jecp.2014.11.007

Klagsbrun, M., & Bowlby, J. (1976). Responses to separation from parents: A clinical test for young children. *British Journal of Projective Psychology & Personality Study, 21,* 7–21.

Kramer, L., & Kowal, A.K.(2005). Sibling relationship quality from birth to adolescence: The enduring contributions of friends. *Journal of Family Psychology, 19,* 503–511. DOI: 10.1037/0893-3200.19.4.503

LaBounty, J., Wellman, H.M., Olson, S., Lagattuta, K. & Liu, D. (2008). Mothers' and fathers' use of internal state talk with their young children. *Social Development, 17,* 757–775.

Last, B., Lawson, G., Breiner, K., Steinberg, L., & Farah, M. (2018). Childhood socioeconomic status and executive function in childhood and beyond. *PLoS ONE, 13.* doi:10.1371/journal.pone.0202964

Lewis, C., Freeman, N., Kyriakidou, C., Maridaki-Kassotaki, K., & Berridge, D. (1996). Social Influences on false belief access: Specific sibling influences or general apprenticeship? *Child Development, 67,* 2930–2947. doi:10.1111/j.1467-8624.1996.tb01896.x

Lillard, A.S., Lerner, M.D., Hopkins, E.J., Dore, R.A., Smith, E.D., & Palmquist, C.M. (2013). The impact of pretend play on children's development: A review of the evidence. *Psychological Bulletin, 139*, 1–34. DOI: 10.1037/a0029321

Long, E., Rutter, M., Kreppner, J., Beckett, C., Castle, J., Groothues, C., Hawkins, A., Stevens, S., & Sonuga-Barke, E.J.S. (2008). Do theory of mind and executive function deficits underlie the adverse outcomes associated with profound early deprivation? Findings from the English and Romanian adoptees study. *Journal of Abnormal Child Psychology, 36*, 1057 –1068.

Main, M., & Solomon, J. (1986). Discovery of an insecure-disorganized/disoriented attachment pattern: Procedures, findings and implications for the classification of behavior. In M. Yogman & T. Brazelton (Eds.), *Affective Development in Infancy* (pp. 95–124). Ablex: Norwood, NJ.

Marchetti, A., Castelli, I., Sanvito, L., & Massaro, D. (2014). Is a bird in the hand worth two in the future? Intertemporal choice, attachment and theory of mind in school-aged children. *Frontiers in Psychology, 5*. doi:10.3389/fpsyg.2014.00483

Meins, E., Centifanti, L., Fernyhough, C., & Fishburn, S. (2013). Maternal mind-mindedness and children's behavioral difficulties: Mitigating the impact of low socioeconomic status. *Journal of Abnormal Child Psychology, 41*, 543–553. doi:10.1007/s10802-012-9699-3

Meins, E., Fernyhough, C., Fradley, E., & Tuckey, M. (2001). Rethinking maternal sensitivity: Mothers' comments on infants' mental processes predict security of attachment at 12-months. *Journal of Child Psychology and Psychiatry, 42*, 637–648. doi:10.1017/S0021963001007302

Milligan, K., Astington, J., & Dack, L. (2007). Language and theory of mind: Meta-analysis of the relation between language ability and false-belief understanding. *Child Development, 78*, 622–646. doi:10.1111/j.1467-8624.2007.01018.x

Noble, K., McCandliss, B., & Farah, M. (2007). Socioeconomic gradients predict individual differences in neurocognitive abilities. *Developmental Science, 10*, 464–480. doi:10.1111/j.1467-7687.2007.00600.x

O'Reilly, J., & Peterson, C. (2014). Maltreatment and advanced theory of mind development in school-aged children. *Journal of Family Violence, 30*, 93–102. doi:10.1007/s10896-014-9647-9

Paine, A., Pearce, H., van Goozen, S., de Sonneville, L., & Hay, D. (2018). Late, but not early, arriving younger siblings foster firstborns' understanding of second-order false belief. *Journal of Experimental Child Psychology, 166*, 251–265. doi:10.1016/j.jecp.2017.08.007

Pearson, R., & Pillow, B. (2016). Mother–child conversation and children's social understanding during middle childhood. *Journal of Genetic Psychology, 177*, 103–121. doi:10.1080/00221325.2016.1188054

Perner, J., & Wimmer, H. (1985). "John thinks that Mary thinks that...": Attribution of second-order beliefs by 5- to 10-year-old children. *Journal of Experimental Child Psychology, 39*, 437–471. doi:10.1016/0022-0965(85)90051-7

Piaget, J. (1959). *The Language and Thought of the Child*. London: Routledge.

Piaget, J. & Inhelder, B. (1969). *The Psychology of the Child*. New York: Basic Books.

Raffington, L., Prindle, J., & Shing, Y. (2018). Income gains predict cognitive functioning longitudinally throughout later childhood in poor children. *Developmental Psychology, 54*, 1232–1243. doi:10.1037/dev0000529

Raley, S., Bianchi, S., & Wang, W. (2012). When do fathers care? Mothers' economic contribute and fathers' involvement in child care. *American Journal of Sociology, 117*, 1422–1459. doi:10.1086/663354

Ronald, A., Viding, E., Happé, F., & Plomin, R. (2006). Individual differences in theory of mind ability in middle childhood and links with verbal ability and autistic traits: A twin study. *Social Neuroscience, 1*, 412–425. doi:10.1080/17470910601068088

Ruffman, T., Slade, L., & Crowe, E. (2002). The relation between children's and mothers' mental state language and theory-of-mind understanding. *Child Development, 73*, 734–751. doi:10.1111/1467-8624.00435

Schwebel, D.C., Rosen, C.S., & Singer, J.L. (1999). Preschoolers' pretend play and theory of mind: The role of jointly constructed pretence. *British Journal of Developmental Psychology, 17*, 333–348. DOI: 10.1348/026151099165320

Semeijn, M. (2019). Interacting with fictions: The role of pretend play in theory of mind acquisition. *Review of Philosophy and Psychology, 10*, 113–132. DOI: 10.1007/s13164-018-0387-2

Tafreshi, D., & Racine, T. (2016). Children's interpretive theory of mind: The role of mothers' personal epistemologies and mother-child talk about interpretation. *Cognitive Development, 39*, 57–70. doi:10.1016/j.cogdev.2016.04.003

Turnbull, W., Carpendale, J., & Racine, T. (2008). Relations between mother-child talk and 3- to 5-year-old children's understanding of belief: Beyond mental state terms to talk about the mind. *Merrill-Palmer Quarterly, 54*, 367–385. doi:10.1353/mpq.0.0004.

Vinden, P. (2001). Parenting attitudes and children's understanding of mind. A comparison of Korean American and Anglo-American families. *Cognitive Development, 16*, 793–809. doi:10.1016/S0885-2014(01)00059-4

Volling, B. (2012). Family transitions following the birth of a sibling: An empirical review of changes in the firstborn's adjustment. *Psychological Bulletin, 138*, 497–528. doi:10.1037/a0026921

Vygotsky, L.S. (1978). *Mind in Society: The Development of Higher Psychological Processes*. Cambridge, MA: Harvard University Press.

Wang, Z., Devine, R., Wong, K., & Hughes, C. (2016). Theory of mind and executive function during middle childhood across cultures. *Journal of Experimental Child Psychology, 149*, 6–22. doi:10.1016/j.jecp.2015.09.028

Wellman, H., & Liu, D. (2004). Scaling of theory-of-mind tasks. *Child Development, 75*, 523–541. doi:10.1111/j.1467-8624.2004.00691.x

White, N., & Hughes, C. (2017). *Why Siblings Matter: The Role of Brother and Sister Relationships in Development and Well-Being* (1st ed.). UK: Routledge.

6 Friendships and theory of mind in middle childhood and adolescence

Elian Fink

Early friendships are children's formative social experience outside the family, and once children start school, peer relationships more broadly, and friendships in particular, take on increasing significance for development. Even young children themselves appreciate the importance of having friends at school (Danby et al., 2012; O'Farrelly et al., 2019), and by adolescence, friendships are crucial for social and emotional wellbeing (Bagwell & Schmidt, 2013). While there is a strong research tradition studying the role of family interactional styles on children's theory of mind (ToM) development (see Chapter 5 of this volume), very little research has examined the way in which ToM influences and is influenced by friendship relationships in middle childhood, with even less work examining these associations longitudinally or in adolescence.

In the current chapter, I first outline the role of friendship for children's development and wellbeing from middle childhood through adolescence. I then outline some of the possible mechanisms linking theory of mind (ToM) to children's friendship relationships, before turning to an evaluation of the existing empirical literature that has attempted to understand how ToM and friendship may be associated across different stages of development. Finally, I conclude by highlighting some challenges facing this research and those questions that are still outstanding.

Children's friendships in middle childhood and adolescence

Prior to the start of formal schooling, caregivers and siblings tend to comprise children's first stable social relationships; however, once children begin school, they spend an increasing proportion of their daily social interactions with peers, replacing time previously spent in the company of siblings and caregivers (Gifford-Smith & Brownell, 2003). From primary to secondary school, the relationships children have with their peers become increasingly stable, intimate, and personally meaningful. In contrast to social interactions with caregivers and siblings, exposure to a wider peer group in the context of school provides the opportunity for children to select the specific peers with whom they prefer to interact frequently. From the peer group, children form friendships; a stable dyadic relationship based on mutual liking, reciprocity, and support. Unlike relationships with parents, siblings, or teachers, friendships are a relationship built on equality, often described as a 'horizontal' relationship, unlike other dyadic relationships (e.g., parent–child, sibling–child) that comprise an inherent imbalance with respect to age, power, etc. (Bagwell & Schmidt, 2013).

While reciprocity and mutual liking remain at the core of friendships throughout the lifespan, what children do with their friends clearly changes with development. During the early years of middle childhood, friends spend the majority of their time engaging in imaginative pretend and fantasy play; these interactions are typically sustained and positive (Gifford-Smith & Brownell, 2003). However, by the later years of middle childhood, the focus for friendship dyads shifts to shared norms and personal qualities that correspond to a growing awareness of others. Friends of this age spend much of their time in animated conversation and playing structured games. The developing interpersonal awareness that starts in middle childhood clearly develops further, and by adolescence, friendships rely on open and honest dyadic exchanges of self-disclosure and affection (Bagwell & Schmidt, 2013; Parker & Gottman, 1989). These developmental contrasts reflect differences in the function of friendships across childhood, with the purpose of early friendships being to share enjoyment and entertainment, while friendships in adolescence, in addition to providing an opportunity to share enjoyment, provide adolescents with space to safely explore identity and self-understanding. Given that aspects of friendship change with development, it is likely that the specific predictors of friendship and the effect of friendship on children's social and cognitive outcomes likely differ with development also.

The developmental significance of children's friendships

A number of studies have demonstrated the importance of friendships for later child and adolescent adjustment, with the long-term implications of friendlessness including both socio-emotional difficulties and poor academic achievement and motivation at school (Ladd & Troop-Gordon, 2003; Nangle et al., 2003; Wentzel et al., 2004; Wentzel & Caldwell, 1997). It has even been proposed that without the intimacy and collaboration afforded by friendship interactions in childhood and adolescence, young people would fail to develop social competencies necessary to form and navigate adult relationships successfully (Gifford-Smith & Brownell, 2003). Providing some support for this statement is a study following 551 children from middle childhood to early adolescence which found that friendlessness at ages 10 to 11 years predicted increased depression and loneliness at age 12 to 13 years (Pedersen et al., 2007). Furthermore, Bagwell and colleagues (1998), in a 12-year longitudinal study, found that having a reciprocated friendship in middle childhood was associated with greater adult adjustment and wellbeing, while children without a reciprocated friend were more likely to experience poor mental health outcomes in adulthood.

When exploring the importance of friendship in children's lives, and the role of ToM for friendship interactions, it is important to distinguish between friendships and children's broader peer relationships, which is often assessed as the degree to which the child is well-liked within the classroom. The central distinction between friendship and peer liking (also referred to as peer acceptance, social preference, or popularity) is that for friendships, by definition, the liking has to be reciprocal (Bagwell & Schmidt, 2013). While both having a friend and being well-liked by peers are important for healthy development, it is possible to be well-liked within the peer group but lack a reciprocated friendship, or to have a reciprocated friendship and be not well-liked by the peer group. In fact, the presence of a reciprocated friendship appears to serve as a buffer against the negative repercussions of being disliked within the peer group. Indeed, in an Australian study, together with colleagues we found that 23% of five-year-old children rated by their peers as being well-liked did not have a reciprocated best friend, while 53% of children who were rejected by the peer group did have a reciprocated best friend (Fink et al., 2015; see also Gest et al., 2001). Of course, being liked by one's peers and friendship are not independent; clearly, a child that develops his or her social skills in the context of a close friendship may then use these skills when interacting with the broader peer group, which may influence their position in this peer group, and the degree to which a child is liked by their peer group will impact their opportunities to make a close friendship (e.g., Pedersen et al., 2007).

While the degrees to which children have reciprocated friendships or are well-liked in their peer group are both associated with concurrent and later socio-emotional competence, school adjustment, and academic success, friendships in particular seem to be uniquely related to children's feelings of loneliness and self-worth and to depression in young adulthood (Parker & Asher, 1993). Similarly, in preadolescence, having a friend is uniquely related to lower levels of depression and higher self-worth in adulthood (Bagwell et al., 1998). Given the positive social outcomes associated with having a reciprocated friendship in childhood and the persistent negative outcomes for those that are friendless, it is important to examine those characteristics of children that support the initiation and maintenance of children's friendships. However, before turning to the specific role of ToM for children's friendships, a brief overview of how friendship is assessed in childhood and adolescence is needed.

The measurement of friendship in middle childhood and adolescence

There are three broad approaches to the measurement of children's friendships; (1) the presence (or absence) of a reciprocated friend, (2) the quality of a child's friendship, and (3) characteristics of friendship interactions.

Friendship reciprocity

The most straightforward index of friendship assesses whether children have a reciprocated friend by asking children to nominate their best friend (or top two or three friends) within a closed peer network, such as a classroom. Children who both nominate each other are considered to have a reciprocated friendship. This can be contrasted with broader peer liking in the classroom, which relies on children nominating the top three classmates they like and dislike – the so-called and widely used sociometric interview (Coie et al., 1982) – and as such, peer likability relies on being liked by the majority of one's classmates and disliked by relatively few.

Employing nominations to determine the presence of a reciprocated friendship has been shown to be a reliable method to measure friendship in childhood and adolescence (Bagwell & Schmidt, 2013). However, clearly there are limitations to this approach. For example, it relies on the participation of whole closed-networks, typically classrooms, with the decreasing proportion of children who participate increasing the inaccuracy of the measure. Furthermore, the presence of reciprocated friendships outside the closed peer network is unknown.

Clearly, assessing whether a child has a reciprocated friendship does not capture the quality of the interaction between friends, a more nuanced but arguably challenging-to-measure aspect of friendship in childhood, and may emerge as particularly important to understanding friendship in adolescence given the potential negative influence of deviant friendships (e.g., Piehler & Dishion, 2007). From the point of view of ToM, those friendships that, despite being reciprocal, are characterized as particularly conflictual, unbalanced, or unsatisfying may show a different pattern of association to reciprocal friendships with greater trust, intimacy, and harmony.

Friendship quality

The second approach to measuring friendship attempts to capture children's own perceptions of the quality of their friendship interactions. There are several reliable and validated self-report measures of friendship quality (e.g., Bukowski et al., 1994; Ladd et al., 1996; Parker & Asher, 1993). Most measures assess both positive friendship features, such as intimacy and support, and negative friendship features, such as conflict and inequality/balance of power (Bagwell & Schmidt, 2013). Research has shown that positive features and negative features of friendships form two independent dimensions of friendship quality (Berndt, 2002).

To assess friendship quality in young children, Dunn and colleagues developed the semi-structured Friendship Interview to determine the degree to which young children liked their friends and had insight into their friends' preferences and feelings, as well as how conflict was resolved within the friendships (Dunn et al., 2002) based on children's responses to 12 open-ended questions, such as 'What makes [friend] sad or upset?', 'What do you really like about [friend]?, and 'Is there anything you don't like about [friend]?'. The Friendship Features Interview uses a similar methodology with 24 open-ended interview questions (e.g., 'Does [friend] say nice things to you?' and 'Does [friend] ever boss you around?') to assess aspects of validation, self-disclosure, and exclusivity in young children's friendships (Ladd et al., 1996).

For older children and adolescents, friendship quality is typically assessed using a questionnaire. For example, the Friendship Qualities Scale (Bukowski et al., 1994) assesses the quality of older children's and early adolescents' friendships on multiple dimensions, including companionship (e.g., 'Sometimes my friend and I just sit around and talk'), conflict ('I can get into fights with my friend'), help (e.g., 'My friend helps me when I am having trouble with something'), security (e.g., 'If my friend or I do something that bothers the other one of us, we can make up easily'), and closeness (e.g., 'Sometimes my friend does things for me, or makes me feel special'). As expected, children rated friends higher than non-friends on this scale. Of course, perceptions of friendship quality may be influenced by child characteristics not directly associated with the friendship, such as self-concept, linguistic competence, and, importantly, ToM understanding (Gifford-Smith & Brownell, 2003).

Characteristics of friendship interactions

The third approach to assessing friendship in children and adolescents involves coding observed behaviors within interactions between friends. This final approach overlaps with both measures of friendship quality and friendship reciprocity. For example, observations of children's interactions with peers are also sometimes used to identify friends in young children (e.g., Howes, 1996), while in adolescence, specific features of observed interactions are used to infer friendship quality. What sets this measurement approach apart from the two preceding approaches is the focus on observing what children *do* together in their interactions.

Typically, characteristics of peer interactions such as proximity, frequency, and affective quality are used to infer friendship in younger children (Gifford-Smith & Brownell, 2003). For example, Howes and Phillipsen (1992) assessed friendship by coding the degree to which children played closely together (within three feet of each other) and expressed positive emotions across a number of different observation windows at nursery school. In another study, Youngblade et al. (1993) coded five-year-old children's friendship interactions during play at the level of the dyad on a number of dimensions, including positive and negative connectedness (e.g., joint pleasure/disagreements), proximity (e.g., time spent close to each other during play), and competition (e.g., degree to which children in the dyad make explicit comparisons of their own achievements or performance).

In middle childhood and adolescence, peer interactions tend to be coded for more complex aspects of friendship, such as conflict and conflict resolution, intimacy, shared affect, cooperation, and self-disclosure, and then are used to infer the features of the interaction that distinguish friends from non-friends. For example, Hartup and colleagues (1993) found that friendship dyads compared to non-friendship dyads in middle childhood were more likely to exhibit conflict while playing a board game together. While, Brendgen and colleagues (2001) rated adolescents' observed friendship interactions on a number of dimensions, including positive/negative emotions, assertiveness, and self-disclosure, and found considerable overlap between observed behaviors and adolescents' own ratings of friendship quality via questionnaire.

Given these varied means by which to assess children's friendships, it becomes important not only to understand the broad link between ToM and friendship but also to examine if ToM is related to a specific index of friendship.

Friendship and theory of mind

In a meta-analysis comparing the social and cognitive features of friends and non-friends, Newcomb and Bagwell (1995) found that friendships were represented by greater reciprocal and intimate affiliation, more intense social activity, and effective conflict resolution compared to non-friend interactions (see also Hartup, 1996). This highlights both that friendship interactions likely have a different quality compared with non-friend interactions and that a degree of shared understanding is necessary for friendship interactions.

Crucially, initiating and maintaining a friendship requires a grasp of the friends' beliefs, intentions, and desires, and how these may be similar or different from one's own. As such, those children who lag behind their peers with respect to understanding another's thoughts and feelings may struggle to forge close friendships with their peers and sustain them over time. ToM may be especially important when children enter a new social setting (such as the transition to formal schooling) as children are not able to rely on previous understanding of peers' preferences, typical behaviors, or emotional responses to help guide their understanding of the unfolding social interaction.

In addition to being the consequence of ToM understanding, friendships and the intimacy and access to the thoughts and feelings of others they afford also likely provide children with the opportunities to hone their ToM understanding (Hughes & Devine, 2015). From a theoretical standpoint, at least, there are strong grounds to suggest that ToM will both facilitate the formation and maintenance of friendships (Hughes & Dunn, 1998), and provide children with the social context needed to improve ToM abilities.

There are a number of features of children's friendship interactions that may both rely on and foster ToM skills. First, during social pretend play, children co-create an imaginative narrative, align their interests, discuss pretend roles and the thoughts, feelings, and actions of the characters, and invest in creating a harmonious pretend play space (Dunn & Brophy, 2005). Empirical research has shown that both the quality (Astington & Jenkins, 1995; Taylor & Carlson, 1997) and quantity (Hughes & Dunn, 1997) of young children's pretend play with friends is associated with ToM understanding. For example, Astington and Jenkins (1995) found that children who made joint plans and assigned their friend roles in the context of pretend play had greater ToM understanding than children who engaged in these behaviors less frequently. Importantly, high-quality pretend play is much more likely in the context of a friendship than for children who are familiar peers (e.g., Werebe & Baudonniere, 1991).

Second, learning about the inner states of others is critical for the development of close relationships, which is often fostered through explicit communication in the context of a close dyadic relationship (Dunn & Brophy, 2005). It is no coincidence then that associations have been found between ToM and children's talk about thoughts and feelings with parents, siblings, and friends (e.g., Brown et al., 1996; Hughes & Dunn, 1998). Of particular interest for the current chapter is the specific association between mental state talk in the context of friendships (as opposed to unacquainted peers). Children's competence in discussing their own mental states promotes intimate interactions with peers, while an understanding that others may have different thoughts, feelings, and desires supports effective conflict resolution. Hughes and Dunn (1998) examined the association between mental state talk in the context of friendship and found that those children who engaged in greater mental state talk with their friends (as reported by teachers) at 3 years 11 months were more likely to have greater ToM understanding both concurrently and at five years of age. Importantly, earlier ToM did not predict mental state talk with the friend at five years of age, highlighting the potentially directional role of friendship interactions for later ToM development, at least in early childhood.

While there is limited longitudinal research on the role of mental state talk for friendships in middle childhood and adolescence, plausibly, as friendships increasingly rely on intimate disclosures and serve to support identity formation, mental state talk in the context of friendships as children develop is likely to be of similar if not greater importance than in early childhood, with the direction of influence shifting such that greater ToM in middle childhood and adolescence may support deeper friendship interactions.

Third, experiencing and managing conflict in the context of friendship interactions likely both rely on and serve to enhance children's ToM. While some studies have shown that children with greater ToM are less likely to experience conflict in their friendship relationship (Dunn & Cutting, 1999), when conflict does arise within friendship interactions, those children with greater ToM at age four engaged in more sophisticated conflict resolution strategies with their friends that specifically accounted for another's point of view compared to those children with less sophisticated ToM (Dunn & Herrera, 1997). In adolescence, the quality of the friendship relationship as identified by both friends significantly predicts conversational quality when discussing social dilemmas (McDonald et al., 2014), with those adolescents reporting greater friendship quality more likely to use sophisticated reasoning strategies to resolve the social dilemmas than those friendship dyads that reported low friendship quality, or who disagreed on the quality of the friendship.

What is missing from much of the empirical literature is a direct comparison of ToM in children with and without reciprocal friendships, making it challenging to evaluate whether the pretend play, mental state talk, and conflict resolution that is afforded by friendships in particular are critical for ToM or whether more transient peer interactions may serve a similar role for ToM. Adding to the complexity in evaluating the role of ToM for friendship is the fact that the manner in which children use their ToM understanding likely shifts with development (Aboud & Mendleson, 1996). Younger children may rely on ToM to engage in pretend play or share a joke with a friend. As children get older, however, understanding the thoughts and feelings of others becomes increasingly important to resolve conflict, develop deeper intimacy, and cultivate shared preferences, in addition to navigating interactions with a number of different friends, all with potentially contrasting thoughts, feelings, and desires.

I turn next to an examination of the empirical literature that has examined the concurrent and longitudinal role of ToM for children's friendships. The majority of research examining the concurrent and longitudinal association between ToM and children's friendships comes from studies examining the association between specific characteristics of preschool-aged play with a reciprocated friend and ToM understanding. As such, I start by briefly summarizing the association between friendship interactions and ToM in young children, as this work was foundational in influencing later research in middle childhood and adolescence.

Friendship and Theory of Mind in young children

The earliest studies in this area suggested that children with friends were better able to take the perspectives of others (e.g., McGuire & Weisz, 1982) but it was not until the work of Judy Dunn and colleagues that provided a clearer understanding of how ToM may come to support children's friendship interactions in early childhood. Across a number of ground-breaking longitudinal studies, Dunn undertook detailed work examining how ToM in toddlerhood and preschool-aged children was associated with multiple aspects of children's friendship interactions. For example, Slomkowski and Dunn (1996) showed that greater ToM at 40 months was associated with more connected conversations with friends at 47 months, and in turn, was associated with greater self-disclosure with a friend. In addition, ToM facilitated friendships at age four by supporting effective conflict resolution that specifically accounted for another's point of view (Dunn & Herrera, 1997). Despite an impressive body of research investigating the characteristics of friendship interactions that are associated concurrently and longitudinally with ToM, Dunn's work focuses on those children with a reciprocated friendship, making it difficult to examine how ToM supports the initiation of friendship or, indeed, the implications of friendlessness on children's ToM understanding.

More recently, Peterson and Siegal (2002) investigated the independent role of both reciprocated friendships and peer-liking play for preschool-aged children's ToM. While they found that peer acceptance and friendship reciprocity were both associated with greater ToM understanding, when examined together, friendship reciprocity was a significant unique predictor of ToM, controlling for language ability and peer acceptance. Importantly, they found that preschoolers who were not well-liked by the peer group (i.e., had rejected sociometric status) but nonetheless had a stable reciprocated friendship had more sophisticated ToM than those rejected children who did not have a reciprocated friendship.

Together, work on the association between ToM and friendship prior to the start of formal schooling suggests that the interactions afforded by having a reciprocated friend are uniquely important for children's developing ToM understanding, with concurrent and longitudinal associations between children's ToM and friendship interactions implying that those children with more sophisticated ToM experience greater intimacy within their friendship interactions.

Theory of mind and friendship in middle childhood

Children's social environments are transformed once they enter school, and friends increasingly hold more importance than family interactions as children spend more time in the company of their peers (Parker et al., 2006). The role of ToM at the transition to formal schooling has received particular attention as it is likely that children's social reputations become less malleable with time (e.g., Fink et al., 2014), and supporting those children to make meaningful relationships with their peers early on will likely have important implications for later social interactions with the peer group.

One study in particular helps to unpack why ToM appears to be so important for friendship at the start of middle childhood. Hughes et al. (2011) assessed ToM at age six using a battery of tasks including first and second-order false belief and belief-based emotion tasks, and observed children in dyadic play with a teacher-nominated best friend for 15 minutes. They found that ToM was associated with the degree to which children spoke about mental states, such as thoughts, feelings, and desires, with their friends (even when accounting for how much their friends may have discussed these topics). Furthermore, ToM at age three uniquely predicted mental state talk with friends over and above the concurrent association with ToM at age six. The ability to discuss mental states competently likely promotes positive and intimate interactions with peers, an awareness of differences in points of view and the importance of reciprocity, as well as the ability to resolve conflicts, all critical for friendship.

Only children with a reciprocated friend were included in the Hughes et al. (2011) study. To address the gap in the literature examining the possible link between friendlessness and poor ToM, my colleagues and I explored the concurrent and longitudinal implications of ToM understanding in children with and without a reciprocated friendship at the start of school, when children were five years of age (Fink et al., 2015). In this study, comprising 114 children, we found that in the first year of school, 71% of children had a reciprocated friendship, assessed using a nomination procedure, while the remaining children were not nominated at all by their peers as one of their top three friends in the classroom. Those children that had formed a reciprocated friendship with a classroom peer outperformed those without a friend on measures of ToM, as assessed by a battery of tasks comprising unexpected contents, unexpected transfer, and belief-based emotion items. Importantly, ToM was uniquely predictive of reciprocal friendship status over and above children's performance on a task involving delay of gratification, peer liking, and observed prosocial behavior with peers; over and above these other social and cognitive factors, every standard deviation gain in ToM increased the likelihood of having a reciprocated friendship by 1.8.

We then revisited these children two years later, when they were seven years of age and in their third year of formal schooling, and found that 21% of children had lost a friend since starting school, while 22% had made a reciprocated friend in the intervening years. The majority of children (48%) had a reciprocal friend at both time-points, although this was not necessarily the same friend at both ages. Importantly, there was also a small group of children who were friendless at both five and seven years of age (9%). When examining the socio-cognitive skills that differentiated these 'chronically friendless' children from their peers, we found that while they were equally linguistically capable, prosocial, and able to delay gratification, they did show significantly poorer ToM understanding. That is, their comparative difficulty taking on the perspective of others at school entry compared to their peers appeared to be a critical impediment to both making and maintaining friendships with their peers during the first years of primary school.

While Fink et al. (2015) contributed to the literature by explicitly including children without a reciprocated friendship into the design, friendship quality was not assessed, meaning that nuances in the experience of children's friendships were not accounted for. Given the body of research that has shown that specific features of children's friendships (e.g., conflict resolution, insight, etc.) are explicitly linked to ToM, further studies examining both the reciprocal nature and the quality of friendship are clearly needed. Nonetheless, the fact that ToM was uniquely associated with the presence/absence of a reciprocated friend over two years, over and above children's peer liking, has important implications for our understanding of the importance of ToM in middle childhood for children's social relationships, especially given recent findings that show that reciprocated friendships in children between 7 and 11 years of age are of better quality than non-reciprocated friendships (Maunder & Monks, 2019).

Other work focusing on the association between ToM and friendship in middle childhood has focused on friendship quality rather than reciprocated friendship status. A recent study by Miller and colleagues (2018) examined the extent to which ToM was associated with a host of cognitive and social factors, including friendship quality. The sample comprised 81 children between seven and ten years of age, who completed four Faux Pas task items (Banerjee et al., 2011) and a perspective-taking task (Lagattuta et al., 2010). Friendship quality was assessed using Parker and Asher's (1993) widely used Friendship

Quality Questionnaire, which children completed after naming their own best friend. A total friendship quality score was determined by summing the positive subscales (validation, conflict resolution, companionship, helpfulness, and intimate disclosure) and a reverse-scored conflict subscale. No significant bivariate associations between friendship quality and children's ToM emerged for the overall sample; however, for boys only, greater faux pas understanding was associated with *poorer* overall friendship quality, which was likely driven by greater conflict.

When including other social and cognitive child characteristics (i.e., sex, age, executive functioning, and language ability) as predictors of children's ToM, friendship quality significantly and uniquely predicted faux pas understanding, such that greater overall friendship quality was associated with poorer faux pas understanding (not perspective-taking). Predicting perspective-taking, there was only a significant gender by friendship quality interaction, such that for boys, there was no difference in perspective-taking as a function of friendship quality, while for girls, as friendship quality increased, perspective-taking was predicted to decrease. Miller et al. (2018) present two possible interpretations of their intriguing findings. First, this study may suggest that some children may use their ToM to exert control to maintain their friendship relationship, resulting in decreased friendship quality, or, second, there is the possibility that girls with greater ToM are simply more sensitive to the typical fluctuations in friendships and attribute poorer relationship quality to their best friend as a result. This second interpretation fits well with the findings that children with greater ToM in middle childhood are more sensitive to teacher criticism than those with less sophisticated ToM (Cutting & Dunn, 2002).

Other studies have examined friendship interactions in young school-aged children as an outcome of earlier ToM. For example, Maguire and Dunn (1997) found that ToM (in addition to emotion understanding) at 40 months predicted the frequency of children's pretend play with a friend during the first year of formal schooling when children were six years of age, as well as self-disclosures to a friend. Greater play complexity (which comprised behaviors that demonstrated an understanding and appreciation of another's interests) in turn predicted children's mixed emotion understanding at the end of the school year seven months later.

Together, these studies focusing on ToM and friendship in middle childhood present a mixed picture of the role of ToM for friendship. On one hand, ToM seems crucial for the presence of a reciprocal friend and competent friendship interactions both concurrently and longitudinally, while, on the other hand, the quality of children's friendship appears to hinge on poorer ToM, although this may be the result of children's sophisticated ToM increasing the salience of negative aspects of friendship rather than sophisticated ToM explicitly employed to engage in greater conflict within friendship. Clearly, in order to disentangle this knotted issue, longitudinal research using multiple measures of both friendship and ToM at each time-point is sorely needed. Of those studies that have examined ToM and friendship longitudinally, positive friendship features appear to both predict later ToM (e.g., Slomkowski & Dunn, 1996) and be a consequence of earlier ToM (e.g., Fink et al., 2015; Hughes et al., 2011). However, it should be noted that these studies were not designed to assess comprehensively competing directional hypotheses, with the directionality between ToM and friendship possibly an artifact of the research design. Unfortunately, existing research on ToM and friendship in adolescence does not provide much additional clarity.

Theory of mind and friendship in adolescence

Given the paucity of work examining ToM in general in adolescence compared to early childhood, the fact there are relatively few studies specifically examining the association between ToM and friendship in adolescence is unsurprising. Nonetheless, given the increasingly important role played by adolescent friendships in providing emotional support (e.g., Laursen & Mooney, 2008) and later associations between friendships in adolescence and adult adjustment (Bagwell et al., 1998), the lack of research in this area is a notable omission.

One exception is the work by Białecka-Pikul and colleagues (2017) who conducted a large study of over 300 Polish adolescents between 13 and 16 years of age to examine the degree to which participants' perceptions of their friendships were associated with their cognitive ToM skills. Using the Friendship Questionnaire (Baron-Cohen & Wheelwright, 2003), a measure originally designed to examine sex differences in relationship quality, and a modified version of the Hinting task (Corcoran et al., 1995), which has been predominantly employed as a measure of ToM in psychiatric populations, some modest associations between specific features of adolescents' friendship styles and ToM emerge. Namely, a small positive association between ToM and emotional closeness (capturing the perception of friendships as intimate), and a negative association between ToM and the so-called social mirror subscale, which captures the extent to which participants feel their friendships provide some information about themselves (after controlling for age, sex, and language ability). Self-disclosure and need for affiliation were unrelated to ToM once language ability, sex, and age were controlled. While this study is commendable in that it breaks new ground by explicitly examining the role of ToM for friendship quality in adolescence, the choice of tasks to assess both ToM and friendship quality makes the generalizability of the findings challenging to determine.

Instead of relying on task-based measures of ToM, other studies in adolescence have asked participants to report on their own perspective-taking ability, and then examined the association between this index of ToM and friendship. For example, Smith and Rose (2011) found that 13-year-olds' own perceptions of their social perspective-taking ability were positively associated with friendship quality (assessed using an adapted version of Parker & Asher's [1993] Friendship Quality Questionnaire). Importantly, this study both ensured that participants were reporting on the quality of a reciprocated friendship and accounted for the dyadic nature of friendship by conducting multi-level models. In another study, Ackermann and colleagues (2019) examined the link between friendship quality and self-reported perspective-taking (as assessed using the cognitive subscale of the Interpersonal Reactivity Index [Davis, 1983]) in a sample of 261 adolescents approximately 14 years of age with and without disruptive behavioral disorders. They found that self-reported perspective-taking abilities were associated with more positive friendship qualities and fewer negative friendship qualities and, interestingly, the positive association between perspective-taking and positive friendship quality remained even when clinical status and aggression were controlled.

Notwithstanding the variation and potential measurement issues associated with assessments of ToM in middle childhood adolescence (see Chapter 3 of this volume), these studies suggest that a modest association between friendship and ToM exists in adolescence, broadly mirroring those found in younger age groups. However, given the concurrent nature of the design of the studies reviewed above, the directionality of this association is difficult to ascertain. Clearly, further research using longitudinal studies and comprehensive measures of friendship that examine both the reciprocated nature of the relationship in addition to the specific features of that relationship is needed at this age group also.

Existing challenges and future research

Perhaps the biggest challenge encountered when attempting to evaluate the existing literature on the link between ToM and friendship is the fact that the inherently dyadic nature of friendship interactions has been overlooked. Blieszner and Roberto (2003) argue that friendships are the 'ideal relationship for studying reciprocal developmental influences' (p.161), an assertion reflected in research, mainly in adolescence, on the dyadic influence of friendship quality on various socio-emotional outcomes, including moral reasoning (McDonald et al., 2014), social information processing, loneliness (Spencer et al., 2013), and empathy (Chow et al., 2013). In younger children, individual child characteristics have also been shown to influence the quality of friendship interactions; for example, Grotpeter and Crick (1996) found that those children who play with less socially skilled peers tend to have less intimate and more conflictual friendships. A similar argument on the importance of examining the social context has been made for understanding the development of ToM understanding (e.g., Carpendale & Lewis, 2004).

However, a dyadic approach examining the reciprocal influence of friends' ToM for friendship has rarely been conducted (for an exception see Dunn & Cutting, 1999). Nor, more broadly, has the dyadic context been typically controlled (e.g., using multi-level modeling) when attempting to understand the association between ToM and specific characteristics of children's friendship interactions. That is, children are observed interacting with their friends but the non-independent nature of this interaction is not accounted for when examining how ToM might be associated with aspects of this interaction.

Some recent studies taking advantage of advances and accessibility of dyadic statistical approaches have demonstrated the importance of understanding the social context of children's interactions. For example, together with colleagues, I highlighted the importance of the dyad for explaining five-year-old children's social pretend play behaviors (Gibson et al., 2020). In this large study, which included observations of negotiation and enactment of pretend play in 134 peer dyads, the degree to which an individual child's play behavior was dependent on his/her partner's play behavior was investigated. We found that between 22% and 44% of the variability in children's pretend play with a peer could be attributable to the dyad before any individual-level characteristics of the child were included in the multi-level model, and when individual-level characteristics were included (i.e., sex, age, and expressive and receptive language ability) they explained only a very small proportion of this variability (e.g., 1.6% of variance in negotiation was accounted for by individual-level characteristics). The non-independence of dyadic pretend play is of particular importance for ToM as many studies have shown an association between ToM and features of pretend play in young children (e.g., Astington & Jenkins, 1995).

Work by Etel and Slaughter (2019) has found similar results for the importance of the peer-dyad in explaining cooperation and coordination during play. Crucially, Etel and Slaughter also looked at the effects of ToM on interactions within the peer-dyad and found a specific reciprocal influence of play-partner ToM in three- to five-year-old children's cooperation. Neither Gibson et al. (2020) nor Etel and Slaughter (2019) specifically examined friendship interactions. However, together, these findings highlight both the importance of the social context for children's interactions as well as the potential for specific reciprocal effects of play-partners' ToM for child–peer interactions.

A promising area of future research that may provide an additional perspective on the role of ToM for friendships is the examination of how ToM within a friendship relationship supports and influences both the child's own and their friend's ratings of friendship quality and interactions. While for younger children, free-play paradigms are commonly employed to observe friendship interactions, by middle childhood and adolescence, free play may not always be developmentally appropriate. For older children, friendship interactions may be observed during collaborative construction (e.g., origami folding), planning of joint activities (e.g., a fun weekend together), and discussion of moral dilemmas (McDonald et al., 2014; Menzer et al., 2012). Using Actor–Partner Interdependence Modeling, for example, the role of an individual child's ToM for both their own and their friends' behavior during these interactions may be examined. Furthermore, contrasting the role of ToM in these dyadic interactions for friend versus non-friend pairs will also shed further light on the specific role of friendship for ToM.

A second challenge facing researchers attempting to understand the role of ToM for children's friendships is the broad range of friendship experiences. While a focus on friendship quality rather than (or in combination with) friendship reciprocity goes some way to understanding better the nuance within children's friendship interactions, more focused attention is still needed. For example, the quality of a friendship is not necessarily associated with how socially adaptive the friendship might be. Research by Ackerman and colleagues (2019) showed no significant difference in friendship quality between adolescents with and without disruptive behavioral disorders. In another study, it was found that adolescents who reported their friendship quality to be high in both negative and positive features increased in their disruptiveness over the course of a school year (Berndt & Keefe, 1995), suggesting that a closer friendship (i.e., one characterized by many positive friendship qualities) increases the opportunity to practice negative interactions (i.e., negative friendship qualities; Berndt, 2002).

So far within the existing literature on ToM and friendship, there tends to be the inherent assumption that ToM supports positive social interactions and friendship interactions; however, of course, ToM understanding is a socially neutral tool and may be used to engage in antisocial behavior (e.g., the link between ToM and bullying behavior; Smith, 2017; Fink et al., 2020). As noted above, ToM was found to be associated with lower levels of friendship quality for girls (Miller et al., 2018), providing some support that the use of conflict and coercion within friendships as well as intimacy is associated with ToM understanding. More research is clearly needed to understand how and under what contexts ToM may facilitate or buffer against the development of negative friendship features.

Finally, an issue that has often been encountered when examining the link between ToM and children's social outcomes is the distinction between children's ToM ability and the proclivity to employ ToM in social interactions. Flannery and Smith (2017) examined the association between adolescents' ability to take the perspective of others using the Social Perspective Taking task (Bosacki & Wilde 1999) and their tendency to do so in the context of their friendship relationship and found that ToM ability was not associated with the tendency to take the perspective of another in friendship. This research may explain the modest findings linking ToM and friendship in middle childhood and adolescence.

Conclusions

Like any research that examines the social antecedents and consequences of children's ToM, exploring the association between ToM and friendship is nuanced. Understanding this nuance in middle childhood and adolescence is made harder still by the small number of studies in these age groups, and the diversity of measures employed both with respect to ToM and friendship. Nonetheless, the research does tentatively suggest that the association between these two constructs in middle childhood and adolescence is similar to that found in early childhood. Greater ToM is generally associated with the presence of a reciprocal friend and mostly higher-quality friendships. Longitudinal studies are needed to understand better the direction of influence or, indeed, if the role of ToM for friendship formation, maintenance, and day-to-day interactions changes with the increasing developmental importance of friendship in young people's lives.

References

Aboud, F.E., & Mendleson, M.J. (1996). Determinants of friendship selection and quality: Developmental perspectives. In W.M. Bukowski, A.F. Newcomb, & W.W. Hartup (Eds.), *The Company They Keep: Friendship in Childhood and Adolescence* (pp. 87–112). Cambridge, UK: Cambridge University Press.

Ackermann, K., Martinelli, A., Bernhard, A., Freitag, C. M., Büttner, G., & Schwenck, C. (2019). Friendship quality in youth with and without disruptive behavior disorders: The role of empathy, aggression, and callousness. *Child Psychiatry and Human Development, 50*(5), 776–788.

Astington, J.W., & Jenkins, J.M. (1995). Theory of mind development and social understanding. *Cognition and Emotion, 9*(2–3), 151–165. doi:10.1080/02699939508409006.

Bagwell, C.L., Newcomb, A.F., & Bukowski, W.M. (1998). Preadolescent friendship and peer rejection as predictors of adult adjustment. *Child Development, 69*(1), 140–153.

Bagwell, C.L., & Schmidt, M.E. (2013). *Friendships in Childhood and Adolescence*. New York: Guilford Press.

Banerjee, R., Watling, D., & Caputi, M. (2011). Peer relations and the understanding of faux pas: Longitudinal evidence for bidirectional associations. *Child Development, 82*(6), 1887–1905.

Baron-Cohen, S., & Wheelwright, S. (2003). The friendship questionnaire: An investigation of adults with Asperger syndrome or high-functioning autism, and normal sex differences. *Journal of Autism and Developmental Disorders, 33*(5), 509–517. doi:10.1023/a:1025879411971.

Berndt, T.J. (2002). Friendship quality and social development. *Current Directions in Psychological Science, 11*(1), 7–10.

Berndt, T.J., & Keefe, K. (1995). Friends' influence on adolescents' adjustment to school. *Child Development, 66*(5), 1312–1329.

Białecka-Pikul, M., Kołodziejczyk, A., & Bosacki, S. (2017). Advanced theory of mind in adolescence: Do age, gender and friendship style play a role? *Journal of Adolescence, 56*, 145–156. doi:10.1016/j.adolescence.2017.02.009.

Blieszner, R., & Roberto, K.A. (2003). Friendship across the life span: Reciprocity in individual and relationship development. In F.R. Lang & K.L. Fingerman (Eds.), *Growing Together: Personal Relationships across the Life Span* (pp. 159–182). Cambridge: Cambridge University Press.

Bosacki, S., & Wilde Astington, J. (1999). Theory of mind in preadolescence: Relations between social understanding and social competence. *Social Development, 8*(2), 237–255.

Brendgen, M., Markiewicz, D., Doyle, A.B., & Bukowski, W.M. (2001). The relations between friendship quality, ranked-friendship preference, and adolescents' behavior with their friends. *Merrill-Palmer Quarterly, 47*, 395–415.

Brown, J.R., Donelan-McCall, N., & Dunn, J. (1996). Why talk about mental states? The significance of children's conversations with friends, siblings, and mothers. *Child Development, 67*(3), 836–849.

Bukowski, W.M., Hoza, B., & Boivin, M. (1994). Measuring friendship quality during pre- and early adolescence: The development and psychometric properties of the friendship qualities scale. *Journal of Social and Personal Relationships, 11*(3), 471–484.

Carpendale, J.I.M., & Lewis, C. (2004). Constructing an understanding of mind: The development of children's social understanding within social interaction. *Behavioral and Brain Sciences*, *27*(1), 79–96. doi:10.1017/S0140525X04000032.

Chow, C.M., Ruhl, H., & Buhrmester, D. (2013). The mediating role of interpersonal competence between adolescents' empathy and friendship quality: A dyadic approach. *Journal of Adolescence*, *36*(1), 191–200. doi:10.1016/j.adolescence.2012.10.004.

Coie, J.D., Dodge, K.A., & Coppotelli, H. (1982). Dimensions and types of social status: A cross-age perspective. *Developmental Psychology*, *18*(4), 557–570. doi:10.1037/0012-1649.18.4.557.

Corcoran, R., Mercer, G., & Frith, C.D. (1995). Schizophrenia, symptomatology and social inference: Investigating "theory of mind" in people with schizophrenia. *Schizophrenia Research*, *17*(1), 5–13. doi:10.1016/0920-9964(95)00024-G.

Cutting, A.L., & Dunn, J. (2002). The cost of understanding other people: Social cognition predicts young children's sensitivity to criticism. *Journal of Child Psychology and Psychiatry, and Allied Disciplines*, *43*(7), 849–860. doi:10.1111/1469-7610.t01-1-00047.

Danby, S., Thompson, C., Theobald, M., & Thorpe, K. (2012). Children's strategies for making friends when starting school. *Australasian Journal of Early Childhood*, *37*(2), 63–71. doi:10.1177/183693911203700210.

Davis, M.H. (1983). Measuring individual differences in empathy: Evidence for a multidimensional approach. *Journal of Personality and Social Psychology*, *44*(1), 113.

Dunn, J., & Brophy, M. (2005). Communication, relationships, and individual differences in children's understanding of mind. In J.W. Astington & J.A. Baird (Eds.), *Why Language Matters for Theory of Mind* (pp. 50–69). New York, NY: Oxford University Press.

Dunn, J., & Cutting, A.L. (1999). Understanding others, and individual differences in friendship interactions in young children. *Social Development*, *8*(2), 201–219.

Dunn, J., Cutting, A.L., & Fisher, N. (2002). Old friends, new friends: Predictors of children's perspective on their friends at school. *Child Development*, *73*(2), 621–635. doi:10.1111/1467-8624.00427.

Dunn, J., & Herrera, C. (1997). Conflict resolution with friends, siblings, and mothers: A developmental perspective. *Aggressive Behavior*, *23*(5), 343–357.

Etel, E., & Slaughter, V. (2019). Theory of mind and peer cooperation in two play contexts. *Journal of Applied Developmental Psychology*, *60*, 87–95. doi:10.1016/j.appdev.2018.11.004.

Fink, E., Begeer, S., Hunt, C., & de Rosnay, M. (2014). False-belief understanding and social preference over the first 2 years of school: A longitudinal study. *Child Development*, *85*(6), 2389–2403. doi:10.1111/cdev.12302.

Fink, E., Begeer, S., Peterson, C.C., Slaughter, V., & de Rosnay, M. (2015). Friendlessness and theory of mind: A prospective longitudinal study. *British Journal of Developmental Psychology*, *33*(1), 1–17. doi:10.1111/bjdp.12060.

Fink, E., de Rosnay, M., Patalay, P., & Hunt, C. (2020). Early pathways to bullying: A prospective longitudinal study examining the influences of theory of mind and social preference on bullying behaviour during the first 3 years of school. *British Journal of Developmental Psychology*. doi:10.1111/bjdp.12328.

Flannery, K.M., & Smith, R.L. (2017). The effects of age, gender, and gender role ideology on adolescents' social perspective-taking ability and tendency in friendships. *Journal of Social and Personal Relationships*, *34*(5), 617–635.

Gest, S.D., Graham-Bermann, S.A., & Hartup, W.W. (2001). Peer experience: Common and unique features of number of friendships, social network centrality, and sociometric status. *Social Development*, *10*(1), 23–40.

Gibson, J.L., Fink, E., Torres, P.E., Browne, W.V., & Mareva, S. (2020). Making sense of social pretense: The effect of the dyad, sex, and language ability in a large observational study of children's behaviors in a social pretend play context. *Social Development, 29*(2), 526–543. doi:10.1111/sode.12420.

Gifford-Smith, M.E., & Brownell, C.A. (2003). Childhood peer relationships: Social acceptance, friendships, and peer networks. *Journal of School Psychology, 41*(4), 235–284.

Grotpeter, J.K., & Crick, N.R. (1996). Relational aggression, overt aggression, and friendship. *Child Development, 67*(5), 2328–2338.

Hartup, W.W. (1996). The company they keep: Friendships and their developmental significance. *Child Development, 67*(1), 1–13.

Hartup, W.W., French, D.C., Laursen, B., Johnston, M.K., & Ogawa, J.R. (1993). Conflict and friendship relations in middle childhood: Behavior in a closed-field situation. *Child Development, 64*(2), 445–454.

Howes, C. (1996). The earliest friendships. In W.M. Bukowski, A.F. Newcomb, & W.W. Hartup (Eds.), *The Company They Keep: Friendship in Childhood and Adolescence* (pp. 66–86). Cambridge, UK: Cambridge University Press.

Howes, C., & Phillipsen, L. (1992). Gender and friendship: Relationships within peer groups of young children. *Social Development, 1*(3), 230–242.

Hughes, C., & Devine, R. (2015). Individual differences in theory of mind from preschool to adolescence: Achievements and directions. *Child Development Perspectives, 9*(3), 149–153.

Hughes, C., & Dunn, J. (1997). "Pretend you didn't know": Preschoolers' talk about mental states in pretend play. *Cognitive Development, 12*(4), 477–497.

Hughes, C., & Dunn, J. (1998). Understanding mind and emotion: Longitudinal associations with mental-state talk between young friends. *Developmental Psychology, 34*(5), 1026–1037.

Hughes, C., Ensor, R., & Marks, A. (2011). Individual differences in false belief understanding are stable from 3 to 6 years of age and predict children's mental state talk with school friends. *Journal of Experimental Child Psychology, 108*(1), 96–112. doi:10.1016/j.jecp.2010.07.012.

Ladd, G.W., Kochenderfer, B.J., & Coleman, C.C. (1996). Friendship quality as a predictor of young children's early school adjustment. *Child Development, 67*(3), 1103–1118.

Ladd, G.W., & Troop-Gordon, W. (2003). The role of chronic peer difficulties in the development of children's psychological adjustment problems. *Child Development, 74*(5), 1344–1367.

Lagattuta, K.H., Sayfan, L., & Blattman, A.J. (2010). Forgetting common ground: Six- to seven-year-olds have an overinterpretive theory of mind. *Developmental Psychology, 46*(6), 1417.

Laursen, B., & Mooney, K.S. (2008). Relationship network quality: Adolescent adjustment and perceptions of relationships with parents and friends. *American Journal of Orthopsychiatry, 78*(1), 47–53.

Maguire, M.C., & Dunn, J. (1997). Friendships in early childhood, and social understanding. *International Journal of Behavioral Development, 21*(4), 669–686.

Maunder, R., & Monks, C.P. (2019). Friendships in middle childhood: Links to peer and school identification, and general self-worth. *British Journal of Developmental Psychology, 37*(2), 211–229.

McDonald, K.L., Malti, T., Killen, M., & Rubin, K.H. (2014). Best friends' discussions of social dilemmas. *Journal of Youth and Adolescence, 43*(2), 233–244. doi:10.1007/s10964-013-9961-1.

McGuire, K.D., & Weisz, J.R. (1982). Social cognition and behavior correlates of preadolescent chumship. *Child Development, 53*(6), 1478–1484.

Menzer, M.M., McDonald, K.L., Rubin, K.H., Rose-Krasnor, L., Booth-LaForce, C., & Schulz, A. (2012). Observed gossip moderates the link between anxious withdrawal and friendship quality in early adolescence. *International Journal of Developmental Science, 6*(3–4), 191–202.

Miller, S.E., Reavis, R.E., & Avila, B.N. (2018). Associations between theory of mind, executive function, and friendship quality in middle childhood. *Merrill-Palmer Quarterly, 64*(3), 397–426.

Nangle, D.W., Erdley, C.A., Newman, J.E., Mason, C.A., & Carpenter, E.M. (2003). Popularity, friendship quantity, and friendship quality: Interactive influences on children's loneliness and depression. *Journal of Clinical Child and Adolescent Psychology: The Official Journal for the Society of Clinical Child and Adolescent Psychology, American Psychological Association, Division 53, 32*(4), 546–555.

Newcomb, A.F., & Bagwell, C.L. (1995). Children's friendship relations: A meta-analytic review. *Psychological Bulletin, 117*(2), 306.

O'Farrelly, C., Booth, A., Tatlow-Golden, M., & Barker, B. (2019). Reconstructing readiness: Young children's priorities for their early school adjustment. *Early Childhood Research Quarterly*. doi:10.1016/j.ecresq.2018.12.001.

Parker, J.G., & Asher, S.R. (1993). Friendship and friendship quality in middle childhood: Links with peer group acceptance and feelings of loneliness and social dissatisfaction. *Developmental Psychology, 29*(4), 611–621.

Parker, J.G., & Gottman, J. (1989). Social and emotional development in a relational context: Friendship interaction from early childhood to adolescence. In T.J. Berndt & G.W. Ladd (Eds.), *Peer Relationships in Child Development* (pp. 95–131). New York: Wiley.

Parker, J.G., Rubin, K.H., Erath, S.A., Wojslawowicz, J.C., & Buskirk, A.A. (2006). Peer relationships, child development, and adjustment: A developmental psychopathology perspective. In D. Cicchetti & D. Cohen (Eds.), *Developmental Psychopathology: Vol 1 Theory and Method*, Vol. 1 (pp. 419–493). Hoboken, NJ: Wiley.

Pedersen, S., Vitaro, F., Barker, E.D., & Borge, A.I. (2007). The timing of middle-childhood peer rejection and friendship: Linking early behavior to early-adolescent adjustment. *Child Development, 78*(4), 1037–1051. doi:10.1111/j.1467-8624.2007.01051.x.

Peterson, C.C. & Siegal, M. (2002). Mindreading and moral awareness in popular and rejected preschoolers. *British Journal of Developmental Psychology, 20*, 205–224.

Piehler, T.F., & Dishion, T.J. (2007). Interpersonal dynamics within adolescent friendships: Dyadic mutuality, deviant talk, and patterns of antisocial behavior. *Child Development, 78*(5), 1611–1624.

Slomkowski, C., & Dunn, J. (1996). Young children's understanding of other people's beliefs and feelings and their connected communication with friends. *Developmental Psychology, 32*(3), 442–447.

Smith, P.K. (2017). Bullying and theory of mind: A review. *Current Psychiatry Reviews, 13*(2), 90–95.

Smith, R.L., & Rose, A.J. (2011). The "cost of caring" in youths' friendships: Considering associations among social perspective taking, co-rumination, and empathetic distress. *Developmental Psychology, 47*(6), 1792–1803. doi:10.1037/a0025309.

Spencer, S.V., Bowker, J.C., Rubin, K.H., Booth-LaForce, C., & Laursen, B. (2013). Similarity between friends in social information processing and associations with positive friendship quality and conflict. *Merrill-Palmer Quarterly, 59*(1), 106–131.

Taylor, M., & Carlson, S.M. (1997). The relation between individual differences in fantasy and theory of mind. *Child Development, 68*(3), 436–455.

Wentzel, K.R., Barry, C.M., & Caldwell, K.A. (2004). Friendships in middle school: Influences on motivation and school adjustment. *Journal of Educational Psychology, 96*(2), 195.

Wentzel, K.R., & Caldwell, K. (1997). Friendships, peer acceptance, and group membership: Relations to academic achievement in middle school. *Child Development, 68*(6), 1198–1209.

Werebe, M.G., & Baudonniere, P.-M. (1991). Social pretend play among friends and familiar preschoolers. *International Journal of Behavioral Development, 14*(4), 411–428.

Youngblade, L.M., Park, K.A., & Belsky, J. (1993). Measurement of young children's close friendship: A comparison of two independent assessment systems and their associations with attachment security. *International Journal of Behavioral Development, 16*(4), 563–587.

7 Theory of mind and peer relationships in middle childhood and adolescence

Sandra Bosacki

This chapter explores theoretical and empirical considerations about the reciprocal relations between the ability to understand mental states of oneself and others, or theory of mind (ToM), and peer relationships during middle childhood and adolescence. More specifically, I will outline mostly social contextual factors that influence the developmental connections between ToM and social behavior, specifically peer relations, during middle childhood and adolescence. Finally, I will outline research that supports the claim that children's and adolescents' ToM abilities are developed in part through interactions that occur among mainly cognitive, emotional, and social-cultural factors.

Importance of peer relations in childhood and adolescence

Why study peer relations in childhood and adolescence? Middle childhood and adolescence are a time when children become more cooperative in relationships, as they become increasingly cognizant of the need to establish and maintain friendly, cooperative, and collaborative exchanges with their peers (Steinhoff & Keller, 2020). Developmental research suggests that for social-cultural and psycho-biological reasons, peer relations become increasingly important into later childhood and adolescence (Bagwell & Bukowski, 2018). Regarding the development of attachment relations, as children enter middle childhood, the emphasis of relationships tends to shift from mainly child–parent relations to peer–peer relations (Adler & Adler, 1998; Bandura, 1986). Studies also suggest that there is a heightened sensitivity to sociocultural signals in one's environment about gender-role stereotypes such as the emphasis on kindness in girls and independence in boys (Blakemore, 2018; Yun 2020). Finally, past research illustrates that changes in the body that accompany puberty may underlie advances in social-cognitive and emotional skills such as inhibitory control, emotion recognition, and compassion for self and others (Greenspan & Deardorff, 2014; Theodoraki et al., 2020).

Children's peer culture (i.e., shared actions, symbols, communicative practices) provides a fertile context to study ToM and peer relations throughout middle childhood and adolescence (Bosacki, 2016). Peer relationships expand as children participate in increased social interactions with same- and opposite-gender peers (Furman, 1996). For both same- and opposite-gender classmates (Adler & Adler, 1998), power dynamics among peers also begin to shift due to competing motives and needs (Artingter et al., 2014;). Given the increasingly complex social rules, rules of decorum, and patterns of communication (Bosacki, 2016; Ronchi et al., 2020), children and adolescents continue to develop their socio-communicative abilities, and also understand what it means to feel lonely in that one can be surrounded by others but feel alone (Spithoven et al., 2017). Studies show that within the context of peer relations, ToM skills can be used to pursue both self-interest and prosocial goals depending on the motives of the child (Doeyneus, 2017).

In addition to the increased importance of peer relationships, during middle childhood and adolescence, times of solitude and personal free time also increase (Eggum-Wiliams et al., 2019). Together with an increase in self-consciousness and self-focus (Blakemore, 2018), such times of aloneness provide opportunities for reflection and contemplation (Eggum-Williams et al., 2019; Owen & Willoughby, 2020), but also for rumination and possible feelings of loneliness, as well as envy of others (Coplan et al., 2019). The increase in cognitive abilities to compare oneself to others and also to reflect and focus on one's thoughts, emotions, and motives enables older children and adolescents to use ToM as a tool to either act prosocially and create social affiliations, or use their ToM to manipulate others and serve their needs (Bosacki et al., 2019). For example, dependent upon their social motives (i.e., to either help self or others), an older child or adolescent with advanced ToM skills may use their ability to either act altruistically to benefit others or act selfishly to use their skills to plan revenge or ways to manipulate others for personal gains (Viding & McCory, 2019). Compared with early childhood, this combination of increased proficiency in ToM skills (Hughes & Devine, 2015), the increase in self-focus and social comparison (Sommerville, 2013), complexity in peer relations (Rivenbark et al., 2019), and increased time alone make the study of relations between ToM and peer relationships in childhood and adolescence particularly fascinating.

Measurement of peer relations

A major challenge that continues to exist for researchers is how to measure accurately the complexity of peer relations during childhood and adolescence. Most commonly, studies include perceptions of children's peer relations, such as questions that focus on how one prefers to spend time (i.e., either with others or alone), peer nominations where children select the children they prefer most and least in a specific social setting (e.g., the classroom), and also reciprocated friendships (e.g. list the top three children in your class that you would like to spend time with) (Rubin et al., 2006). Sociometrics also include peer ratings of peer status and reputation, including popularity, as such ratings can be collected by teachers or peers (Fu et al., 2016; Rivenbark et al., 2019). In addition to peer reports, in middle childhood, especially during the later years of elementary school that involve students being in close contact with their teachers for the majority of the school year, teacher reports as well as parent reports are also often used as a measure of peer relations (Hipson et al., 2019; Slaughter et al., 2015; Smith et al., 2018).

As relationships continue to grow in complexity throughout middle childhood and into adolescence (Corsano et al., 2020), researchers can focus on self-report measures that explore the more subtle psychological and emotional aspects of peer relations. For example, some studies measure how peers perceive the quality of attachment or emotional closeness of their relationships with their peers, such as whether or not they consider a peer their best friend (indicating high or strong attachment), or a casual acquaintance (indicating low or weak attachment) (Białecka-Pikul et al., 2017; McElwain et al., 2019). In addition, compared with early childhood, measurements of peer relations in adolescence often use narrative and open-ended tasks such as drawings and stories (e.g. draw a picture of someone bullying in school) (Bosacki et al., 2006, 2012), as well as more detailed stories about perceptions of qualities of friendship and peer interactions (Bosacki et al., 2019; Peplak et al., 2020).

Theory of mind and peer relations: Theoretical accounts

Theoretical models of development emphasize the role social life and interactions play in social-cognitive skills such as ToM, emotion recognition, and self-awareness or insight (Bandura, 1999; Tudge & Winterhoff, 1993). Theory of mind is thought to play a key role in social interactions and is viewed as necessary for the formation of adaptive relationships, particularly during middle childhood and adolescence (Bosacki et al., 2019; Caputi et al., 2012, 2020; Crick & Dodge, 1994). As social-cognitive skills further develop as children mature, more advanced ToM ability is often referred to as including a combination of skills such as social reasoning skills, emotion recognition, recognition of ambiguity, and social transgressions such as faux pas (Couette et al., 2020; Hughes & Devine, 2015; Osterhaus et al., 2016).

Although many theories to date try to explain the connections between ToM and social interactions among youth, current ToM studies tend to focus on the following three. First, social-constructivist theory predicts that social experiences help children to develop and hone their ToM skills (Caputi et al., 2020; Carpendale & Lewis, 2015). Such theories predict that cooperative and prosocial interactions such as helping and comforting others may lead to high levels of ToM skills (Beauchamp & Anderson, 2010). Second, social outcomes theorists argue that skilled mindreaders, due to their social information processing abilities, are better at building social relationships and more secure friendships (Crick & Dodge, 1994; Spithoven et al., 2017). That is, this theory suggests that researchers should investigate children's performance on ToM tasks as a way of investigating the cognitive roots of sociability and social withdrawal. For example, a longitudinal study showed that at age five, low levels of ToM predicted chronic friendlessness at age seven, and suggested that ToM development plays a role in how children form and maintain reciprocal friendships (Fink et al., 2015; Wellman, 2015).

Finally, the third theory is a combination of the two that suggests ToM and peer relations are linked due to some other common factor. That is, such theoretical models predict that the ToM–peer relations link may also be affected indirectly by self-cognitions and self-affect (Bosacki et al., 2000, 2019), genetic influences such as temperament (DiLalla & John, 2020), or other aspects of personality such as conscientiousness or narcissism (Artinger et al., 2014), or social motivations (Doenyeus, 2017). External influences such as exposure to teachers', parents', media's, and religion's attitudes towards social-moral behavior have also been found to influence relations between ToM and peer relations (Roberts et al., 2020; Van Doesum et al., 2013).

For example, studies that illustrate the indirect influence of other factors on ToM and peer relations show that children with high levels of ToM and social anxiety may misinterpret social events that appear ambiguous or difficult to read (Nikolić et al., 2019). Other studies show that some adolescents who experience social anxiety but are skilled at reading social cues may also be overly sensitive to the disrespect or judgment of others, and use more aggressive or spiteful strategies and retaliation (McDonald & Asher, 2018). Such misinterpretations may lead to miscommunication among peers and have a negative influence on friendship formation (Nikolić et al., 2019). Finally, studies with adolescents show that the combination of high levels of ToM and low self-worth may also have negative outcomes in terms of feeling lonely or the desire for social connection (Bosacki et al., 2019), lower levels of social competence and self-compassion (Bosacki et al., 2018), social anxiety, and perceptions of peer acceptance (Bosacki, 2000; Nikolić et al., 2019).

On the one hand, studies with children and adolescents show that successful peer interactions require friendlier, kinder, and more self-regulated prosocial actions such as sharing, cooperation, and feelings of gratitude (Bosacki et al., 2018; Slaughter et al., 2015; Viana et al., 2020). However, on the other hand, peer relationships provide a valuable context for practicing and learning ToM-related skills such as deception and the concealment of social or selfish motivations (Banerjee et al., 2011; Jones et al., 2010; Sutton et al., 1999b; Sutton & Keough, 2000; Williams et al., 2016), conflict resolution, and negotiation (Tomasello, 2000). In other words, peer relationships at school may provide a social context that shapes and/or is shaped by ToM and emotional understanding skills because it requires the coordination of different perspectives and emotions (Carpendale & Lewis, 2015; Kwan et al., 2015; van Ryzin & Roseth, 2019).

Recently, Foster et al. (2020) applied moral disengagement theory to explore how children justified deception and found that boys were more likely than girls to express moral disengagement within the classroom (see Foster et al., 2019 for a review of moral disengagement theory). Therefore, more research is needed to link ToM skills and moral reasoning to prosocial and anti-social behavior as researchers try to understand how gender and culture play a role in the existing puzzles regarding the disconnect between moral cognition and moral action. Such studies may help us to make sense of how ToM plays a role in the process of children's and adolescents' moral disengagement (Minnameier, 2012; Peplak et al., 2020). In the following sections, I will outline supporting research that attempts to explore the question of how ToM relates to peer interactions (for better or worse) and how trajectories change during childhood and adolescence. To conclude, I will outline implications for future research and educational interventions to promote social-cognitive skills and the formation of compassionate, prosocial, and peaceful behaviors and supportive peer relationships.

ToM and peer relations in childhood and adolescence: Research

Compared with early childhood where ToM is important for learning how to play with others in a prosocial nature (e.g., sharing and cooperating) (Moore et al., 2011), as children approach adolescence, their social worlds grow in complexity, and their school life plays a greater role in their social and cognitive development (Lecce et al., 2019). In particular, during middle and late childhood, children's play experiences with peers and friends begin to make greater cognitive demands on their ability to engage in coordinated interactions and pretense that involves cooperation and collaborative problem-solving (Bagwell & Bukowski, 2018; Endedijk et al., 2015; van den Berg et al., 2017). At the same time, emotionally close peer relationships also satisfy social and emotional needs, which in turn contribute to prosocial behaviors and psychological wellbeing (Sullivan, 1953). For example, studies show that perceived increased emotional closeness among friends is related to higher levels of mindreading in adolescents (Białecka-Pikul et al., 2020).

Middle childhood and adolescence are also periods when children's social and communication skills continue to develop, which has implications for the ability to co-construct or negotiate a mutually agreed-upon play scenario (Cassidy et al., 2003). For example, the use of shared meanings with friends during play and leisure activities during childhood and adolescence can help to increase ToM abilities, such as learning to take the perspectives of others and recognize emotions in others (Bosacki et al., 2019). Slaughter et al. (2015) conducted a meta-analysis of 20 studies on ToM and popularity in children ages two to ten years. Results revealed higher peer-group popularity correlated moderately with higher ToM test scores. A corresponding negative relation between lower levels of ToM understanding and greater rejection by peers was also found, although of weaker absolute magnitude. This association was found at all ages within this wide range and was just as apparent when popularity was measured with either teacher or peer ratings. The majority of past studies suggest a bi-directional relation between ToM skills and peer relations (Bosacki, 2015; Carpendale & Lewis, 2004; Jenkins & Astington, 2000; Longobordi et al., 2019), in that social cognitive abilities may influence, and be influenced by, peer relationships. The following sections thus explore the dynamic interplay between ToM and peer relationships during middle childhood and adolescence.

Extant theory and research show that peer relationships are vital for psychosocial adjustment from childhood through adolescence (Bosacki, 2016; Carpendale & Lewis, 2004; Sullivan, 1953; Trivers, 1971). During middle childhood, children spend increasingly more time with their peers outside the home environment (Bagwell & Bukowski, 2018). As children make the transition from childhood to adolescence, peer relationships continue to grow in novelty, complexity, and ambiguity (Zimbardo, 1977), and become more challenging as school contexts and peer circles change (Hughes, 2011, 2016; Hughes & Leekam, 2004; Ronchi et al., 2020).

Research on theory of mind and peer relations suggests that theory of mind is socially neutral. For example, some studies show that high levels of advanced theory of mind (ToM) abilities led to social competence and prosocial behaviors and emotions such as gratitude in middle childhood and adolescents (Bosacki & Astington, 1999; Bosacki et al., 2006, 2018; Longobardi et al., 2016, 2019). However, other studies suggest that this may not always be the case. That is, some studies show that children may use their proficiency in ToM to manipulate strategically and harm others instead of acting prosocially towards them (Barlow et al., 2010; Caravita et al., 2009; Roberts et al., 2020; Sutton et al., 1999a, 1999b).

To date, researchers remain puzzled as to what kind of role (if any) ToM plays in the link between moral cognition and moral action within peer relations. That is, how do children's ToM skills such as emotion recognition and perspective-taking relate to complex moral emotional experiences including pride, humility, shame, remorse, and envy, among others? For example, one puzzle that continues to elude researchers is what role ToM skills play in the socio-emotional and cognitive processes of schadenfreude, or the happy victimizer phenomena (e.g., feeling happy when observing a peer's misfortune, or harming another peer) (Arsenio & Lover, 1995), and whether this changes across time, gender, and culture. Another conundrum that continues to baffle researchers is that current studies on ToM and peer relations assess the ability to mentalize, and not the propensity, that is, a child's motivation to consider the minds of another peer in a social situation or their will to use their skill (ToM).

In addition, such a developed ability to read others' mental states may lead to an increase in sensitivity to social cues, criticism, and negative evaluations or judgments, and feelings of loneliness (Cutting & Dunn, 2002; Gardner et al., 2005). Thus, it is an important developmental task to understand the factors that contribute to this behavioral divergence for children and adolescents with advanced ToM understanding. Such research also has significant practical implications for anti-bullying and peace-building educational programs (O'Driscoll et al., 2018; Taylor, 2020). Such research may also further the development of combinations of compassionate mindfulness programs that combine positive youth development and social-cognitive learning interventions that promote connections among moral reasoning and critical, philosophical, psychological thinking and critical action and prosocial behavior (Heberle et al., 2020; Lecce et al., 2014; Troop-Gordon & Unhjem, 2018).

Cross-sectional studies with primary school–aged children who possess advanced levels of ToM abilities show that such a propensity may be associated with divergent psychological and behavioral outcomes such as prosocial behaviors (e.g., Longibardo et al., 2019; Moore et al., 2011), whereas some longitudinal studies with school-aged children and early adolescents show that impaired ToM may lead to aggressive/bullying behaviors (e.g., Bosacki, 2015; Long & Li, 2020). Other cross-sectional studies in middle childhood find no direct connections between ToM and peer relations and social orientations such as social withdrawal and sociability (Pequet & Warnell, 2020; Van der Graaff et al., 2018).

In terms of behavioral outcomes, these have been termed 'nice ToM behaviors' such as cooperative, shared play, and 'nasty ToM behaviors' such as Machiavellianism, relational aggression, and selfish behavior. For example, school-aged children who chose to use their mentalizing abilities for prosocial purposes such as helping and caring for others (Longibardo et al., 2019) are more likely to serve as assertive and caring defenders in a school bullying scenario (Yun, 2020). In contrast, longitudinal studies have found that school-aged children may choose to use their advanced mindreading skills to engage in antisocial and aggressive behaviors such as harming and controlling others (Renouf et al., 2010). Additional studies show that children often labeled by others as prosocial, as well as those labeled as bullies or anti-social, have significantly better second-order ToM understanding than bully-victims and victims (Gasser & Keller, 2009). Cross-sectional studies with school-aged children and adolescents with conduct problems and callous-unemotional traits have also found no differences in mentalizing abilities as compared with typically developing children (O'Nions et al., 2014; Roberts et al., 2020).

In terms of psychosocial outcomes of high levels of ToM skills, the ability to recognize and understand thoughts and emotions in others may also lead to increased sensitivity to social evaluations that may be either negative (criticism) or positive (praise) (Sommerville, 2013). As children approach adolescence, they usually experience a period of social reorienting and re-adaptation, where the opinions and evaluations of peers become more valuable than those of family members (Van der Wal et al., 2017). A recent longitudinal study on social and moral reasoning skills showed that higher mental reasoning in middle childhood was related to reports of higher friendship quality in adulthood (Steinhoff & Keller, 2020).

Within peer relations, children with advanced ToM skills may also use their mindreading or intention- and emotion-recognition abilities to monitor the facial emotions and social actions of others (Qualter et al., 2013). Such skills may also foster children's abilities to imagine or fantasize about social scenarios that include their peers. For example, children who create negative or harmful fantasies may be more susceptible to periods of worry and rumination about what their peers might be thinking and saying about them. Subsequently, these children may also experience higher levels of stress and anxiety due to the imagined emotional experiences of possible threat and negative social peer evaluation (Ronchi et al., 2020).

Some researchers claim that the divergence in behavioral and psychological outcomes is too complex to be explained by a lack of moral competence, ToM, or empathy (Minnameier, 2012; Weinstein & Ryan, 2010). A combination of theories may lend themselves better to a more social-cognitive and motivational explanation – particularly if this more comprehensive approach sheds light on why some children and adolescents develop the stance of a happy victimizer (Arsenio et al., 2006; Peplak et al., 2020) and develop ill-judged, negative desires and goals (Arsenio & Lover, 1995; Krettenauer et al., 2019; Yuill et al., 1996). Furthermore, self- versus other-oriented social motivations may in part determine the proclivity of social-cognitive abilities such as ToM. In particular, such motivations may help children to decide if they will use their moral reasoning and emotional competencies in social interactions to act either for fairness and prosocial reasons (other-oriented motivation) or selfishly (self-oriented motivation), or to follow social conventions (Blake et al., 2015).

Perhaps ToM skills may help some young people to disengage morally by cognitively diverting social-moral and empathic emotions such as compassion to avoid negative feelings such as guilt or shame about manipulating others (Preckel et al., 2018). Research has yet to explore possible moderators and mediators of how and why children use ToM to influence peer relations. In addition, more studies need to explore ToM and peer relations from a social-information processing framework that suggests social actions are influenced by the understanding of one's intentions and attributions about a social situation (Crick & Dodge, 1994; Dodge & Coie, 1987). Such skills involve attributions and outcome expectancies that help young people to make sense of social events, particularly ones that remain subtle and ambiguous, particularly within the school context (Bosacki et al., 2019; Long & Li, 2020).

'Nice' Theory of Mind: Theory of Mind and prosocial behavior

Theory of mind skills, including the ability to recognize emotions in others and understand that others have different perspectives, are an essential component of the everyday life of children and adolescents (Eisenberg & Miller, 1987). Although some cross-sectional research with children shows that emotion recognition and ToM are likely to lead to increased prosocial behavior in children and adolescents (Sierksma et al., 2015), others show weak or mixed relations. For example, studies with adolescents show that high levels of ToM may not consistently lead to either more prosocial behaviors (Van der Graaff et al., 2018) or more bullying, given that the magnitude of the ToM–prosocial behavior association in meta-analyses is found to be significant but weak ($r = .19$) (Imuta et al., 2016).

Research on peer relations and bullying situations shows that children who exhibit higher levels of ToM and emotion-recognition skills are more likely to help other children and comfort the victims of a bullying situation (Van Ryzin & Roseth, 2019; Yun, 2020). In addition, studies with young children show that high levels of ToM and emotion recognition are related to high levels of peer action–coordination behaviors, including cooperative learning and sharing (Grüneisen et al., 2015; Tomasello, 1999; Viana et al., 2020). That is, children may use their ToM and emotion recognition skills to help others, solve social problems and conflicts, and be kind, honest, respectful, and equitable to others, as well as caring and supportive friends. Advanced ToM skills may also help children to develop a sense of social competence in that they may be able to decipher socially ambiguous settings, or those with incongruent emotional messages (e.g., positive verbal expression, negative facial emotional expression) (Bosacki, 2000; Morningstar et al., 2019). An improved ability to read the emotions of others may help those youth who feel rejected or ignored by their peers. A study by Morningstar et al. (2019) found that lonely teenagers showed a high ability to recognize emotion in vocalizations that suggest social affiliation or friendliness, but scored low on recognizing the expression of fear in others' voices. Thus, perhaps lonely individuals are more attuned to the positive expressions of others and either avoid or misread fear and other negative emotions such as anger in others' facial and vocal expressions. The ability to recognize emotions in faces and voices may help youth to understand friendly and positive gestures over fearful or negative ones. Future research needs to explore how such social-emotional skills may influence young people's abilities to engage in social interaction and form friendships.

'Nasty' Theory of Mind: Antisocial behavior, loneliness, and social anxiety

When children choose to use their ToM to manipulate or harm others, the ability to understand mental states in others is often accompanied by an emotional drive or need to get the quickest and most elaborate internal representations of others' mental states in social situations (Esperger & Bereczkei, 2012). Past studies show that adolescents and young adults who are high in Machiavellianism are more likely to show spontaneous mentalization (Schaefer et al., 2018), which may also serve as a motivational aspect of mindreading (DiLalla & John, 2020). However, researchers suggest that the highly developed spontaneous mentalization ability of Machiavellians may not be coupled with other elements of mentalization, such as self-insight or self-compassion (Jones & Paulhus, 2009). Such a disconnect between understanding mental states in self and others may prevent children and adolescents from recognizing their own and others' emotions.

Another cross-sectional study on mentalizing in 11- to 16-year-old boys with callous-unemotional (CU) and conduct problems (CP) found that compared with typically developing (TD) boys, CP-CU boys scored lower on advanced ToM tasks, but did not differ from the TD group in mind-mindedness or social reasoning (Roberts et al., 2020). A recent longitudinal study with 8- to 11-year-old children showed that ToM at age eight (measured using a cartoon task) was a negative predictor of teachers' ratings of relational and physical aggression at age 11 (Holl et al., 2018). In contrast, a cross-sectional study with school-aged children showed that higher levels of ToM skills measured by the understanding of the mental state of the listener when an individual makes a socially inappropriate comment or faux pas was related to lower levels of scores on Machiavellianism (Barlow et al., 2010).

Such findings suggest that although the ability to represent mental states may remain intact in terms of peer relations, some children are less likely to update mental state inferences as a function of different minds. The diverse combination of findings on ToM and peer relations in childhood and adolescence support the idea that other social-cognitive skills may or may not accompany high spontaneous mentalization such as emotion recognition, beliefs about reciprocity and aggression, social goals (relationship or reputation maintenance and regulation) (McDonald & Asher, 2018), and self-reflection (Conway et al., 2019). Such an eclectic and unbalanced social skills toolkit may help to determine if advanced mindreading leads to prosocial and pacifist or Machiavellian and revengeful outcomes (DiLalla & John, 2020; Esperger & Bereczkei, 2012; Recchia et al., 2019).

Overall, children's Machiavellian characteristics may interact with cognitive patterns to perceive social interactions in a different light than their peers, which may result in the use of ToM skills for manipulative or harmful purposes. Within such social interactions, these children are likely to be guided by self-serving interests and beneficial motivations (Doeyneus, 2017; McCombs & Marzano, 1990; Repacholi et al., 2003). Such results support past research that emphasizes how personal motivation and self-agency plays a key role in the shaping of how one uses ToM ability within social action. For example, within children's and adolescents' peer context, studies show that ToM skills may be involved in the use of humor, such as aggressive humor (e.g. irony, sarcasm, cynical hostility) (Zajączkowska & Abbot-Smith, 2020) or affiliative or friendly humor (Bosacki, 2013; Fritz, 2020). The question is, how does a child or adolescent learn how to use their ToM skills to apply humor in a kind or cruel way, and for what purpose and why? How do they acquire the skill of ToM and the will to either help or hurt others?

Researchers will need to continue to explore this question, particularly within the dynamics of best friendships and the larger peer culture. There is a need to find measures that distinguish between those who are unaware that they offend or hurt others and those who are aware that they are hurtful, but do not care enough, or lack the desire to modify their beliefs and behaviors (Preckel et al., 2018). As McElwain et al. (2019) suggest, future research needs to explore how parent–child attachments affect ToM and friendships, especially given that children who were securely attached to their mothers were more likely than insecurely attached children to use their ToM skills in prosocial ways. Teacher–student relationships have also been shown to influence peer interactions in middle childhood, as a recent cross-sectional study found a positive link between conflictual teacher–student attachment and anti-social peer relations (Baroncelli & Ciucci, 2020). A recent cross-sectional study also shows increased levels of adolescents' psychological school engagement related to increased levels of ToM skills (Bosacki et al., 2019). Given the complexity of peer–peer and teacher–student relationships within the school context, more work is needed to understand how school-level norms of psychosocial behavior and overall school climate influence ToM development in children and adolescents (Schacter & Juvonen, 2018).

Being skilled in ToM may also lead to peer recognition in terms of popularity (Closson & Watanabe, 2018). For example, past studies suggest that children who are approved of and perceived by their peers as 'cool' may demonstrate social savviness or high levels of ToM (Jamison et al., 2015). That is, studies show that such children may be attuned to relational aggressive characteristics that include the ability to interpret and value the mental state of the peer group as a whole (rather than the emotional state of one's best friend) (Bloustien, 2003). This ability may help children judged as 'cool' to maintain social status such as popularity, as peer relations and coolness are in flux during preadolescence (Adler & Adler, 1998; Wilson & Jamison, 2019).

As discussed earlier, ToM skills may also enable children and adolescents to feel complex, moral emotions such as schadenfreude, which may play a role in peer relations (Peplak et al., 2020). Past studies show that children as young as four and five years understand and experience schadenfreude within peer relations (Schulz et al., 2013), particularly when one has a desire or goal to harm another (van Dijk et al., 2011; Yuill et al., 1996). Studies also show that feelings of schadenfreude impair social relationships in that high levels of schadenfreude (as opposed to sympathy and compassion) lead to fewer helping behaviors (Schulz et al., 2013). Further, studies show that negative self-conscious feelings, such as jealousy and schadenfreude, may be damaging to interpersonal relationships (McDonald & Asher, 2018; Peplak et al., 2020), and suggest the need for future research on links between social-cognitive factors and self-conscious feelings, particularly within the social context of the classroom.

Moderating influences on Theory of Mind and peer relationships

Past studies on gender-influenced social cognition and peer relations suggest a complex interaction of endogenous (hormones) and exogenous factors (social experiences from peers, parents, teachers) influence how gender plays a role in social-cognitive development (Baroncelli & Ciucci, 2020; Białecka-Pikul et al., 2017; Card et al., 2008). In studies of gender differences in ToM and perceptions of friendship, significant gender differences are often reported in empathic concern and prosocial behavior (Bosacki et al., 2006; Białecka-Pikul et al., 2020), with girls outperforming boys in childhood and adolescence (Smith et al., 2018; Van der Graaff et al., 2014). Studies also show that the positive influence of empathic concern, perspective-taking, and language ability on prosocial behavior was stronger among boys than among girls (Hipson et al., 2019; Longobardi et al., 2016). However, compared with boys, longitudinal studies also find that girls obtain higher levels of empathy and prosocial behaviors across childhood and adolescence (Bosacki et al., 2019; Van der Graaff, 2018).

In the meta-analysis by Imuta et al. (2016), the relation between ToM and prosocial behavior was stronger in girls than in boys – although it reached the significance level in both groups. However, over the past decade, researchers have cautioned against studies focused on gender-related differences, and advise researchers to switch focus to gender similarities as well as gender-role orientations (Bosacki et al., 2019; Hyde, 2005; Nielson et al., 2020). For example, in a cross-sectional study of early adolescents, irrespective of self-identified gender, participants who scored high on perceived stereotypical feminine gender orientation and low on perceived self-worth scored the highest in advanced ToM tasks, although received the lowest peer-ratings of social competence (Bosacki, 2000). In addition, as an alternative to using stereotypes such as gender or ethnicity for grouping variables, future studies could conduct group difference analysis with personality characteristics, and to capture gender fluidity in children and adolescents, more nuanced identifications of gender (Long & Li, 2020; Sellers et al., 1998). For example, to investigate individual differences in children's ToM skills, friendship experiences, and prosocial behavior, researchers could group children according to their level of social orientations or preferences (e.g., social withdrawal or social approach), and then explore the influence of gender and cultural context (Bosacki et al., 2020 under review; Nikolić et al., 2019). Thus, as Yun (2020) suggests, to investigate gender-related differences in ToM and peer relations, perhaps researchers need to change the emphasis to 'which girls and which boys' instead of 'girls versus boys'.

Regarding ToM and peer relations, studies suggest that the direction of children's and adolescents' social and moral cognitions and motivations vary across genders and cultural contexts (Long & Li, 2020; McGuire et al., 2018). For example, Barlow et al. (2010) found that for 8- to 11-year-old children, advanced ToM as measured by faux pas understanding, but not false belief understanding (FBU), was negatively related to Machiavellianism. In addition, results showed that compared with girls, boys with high levels of ToM were more likely to engage in Machiavellian strategies such as emotion manipulation to achieve their goals. Such a finding suggests that compared with girls, boys were more likely to use their advanced mindreading or intention recognition to take advantage of their peers (Barlow et al., 2010).

Further, only the children with high levels of faux pas understanding, and not false belief understanding, were more likely to report Machiavellian characteristics. Accordingly, different aspects of mental state understanding may be differentially involved in Machiavellianism and bullying. Such speculations require future research to explore this issue further with adolescents, particularly in relation to theories that try to link together moral thought and action. For example, the social-cognitive process of moral disengagement allows children to justify morally unacceptable actions without feeling guilt, shame, or self-condemnation (Bandura, 2016).

Gender may also play a role in the associations between children's Machiavellian characteristics and their play with their peers. Currently, sex differences research remains mixed and contradictory in that some studies find no gender-related differences in the links between ToM and prosocial play and antisocial behavior and bullying (Gasser & Keller, 2009; Gini, 2006; Holl et al., 2018; Leach et al., 2019; Lecce et al., 2019; McElwain et al., 2019; Yun, 2020). In contrast, some studies show that in early and middle childhood, boys engage in more frequent rough and tumble (R&T) play than girls, which includes a balance between cooperation and competition that may be a precursor to aggression and conflict in adolescence (Kung et al., 2018; Lew-Levy et al., 2020). Studies also show that compared with boys, in middle childhood, girls who are more competent in ToM, affective empathy, and emotion regulation are less likely to manipulate their peers (Barlow et al., 2010; Hipson et al., 2019) and more likely to cooperate with others (Viana et al., 2020). This distinction is also important for the play and relational/indirect aggression literature, where relational or social aggression and social dramatic and pretend play is mostly associated with girls (Leach et al., 2019).

Cultural experiences may also influence social cognition and peer relations in childhood and adolescence. For example, past studies show that collectivistic and interdependent cultures facilitate perspective-taking and empathy more than individualistic and independent cultures (Lu et al., 2008). Other studies found that Chinese children and youth show more of an other-oriented bias, whereas European youth show an egocentric or self-oriented bias (Kwan et al., 2015). In addition, some studies show that often children from collectivistic countries (e.g., China, Korea) score higher on ToM measures than children from individualistic cultures (e.g., the United States) (Tomasello, 2000; Wellman & Liu, 2004).

Possible reasons for such contradictory gender- and culture-related findings among ToM and peer relations could include a lack of gender- and culturally-sensitive measures to examine the multidimensional aspect of advanced ToM abilities and complex peer relationships during older childhood and adolescence (Long & Li, 2020). Another possible reason could be the absence of gender- and culturally-specific analyses, where the patterns may differ across genders as well as cultural and socio-economical contexts (Yun, 2020). A third possible reason could be due to changing definitions of gender and cultural identity, and ways to measure the influence of one's gender-role orientation, and gender and cultural identity on ToM abilities. In any case, further research needs to explore the intersectionality of gender, culture, and socioeconomic status in the links between ToM and peer relations (Nielson et al., 2020).

Implications

Interventions are needed to teach children how to apply their ToM skills to the peer context in prosocial and meaningful ways. For example, programs that highlight the importance of emotion recognition and regulation, affective empathy, and compassion could strengthen social decision-making abilities. Such learned skills may lead to prosocial behaviors and the formation and maintenance of caring and supportive friendships. Such interventions that draw on extant social-cognitive behavioral and compassion-focused mindfulness programs may present other outlets for students to enact their self-oriented motivations that are less harmful to those around them (Clear et al., 2019).

Programs that focus on perspective-taking, emotion recognition, self-awareness, and regulation may help children and adolescents to develop conflict negotiation and social problem-solving skills (McCombs & Marzano, 1990; Taylor, 2020). Such programs may be especially valuable for children and adolescents, particularly those who are sensitive to social judgment and social anxiety–prone (Jungert & Perrin, 2019). Such programs could include cooperative learning activities such as group role-play, 'think-aloud' activities, brainstorming, and explicit instruction in social problem-solving, social coordination, or peer action coordination (Van Ryzin & Roseth, 2019; Viana et al., 2020) and emotional recognition and regulation (Van Loan et al., 2019).

Future studies need to study the many uses of ToM in social settings across cultures and longitudinally – from early childhood through to early adulthood. Studies also need to combine multiple methods including the use of more qualitative and narrative tasks such as asking children and adolescents to describe what bullying and friendship mean to them either in written and/or graphic form, and how they would think, feel, and act in bullying and friendship scenarios (Bosacki et al., 2006; McAdams & McLean, 2013). Such multi-method explorations may help researchers to understand how children and adolescents use ToM skills as a social tool to either help or harm others and lead to disturbances in children's and adolescents' socio-cognitive abilities (advanced or deficit).

Theory of mind as a double-edged sword in real-world social functioning may influence children and adolescents to either approach others and be sociable, or fear and avoid or confront others in social situations. Early prevention or intervention efforts need to target peer aggression, as well as loneliness and social anxiety, and focus on children's ToM abilities such as perspective-taking and emotion recognition (Jungert & Perrin, 2019; Hipson et al., 2019; Koerber & Osterhaus, 2019; Ronchi et al., 2020). For example, emotional literacy programs, such as those that encourage students to read fiction novels and films and consider the perspectives and emotions of novel characters, may help to promote ToM ability skills and promote prosocial peer relations and social functioning (Bosacki et al., 2019; Caputi et al., 2020; Longobardi et al., 2019). Developmental conflict resolution and peace-building programs (Taylor, 2020) that focus on helping intentions and acts of kindness, cooperation, and respect may also be of use in helping to strengthen ToM skills in middle childhood and adolescence (O'Driscoll et al., 2018).

Alternatively, for students with advanced mindreading, activities could focus on tackling the tendency to over-focus and engage in ruminative, or excessive mindreading. Teachers could create activities that focus on how to cope with heightened self-consciousness, low self-worth or value, and sensitivity to others' opinions. Most importantly, as influential role-models and emotional socializers, teachers can provide verbal and non-verbal examples of emotion management, thoughtfulness, compassion, and prosocial behavior in the classroom (Baroncelli & Ciucci, 2020). For example, in the day-to-day school routine and student-teacher conversations, teachers can use mental state language throughout the day and also encourage students to do so by means of a personal reflective journal on one's learning journey. Drawings, comics, and personal written narratives can also be used to assess students' mental reasoning abilities (e.g., ToM, mind-mindedness, emotion recognition) (Bosacki et al., 2019; Holl et al., 2018; Recchia et al., 2019; Vendeville et al., 2018) and perceptions of bullying and friendship experiences (Bosacki et al., 2006). Such psychological language, or the verbalization of epistemic cognition within the classroom, may provide direct scaffolding of children's and adolescents' mentalistic understanding of social situations, which in turn may promote epistemic volition or the will to engage in prosocial peer relations (Kerwer et al., 2020).

Future questions and conclusions

Given these complexities, the question remains as to why the socio-communicative and moral developmental trajectories of children with either high or low levels of ToM diverge, and how such trajectories change according to age, gender, and culture – especially during the approach to adolescence. For example, why do studies show a divergence in the links between ToM skills and social-moral behavior within the peer context? Why are there so few longitudinal studies on ToM and peer relations that examine the influence of culture, social status, and gender, and the intersectionality among all three?

In sum, as reviewed in the previous sections, the emergent and contradictory status of research on social cognition and social behavior in middle childhood and adolescence suggests that ToM is a double-edged sword in terms of peer relations. That is, high levels of ToM skills may promote bonds with peers, as high levels of ToM and emotion recognition skills may increase the desire to connect and heighten attention to social cues, and may promote bonding within an established pair (or group) (Morningstar et al., 2019). In addition, studies with adolescents show that ToM may affect the need for solitude or being alone, which may be accompanied by feelings of shyness and loneliness or a perceived lack of emotional connections with others (Bosacki et al., 2019). Alternatively, ToM may also relate to feelings of loneliness, or an emotional craving to be away from others and to reconnect with oneself (Coplan et al., 2019).

The complex connections between ToM and social orientations may add to the ongoing debate of whether or not higher levels of ToM and higher levels of social maladjustment are explained by either the deficit (i.e., low ToM leads to higher aggression, feelings of loneliness) or hypersensitivity model (i.e., high ToM leads to over-sensitivity to others' judgments and evaluations, which leads to higher levels of aggression and feelings of loneliness) (Bosacki et al., 2019; Devine & Hughes, 2013). As mentioned earlier, given the diverse and eclectic mix of skills involved with mentalization and the role they play in peer relations, with ToM and social moral reasoning having mixed relations, researchers need to carefully unravel how and why some children excel in some skills and perhaps have deficits in others that may affect their social action accordingly. Future studies need to explore how children and adolescents learn the multiple dimensions of ToM, and the social motivations underlying how and why they decide to use such skills to help, harm, or ignore others (Bosacki et al., 2019; Doeynus et al., 2017). Building on past studies with younger children that showed links between ToM and reticent or onlooker behavior in social play (Moore et al., 2011), studies in middle childhood and adolescence need to explore the role of ToM in the nuanced social behaviors involved in peer relations such as competition, conflict, and revenge among peers and best friends (Recchia et al., 2019), social initiative or assertiveness, and social reticence or wariness.

Overall, researchers need to continue to explore the role of genetic, neurobiological, and social-cultural factors associated with ToM development, emotion regulation, and prosocial and antisocial behavior among children and adolescents. An increase in cross-cultural, longitudinal, and person-centered studies are needed to examine the complex relations between ToM and peer relations as individuals journey through childhood and adolescence. To explore the complex within-subject differences, researchers should also take a more person-centered approach to explore how individual patterns change in ToM skills in connection with peer relations and social orientations (Hassan et al., 2020).

To explain the mechanisms underlying the ToM development and peer relationships of children and adolescents, future research could also explore the role that social motivations (approach or avoid others) and emotional knowledge play in young people's social cognition and peer relations. Researchers could explore what role other social-cognitive skills such as mind-mindedness (i.e., the belief that others are intentional agents with mental states), social mindfulness (Bosacki et al., 2018; Clear et al., 2019), and executive function (i.e., planning, cognitive flexibility) play in children's and adolescents' social decision-making processes (Devine & Hughes, 2014; Lecce et al., 2019; Pequet & Warnell, 2020).

More specifically, what role do goals and emotional sensitivity play in gender- and culturally informed developmental patterns in the links among social reasoning, self-awareness, and prosocial and harmful behavior with one's peers? Studies with preschool and school-aged children suggest links between ToM and social functioning and wellbeing (Caputi et al., 2017; Devine et al., 2016; Jenkins & Astington, 2000). More elaborate training studies with older children and adolescents would also be useful to examine whether the links between ToM and social competence are bi-directional or asymmetrical (i.e., early ToM leads to later success in social functioning but not vice versa) (Lecce et al., 2019). Such experimental studies will help researchers test if changes in ToM performance can change peer relations and friendships in real-life situations (Wellman, 2015).

Building on past training studies that use conversation-based training in ToM with middle-school children (Caputi et al., 2020; Lecce et al., 2014; Lecce & Bianco, 2018) to promote prosocial peer relations, training studies that aim to develop ToM skills can incorporate discussing and writing about intentional kind acts with self and peers (Harwood & Kocovski, 2017), reading and writing fiction, viewing silent films and cartoons followed by discussion (Devine & Hughes, 2013), viewing and creating art (Zabelina et al., 2020), and engaging in dramatic arts (Goldstein & Winner, 2012). Other training studies could incorporate tasks that include listening to peers and 'eavesdropping' on gossip (Caivano et al., 2020) or other peer social conversations, which would also be useful (Gola, 2012), as well as the incorporation of online or remote social interactions such as engagement with social media.

Such a research agenda will require collaborations with educators, neurobiologists, and neuroscientists across the globe to co-create developmentally appropriate interdisciplinary and inclusive psychoeducational programs that address ToM skills and peer relations. In sum, future research on ToM and peer relations will enrich our understanding of the fluid and multi-faceted nature of peer relations during childhood and adolescence by discovering more nuanced and hidden features of the peer ecology.

References

Adler, P., & Adler, P. (1998). *Peer Power: Preadolescent Culture and Identity*. New Brunswick, NJ: Rutgers University Press.

Arsenio, W.F., Gold, J., & Adams, E. (2006). Children's conceptions and displays of moral emotions. In M. Killen & J.G. Smetana (Eds.), *Handbook of Moral Development* (pp. 581–609). Erlbaum, NJ: Mahwah.

Arsenio, W.F., & Lover, A. (1995). Children's conceptions of sociomoral affect: Happy victimizers, mixed emotions, and other expectancies. In M. Killen &D. Hart (Eds.), *Morality in Everyday Life: Developmental Perspectives* (pp. 87–128). New York, NY: Cambridge University Press.

Artinger, F., Exadaktylos, F., Koppel, H., & Sääksvuori, L. (2014). In others' shoes: Do individual differences in empathy and theory of mind shape social preferences? *PLOS ONE*, *9*(4), e92844. doi:10.1371/journal.pone.0092844

Bagwell, C.L., & Bukowski, W.M. (2018). Friendship in childhood and adolescence: Features, effects, and processes. In W.M. Bukowski, B. Laursen, & K.H. Rubin (Eds.), *Handbook of Peer Interactions, Relationships, and Groups* (2nd ed.) (pp. 371–390). New York, NY: Guilford.

Bandura, A. (1986). *Social Foundations of Thought and Action: A Social Cognitive Theory.* Englewood Cliffs, NJ: Prentice-Hall.

Bandura, A. (1999). Social cognitive theory: An agentic perspective. *Asian Journal of Social Psychology, 2*, 21–41.

Bandura, A. (2016). *Moral Disengagement: How People Do Harm and Live with Themselves.* New York City, NY: Worth Publishers.

Banerjee, R., Watling, D., & Caputi, M. (2011). Peer relations and the understanding of faux pas: Longitudinal evidence for bidirectional associations. *Child Development, 82*(6), 1887–1905. doi:10.1111/j.1467-8624.2011.01669.x

Barlow, A., Qualter, P., & Stylianou, M. (2010). Relationships between Machiavellianism, emotional intelligence and theory of mind in children. *Personality and Individual Differences, 48*(1), 78–82. doi:10.1016/j.paid.2009.08.021

Baroncelli, A., & Ciucci, E. (2020). Bidirectional effects between callous-unemotional traits and student-teacher relationship quality among middle school students. *Journal of Abnormal Child Psychology.* doi:10.1007/s10802-019-00595-6

Beauchamp, M., & Anderson, V. (2010). SOCIAL: An integrative framework for the development of social skills. *Psychological Bulletin, 136*(1), 39–64.

Białecka-Pikul, M., Kołodziejczyk, A., & Bosacki, S. (2017). Advanced theory of mind in adolescence: Do age, gender and friendship style play a role? *Journal of Adolescence, 56*, 145–156.

Białecka-Pikul, M., Szpak, M., Zubek, J., Bosacki, S., & Kołodziejczyk, A. (2020). The psychological self and advanced theory of mind in adolescence. *Self and Identity, 19*(1), 85–104. doi:10.1080/15298868.2018.1538900

Blake, P.R., McAuliffe, K., Corbit, J., Callaghan, T.C., Barry, O., Bowie, A., … & Warneken, F. (2015). The ontogeny of fairness in seven societies. *Nature, 528*(7581), 258–261. doi:10.1038/nature15703

Blakemore, S.-J. (2018). *Inventing Ourselves: The Secret Life of the Teenage Brain.* New York: Doubleday.

Bloustien, G. (2003). *Girl Making: A Cross-Cultural Ethnography on the Processes of Growing Up Female.* New York, NY: Berghahn Books.

Bosacki, S. (2000). Theory of mind and self-concept in preadolescents: Links with gender and language. *Journal of Educational Psychology, 92*(4), 709–717.

Bosacki, S. (2013). A longitudinal study of children's theory of mind, self-concept, and perceptions of humor in self and other. *Social Behavior and Personality: An International Journal, 41*(4), 663–674.

Bosacki, S. (2015). Children's theory of mind, self-perceptions, and peer relations: A longitudinal study. *Infant and Child Development, 24*(2), 175–188. doi:10.1002/icd.1878

Bosacki, S. (2016). *Social Cognition in Middle Childhood and Adolescence: Integrating the Personal, Social, and Educational Lives of Young People.* Oxford, UK: Wiley Publications.

Bosacki, S., & Astington, J.W. (1999). Theory of mind in preadolescence: Relations between social understanding and social competence. *Social Development, 8*(2), 237–255. doi:10.1111/1467-9507.00093

Bosacki, S., Harwood, D., & Sumaway, C. (2012). Being mean: Children's gendered perceptions of peer teasing within the classroom. *Journal of Moral Education, 41*(4), 473–489. doi:10.1080/03057240.2012.690728

Bosacki, S., Marini, Z., & Dane, A. (2006). Voices from the classroom: Pictorial and narrative representations of children's bullying experiences. *Journal of Moral Education, 35*(2), 231–245.

Bosacki, S., Moreira, F., Sitnik, V., Andrews, K., & Talwar, V. (2019). Theory of mind, emotion knowledge, and school engagement in emerging adolescents. *International Electronic Journal of Elementary Education, 11*(5), 529–538.

Bosacki, S., Moreira, F.P., Sitnik, V., Andrews, K., & Talwar, V. (2020). Theory of mind, self-knowledge, and perceptions of loneliness in emerging adolescents. *Journal of Genetic Psychology*, 181(1), 14–31. doi:10.1080/00221325.2019.1687418

Bosacki, S., Sitnik, V., Dutcher, K., & Talwar, V. (2018). Gratitude, social cognition, and well-being in emerging adolescents. *The Journal of Genetic Psychology*. doi:10.1080/00221325.2018.1499607

Bosacki, S., Sitnik, V., Moreira, F., & Talwar, V. (2019). Emerging adolescents' theory of mind and perceptions of self and play. Symposium paper presented at the biennial meeting of the Society for Research in Child Development. Baltimore, MD.

Caivano, O., Leduc, K., & Talwar, V. (2020). When is gossiping wrong? The influence of valence and relationships on children's moral evaluations of gossip. *British Journal of Developmental Psychology*. doi:10.1111/bjdp.12319

Caputi, M., Cugnata, F., & Brombin, C. (2020). Theory of mind and loneliness: Effects of a conversation-based training at school. *International Journal of Psychology: Journal International de Psychologie*. doi:10.1002/ijop.12707

Caputi, M., Lecce, S., Pagnin, A., & Banerjee, R. (2012). Longitudinal effects of theory of mind on later peer relations: The role of prosocial behavior. *Developmental Psychology, 48*(1), 257–270. doi:10.1037/a0025402

Caputi, M., Pantaleo, G., & Scaini, S. (2017). Do feelings of loneliness mediate the relationship between sociocognitive understanding and depressive symptoms during late childhood and early adolescence? *The Journal of Genetic Psychology, 178*(4), 207–216. doi:10.1080/00221325.2017.1317629

Caravita, S.C.S., Di Blasio, P., & Salmivalli, C. (2009). Unique and interactive effects of empathy and social status on involvement in bullying. *Social Development, 18*(1), 140–163. doi:10.1111/j.1467-9507.2008.00465.x

Card, N.A., Stucky, B.D., Sawalani, G.M., & Little, T.D. (2008). Direct and indirect aggression during childhood and adolescence: A meta-analytic review of gender differences, intercorrelations, and relations to maladjustment. *Child Development, 79*(5), 1185–1229. doi:10.1111/j.1467-8624.2008.01184.x

Carpendale, J., & Lewis, C. (2004). Constructing an understanding of mind: The development of children's social understanding within social interaction. *Behavioral and Brain Sciences, 27*(1), 79–151.

Carpendale, J., & Lewis, C. (2015). The development of social understanding. In R.M. Lerner, L.S. Liben, & U. Mueller (Eds.), *Handbook of Child Psychology and Developmental Science, Cognitive Processes*, Vol 2 (pp. 425–458). Hoboken, NJ: Wiley. doi:10.1002/9781118963418.childpsy210

Cassidy, K.W., Werner, R.S., Rourke, M., Zubernis, L.S., & Balaraman, G. (2003). The relationship between psychological understanding and positive social behaviors. *Social Development, 12*(2), 198–221. doi:10.1111/1467-9507.00229

Clear, S., Zimmer-Gembeck, M., Duffy, A., & Barber, B. (2019). Internalizing symptoms and loneliness: Direct effects of mindfulness and protection against the negative effects of peer victimization and exclusion. *International Journal of Behavioral Development*, 1–11. doi:10.1177/0165025419876358

Closson, L., & Watanabe, L. (2018). Popularity in the peer group and victimization within friendship cliques during early adolescence. *Journal of Early Adolescence, 38*(3), 327–351. doi:10.1177/0272431616670753

Conway, J., Catmur, C., & Bird, G. (2019). Understanding individual differences in theory of mind via representation of minds, not mental states. *Psychonomic Bulletin and Review, 26*(3), 798–812. doi:10.3758/s13423-018-1559-x

Coplan, R.J., Ooi, L.L., & Baldwin, D. (2019). Does it matter when we want to be alone? Exploring developmental timing effects in the implications of unsociability. *New Ideas in Psychology, 53*, 47–57.

Corsano, P., Musetti, A., & Favari, D. (2020). Self-concept, loneliness, and voluntary aloneness during late childhood. *Current Psychology*. doi:10.1007/s12144-020-00675-7

Couette, M., Mouchabac, S., Bourla, A., Nuss, P., & Ferreri, F. (2020). Social cognition in post- traumatic stress disorder: A systematic review. *British Journal of Clinical Psychology*. doi:10.1111/bjc.12238

Crick, N.R., & Dodge, K.A. (1994). A review and reformulation of social information-processing mechanisms in children's social adjustment. *Psychological Bulletin, 115*(1), 74–101.

Cutting, A., & Dunn, J. (2002). The cost of understanding other people: Social cognition predicts young children's sensitivity to criticism. *Journal of Child Psychology and Psychiatry, and Allied Disciplines, 43*(7), 849–860. doi:10.1111/1469-7610.t01-1-00047

Devine, R.T., & Hughes, C. (2013). Silent films and strange stories: Theory of mind, gender, and social experiences in middle childhood. *Child Development, 84*(3), 989–1003.

Devine, R.T. & Hughes, C. (2014). Relations between false belief understanding and executive function in early childhood: A meta-analysis. *Child Development, 85*, 1777–1794.

DiLalla, L., & John, S. (2020). A genetically informed examination of the relations between inaccurate emotion expression and recognition and experiencing peer victimization. *Social Development, 29*(2), 391–410.

Doenyas, C. (2017). Self versus other oriented social motivation, not lack of empathic or moral ability, explains behavioral outcomes in children with high theory of mind abilities. *Motivation and Emotion, 41*(6), 683–697.

Dodge, K.A., & Coie, J.D. (1987). Social-information-processing factors in reactive and proactive aggression in children's peer groups. *Journal of Personality and Social Psychology, 53*(6), 1146.

Eggum-Williams, N.D., An, D., Zhang, L., & Costa, M. (2019). Co-occurrence of cross- informant agreement on shyness, unsociability, and social avoidance during early adolescence. *Social Development, 29*, 73–88.

Eisenberg, N., & Miller, P. (1987). The relation of empathy to prosocial and related behaviors. *Psychological Bulletin, 101*(1), 91–119. doi:10.1037/0033-2909.101.1.91

Endedijk, H.M., & Cillessen, A.H.N. (2015). Computerized sociometric assessment for preschool children. *International Journal of Behavioral Development, 39*(4), 383–388. doi:10.1177/0165025414561706

Esperger, Z., & Bereczkei, T. (2012). Machiavellianism and spontaneous mentalization: One step ahead of others. *European Journal of Personality, 26*(6), 580–587. doi:10.1002/per.859

Fink, E., Begeer, S., Peterson, C.C., Slaughter, V., & de Rosnay, M. (2015). Friends, friendlessness, and the social consequences of gaining a theory of mind. *British Journal of Developmental Psychology, 33*(1), 1–17. doi:10.1111/bjdp.12080

Foster, I., Wyman, J., & Talwar, V. (2020). Moral disengagement: A new lens with which to examine children's justifications for lying. *Journal of Moral Education*. doi:10.1080/03057240.2019.1656057

Fritz, H. (2020). Why are humor styles associated with well-being, and does social competence matter? Examining relations to psychological and physical well being, reappraisal, and social support. *Personality and Individual Differences, 154*. doi:10.1016/j.paid.2019.109641

Fu, G., Heyman, G.D., Qian, M., Guo, T., & Lee, K. (2016). Young children with a positive reputation to maintain are less likely to cheat. *Developmental Science, 19*(2), 275–283.

Furman, W. (1996). The measurement of children and adolescent's perceptions of friendships: Conceptual and methodological issues. In W.M. Bukowski, A.F. Newcomb, & W.W. Hartup (Eds.), *The Company They Keep: Friendships in Childhood and Adolescence* (pp. 41–65). Cambridge, MA: Cambridge University Press.

Gardner, W., Pickett, C.L., Jefferis, V., & Knowles, M. (2005). On the outside looking in: Loneliness and social monitoring. *Personality and Social Psychology Bulletin, 31*(11), 1549–1560.

Gasser, L., & Keller, M. (2009). Are the competent the morally good? Perspective taking and moral motivation of children involved in bullying. *Social Development, 18*(4), 798–816. doi:10.1111/j.1467-9507.2008.00516.x

Gini, G. (2006). Social cognition and moral cognition in bullying: What's wrong? *Aggressive Behavior, 32*(6), 528–539. doi:10.1002/ab.20153

Gola, A. (2012). Mental verb input for promoting children's theory of mind: A training study. *Cognitive Development, 27*(1), 64–76.

Goldstein, T., & Winner, E. (2012). Enhancing empathy and theory of mind. *Journal of Cognition and Development, 13*(1), 19–37.

Greenspan, L., & Deardorff, J. (2014). *The New Puberty: How to Navigate Early Development in Today's Girls*. New York: Rodale.

Grueneisen, S., Wyman, E., & Tomasello, M. (2015). "I know you don't know I know…" Children use second-order false-belief reasoning for peer coordination. *Child Development, 86*(1), 287–293. doi:10.1111/cdev.12264

Harwood, E.M., & Kocovski, N.L. (2017). Self-compassion induction reduces anticipatory anxiety among socially anxious students. *Mindfulness, 8*(6), 1544–15511551. doi:10.1007/s12671-017-0721-2

Hassan, R., Poole, K., & Schmidt, L. (2020). Revisiting the double-edged sword of self-regulation: Linking shyness, attentional shifting, and social behavior in preschoolers. *Journal of Experimental Child Psychology, 196*, 104842.

Heberle, A., Rapa, L., & Farago, F. (2020). Critical consciousness in children and adolescents: A systematic review, critical assessment, and recommendations for future research. *Psychological Bulletin, 146*(6), 525–551. doi:10.1037/bul0000230

Hipson, W., Coplan, R., & Séguin, D. (2019). Active emotion regulation mediates links between shyness and social adjustment in preschool. *Social Development, 28*(4), 893–907.

Holl, A., Kirsch, F., Rohlf, H., Krahé, B., & Elsner, B. (2018). Longitudinal reciprocity between theory of mind and aggression in middle childhood. *International Journal of Behavioral Development, 42*(2), 257–266.

Hughes, C. (2011). Social *Understanding* and *Social Lives*: From *Toddlerhood Through* to the *Transition* to *School*. London: Psychology Press. doi:0.4324/9780203813225

Hughes, C. (2016). Theory of mind grows up: Reflections on new research on theory of mind in middle childhood and adolescence. *Journal of Experimental Child Psychology, 149*, 1–5. doi:10.1016/j.jecp.2016.01.017

Hughes, C., & Devine, R.T. (2015). Individual differences in theory of mind from preschool to adolescence: Achievements and directions. *Child Development Perspectives, 9*(3), 149–153.

Hughes, C., & Leekam, S. (2004). What are the links between theory of mind and social relations? Review, reflections and new directions for studies of typical and atypical development. *Social Development, 13*(4), 590–619. doi:10.1111/j.1467-9507.2004.00285.x

Hyde, J.S. (2005). The gender similarities hypothesis. *American Psychologist, 60*(6), 581–592. doi:10.1037/0003-066X.60.6.581

Imuta, K., Henry, J.D., Slaughter, V., Selcuk, B., & Ruffman, T. (2016). Theory of mind and prosocial behavior in childhood: A meta-analytic review. *Developmental Psychology, 52*(8), 1192–1205. doi:10.1037/dev0000140

Jamison, R.S., Wilson, T., & Ryan, A. (2015). Too cool for school? The relationship between coolness and academic reputation in early adolescence. *Social Development, 24*(2), 384–403. doi:10.1111/sode.12097

Jenkins, J.M., & Astington, J.W. (2000). Theory of mind and social behavior: Causal models tested in a longitudinal study. *Merrill-Palmer Quarterly, 46*, 203–220.

Jones, A., Happé, F., Gilbert, F., Burnett, S., &Viding, E. (2010). Feeling, caring, knowing: Different types of empathy deficit in boys with psychopathic tendencies and autism spectrum disorder. *Journal of Child Psychology and Psychiatry, and Allied Disciplines, 51*(11), 1188–1197. doi:10.1111/j.1469-7610.2010.02280.x

Jones, D., & Paulus, D. (2009). Machiavellianism. In M.R. Leary & R.H. Hoyle (Eds.), *Handbook of Individual Differences in Social Behavior* (pp. 93–108). New York, NY: Guilford Press.

Jungert, T., & Perrin, S. (2019). Trait anxiety and bystander motivation to defend victims of school bullying. *Journal of Adolescence*, 77, 1–10.

Kerwer, M., Rosman, T., Wedderhoff, O., & Chasiotis, A. (2020). Disentangling the process of epistemic change: The role of epistemic volition. *British Journal of Educational Psychology*. doi:10.1111/bjep.12372

Koerber, S., & Osterhaus, C. (2020). Some but not all aspects of (advanced) theory of mind predict loneliness. *British Journal of Developmental Psychology, 38*(1), 144–148. doi:10.1111/bjdp.12302

Krettenauer, T., Bauer, K., & Sengsavang, S. (2019). Fairness, prosociality, hypocrisy, and happiness: Children's and adolescents' motives for showing unselfish behaviour and positive emotions. *British Journal of Developmental Psychology, 37*(4), 505–518.

Kung, K.T.F., Li, G., Golding, J., & Hines, M. (2018). Preschool gender-typed play behavior at age 3.5 years predicts physical aggression at age 13 years. *Archives of Sexual Behavior, 47*(4), 905–914. doi:10.1007/s10508-017-1005-6

Kwan, V.S.Y., Li, Y.J., White, A.E., & Jacobson, R.P. (2015). Cultural worldview and cognition. In S. Ng & A.Y. Lee (Eds.), *Handbook of Culture and Consumer Behavior* (pp. 13–33). New York, NY: Oxford University Press.

Leach, J., Howe, N., & DeHart, G. (2019). "Let's make a place where giants live!": Children's communication during play with siblings and friends from early to middle childhood. *Infant and Child Development*. doi:10.1002/icd.2156

Lecce, S., & Bianco, F. (2018). Working memory predicts changes in children's theory of mind during middle childhood: A training study. *Cognitive Development, 47*, 71–81.

Lecce, S., Bianco, F., Devine, R.T., Hughes, C., & Banerjee, R. (2014). Promoting theory of mind during middle childhood: A training program. *Journal of Experimental Child Psychology, 126*, 52–67.

Lecce, S., Ceccato, I., & Cavallini, E. (2019). Theory of mind, mental state talk and social relationships in aging: The case of friendship. *Aging and Mental Health, 23*(9), 1105–1112. doi:10.1080/13607863.2018.1479832

Lecce, S., Ceccato, I., Rosi, A., Bianco, F., Bottiroli, S., & Cavallini, E. (2019). Theory of mind plasticity in aging: The role of baseline, verbal knowledge, and executive functions. *Neuropsychological Rehabilitation, 29*(3), 440–455.

Lew-Levy, S., Boyette, A., Crittenden, A., Hewlett, B., & Lamb, M. (2020). Gender-typed and gender-segregated play among Tanzanian Hadza and Congolese BaYaka Hunter-Gatherer children and adolescents. *Child Development.* doi:10.1111/cdev.13306

Long, Y., & Li, Y. (2020). The longitudinal association between social status insecurity and relational aggression: Moderation effects of social cognition about relational aggression. *Aggressive Behavior,* 1–13. doi:10.1002/ab.21872

Longobardi, E., Spataro, P., & Rossi-Arnaud, C. (2016). Relations between theory of mind, mental state language and social adjustment in primary school children. *European Journal of Developmental Psychology, 13*(4), 424–438. doi:10.1080/17405629.2015.1093930

Longobardi, E., Spataro, P., & Rossi-Arnaud, C. (2019). Direct and indirect associations of empathy, theory of mind, and language with prosocial behavior: Gender differences in primary school children. *The Journal of Genetic Psychology, 180*(6), 266–279.

Lu, H., Su, Y., & Wang, Q. (2008). Talking about others facilitates theory of mind in Chinese preschoolers. *Developmental Psychology, 44*(6), 1726–1736. doi:10.1037/a0013074

McAdams, D.P., & McLean, K.C. (2013). Narrative identity. *Current Directions in Psychological Science, 22*(3), 233–238. doi:10.1177/0963721413475622

McCombs, B.L., & Marzano, R.J. (1990). Putting the self in self-regulated learning: The self as agent in integrating will and skill. *Educational Psychologist, 25*(1), 51–69. https://doi-org.proxy.library.brocku.ca/10.1207/s15326985ep2501_5

McDonald, K.L., & Asher, S.R. (2018). Pacifists and revenge-seekers in response to unambiguous peer provocation. *Journal of Youth and Adolescence, 47*(9), 1907–1925. doi:10.1007/s10964-017-0767-4

McElwain, N., Ravindran, N., Emery, H., & Swartz, R. (2019). Theory of mind as a mechanism linking mother–toddler relationship quality and child–friend interaction during the preschool years. *Social Development, 28*, 998–1015.

McGuire, L., Rizzo, M.T., Killen, M., & Rutland, A. (2018). The development of intergroup resource allocation: The role of cooperative and competitive in-group norms. *Developmental Psychology, 54*(8), 1499–1506. doi:10.1037/dev0000535

Minnameier, G. (2012). A cognitive approach to the 'happy victimiser'. *Journal of Moral Education, 41*(4), 491–508.

Moore, C., Bosacki, S.L., & Macgillivray, S. (2011). Theory of mind and social interest in zero-acquaintance play situations. *Child Development, 82*(4), 1163–1172.

Morningstar, M., Nowland, R., Dirks, M., & Qualter, P. (2019). Loneliness and the recognition of vocal socioemotional expressions in adolescence. Cognition and Emotion. doi:10.1080/02699931.2019.1682971

Nielson, M., Xiao, S., & Padilla-Walker, L. (2020). Gender similarity in growth patterns of support toward friends during young adulthood. *Social Development.* doi:10.1111/SODE.12419

Nikolić, M., van der storm, L., Colonnesi, C., Brummelman, E., Kan, K., & Bögels, S. (2019). Are socially anxious children poor or advanced mindreaders? *Child Development, 90*(4), 1425–1441.

O'Driscoll, D., Taylor, L.K., & Dautel, J. (2018). Intergroup resource distribution among children living in segregated neighborhoods amid protracted conflict. *Peace and Conflict: Journal of Peace Psychology, 24*(4), 464–474. doi:10.1037/pac0000348

O'Nions, E., Sebastian, C.L., McCrory, E., Chantiluke, K., Happé, F., & Viding, E. (2014). Neural bases of theory of mind in children with autism spectrum disorders and children with conduct problems and callous-unemotional traits. *Developmental Science, 17*(5), 786–796. doi:10.1111/desc.12167

Osterhaus, C., Koerber, S., & Sodian, B. (2016). Scaling of advanced theory-of-mind tasks. *Child Development, 87*(6), 1971–1991. doi:10.1111/cdev.12566

Owen, D., & Willoughby, T. (2020). A longitudinal person-centered examination of affinity for aloneness among children and adolescents. *Child Development.* doi:10.1111/cdev.13411

Peplak, J., Ali, S., & Malti, T. (2020). Adolescents' Narratives of Schadenfreude. *Journal of Research on Adolescence: The Official Journal of the Society for Research on Adolescence.* doi:10.1111/jora.12565

Pequet, A., & Warnell, K. (2020). Thinking of you: Relations between mind-mindedness, theory of mind, and social anxiety traits in middle childhood and adulthood. *Social Development.* doi:10.1111/SODE.12468

Preckel, K., Kanske, P., & Singer, T. (2018). On the interaction of social affect and cognition: Empathy, compassion and theory of mind. *Current Opinion in Behavioral Sciences, 19*, 1–6.

Qualter, P., Rotenberg, K., Barrett, L., Henzi, P., Barlow, A., Stylianou, M., & Harris, R.A. (2013). Investigating hypervigilance for social threat of lonely children. *Journal of Abnormal Child Psychology, 41*(2), 325–338.

Recchia, H., Wainryb, C., & Pasupathi, M. (2019). "I wanted to hurt her": Children's and adolescents' experiences of desiring and seeking revenge in their own peer conflicts. *Social Development, 28*(4), 840–853. doi:10.1111/sode.12370

Renouf, A., Brendgen, M., Séguin, J.R., Vitaro, F., Boivin, M., Dionne, G., … & Pérusse, D. (2010). Interactive links between theory of mind, peer victimization, and reactive and proactive aggression. *Journal of Abnormal Child Psychology, 38*(8), 1109–1123. doi:10.1007/ s10802-010-9432-z

Repacholi, B., Slaughter, V., Pritchard, M., & Gibbs, V. (2003). Theory of mind, Machiavellianism, and social functioning in childhood. In B. Repacholi & V. Slaughter (Eds.), *Individual Differences in Theory of Mind: Implications for Typical and Atypical Development* (pp. 67–97). New York: Psychology Press.

Rivenbark, J.G., Copeland, W.E., Davisson, E.K., Gassman-Pines, A., Hoyle, R.H., Piontak, J.R., … & Odgers, C.L. (2019). Perceived social status and mental health among young adolescents: Evidence from census data to cellphones. *Developmental Psychology, 55*(3), 574–585. doi:10.1037/dev0000551

Roberts, R., McCrory, E., Bird, G., Sharp, M., Roberts, L., & Viding, E. (2020). Thinking about others' minds: Mental state inference in boys with conduct problems and callous-unemotional traits. *Journal of Abnormal Child Psychology.* doi:10.1007/ s10802-020-00664-1

Ronchi, L., Banerjee, R., & Lecce, S. (2020). Theory of mind and peer relationships: The role of social anxiety. *Social Development, 29*(2), 478–493. doi:10.1111/SODE.12417

Rubin, K.H., Bukowski, W.M., & Parker, J.G. (2006). *Peer Interactions, Relationships, and Groups.* Hoboken, NJ: John Wiley.

Schacter, H., & Juvonen, J. (2018). You've got a friend(ly school): Can school prosocial norms and friends similarly protect victims from distress? *Social Development*. doi:10.1111/sode.12281

Schaefer, J.D., Moffitt, T.E., Arseneault, L., Danese, A., Fisher, H.L., Houts, R., ... & Caspi, A. (2018). Adolescent victimization and early-adult psychopathology: Approaching causal inference using a longitudinal twin study to rule out noncausal explanations. *Clinical Psychological Science: A Journal of the Association for Psychological Science, 6*(3), 352–371. doi:10.1177/2167702617741381

Schulz, K., Rudolph, A., Tscharaktschiew, N., & Rudolph, U. (2013). Daniel has fallen into a muddy puddle—Schadenfreude or sympathy? *British Journal of Developmental Psychology, 31*(4), 363–378. https://doi.org/10.1111/bjdp.12013

Sellers, R.M., Smith, M.A., Shelton, J.N., Rowley, S.A.J., & Chavous, T.M. (1998). Multidimensional model of racial identity: A reconceptualization of African American racial identity. *Personality and Social Psychology Review: An Official Journal of the Society for Personality and Social Psychology, Inc, 2*(1), 18–39. doi:10.1207/s15327957pspr0201_2

Sierksma, J., Thijs, J., & Verkuyten, M. (2015). In-group bias in children's intention to help can be overpowered by inducing empathy. *British Journal of Developmental Psychology, 33*(1), 45–56. doi:10.1111/bjdp.12065

Slaughter, V., Imuta, K., Peterson, C.C., & Henry, J.D. (2015). Meta-analysis of theory of mind and peer popularity in the preschool and early school years. *Child Development, 86*(4), 1159–1174. doi:10.1111/cdev.12372

Smith, S., Dutcher, K., Aksar, M., Talwar, V., & Bosacki, S. (2018). Emotional competencies in emerging adolescence: Relations between teacher ratings and student self-reports. *International Journal of Adolescence and Youth*. doi:10.1080/02673843.2018.1455059

Somerville, L. (2013). Special issue on The teenage brain: Sensitivity to social evaluation. *Current Directions in Psychological Science, 22*(2), 121–127. doi:10.1177/0963721413476512

Spithoven, A., Bijttebier, P., & Goossens, L. (2017). It is all in their mind: A review on information processing bias in lonely individuals. *Clinical Psychology Review, 58*, 97–114.

Steinhoff, A., & Keller, M. (2020). Pathways from childhood sociomoral sensitivity in friendship, insecurity, and peer rejection to adult friendship quality. *Child Development*. doi:10.1111/cdev.13381

Sullivan, H.S. (1953). *The Interpersonal Theory of Psychiatry*. New York, NY: Norton.

Sutton, J., & Keogh, E. (2000). Social competition in school: Relationships with bullying, Machiavellianism and personality. *British Journal of Educational Psychology, 70*(3), 443–456. doi:10.1348/000709900158227

Sutton, J., Smith, P., & Swettenham, J. (1999a). Bullying and 'theory of mind': A critique of the 'social skills deficit' view of anti-social behaviour. *Social Development, 8*(1), 117–127. doi:10.1111/1467-9507.00083

Sutton, J., Smith, P., & Swettenham, J. (1999b). Social cognition and bullying: Social inadequacy or skilled manipulation? *British Journal of Developmental Psychology, 17*(3), 435–450. doi:10.1348/026151099165384

Taylor, L. (2020). The developmental peacebuilding model (DPM) of children's prosocial behaviors in settings of intergroup conflict. *Child Development Perspectives*. doi:10.1111/cdep.12377

Theodoraki, T.E., McGeown, S.P., Rhodes, S.M., & MacPherson, S.E. (2020). Developmental changes in executive functions during adolescence: A study of inhibition, shifting, and working memory. *British Journal of Developmental Psychology, 38*(1), 74–89. doi:10.1111/bjdp.12307

Tomasello, M. (1999). Having intentions, understanding intentions, and understanding communicative intentions. In P. Zelazo, J. Astington, & D. Olson (Eds.), *Developing Theories of Intention: Social Understanding and Self-Control* (pp. 63–75). Mahwah, NJ: Lawrence Erlbaum Associates.

Tomasello, M. (2000). *The Cultural Origin of Human Cognition*. Cambridge, MA: Harvard University Press.

Trivers, R.L. (1971). The evolution of reciprocal altruism. *The Quarterly Review of Biology, 46*(1), 35–57.

Troop-Gordon, W., & Unhjem, L. (2018). Is preventing peer victimization sufficient? The role of prosocial peer group treatment in children's socioemotional development. *Social Development, 27*(3), 619–635.

Tudge, J., & Winterhoff, P. (1993). Vygotsky, Piaget, and Bandura: Perspectives on the relations between the social world and cognitive development. *Human Development, 36*(2), 61–81. doi:10.1159/000277297

van den Berg, Y., Deutz, M., Smeekens, S., & Cillessen, A. (2017). Developmental pathways to preference and popularity in middle childhood. *Child Development, 88*(5), 1629–1641. doi:10.1111/cdev.12706

Van der Graaff, J., Branje, S., De Wied, M., Hawk, S., Van Lier, P., & Meeus, W. (2014). Perspective taking and empathic concern in adolescence: Gender differences in developmental changes. *Developmental Psychology, 50*(3), 881–888. doi:10.1037/a0034325

Van der Graaff, J., Carlo, G., Crocetti, E., Koot, H.M., & Branje, S. (2018). Prosocial behavior in adolescence: Gender differences in development and links with empathy. *Journal of Youth and Adolescence, 47*(5), 1086–1099. doi:10.1007/s10964-017-0786-1

Van der Wal, R., Karremans, J., & Cillessen, A. (2017). Causes and consequences of children's forgiveness. *Child Development Perspectives, 11*(2), 97–101.

van Dijk, W., Ouwerkerk, J., Wesseling, Y., &van Koningsbruggen, G. (2011). Towards understanding pleasure at the misfortunes of others: The impact of self-evaluation threat on Schadenfreude. *Cognition and Emotion, 25*(2), 360–368. doi:10.1080/02699931.2010.487365

Van Doesum, N., Van Lange, D., & Van Lange, P. (2013). Social mindfulness: Skill and will to navigate the social world. *Journal of Personality and Social Psychology, 105*(1), 86–103. doi:10.1037/a0032540

Van Loan, C., Garwood, J., Smith, S., & Daunic, A. (2019). Take CHARGE! A randomized controlled trial of a social problem-solving curriculum to support students with emotional and behavioral disorders. *Journal of Emotional and Behavioral Disorders, 27*(3), 143–153.

Van Ryzin, M., & Roseth, C. (2019). Effects of cooperative learning on peer relations, empathy, and bullying in middle school. *Aggressive Behavior*. doi:10.1002/ab.21858

Vendeville, N., Blanc, N., & Brechet, C. (2018). Tears for girls and teeth for boys: The influence of gender on children's depiction of sadness and anger in their drawings. *Educational Psychology, 38*(7), 927–944. doi:10.1080/01443410.2018.1461810

Viana, K.M.P., Zambrana, I.M., Karevold, E.B., & Pons, F. (2020). Emotions in motion: Impact of emotion understanding on children's peer action coordination. *Cognition and Emotion*, 34(4), 831–838. doi:10.1080/02699931.2019.1669535

Viding, E.,&McCrory, E. (2019). Towards understanding atypical social affiliation in psychopathy. *The Lancet Psychiatry, 6*(5), 437–444. doi:10.1016/S2215-0366(19)30049-5

Weinstein, N., & Ryan, R.M. (2010). When helping helps: Autonomous motivation for prosocial behavior and its influence on well-being for the helper and recipient. *Journal of Personality and Social Psychology, 98*(2), 222–244. doi:10.1037/a0016984

Wellman, H. (2015). Commentary: Friends, friendlessness, and social cognition. *British Journal of Developmental Psychology, 33*(1), 24–26.

Wellman, H.M., & Liu, D. (2004). Scaling of theory-of-mind tasks. *Child Development, 75*(2), 523–541.

Williams, S., Moore, K., Crossman, A.M., & Talwar, V. (2016). The role of executive functions and theory of mind in children's prosocial lie-telling. *Journal of Experimental Child Psychology, 141*, 256–266. doi:10.1016/j.jecp.2015.08.001

Wilson, T.M., & Jamison, R. (2019). Perceptions of same-sex and cross-sex peers: Behavioral correlates of perceived coolness during middle childhood. *Merrill-Palmer Quarterly, 65*(1), 1–27. doi:10.13110/merrpalmquar1982.65.1.0001

Yuill, N., Perner, J., Pearson, A., Peerbhoy, & van den Ende, J. (1996). Children's changing understanding of wicked desires: From objective to subjective and moral. *British Journal of Developmental Psychology, 14*(4), 457–475.

Yun, H. (2020). New approaches to defender and outsider roles in school bullying. *Child Development*, 91, e814–e832. DOI: 10.1111/cdev.13312

Zabelina, D., White, R., Tobin, A., & Thompson, L. (2020). The role of mindfulness in viewing and making art in children and adults. *Mindfulness*. doi:10.1007/s12671-020-01474-8

Zajączkowska, M., & Abbot-Smith, K. (2020). "Sure I'll help—I've just been sitting around doing nothing at school all day": Cognitive flexibility and child irony interpretation. *Journal of Experimental Child Psychology, 199*. http://www.ncbi.nlm.nih.gov/pubmed/104942

Zimbardo, P.G. (1977). *Shyness: What It Is and What to Do About It*. New York: Jove.

8 Theory of mind goes to school

Serena Lecce

The present chapter examines theory of mind (ToM) in relation to children's school life and school accomplishments in order to find out if and how understanding others' minds helps children to face the demands of school. The general premise is that children's ToM is just as important as other factors, such as numeracy and literacy, in enhancing school achievement. The chapter is organized into four main sections. The first focuses on the associations between children's ToM and school achievement in the two main areas of reading comprehension and mathematics. The second examines the mechanisms that underlie these associations, focusing on the role played by social (i.e., social relationships and competence), metacognitive (i.e., sensitivity to criticism, metamemory, meta-reading, belief about learning), and high-level language (i.e., mental state talk and figurative language) variables. The third section has a practical angle and focuses on how school-based activities and school setting–related variables (e.g., teachers' teaching style, classroom composition) impact ToM; it also presents an overview of existing ToM training studies. The fourth section addresses the theoretical and methodological implications of existing findings and proposes a theoretical framework, the 'ToM at school framework', to guide future research.

Theory of mind and school achievement

Studies of ToM and children's school achievement have traditionally been conducted under the heading of 'school readiness', defined as children's ability to meet everyday social and practical challenges (Hughes et al., 2015). Work in this area has shown significant and unique relations between individual differences in preschoolers' false belief (FB) understanding and their general success in learning (Wellman, 2016). It is only in recent times that researchers have examined the potential impact that individual differences in children's advanced ToM have on specific dimensions of academic achievement, reading comprehension, and mathematical skills during middle childhood and adolescence. Below I discuss these three topics in turn.

Reading comprehension

There are several reasons to hypothesize that ToM has a role in children's reading comprehension. Theoretically, several models of reading comprehension implicitly refer to and implicate ToM skills. For example, Bruner (1987) has proposed that understanding stories hinges on bringing together the 'landscape of consciousness' (i.e., characters' mental states) with the 'landscape of actions' (i.e., physical events), and ToM is clearly implicated in the former. Cain et al. (2001) and, more recently, Dore et al. (2018) have examined the ability necessary to understand a text and have argued that children's ToM plays an important role. Cain and colleagues have proposed that reading comprehension depends on children's ability to assume characters' perspectives, which allows them to create a mental model of the text itself (Cain et al., 2001). Dore and colleagues have highlighted that ToM allows children to make inferences about characters' mental states (Dore et al., 2018), thus improving reading comprehension.

The second reason for hypothesizing a link between ToM and reading comprehension emerges from studies on children with Autism Spectrum Disorders (ASD) who, in addition to experiencing ToM difficulties (Happé, 2015), show limited reading comprehension (Lindgren et al., 2009; Minshew et al., 1994) that could not be explained by general IQ level (Jones et al., 2009; McIntyre et al., 2018) and that appear to be explained by ToM difficulties (McIntyre et al., 2018; Ricketts et al., 2013).

Direct support for the influence of ToM on reading comprehension in typically developing children comes from longitudinal studies. At least three issues should be carefully considered here. The first concerns the role that potentially confounding variables may have in the relation between ToM and reading comprehension. Performance in reading comprehension and in ToM involves a number of skills, such as executive function and language, which raises the question of whether ToM shows unique associations with reading comprehension (Guajardo & Cartwright, 2016). The second issue that deserves attention is methodological and concerns the fact that many of the tasks used to assess advanced ToM, for example, the Faux Pas (Baron-Cohen et al., 1999) and Strange Stories tasks (White et al., 2009), are very similar to classic reading comprehension tasks in that they require children to read short passages and answer inferential questions. Thus, it is possible that the associations between ToM and reading comprehension are superficial rather than genuine and reflect similarities in the tasks. The third issue concerns the direction of the relation between ToM and reading comprehension. Although there are reasons for expecting that ToM predicts later reading comprehension, it is also possible that reading comprehension predicts later ToM. Reading may provide readers with extra practice in the same inferential processes that are involved in real-world social cognition (Oatley, 2016). Dodell-Feder and Tamir (2018) recently conducted a meta-analysis of 53 effect sizes from 14 studies on young adults and demonstrated that, compared with nonfiction reading and no reading, fiction reading leads to a small, statistically significant improvement in social cognitive performance (g = .15–.16). Cross-cultural research has provided data compatible with the view that reading positively affects children's ToM. Indeed, three different studies have shown that children in the UK outperform peers from Italy (Lecce & Hughes, 2010), Hong Kong (Hughes et al., 2018), and Japan (Hughes et al., 2014) on ToM skills, despite being matched for age, gender, and verbal ability. Crucially, in the UK children start school a year earlier than children in Italy and Japan (Hughes et al., 2014), which suggests a possible role for school experience in children's development of ToM. Furthermore, Lysaker et al. (2011) showed that an eight-week relationally oriented reading intervention led to improvements in ToM in children in Year 2 and Year 3.

My colleagues and I conducted two studies to address each of the issues previously discussed: Confounding variables, overlap between ToM and reading tasks modality, and the direction of association (Lecce, Bianco, & Hughes, 2021). The first study examined whether the (expected) association between ToM and reading comprehension was independent of the roles of family affluence, verbal ability, and working memory and of the type of task used to test ToM skills. Results from a sample of 157 children between nine and ten years of age showed a significant association between reading comprehension and both the Strange Stories (White et al., 2009), a classic static verbal ToM task, and the Animations task (Castelli et al., 2000), a nonverbal, dynamic task that uses short clips of moving triangles as prompts (r = .45 for both tasks). These associations were independent of family affluence, verbal ability, and working memory (r = .36 and .43 for the Strange Stories and Animation tasks, respectively). The second study had a longitudinal design and allowed us to address the issue of the direction of the associations between ToM and reading comprehension. ToM at age nine explained 10% of the variance in reading comprehension at age ten, even when controlling for children's verbal ability, maternal education, and earlier reading comprehension. Results also showed a significant effect of children's early reading comprehension on later ToM (15% of explained variance). These findings show that understanding a text requires, and at the same time promotes, the identification of the relations between characters and their mental states. Whether or not this finding applies to nonfictional narratives is an open question for future research.

Mathematical skills

Literature on the effects of children's ToM on mathematical skills is relatively scarce. Two exceptions are worth mentioning here. The first is a correlational study by Cantin and colleagues on a sample of 93 seven- to ten-year-old children (Cantin et al., 2016). Using path analyses, the authors showed no significant associations between ToM and a composite score of mathematics performance assessed using the Math Problem Solving, Numerical Operations, and Math Fluency measurements of the Wechsler's scale. The second is the study cited above (Lecce, Bianco, & Hughes, 2021) that included a measure of mathematical ability (together with that of reading comprehension) assessing four specific abilities: Judgment of numerosity, transformation from letters into numbers, and ordering numbers in increasing and decreasing size. In line with Cantin et al. (2016), my colleagues and I found no significant cross-sectional or longitudinal relations between ToM and mathematical skills. Taken together, these studies suggest that ToM has a minor role in children's mathematical ability. However, the strength of the relations between these two variables may change depending on the specific aspect of mathematical performance considered. Lockl and collaborators reported a moderate relation between those dimensions of mathematical skills touching on mental representation, such as problem-solving, but not on arithmetic tasks (Lockl et al., 2017). More generally speaking, ToM may help to solve those mathematical tasks that require the ability to reason about hypothetical entities and to operate with different mental representations. For example, Osterhaus and colleagues (2017) showed in a sample of eight- to nine-year-old children a significant influence of social cognition (as evaluated via several items taken from various methodologically distinct tasks such as second-order FB, Eyes, and Strange Stories) on epistemological understanding, which in turn is closely related to the development of experimentation skills.

The research reported in this section shows that individual differences in ToM are implicated in children's school performance, especially in reading comprehension. This section highlights the bidirectional link between children's ToM and their reading comprehension; it also stresses the need to adopt longitudinal designs and to measure children's ToM using a variety of tasks that differ in modality in order to gain a deeper understanding of the nature of the associations between children's ToM and school performance.

Theory of mind and school achievement: Underlying mechanisms

Having shown that ToM influences children's learning outcomes, it is important to understand the mechanisms underlying this association. In this section, I focus on three mechanisms involving social competence and social relationships, metacognition, and high-level language.

Social competence and social relationships

Children's social competence and social relationships with peers and teachers represent an obvious way through which ToM can influence children's school achievement. Existing research on children in middle childhood and adolescence has shown that ToM is associated (please note that the effect sizes range from weak to moderate in strength) with the degree to which children are accepted by their peers (or are friendless) and the frequency with which they engage in socially mature and competent behaviors (Banerjee et al., 2011; Lecce & Devine, in press; Peterson et al., 2007; Roorda et al., 2011; Slaughter et al., 2015). Crucially, social competence and relationships predict desirable school-related outcomes (Hamre & Pianta, 2001; Pianta & Stuhlman, 2004; Roorda et al., 2011). Indeed, a growing body of research shows that relationships with teachers significantly contribute to school engagement and school performance with associations that were medium to large for engagement and small to medium for achievement (Roorda et al., 2011). In a similar vein, peer relationships and group membership have been found to predict later achievement (Wentzel & Caldwell, 1997). These associations between social relationships and school outcomes reflect the significance of social behavior patterns. While prosocial and socially competent behaviors foster school engagement and success (Caprara et al., 2000), peer problems are risk factors for school outcomes (Campbell et al., 2006; Fergusson & Horwood, 1995). Children experiencing social exclusion and rejection are more likely to get distracted from learning situations (Welsh et al., 2001), to be less involved in classroom activities (Buhs et al., 2006), and to be excluded from a number of social situations that facilitate successful school outcomes (Chen et al., 1997).

In light of these associations, my colleagues and I tested the hypothesis that children's social adjustment mediates the link between ToM and school achievement (Lecce et al., 2017). This study had a longitudinal design coupled with a multi-informant and multi-indicator approach and showed that social competence at age seven (indexed by an aggregate score of peer relationships and social skills) mediated the relation between ToM at age five and school achievement (indexed by teachers' ratings of academic competence and children's performance on reading comprehension and math tests) at age eight. Altogether these findings suggest that ToM can have an indirect effect on children's academic achievement via social competence and relationships.

Metacognition

The second pathway through which ToM influences learning outcomes is children's metacognition. In discussing this topic, I focus on two constructs that have attracted researchers' attention: Sensitivity to criticism, and meta-knowledge. Children's sensitivity to criticism refers to children's understanding of other people's negative comments about them. Previous studies have operationalized this construct by measuring children's tendency to rate their own ability as being lower when criticized than when they are not criticized by their teachers (Heyman et al., 1992). Research has consistently found that ToM explained unique variance in later sensitivity to criticism (Cutting & Dunn, 2002; Hughes, 2011; Lecce et al., 2011; Mizokawa, 2015; Mizokawa & Lecce, 2017). While this association has been originally interpreted as reflecting a 'cost' of understanding other people (Cutting & Dunn, 2002), in the school context, sensitivity to criticism can represent an advantage in the process of learning. Criticism and feedback from teachers constitute important learning opportunities, which allow children to improve their strategies for learning (Frese & Altman, 1989; Gully et al., 2002; Matsumura et al., 2002; Torgesen,

2002). My colleagues and I provided data to support this view and showed that sensitivity to criticism at six years of age mediated the effect of ToM at five years on academic achievements at seven years (Lecce et al., 2011) and ten years of age (Lecce et al., 2014c). Children with more advanced ToM were more sensitive to teachers' criticism, and this deeper understanding, in turn, promoted their achievement performance. These results are also in line with data provided by Mizowaka (2015) on a sample of 89 Japanese six-year-olds, according to which sensitivity to criticism not only affects school outcomes but also promotes children's motivation to keep trying.

Overall, therefore, children whose advanced mindreading skills make them particularly sensitive to criticism seem to be particularly good at the metacognitive process of reflecting on learning. The link between ToM and metaknowledge (a person's awareness/knowledge about his/her own knowledge) provides another clue as to how individual differences in children's understanding of mind might relate to academic outcomes. The rationale for this position is that ToM equips children with a form of knowledge about the mind (i.e., mental states can change over time and influence behavior) upon which they can rely when asked to perform a cognitive task, such as remembering or reading (Bartsch & Estes, 1996; Kuhn, 2009; Wellman, 1985). Thus, ToM potentially allows children to understand that knowledge depends on access to that topic (i.e., study), that learning is a process of knowledge change, and that their knowledge does not replicate reality and can be inaccurate. Specifically, ToM represents a crucial starting point for the development of children's knowledge about how their own mind works when learning, how to use their mind, which variables affect their mind, and what strategies maximize learning. ToM can therefore be considered as a critical precursor to the development of different areas of metacognition. Take, for example, metamemory, namely the knowledge and beliefs about one's own memory, memory-relevant variables, and potentially applicable memory strategies (Wellman, 1977). Metamemory hinges on understanding the meaning of cognitive state terms (e.g., remembering) and the process of knowledge acquisition, which are crucial aspects of ToM. From an empirical stance, the relation between children's ToM and metamemory has been investigated in a number of studies involving young children from different European countries (Lecce et al., 2014a, 2015b; Lockl & Schneider, 2006). Another dimension of metacognition that is linked to ToM is metaknowledge about reading, or 'meta-reading'. Children's understanding of the interpretative nature of mental states represents a crucial predictor of their understanding that a text can be interpreted in different ways by different people, and that there are different strategies for reading and understanding a text (Lecce et al., 2010). Other studies in this field have adopted a wider perspective and examined ToM in relation to the broader aspect of beliefs about learning, namely children's thoughts about the nature of the learning process. Individual differences in children's ToM correlate with and predict those in constructivist beliefs, according to which learning implies a conceptual change from not knowing to knowing, rather than those in reproductive beliefs (i.e, viewing learning as performing assigned tasks and memorizing) (Lecce et al., 2015a).

Although nobody has directly tested the mediating role of metacognition in the associations between ToM and educational outcomes, this model is plausible. Kuhn (2000) has proposed a theoretical model in which ToM is considered as a precursor of a meta-strategic knowing, which focuses on the impact of cognitive processes on task performance. Empirically, several studies have demonstrated, as outlined above, that ToM promotes the development of metacognition in several areas (e.g., metamemory, meta-reading, and beliefs about learning) and that metacognition has a profound impact on school outcomes, such as reading comprehension (Chan & Law, 2003; Chan & Sachs, 2001; Orasanu, 1986; Paris et al., 1984).

High-level language

Another way through which individual differences in ToM may impact children's school achievement is via high-level language skills. While the issue of the relations between ToM and language has traditionally been examined to understand the role that children's verbal ability and verbal input have on ToM (Devine & Hughes, 2019; Milligan et al., 2007), this section takes a different perspective and examines the role that ToM has on children's high-level language skill development: Mental state talk (MST) and pragmatic skills.

The study of MST represents a hot topic in the developmental literature. Recent literature has shown that individual differences in children's ToM during middle childhood correlate with the frequency of cognitive state talk one year later (Lecce et al., 2010), suggesting that ToM acts as a promoter of children's use (and possibly understanding) of mental-state terms. Coupled with findings that MST correlates with metacognition (Lockl & Schneider, 2006), these results suggest that MST drives (at least in part) the positive effect of ToM on school performance. ToM skills may support the enrichment of children's mental-state vocabulary and understanding and this, in turn, may facilitate further development of metacognitive skills and enable children to benefit from increasingly complex methods of instruction.

ToM is also linked to another form of advanced language skills: Figurative language and, in particular, metaphor understanding. Understanding metaphors is a complex task requiring the ability to adjust the literal meaning of words and infer the speaker's meaning based on the communicative context (Carston, 2010). On this basis, and considering the fact that metaphors often refer to emotions and mental states (Kövecses, 2000), researchers have shown that those clinical conditions, such as Autism Spectrum Disorder (ASD) and schizophrenia, which are characterized by a deficit in ToM, also show a disadvantage in metaphor understanding (Bosia et al., 2016; Kalandadze et al., 2019; Vulchanova et al., 2015; Whyte & Nelson, 2015). Regarding the typical population, studies on processing have often pointed to the involvement of ToM brain circuitry (Bambini et al., 2011) in metaphor understanding. A very recent study conducted by my colleagues and I showed a significant correlation (moderate to strong in size) between ToM and metaphor understanding (Del Sette et al., in press) assessed through a classic verbal task. Interestingly, figurative language is frequently used at school, where teachers use it to admonish, to praise, and to express humor and sarcasm (Mio & Katz, 2018; Nippold, 1991). Perhaps more importantly, the use of metaphors facilitates children's learning as it allows for the understanding of new abstract and complex concepts, taking advantage of what is already known, and also enhances memorability (Low, 2008).

This section presents three different pathways through which ToM may influence school outcomes: (1) A social route, by impacting children's social circumstances within their school; (2) a metacognitive route, by influencing different areas of children's metacognition, such as sensitivity to criticism, metamemory, meta-reading, and beliefs about learning; and (3) a linguistic route, by affecting children's mental state talk and figurative language. These pathways are represented in Figure 8.2 at the end of this chapter.

Promoting theory of mind at school

Given the existence and importance of individual differences in ToM for children's cognitive and social development (see also Chapters 6 and 7 of this volume), researchers have started to ask whether ToM can be enhanced during middle childhood and adolescence and whether it is possible to do this within the school context.

In a recent meta-analysis of 45 training studies on 1,529 children (both typically developing and atypically developing) with a mean age of 63 months, Hofmann and colleagues (2016) found that ToM training programs have a moderately strong effect in improving children's ToM skills (compared with a control group), with an effect that was larger for training programs with longer sessions and shorter training periods. Typically, in these training programs, children participated in individual sessions in which they were prompted to reason about story characters' mental states and were required to take alternative perspectives. The majority of training studies were designed either for preschoolers or for older children with clinical conditions.

One notable exception to this trend is the training program that my colleagues and I developed for typically developing children attending primary school (Lecce et al., 2014b). This training (see Table 8.1 for more details) was based on narratives, followed by a series of questions and a language exercise. In the ToM condition, the narratives were about mental states, the language exercises involved mental-state verbs, and the experimenter made substantial use of the mental-state language within sentential complement constructions. In the control condition, the stories were about physical events, the language exercises involved physical verbs, and the experimenter made no use of the mental-state language. A core aspect of this ToM training program is the use of group conversations about mental (or physical) states, which provide

Table 8.1 Description of Lecce and colleagues' ToM training program (2014)

	ToM training	*Control training*
N° sessions	Four of 50 minutes each	
Exercises	Narratives, comprehension questions, language exercise	
Approach	Individual questions followed by group conversations including explanations and corrective feedback	
Theoretical background	Socio-constructivist account	
Focus	Mental states	Physical states
Materials	Mental narratives (two misunderstanding, two double-bluff, two Faux Pas, two persuasion)	Physical narratives

opportunities to elaborate on children's comments, explaining the reasons why their answers are right or wrong and highlighting the existence of different points. We tested the efficacy of this ToM training program (as compared to a control physical one) in six different studies involving a total of 423 children with an age range spanning from seven to ten years. Table 8.2 provides details for each of these training studies.

Overall, results of these studies (see Figure 8.1) showed that the ToM training program was effective in stimulating gains in children's understanding of mind with an average effect size on the practice task (i.e., Strange Stories) that was large (Cohen's d = .89) (Cohen, 1988). The positive effects of training were evident not only in the Strange Stories task but generalized to a far transfer task for which children received no training, the Triangles Animation task (Cohen's d = .69). Furthermore, these positive effects were also evident two months later (Cohen's d = .47) and were due to an increased ability to make context-sensitive inferences about mental states (indexed by the accuracy of mental-state attributions) rather than to increased attention toward mental states (indexed by the frequency of use of mental-state references).

Demonstrating that training can enhance children's ToM supports the claim that individual differences in ToM skills are not merely the result of maturational changes or broad developments in cognitive processing, but are influenced by the specific type of social-environmental input that children receive (Carpendale & Lewis, 2004; Slaughter & De Rosnay, 2017). Accordingly, we recently conducted an exhaustive training study to demonstrate that conversations about mental states, rather than exposure to mental material and self-reflection about mental states, is the core ingredient of this training program (Lecce et al., in prep). Together with a study by Meristo and colleagues on deaf children attending oralist and bimodal/bilingual schools (Meristo et al., 2007), our studies are the first clear demonstration that conversations about the mind in the school environment and, more generally, children's social and communicative experiences during primary school are meaningful for ToM understanding and exert a

Table 8.2 Overview of the ToM training studies on children in middle childhood

Reference	*Participants*	*Control measures*	*ToM measures*	*Follow up*
Lecce, S., Bianco, F., Devine, R., Hughes, C., & Banerjee, R. (2014). Promoting theory of mind in middle childhood: A training program. *Journal of Experimental Child Psychology, 126,* 52–67.	N = 91 *M* age = 9.58; *SD* = .34 Age range = 9.08–10.83	SES (Family Affluence Scale) Verbal ability (WISC-R) Planning (Tower of London) Working memory (WISC-R) Reading comprehension (MT)	Strange Stories	✓
Bianco, F. & Lecce, S. (2016). Translating child development research into practice: Can teachers foster children's theory of mind in primary school? *British Journal of Educational Psychology, 86,* 592–605.	N = 72 *M* age = 8.68; *SD* = .36 Age range = 7.92–9.25	SES (Family Affluence Scale) Verbal ability (PMA) Planning (Tower of London) Working memory (WISC-R) Reading comprehension (MT)	Strange Stories	✓
Bianco, F., Lecce S., & Banerjee, R. (2016). Conversations about mental states and theory of mind development in middle childhood: A training study. *Journal of Experimental Child Psychology, 149,* 41–61.	N = 101 *M* age = 9.62; *SD* = .33 Age range = 8.83–10.42	SES (Family Affluence Scale) Verbal ability (PMA) Planning (Tower of London) Working memory (WISC-R) Reading comprehension (MT)	Strange Stories Animations task	✓
Lecce, S. & Bianco, F. (2018). Working memory predicts children's theory of mind during middle childhood: A training study. *Cognitive Development, 47,* 71–81.	N = 86 *M* age = 9.67; *SD* = .62 Age range = 8.75–11	SES (Family Affluence Scale) Verbal ability (PMA) Working memory (WISC-R) Reading comprehension (MT)	Animations task	X

(*Continued*)

Table 8.2 Continued

Reference	*Participants*	*Control measures*	*ToM measures*	*Follow up*
Bianco, F., Lombardi, E., Massaro, D., Castelli, I., Valle, A., Marchetti, A., &, Lecce, S. (2019). Enhancing advanced ToM skills in Primary school: A training study with 7- to 8-year olds. *Infant and Child Development.*	N = 49 *M* age = 7.60; *SD* = .33 Age range = 6.58–8.25	SES (Family Affluence Scale) Verbal ability (PMA) Inhibition (Fruit Stroop) Shifting (MWCST) Working memory (WISC-R) Reading comprehension (MT)	Strange Stories Animations task	X
Lecce, S., Bianco, F., & Banerjee, R. (in prep.). Let's discuss! Connected mental-state conversations as engine of ToM development in middle childhood.	N = 110 *M* age = 9.50; *SD* = .39 Age range = 8.67–11.33	SES (Family Affluence Scale) Verbal ability (PMA) Inhibition (Arrow) Working memory (WISC-R) Reading comprehension (MT)	Strange Stories Animations task	X

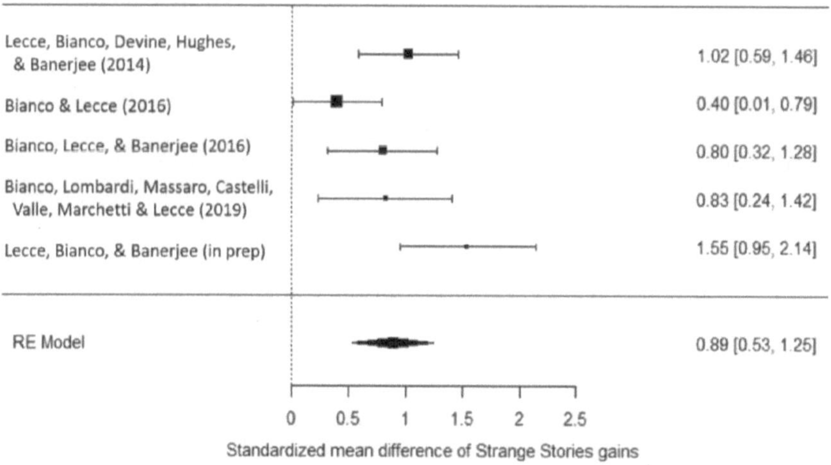

Figure 8.1 Effects of Theory of Mind training.

continued influence on ToM development. Notably, we have also shown that the positive effects of training were independent of individual differences in age, working memory, planning, reading comprehension, family affluence, and verbal ability, as measured before the training. Altogether these results are important as they indicate, first, that the training program we developed promotes a genuine (and relatively durable) change in children's ability to explain social behaviors on the basis of inner states and, second, that the ToM program is suitable for children with different levels of ToM, EF, reading comprehension, verbal ability, and socioeconomic background.

From an educational perspective, the fact that the effect of mental-state conversations was independent of individual differences on all baseline measures is very important, as it suggests that the program activities can be easily conveyed to the whole class group and that it is potentially applicable under real-world school conditions. In addition, the training we developed has at least three other features that make it suitable for application in the context of school life. Firstly, it uses written narratives, which are typical school activities. Secondly, our ToM training program makes considerable use of feedback (with which teachers are very familiar) in order to confirm and expand children's answers. Thirdly, in our program, each training trial follows a predictable sequence in which children work individually and, subsequently, take part in group discussions guided by an adult. This sequence (i.e., individual work followed by group discussion) is a very common one when carrying out classroom-based activities. Starting from these premises, Bianco and Lecce (2016) tested the effectiveness of our training program when implemented by regular class teachers during normal school time. Results showed that the ToM group improved ToM skills significantly more than the control group (Cohen's d = .80).

The aforementioned study by Bianco and Lecce (2016) is the first clear demonstration that teachers can successfully promote their pupils' ToM development during their regular teaching hours. It clearly shows that teachers can have a role in children's ToM development and that programs to convey teachers' best practices on how to improve children's ToM skills should be carefully considered by researchers and educators. Working with teachers, and not directly with children, also has the practical advantage of potentially reaching a large number of children with relatively low cost and little effort involved. The enhancement of ToM competence might provide teachers with a platform to help students to deal successfully with the social and academic challenges of the school context. On a more general note, it is important to consider that a number of school-based activities and school settings–related variables are likely to influence children's ToM. The language and method of instruction used by teachers may potentially promote pupils' understanding of mental states. Indeed, existing research provides strong support for the view that adults' references to mental-state terms (Devine & Hughes, 2019) and use of cognitive-processing language (i.e., instruction that is rich in references to cognitive processes, metacognition, and requests for remembering) positively influence children's ToM development and their school achievement

(Grammer et al., 2016; Zepeda et al., 2019). Another school-related factor that can potentially impact children's ToM is classroom composition. Of note, it is important to recall that existing research has pointed out the importance that diversity has for children's ToM. For example, Cassidy and colleagues have shown that preschoolers whose only sibling is a twin benefit less than those who also have a non-twin sibling (Cassidy et al., 2005), and Deneault et al. (2008) have reported that monozygotic twins (whose cognitive perspectives are likely to be highly overlapping) are slower to gain emotion understanding than dizygotic twins. Thus, an interesting possibility, which should be investigated in the future, is whether the diversity of classroom composition has a role in children's ToM development. One possibility is that the more diverse the classroom is in terms of children's cognitive levels, the more children are likely to increase their mindreading skills. Despite the fact that no research to date has focused on this issue, a very recent study by Smogorzewska and colleagues showed that in inclusive classrooms, the learning of ToM in children with a mild intellectual disability was significantly greater than that of children with a mild intellectual disability in special classrooms (Smogorzewska et al., 2019), thus suggesting that inclusive classrooms maximize ToM development. Whether this is also the case for typically developing children remains an open question for future research.

The findings reported above clearly show that it is possible to support ToM development in middle childhood through school activities that encourage reflection on story characters' mental states and on the meaning of mental state talk. The literature reported herein also highlights that mental-state conversations within the peer school group are crucial in accelerating children's progress in ToM. Such mental-state conversations can easily be proposed by teachers in the context of normal school activities and should be viewed as an important step in the development of effective pedagogy to support pupils' adaptive daily life functioning.

Caveats, conclusions, and new directions

In a shift from traditional research, which has mainly considered the social consequences of individual differences in ToM (Lecce & Devine, in press; Slaughter & de Rosnay, 2017), this chapter focused on the school correlates of children's advanced mindreading skills. The main aim was to provide an overview of the literature linking children's ToM and academic achievement. This topic has historically been overlooked, perhaps because most research on children's ToM comes from developmental rather than educational literature and because traditional studies on school success have overlooked the importance of social skills. Overall, the findings reviewed in this chapter provide compelling evidence that ToM can be viewed as a tool that enables children to develop sophisticated forms of knowledge about mental phenomena, advanced forms of language, and positive social relationships in the school context and, as such, influences school achievement.

The results of this growing body of research are summarized in the 'ToM at school framework' depicted in Figure 8.2. It presents a model that explains the relations between ToM and school outcomes considering underlying mechanisms and highlighting the importance of environmental contextual inputs. This framework makes novel and testable predictions about the relations between ToM and school achievement. Whereas some of these hypotheses have been tested, others provide an agenda for future research. As is clear from the 'ToM at school framework', the relation between ToM and school outcomes is expected to be bidirectional and complex; while it is plausible that children's ToM may help children to achieve better school results, it is also possible that academic achievement, or at least some components of it (i.e., reading comprehension), acts as an engine of children's mindreading abilities, creating a virtuous circle that unfolds over time. As anticipated, empirical findings and theoretical positions show that there is more than one route through which ToM can influence children's school performance during middle childhood: Through social relationships within school (e.g., relationships with peers and teachers) and social competence, impacting children's metacognition (e.g., sensitivity to criticism, metamemory, meta-reading), and through advanced forms of language (e.g., mental state talk and metaphor understanding). Notably, it is entirely possible that these different routes are active at the same time.

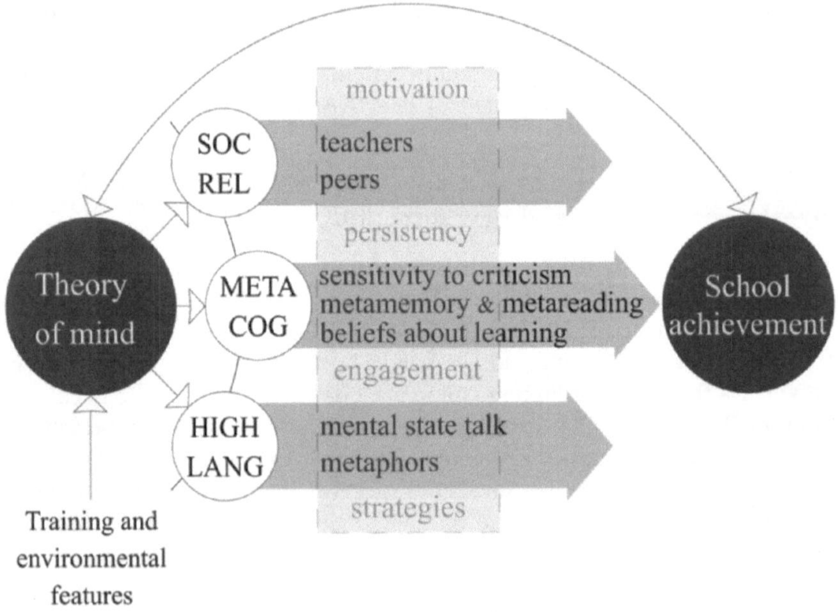

Figure 8.2 Theory of Mind at school framework.

The third set of predictions concerns the relations between social relationships, metacognition, high-level language skills, and school achievement. These relations are unlikely to be simple or direct. The framework that I propose predicts that the expected links between social relationships, metacognition, and high-level language skills and school outcomes could be mediated, in part, by individual differences in children's motivation towards and persistence in school tasks, school engagement, and strategic behaviors. Research clearly shows that children with better social relationships in the classroom, with more advanced metacognitive knowledge and high-level language skills, are more receptive to teachers' input and show superior school performance (Low, 2008; Mizokawa, 2015; Nelson & DeBacker, 2008; Perdue et al., 2009; Zimmerman & Moylan, 2009). Note that these different routes are not mutually exclusive and are likely to influence each other.

This framework also highlights the importance of environmental factors within the school context for children's ToM development. In particular, the adoption of a teaching style characterized by the frequent use of mental-state group conversations helps children's ToM, independently of their initial level of ToM, language, and EF.

The focus on intervention not only provides an opportunity to increase children's school outcomes but also allows researchers to test causal relations (in a controlled and stringent way) between ToM and school success in middle childhood and adolescence. Training ToM provides a way to assess its impact on children's lives and education and should be considered in future research.

From a methodological point of view, cross-lagged longitudinal and training studies on large samples are needed in order to test the predictions of this framework. An additional crucial step for future research is to learn more about the developmental processes that connect ToM with school achievement during adolescence. The majority of studies cited in this chapter focused on children younger than ten years. However, ToM continues to increase during adolescence (e.g., Dumontheil et al., 2010), and studies show that ToM is particularly important in crucial developmental periods characterized by high instability, such as the transition to secondary school (see, for example, Ronchi et al., 2020).

Overall, the proliferation of research into ToM in middle childhood and adolescence is exciting as it provides a valuable platform to investigate the effects that individual differences in mindreading have on children's school achievement. Future research will benefit from integrating developmental and educational literature in order to improve children's wellbeing.

References

Atkinson, L., Slade, L., Powell, D., & Levy, J.P. (2017). Theory of mind in emerging reading comprehension: A longitudinal study of early indirect and direct effects. *Journal of Experimental Child Psychology, 164*, 225–238. doi:10.1016/j.jecp.2017.04.007

Bambini, V., Gentili, C., Ricciardi, E., Bertinetto, P.M., & Pietrini, P. (2011). Decomposing metaphor processing at the cognitive and neural level through functional magnetic resonance imaging. *Brain Research Bulletin, 86*(3–4), 203–216. doi:10.1016/j.brainresbull.2011.07.015

Bandura, A. (2002). Social cognitive theory in cultural context. *Applied Psychology, 51*(2), 269–290. doi:10.1111/1464-0597.00092

Banerjee, R., Watling, D., & Caputi, M. (2011). Peer relations and the understanding of faux pas: Longitudinal evidence for bidirectional associations. *Child Development, 82*(6), 1887–1905. doi:10.1111/j.1467-8624.2011.01669.x

Baron-Cohen, S., O'Riordan, M., Stone, V., Jones, R., & Plaisted, K. (1999). Recognition of faux pas by normally developing children and children with Asperger syndrome or high-functioning autism. *Journal of Autism and Developmental Disorders, 29*(5), 407–418. doi:10.1023/A:1023035012436

Bartsch, K., & Estes, D. (1996). Individual differences in children's developing theory of mind and implications for metacognition. *Learning and Individual Differences, 8*(4), 281–304. doi:10.1016/S1041-6080(96)90020-5

Bianco, F., & Lecce, S. (2016). Translating child development research into practice: Can teachers foster children's theory of mind in primary school? *British Journal of Educational Psychology, 86*(4), 592–605. doi:10.1111/bjep.12125

Bianco, F., Lecce, S., & Banerjee, R. (2016). Conversations about mental states and theory of mind development during middle childhood: A training study. *Journal of Experimental Child Psychology, 149*, 41–61. doi:10.1016/j.jecp.2015.11.006

Bianco, F., Lombardi, E., Massaro, D., Castelli, I., Valle, A., Marchetti, A., & Lecce, S. (2019). Enhancing advanced theory of mind skills in primary school: A training study with 7- to 8-year-olds. *Infant and Child Development.* doi:10.1002/icd.2155

Blair, C., & Raver, C.C. (2015). School readiness and self-regulation: A developmental psychobiological approach. *Annual Review of Psychology, 66*, 711–731. doi:10.1146/annurev-psych-010814-015221

Blair, C., & Razza, R.P. (2007). Relating effortful control, executive function, and false belief understanding to emerging math and literacy ability in kindergarten. *Child Development, 78*(2), 647–663. doi:10.1111/j.1467-8624.2007.01019.x

Borkowski, J.G., & Muthukrishna, N. (1992). Moving metacognition into the classroom: Working models and effective strategy teaching. In M. Pressley, K.R. Harris, & J.T. Guthrie (Eds.), *Promoting Academic Literacy: Cognitive Research and Instructional Innovation* (pp. 477–501). Orlando, FL: Academic Press

Bosco, F.M., Tirassa, M., & Gabbatore, I. (2018). Why pragmatics and theory of mind do not (completely) overlap. *Frontiers in Psychology, 9*, 1453. doi:10.3389/fpsyg.2018.01453

Bosia, M., Arcara, G., Buonocore, M., Bechi, M., Moro, A., Cavallaro, R., & Bambini, V. (2016). Communication in schizophrenia, between pragmatics, cognition and social cognition. In A.M. Di Sciullo (Ed.), *Biolinguistic Investigations on the Language Faculty* (pp. 213–234). Amsterdam: John Benjamins

Bruner, J. (1987). Life as narrative. *Social Research*, 54, 11–32.

Buhs, E.S., Ladd, G.W., & Herald, S.L. (2006). Peer exclusion and victimization: Processes that mediate the relation between peer group rejection and children's classroom engagement and achievement? *Journal of Educational Psychology, 98*(1), 1–13. doi:10.1037/0022-0663.98.1.1

Burhans, K.K., & Dweck, C.S. (1995). Helplessness in early childhood: The role of contingent worth. *Child Development, 66*(6), 1719–1738. doi:10.2307/1131906

Cain, K., Oakhill, J.V., Barnes, M.A., & Bryant, P.E. (2001). Comprehension skill, inference-making ability, and their relation to knowledge. *Memory and Cognition, 29*(6), 850–859. doi:10.3758/BF03196414

Campbell, S.B., Spieker, S., Burchinal, M., Poe, M.D., & NICHD Early Child Care Research Network (2006). Trajectories of aggression from toddlerhood to age 9 predict academic and social functioning through age 12. *Journal of Child Psychology and Psychiatry, and Allied Disciplines*, *47*(8), 791–800. doi:10.1111/j.1469-7610.2006.01636.x

Cantin, R.H., Gnaedinger, E.K., Gallaway, K.C., Hesson-McInnis, M.S., & Hund, A.M. (2016). Executive functioning predicts reading, mathematics, and theory of mind during the elementary years. *Journal of Experimental Child Psychology*, *146*, 66–78. doi:10.1016/j.jecp.2016.01.014

Caprara, G.V., Barbaranelli, C., Pastorelli, C., Bandura, A., & Zimbardo, P.G. (2000). Prosocial foundations of children's academic achievement. *Psychological Science*, *11*(4), 302. doi:10.1111/1467-9280.00260

Carpendale, J.I.M., & Lewis, C. (2004). Constructing an understanding of mind: The development of children's social understanding within social interaction. *Behavioral and Brain Sciences*, *27*(1), 79–151. doi:10.1017/S0140525X04000032

Carston, R. (2010). Lexical pragmatics, ad hoc concepts and metaphor: A relevance theory perspective. *Italian Journal of Linguistics*, *22*, 153–180

Cassidy, K.W., Fineberg, D.S., Brown, K., & Perkins, A. (2005). Theory of mind may be contagious, but you don't catch it From your twin. *Child Development*, *76*(1), 97–106. doi:10.1111/j.1467-8624.2005.00832.x

Castelli, F., Happé, F., Frith, U., & Frith, C. (2000). Movement and mind: A functional imaging study of perception and interpretation of complex intentional movement patterns. *NeuroImage*, *12*(3), 314–325. doi:10.1006/nimg.2000.0612

Cavadel, E.W., & Frye, D.A. (2017). Not just numeracy and literacy: Theory of mind development and school readiness among low-income children. *Developmental Psychology*, *53*(12), 2290–2303. doi:10.1037/dev0000409

Chan, C.K.K., & Law, Y.K. (2003). Metacognitive beliefs and strategies in reading comprehension. In C. McBride & C.H. Chen (Eds.), *Reading Development in Chinese Children* (pp. 171–182). Westport, CT: Praeger

Chan, C.K.K., & Sachs, J. (2001). Beliefs about learning in children's understanding of science texts. *Contemporary Educational Psychology*, *26*(2), 192–210. doi:10.1006/ceps.1999.1045

Chen, X., Rubin, K.H., & Li, D. (1997). Relation between academic achievement and social adjustment: Evidence from Chinese children. *Developmental Psychology*, *33*(3), 518–525. doi:10.1037/0012-1649.33.3.518

Cohen, J. (1988). *Statistical Power Analysis for the Behavioural Sciences*. New York: Academic Press

Cornoldi, C., DeBeni, R., & Fioritto, M.C. (2003). The assessment of self-regulation in college students with and without academic difficulties. *Advances in Learning and Behavioral Disabilities*, *16*, 231–242. doi:10.1016/S0735-004X(03)16009-0

Cutting, A.L., & Dunn, J. (2002). The cost of understanding other people: Social cognition predicts young children's sensitivity to criticism. *Journal of Child Psychology and Psychiatry, and Allied Disciplines*, *43*(7), 849–860. doi:10.1111/1469-7610.t01-1-00047

Del Sette, P., Bambini, V., & Lecce, S. (2020). Longitudinal associations between ToM and metaphors in children. *Journal of Cognition and Development*, *56*, 100958

Deneault, J., Ricard, M., Gouin Décarie, T., Morin, P.L., Quintal, G., Boivin, M., Tremblay, R.E., & Pérusse, D. (2008). False belief and emotion understanding in monozygotic twins, dizygotic twins and non-twin children. *Cognition and Emotion*, *22*(4), 697–708. doi:10.1080/02699930701486896

Denham, S.A. (2006). Social-emotional competence as support for school readiness: What is it and how do we assess it? *Early Education and Development, 17*(1), 57–89. doi:10.1207/s15566935eed1701_4

Denham, S.A., Bassett, H.H., Thayer, S.K., Mincic, M.S., Sirotkin, Y.S., & Zinsser, K. (2012). Observing preschoolers' social-emotional behavior: Structure, foundations, and prediction of early school success. *The Journal of Genetic Psychology, 173*(3), 246–278. doi:10.1080/00221325.2011.597457

Devine, R.T., & Hughes, C. (2013). Silent films and strange stories: Theory of mind, gender, and social experiences in middle childhood. *Child Development, 84*(3), 989–1003. doi:10.1111/cdev.12017

Devine, R.T., & Hughes, C. (2019). Let's talk: Parents' mental talk (not mind-mindedness or mindreading capacity) predicts children's false belief understanding. *Child Development, 90*(4), 1236–1253. doi:10.1111/cdev.12990

Dodell-Feder, D., & Tamir, D.I. (2018). Fiction reading has a small positive impact on social cognition: A meta-analysis. *Journal of Experimental Psychology. General, 147*(11), 1713. doi:10.1037/xge0000395

Doise, W., Mugny, G., James, A.S., Emler, N., & Mackie, D. (2013). *The Social Development of the Intellect* (Vol. 10). Oxford, UK: Pergamon Press.

Dore, R.A., Amendum, S.J., Golinkoff, R.M., & Hirsh-Pasek, K. (2018). Theory of mind: A hidden factor in reading comprehension? *Educational Psychology Review, 30*(3), 1067–1089. doi:10.1007/s10648-018-9443-9

Dumontheil, I., Apperly, I.A., & Blakemore, S.J. (2010). Online usage of theory of mind continues to develop in late adolescence. *Developmental Science, 13*(2), 331–338. doi:10.1111/j.1467-7687.2009.00888.x

Duncan, G.J., Dowsett, C.J., Claessens, A., Magnuson, K., Huston, A.C., Klebanov, P., Pagani, L.S., Feinstein, L., Engel, M., Brooks-Gunn, J., Sexton, H., & Duckworth, K. (2007). School readiness and later achievement. *Developmental Psychology, 43*(6), 1428–1446. doi:10.1037/0012-1649.43.6.1428

Dziobek, I., Fleck, S., Kalbe, E., Rogers, K., Hassenstab, J., Brand, M., Kessler, J., Woike, J.K., Wolf, O.T., & Convit, A. (2006). Introducing MASC: A movie for the assessment of social cognition. *Journal of Autism and Developmental Disorders, 36*(5), 623–636. doi:10.1007/s10803-006-0107-0

Ebert, S. (2015). Longitudinal relations between theory of mind and metacognition and the impact of language. *Journal of Cognition and Development, 16*(4), 559–586. doi:10.1080/15248372.2014.926272

Fergusson, D.M., & Horwood, L.J. (1995). Early disruptive behavior, IQ, and later school achievement and delinquent behavior. *Journal of Abnormal Child Psychology, 23*(2), 183–199. doi:10.1007/BF01447088

Fernández-Sotos, P., Torio, I., Fernández-Caballero, A., Navarro, E., González, P., Dompablo, M., & Rodriguez-Jimenez, R. (2019). Social cognition remediation interventions: A systematic mapping review. *PLOS ONE, 14*(6). doi:10.1371/journal.pone.0218720

Frese, M., & Altman, A. (1989). The treatment of errors in learning and training. In L. Bainbridge & S.A. Quintanilla (Eds.), *Developing Skills with Information Technology* (pp. 65–86). Chichester, UK: John Wiley.

Frye, D., & Ziv, M. (2005). Teaching and learning as intentional activities. In B.D. Homer & C.S. Tamis-LeMonda (Eds.), *The Development of Social Cognition and Communication* (pp. 231–258). Mahwah, NJ: Lawrence Erlbaum Associates Publishers.

Grammer, J.K., Coffman, J.L., Sidney, P., & Ornstein, P.A. (2016). Linking teacher instruction and student achievement in mathematics: The role of teacher language.

Journal of Cognition and Development, 17(3), 468–485. doi:10.1080/15248372.2015.1068777

Guajardo, N., & Cartwright, K. (2016). The contribution of theory of mind, counterfactual reasoning, and executive function to pre-readers' language comprehension and later reading awareness and comprehension in elementary school. *Journal of Experimental Child Psychology, 144*, 27–45. doi:10.1016/j.jecp.2015.11.004

Gully, S.M., Payne, S.C., Kiechel Koles, K.L., & Whiteman, J.A. (2002). The impact of error training and individual differences on training outcomes: An attribute-treatment interaction perspective. *Journal of Applied Psychology, 87*(1), 143–155. doi:10.1037/0021-9010.87.1.143

Hamre, B.K., & Pianta, R.C. (2001). Early teacher–child relationships and the trajectory of children's school outcomes through eighth grade. *Child Development, 72*(2), 625–638. doi:10.1111/1467-8624.00301

Happé, F. (2015). Autism as a neurodevelopmental disorder of mind-reading. *Journal of the British Academy, 3*, 197–209. doi:10.5871/jba/003.197

Heyman, G.D., Dweck, C.S., & Cain, K.M. (1992). Young children's vulnerability to self-blame and helplessness: Relationship to beliefs about goodness. *Child Development, 63*(2), 401–415. http://www.ncbi.nlm.nih.gov/pubmed/1131488

Hofmann, S.G., Doan, S.N., Sprung, M., Wilson, A., Ebesutani, C., Andrews, L.A., Curtiss, J., & Harris, P.L. (2016). Training children's theory-of-mind: A meta-analysis of controlled studies. *Cognition, 150*, 200–212. doi:10.1016/j.cognition.2016.01.006

Hughes, C. (2011). *Social Understanding and Social Lives: From Toddlerhood through to the Transition to School*. London: Psychology Press.

Hughes, C., Daly, I., Foley, S., White, N., & Devine, R.T. (2015). Measuring the foundations of school readiness: Introducing a new questionnaire for teachers—the Brief Early Skills and Support Index (BESSI). *British Journal of Educational Psychology, 85*(3), 332–356. doi:10.1111/bjep.12076

Hughes, C., Devine, R., Ensor, R., Koyasu, M., Mizokawa, A., & Lecce, S. (2014). Lost in translation? comparing British, Japanese, and Italian children's theory-of-mind performance. *Child Development Research Manuscript*. doi:10.1155/2014/893492

Hughes, C., Devine, R.T., & Wang, Z. (2018). Does parental mind-mindedness account for cross-cultural differences in preschoolers' theory of mind? *Child Development, 89*(4), 1296–1310. doi:10.1111/cdev.12746

Izard, C., Fine, S., Schultz, D., Mostow, A., Ackerman, B., & Youngstrom, E. (2001). Emotion knowledge as a predictor of social behavior and academic competence in children at risk. *Psychological Science, 12*(1), 18–23. doi:10.1111/1467-9280.00304

Jones, C.R., Happé, F., Golden, H., Marsden, A.J., Tregay, J., Simonoff, E., Pickles, A., Baird, G., & Charman, T. (2009). Reading and arithmetic in adolescents with autism spectrum disorders: Peaks and dips in attainment. *Neuropsychology, 23*(6), 718–728. doi:10.1037/a0016360

Kalandadze, T., Bambini, V., & Næss, K.B. (2019). A systematic review and meta-analysis of studies on metaphor comprehension in individuals with autism spectrum disorder: Do task properties matter? *Applied Psycholinguistics, 40*(6), 1421–1454. doi:10.1017/S0142716419000328

Kamins, M.L., & Dweck, C.S. (1999). Person versus process praise and criticism: Implications for contingent self-worth and coping. *Developmental Psychology, 35*(3), 835–847. doi:10.1037//0012-1649.35.3.835

Klein, P.D. (1998). The role of children's theory of mind in science experimentation. *The Journal of Experimental Education, 66*(2), 101–124. doi:10.1080/00220979809601398

Koenig, M.A., & Sabbagh, M.A. (2013). Selective social learning: New perspectives on learning from others. *Developmental Psychology, 49*(3), 399–403. doi:10.1037/a0031619
Kövecses, Z. (2000). *Metaphor and Emotion: Language, Culture, and Body in Human Feeling.* New York, NY: Cambridge University Press
Kruger, A.C., & Tomasello, M. (1996). Cultural learning and learning culture. In D.R. Olson and N. Torrance (Ed.), *The Handbook of Education and Human Development* (pp. 369–387). Malden: Blackwell Publishing.
Kuhn, D. (2000). Theory of mind, metacognition, and reasoning: A life-span perspective. In P. Mitchell & K.J. Riggs (Eds.), *Children's Reasoning and the Mind* (pp. 301–326). Hove, UK: Psychology Press/Taylor & Francis
Kuhn, D. (2009). The importance of learning about knowing: Creating a foundation for development of intellectual values. *Child Development Perspectives, 3*(2), 112–117. doi:10.1111/j.1750-8606.2009.00089.x
Kuhn, D., & Dean, D., Jr. (2004). Metacognition: A bridge between cognitive psychology and educational practice. *Theory Into Practice, 43*(4), 268–273. doi:10.1207/s15430421tip4304_4
Kuhn, D., & Pearsall, S. (2000). Developmental origins of scientific thinking. *Journal of Cognition and Development, 1*(1), 113–129. doi:10.1207/S15327647JCD0101N_11
Lecce, S., & Bianco, F. (2018). Working memory predicts changes in children's theory of mind during middle childhood: A training study. *Cognitive Development, 47*, 71–81. doi:10.1016/j.cogdev.2018.04.002
Lecce, S., Bianco, F., & Banerjee, R. (in prep). How best to promote ToM in middle childhood: Comparing the role of mental state conversations with that of mental material.
Lecce, S., Bianco, F., Demicheli, P., & Cavallini, E. (2014a). Training preschoolers on first-order false belief understanding: Transfer on advanced ToM skills and metamemory. *Child Development, 85*(6), 2404–2418. doi:10.1111/cdev.12267
Lecce, S., Bianco, F., Devine, R., Hughes, C., & Banerjee, R. (2014b). Promoting theory of mind during middle childhood: A training program. *Journal of Experimental Child Psychology, 126*, 52–67. doi:10.1016/j.jecp.2014.03.002
Lecce, S., Bianco, F., & Hughes, C. (2021). Reading minds and reading texts: Evidence for independent and specific associations. *Cognitive Development, 57*, 101010. doi:10.1016/j.cogdev.2021.101010
Lecce, S., Caputi, M., & Hughes, C. (2011). Does sensitivity to criticism mediate the relationship between theory of mind and academic achievement? *Journal of Experimental Child Psychology, 110*(3), 313–331. doi:10.1016/j.jecp.2011.04.011
Lecce, S., Caputi, M., & Pagnin, A. (2014c). Long-term effect of theory of mind on school achievement: The role of sensitivity to criticism. *European Journal of Developmental Psychology, 11*(3), 305–318. doi:10.1080/17405629.2013.821944
Lecce, S., Caputi, M., & Pagnin, A. (2015). False-belief understanding at age 5 predicts beliefs about learning in year 3 of primary school. *European Journal of Developmental Psychology, 12*(1), 40–53. doi:10.1080/17405629.2014.949665
Lecce, S., Caputi, M., Pagnin, A., & Banerjee, R. (2017). Theory of mind and school achievement: The mediating role of social competence. *Cognitive Development, 44*, 85–97. doi:10.1016/j.cogdev.2017.08.010
Lecce, S., Demicheli, P., Zocchi, S., & Palladino, P. (2015). The origins of children's metamemory: The role of theory of mind. *Journal of Experimental Child Psychology, 131*, 56–72. doi:10.1016/j.jecp.2014.11.005
Lecce, S., & Devine, R.T. (2021). Social interaction in early and middle childhood: The role of theory of mind. In H.J. Ferguson & E.E.F. Bradford (Eds.), *The Cognitive Basis of Social Interaction Across the Lifespan* (pp. 46–68). Oxford, UK: Oxford University Press.

Lecce, S., & Hughes, C. (2010). "The Italian job?": Comparing theory of mind performance in British and Italian children. *British Journal of Developmental Psychology, 28*(4), 747–766. doi:10.1348/026151009X479006

Lecce, S., Zocchi, S., Pagnin, A., Palladino, P., & Taumoepeau, M. (2010). Reading minds: The relation between children's mental state knowledge and their metaknowledge about reading. *Child Development, 81*(6), 1876–1893. doi:10.1111/j.1467-8624.2010.01516.x

Lindgren, K.A., Folstein, S.E., Tomblin, J.B., & Tager-Flusberg, H. (2009). Language and reading abilities of children with autism spectrum disorders and specific language impairment and their first-degree relatives. *Autism Research: Official Journal of the International Society for Autism Research, 2*(1), 22–38. doi:10.1002/aur.63

Lockl, K., Ebert, S., & Weinert, S. (2017). Predicting school achievement from early theory of mind: Differential effects on achievement tests and teacher ratings. *Learning and Individual Differences, 53*, 93–102. doi:10.1016/j.lindif.2016.11.007

Lockl, K., & Schneider, W. (2006). Precursors of metamemory in young children: The role of theory of mind and metacognitive vocabulary. *Metacognition and Learning, 1*(1), 15–31. doi:10.1007/s11409-006-6585-9

Low, G.D. (2008). Metaphor in Education. In R. Gibbs (Ed.), *The Cambridge handbook of metaphor and thought* (pp. 212–231). Cambridge, UK: Cambridge University Press.

Lysaker, J., Tonge, C., Gauson, D., & Miller, A. (2011). Reading and social imagination: What relationally oriented reading instruction can do for children. *Reading Psychology, 32*, 520–566. doi:10.1080/02702711.2010.507589

Mar, R.A., & Oatley, K. (2008). The function of fiction is the abstraction and simulation of social experience. *Perspectives on Psychological Science: A Journal of the Association for Psychological Science, 3*(3), 173–192. doi:10.1111/j.1745-6924.2008.00073.x

Mar, R.A., Tackett, J.L., & Moore, C. (2010). Exposure to media and theory-of-mind development in preschoolers. *Cognitive Development, 25*(1), 69–78. doi:10.1016/j.cogdev.2009.11.002

Matsumura, L.C., Patthey-Chavez, G.G., Valdés, R., & Garnier, H. (2002). Teacher feedback, writing assignment quality, and third-grade students' revision in lower- and higher-achieving urban schools. *Elementary School Journal, 103*(1), 3–25. doi:10.1086/499713

McIntyre, N.S., Oswald, T.M., Solari, E.J., Zajic, M.C., Lerro, L.E., Hughes, C., Devine, R.T., & Mundy, P.C. (2018). Social cognition and reading comprehension in children and adolescents with autism spectrum disorders or typical development. *Research in Autism Spectrum Disorders, 54*, 9–20. doi:10.1016/j.rasd.2018.06.004

Meristo, M., Falkman, K.W., Hjelmquist, E., Tedoldi, M., Surian, L., & Siegal, M. (2007). Language access and theory of mind reasoning: Evidence from deaf children in bilingual and oralist environments. *Developmental Psychology, 43*(5), 1156–1169. doi:10.1037/0012-1649.43.5.1156

Milligan, K., Astington, J.W., & Dack, L.A. (2007). Language and theory of mind: Meta analysis of the relation between language ability and false-belief understanding. *Child Development, 78*(2), 622–646. doi:10.1111/j.1467-8624.2007.01018.x

Minshew, N.J., Goldstein, G., Taylor, H.G., & Siegel, D.J. (1994). Academic achievement in high functioning autistic individuals. *Journal of Clinical and Experimental Neuropsychology, 16*(2), 261–270. doi:10.1080/01688639408402637

Mio, J.S., & Katz, A.N. (Eds.) (2018). *Metaphor: Implications and Applications*. London: Psychology Press.

Mizokawa, A. (2015). Theory of mind and sensitivity to teacher and peer criticism among Japanese children. *Infant and Child Development, 24*(2), 189–205. doi:10.1002/icd.1877

Mizokawa, A., & Lecce, S. (2017). Sensitivity to criticism and theory of mind: A cross cultural study on Japanese and Italian children. *European Journal of Developmental Psychology, 14*(2), 159–171. doi:10.1080/17405629.2016.1180970

Nelson, R.M., & DeBacker, T.K. (2008). Achievement motivation in adolescents: The role of peer climate and best friends. *The Journal of Experimental Education, 76*(2), 170–189. doi:10.3200/JEXE.76.2.170-190

Nippold, M.A. (1991). Evaluating and enhancing idiom comprehension in language-disordered students. *Language, Speech, and Hearing Services in Schools, 22*(3), 100–106. doi:10.1044/0161-1461.2203.100

Oatley, K. (2016). Fiction: Simulation of social worlds. *Trends in Cognitive Sciences, 20*(8), 618–628. doi:10.1016/j.tics.2016.06.002

Orasanu, J. (1986). *Reading Comprehension from Research to Practice.* Hillsdale, NJ: Erlbaum.

Osterhaus, C., Koerber, S., & Sodian, B. (2017). Scientific thinking in elementary school: Children's social cognition and their epistemological understanding promote experimentation skills. *Developmental Psychology, 53*(3), 450–462. doi:10.1037/dev0000260

Paris, S.G., Cross, D.R., & Lipson, M.Y. (1984). Informed strategies for learning: A program to improve children's reading awareness and comprehension. *Journal of Educational Psychology, 76*(6), 1239–1252. doi:10.1037/0022-0663.76.6.1239

Pelletier, J., & Astington, J.W. (2004). Action, consciousness and theory of mind: Children's ability to coordinate story characters' actions and thoughts. *Early Education and Development, 15*(1), 5–22. doi:10.1207/s15566935eed1501_1

Perdue, N.H., Manzeske, D.P., & Estell, D.B. (2009). Early predictors of school engagement: Exploring the role of peer relationships. *Psychology in the Schools, 46*(10), 1084–1097. doi:10.1002/pits.20446

Peterson, C.C., Slaughter, V.P., & Paynter, J. (2007). Social maturity and theory of mind in typically developing children and those on the autism spectrum. *Journal of Child Psychology and Psychiatry, and Allied Disciplines, 48*(12), 1243–1250. doi:10.1111/j.1469-7610.2007.01810.x

Pianta, R.C., & Stuhlman, M.W. (2004). Teacher-child relationships and children's success in the first years of school. *School Psychology Review, 33*(3), 444–458

Piekny, J., Grube, D., & Maehler, C. (2013). The relation between preschool children's false-belief understanding and domain-general experimentation skills. *Metacognition and Learning, 8*(2), 103–119. doi:10.1007/s11409-013-9097-4

Ray, C.E., & Elliott, S.N. (2006). Social adjustment and academic achievement: A predictive model for students with diverse academic and behavior competencies. *School Psychology Review, 35*(3), 493–501

Ricketts, J., Jones, C., Happé, F., & Charman, T. (2013). Reading comprehension in autism spectrum disorders: The role of oral language and social functioning. *Journal of Autism and Developmental Disorders, 43*(4), 807–816. doi:10.1007/s10803-012-1619-4

Ronchi, L., Banerjee, R., & Lecce, S. (2020). Theory of mind and peer relationships: The role of social anxiety. *Social Development*, 29(2), 478–493. doi:10.1111/sode.12417

Roorda, D.L., Koomen, H.M., Spilt, J.L., & Oort, F.J. (2011). The influence of affective teacher–student relationships on students' school engagement and achievement: A meta-analytic approach. *Review of Educational Research, 81*(4), 493–529. doi:10.3102/0034654311421793

Sharp, C., Fonagy, P., & Goodyer, I. (Eds.) (2008). *Social Cognition and Developmental Psychopathology.* New York, NY: Oxford University Press. doi:10.1093/med/9780198569183.001.0001

Slaughter, V., & De Rosnay, M. (Eds.) (2017). *Theory of Mind Development in Context.* Psychology Press.

Slaughter, V., Imuta, K., Peterson, C.C., & Henry, J.D. (2015). Meta-analysis of theory of mind and peer popularity in the preschool and early school years. *Child Development, 86*(4), 1159–1174. doi:10.1111/cdev.12372

Smogorzewska, J., Szumski, G., & Grygiel, P. (2019). Theory of mind development in school environment: A case of children with mild intellectual disability learning in inclusive and special education classrooms. *Journal of Applied Research in Intellectual Disabilities: JARID, 32*(5), 1241–1254. doi:10.1111/jar.12616

Snow, K.L. (2006). Measuring school readiness: Conceptual and practical considerations. *Early Education and Development, 17*(1), 7–41. doi:10.1207/s15566935eed1701_2

Torgesen, J.K. (2002). The prevention of reading difficulties. *Journal of School Psychology, 40*(1), 7–26. doi::0.1016/S0022-4405(01)00092-9

Ursache, A., Blair, C., & Raver, C.C. (2012). The promotion of self-regulation as a means of enhancing school readiness and early achievement in children at risk for school failure. *Child Development Perspectives, 6*(2), 122–128. doi:10.1111/j.1750-8606.2011.00209.x

Valentine, J.C., & Dubois, D.L. (2005). Effects of self-beliefs on academic achievement and vice versa. Separating the chicken from the egg. In H.W. Marsh, R.G. Craven, & D.M. McInerney (Eds.), *International Advances in Self Research* (pp. 53–78). Greenwich, CT: Information Age.

Vulchanova, M., Saldaña, D., Chahboun, S., & Vulchanov, V. (2015). Figurative language processing in atypical populations: The ASD perspective. *Frontiers in Human Neuroscience, 9*. doi:10.3389/fnhum.2015.00024

Vygotsky, L.S. (1962). *Thought and Language.* Cambridge, MA: MIT Press

Wang, Z. (2010). Mindful learning: Children's developing theory of mind and their understanding of the concept of learning. Publicly accessible Penn Dissertations, Paper 157. https://repository.upenn.edu/edissertations/157

Wellman, H.M. (1977). Preschoolers' understanding of memory-relevant variables. *Child Development, 48*, 1720–1723.

Wellman, H.M. (1985). The origins of metacognition. In S.R. Yussen (Ed.), *Metacognition, Cognition, and Human Performance*, Vol. 1 (pp. 1–31). New York: Academic Press.

Wellman, H.M. (2016). Social cognition and education. *Pensamiento Educativo: Revista de Investigación Educacional Latinoamericana, 53*, 1–23. doi:0.7764/PEL.53.1.2016.14

Welsh, M., Parke, R.D., Widaman, K., & O'Neil, R. (2001). Linkages between children's social and academic competence: A longitudinal analysis. *Journal of School Psychology, 39*(6), 463–482. doi:10.1016/S0022-4405(01)00084-X

Wentzel, K.R., & Caldwell, K. (1997). Friendships, peer acceptance, and group membership: Relations to academic achievement in middle school. *Child Development, 68*(6), 1198–1209. doi:10.1111/j.1467-8624.1997.tb01994.x

White, S., Hill, E., Happé, F.G.E., & Frith, U. (2009). Revisiting the Strange Stories: Revealing mentalizing impairments in autism. *Child Development, 80*(4), 1097–1117. doi:10.1111/j.1467-8624.2009.01319.x

Whyte, E.M., & Nelson, K.E. (2015). Trajectories of pragmatic and nonliteral language development in children with autism spectrum disorders. *Journal of Communication Disorders, 54*, 2–14. doi:10.1016/j.jcomdis.2015.01.001

York, T., Gibson, C., & Rankin, S. (2015). Defining and measuring academic success Travis T. York, Valdosta State University. *Practical Assessment, Research and Evaluation, 20*, 5

Zepeda, C.D., Hlutkowsky, C.O., Partika, A.C., & Nokes-Malach, T.J. (2019). Identifying teachers' supports of metacognition through classroom talk and its relation to growth in conceptual learning. *Journal of Educational Psychology, 111*(3), 522. doi:10.1037/edu0000300

Zimmerman, B.J., & Moylan, A.R. (2009). Self-regulation: Where metacognition and motivation intersect. In D.J. Hacker, J. Dunlosky, & A.C. Graesser (Eds.), *Handbook of Metacognition in Education* (pp. 299–315). New York, NY: Routledge/Taylor & Francis Group.

Ziv, M., Solomon, A., Strauss, S., & Frye, D. (2016). Relations between the development of teaching and theory of mind in early childhood. *Journal of Cognition and Development, 17*(2), 264–284. doi:10.1080/15248372.2015.1048862

Part III

Neurodiversity, disability, and youth mental health

9 Theory of mind in adolescents with autism

Sander Begeer and Anke M. Scheeren

Theory of mind among individuals with autism spectrum disorder (ASD) is a popular, well-documented theme (Jones et al., 2018; Yirmiya et al., 1998). In this chapter, we aim to put some of this literature in perspective, while highlighting a relatively overlooked age group: Autistic adolescents. Note that we alternate between identity-first and person-first language, as per the preference of the autism community (Kenny et al., 2016). Theory of mind research in autism has mostly focused on children. This is partly due to the extremely successful operationalization of theory of mind for this young age group. Core characteristics of ASD such as social communication difficulties have been attributed to a cognitive deficit in mindreading. This so-called 'mindblindness' account of ASD has subsequently been challenged on several fronts. We will focus on how evidence from (early) adolescence provides additional and alternative perspectives on the development of theory of mind in autism. We will highlight atypical theory of mind abilities rather than deficient or even absent theory of mind in autistic individuals. As measures of theory of mind in adolescents are increasingly complex and often require a minimum of intellectual and verbal abilities, this chapter will emphasize findings on normally intelligent participants, thus reducing the generalizability to all autistic adolescents.

Autism

Prevalence rates of ASD are estimated at 1–2% of the population worldwide (Lord et al., 2020). ASD is traditionally viewed as a predominantly male condition, with a male-to-female ratio of 3:1, although recent findings suggest girls and women with autism may be underdiagnosed (Loomes et al., 2017). An ASD diagnosis is given based on behavioral and developmental impairments. Key criteria according to DSM-V (APA, 2013) are (1) limited abilities in social interaction and communication and (2) repetitive, restricted behavior and interests. Put differently, autistic individuals have difficulties navigating the social world and show an insistence on sameness. The current symptoms of ASD remain remarkably close to the original criteria as specified by Kanner in 1944. Kanner (1944) was the first to use the term 'autistic aloneness' to describe a group of children with a shared set of non-social interests and rigid behaviors. He argued that, compared with typically developing children, these children seemed to be scarcely affected by others' emotional states. Although this claim has been nuanced and refuted over the years (Lord et al., 2020), Kanner was one of the first to notice that children with autism seemed to have a limited orientation to others' internal states.

Classic measures of theory of mind

It took a while after Kanner's (1944) observations before the orientation to others' internal states became a central topic in autism research and care. In the early 1980s, theory of mind research finally took off, largely due to the very successful and elegant *false belief* paradigm, a brief and simple measure of theory of mind skills. This paradigm emerged because of a philosopher's reflection (Dennett, 1978) on a paper on chimpanzees (Premack & Woodruff, 1978). This led Austrian researchers (Wimmer & Perner, 1983) to develop the first false belief task, focused on four- to five-year-old children, and set into motion a new direction in developmental psychology (Hughes & Devine, 2015). The test quickly became one of the most popular measures in child psychology, due to its various exceptional qualities: It is very short (administration takes around one minute), it is free, and, when used in the appropriate age range, it is highly reliable. In neurotypical children, most four-year-old children pass the test, showing a basic understanding that people can hold different and false beliefs about the world. Most typically developing three-year-old children, however, fail the test (Hughes et al., 2000; Yirmiya et al., 1998). The emergence of theory of mind research within the field of child psychology influenced and steered the measurement of theory of mind. Most theory of mind tasks are suitable for infants or young children. Moreover, the use of theory of mind tasks for adolescents and adults was initially deemed unnecessary because, as most child psychology textbooks still hold today (e.g., Nolen-Hoeksema et al., 2014), theory of mind emerges in its final form during childhood. In this light, developing theory of mind tests for adolescents and adults would be comparable to developing a walking ability test for this age group. The classic mistake here is that passing the false belief task is taken as an equivalent to possessing a theory of mind.

The classic approach to theory of mind is a focus on an explicit understanding of one's own and others' mental states. This understanding is usually tested with questions about static hypothetical situations. Explicit theory of mind entails the top-down insight of others having mental states, and the ability to make inferences about their behavior based on this insight. This process involves analytic and reflective reasoning. Implicit theory of mind is a more automatic bottom-up system (Low & Perner, 2012). These two are connected: Being in direct interaction with another person enables one to reflect on this interaction. Theory of mind involves the ability to integrate information derived from reflective and analytic capacities with information derived from rapid perceptual and affective mechanisms. The characterization of theory of mind as being either fundamentally implicit or explicit is unhelpful when trying to understand human social behavior. Both implicit and explicit ToM are needed to successfully monitor, analyze, and respond to social interactions.

Theory of mind in autistic children

Shortly after the first publications on theory of mind, a ground-breaking paper on the false belief understanding of autistic children appeared in 1985 (Baron-Cohen et al., 1985). The autistic children performed remarkably poorly on this test compared with age- or IQ-matched children. The central message, therefore, was that autistic children lacked a theory of mind. In retrospect, the terminology used in this paper sounds harsh: Autistic children were found to 'fail to employ a theory of mind…show inability to represent mental states… failing to impute beliefs to others'(p. 43). The paper set the tone for decades of research on the potential link between autism and theory of mind (the paper has been cited over 3,400 times). Even though theory of mind research has made immense contributions to our understanding of autism and its symptoms, the 1985 paper and the dichotomous (pass/fail) nature of the false belief test also (unintentionally) ignited an oversimplified, and possibly stigmatizing, image of the theory of mind abilities in autism. Theory of mind is not an all-or-nothing ability and children with ASD are not completely 'mind blind'. As will be explained later, studies based on other theory of mind measures and older age groups reveal a more nuanced picture of autistic theory of mind abilities, showing similar theory of mind test performances across adolescents with and without ASD.

The impact of age and intelligence on theory of mind

Large individual differences exist across the autism spectrum. Individual factors, such as age, intelligence, and motivation, make a significant impact on the quality and severity of ASD symptoms, as do contextual factors (Lord et al., 2020). Therefore, findings of theory of mind studies in autistic children and adolescents should be evaluated by taking their developmental and intellectual levels into account. When autistic children (with normal intelligence) are around ten years old, they generally pass false belief tasks (Bowler, 1992; Happé, 1994). This indicates that children with ASD may be delayed in their theory of mind development compared with their typically developing peers, but do show progress over time (Steele et al., 2003). Indeed, specific longitudinal progress in ToM mastery has also been found in eight- to nine-year-old children with ASD over the course of 1.5 years (Peterson & Wellman, 2019). Using a specially designed theory of mind scale, researchers were able to target theory of mind growth, indicating progress in the ASD group, albeit not on par with the typically developing groups. Similar approaches for adolescent groups are not yet available. When studying adolescents over time, it is important to consider that the false belief task was originally designed to test theory of mind abilities among three- to four-year-olds. Using such a test in middle childhood or adolescence reduces its validity. More age-appropriate and challenging measures may still show limitations or atypicality in theory of mind in autistic individuals.

In addition to age, intelligence may play an even bigger role in theory of mind development. Intelligence and success on theory of mind measures generally correlate positively in autistic children. In autistic samples, normally intelligent children were suggested to 'solve' the classic false belief tasks by using their analytic skills (Bowler, 1992). To deal with this issue, various 'advanced' theory of mind tasks were developed in order to measure a more complicated, but also more applied theory of mind competence. Some of these theory of mind tasks focused on the understanding of a speaker's and a listener's intentions during hypothetical social interactions. These tests prototypically include non-literal statements such as irony or sarcasm. For instance, someone might comment on the 'nice weather' while it is pouring with rain. These types of advanced theory of mind tasks, including the Strange Stories task (see Figure 9.1) (Happé, 1994; White et al., 2009), generally show reduced theory of mind understanding among participants with autism. The task involves a strong language component and describes rather complex interactions between two or more people. The situations often elicit embedded mental states. These are mental states about mental states. For instance, person A may wonder what person B thinks person C wants.

> Helen waited all year for Christmas because she knew at Christmas, she could ask her parents for a rabbit. Helen wanted a rabbit more than anything in the world. At last Christmas Day arrived, and Helen ran to unwrap the big box her parents had given her. She felt sure it would contain a little rabbit in a cage. But when she opened it, with all the family standing around, she found her present was just a boring old set of encyclopedias, which Helen did not want at all! Still, when Helen's parents asked her how she liked her Christmas present, she said, 'It's lovely, thank you. It's just what I wanted'.
>
> Is it true, what Helen said? Why did she say that to her parents?

Figure 9.1 Sample item from the Strange Stories task (Happé, 1994).

We used stories such as these to study advanced theory of mind abilities in school-aged children and adolescents with and without ASD, all with an intellectual ability within the normal range. Counter to our expectations, we found no support for any impairments in advanced theory of mind reasoning of autistic children (aged 6 to 11 years) and adolescents (aged 12 to 20 years) (Scheeren et al., 2013). Our autistic participants acknowledged and recognized the mental states of story characters to the same extent as their typically developing peers. Not surprisingly, given the strong verbal nature of the test, children and adolescents with a higher verbal ability generally performed better than those with a lower verbal ability. Importantly, only the group of children and adolescents with ASD showed a positive correlation between their physical state reasoning and mental state reasoning, implying a reliance on general logic to understand social stories. Other studies have confirmed the correlation between verbal abilities and theory of mind in ASD samples (Buitelaar et al., 1999; Kaland et al., 2002). Ideally, theory of mind measures should be (more) independent from other abilities and should be a true reflection of theory of mind abilities during everyday social interactions.

Theory of mind problems have traditionally been viewed as an impairment underlying the social symptoms that we see in autism. However, two other 'competing' cognitive theories have been put forward to explain autistic symptomatology as well as theory of mind limitations: (1) A theory of executive functions, stating that those cognitive processes that drive goal-directed behavior are impaired in ASD (e.g., Hughes & Russell, 1993), and (2) a theory of weak central coherence, claiming that individuals with ASD have a detail-focused style of thinking (e.g., Frith & Happé, 1994). Theoretically, it can be argued that various executive functions are required when applying theory of mind. For instance, we need to *inhibit* (but *remember*) our own perspective, while *switching* to another person's point of view. Similarly, central coherence is needed when attributing mental states to others. For instance, only by combining multiple single observations (the raise of an eyebrow, context, posture, verbalizations, eye gaze), we can conclude that another person is being cynical or serious. Empirical studies have also confirmed the links between theory of mind, executive functioning, and central coherence, showing that executive function and central coherence predict theory of mind skills (but not the other way around) in school-aged and preadolescent children with ASD over the course of three years, independently of age and intelligence (Pellicano, 2010). Theory of mind impairments may therefore not fully explain the social difficulties in autism. Still, in adolescents with ASD, theory of mind skills predict autistic symptoms much better than executive functions (Jones et al., 2018).

Alternative approaches to measuring theory of mind

In an earlier study, we used a dynamic and less verbal test to challenge perspective-taking skills, related to theory of mind abilities of adolescents with and without ASD. Two participants were standing on opposite sides of a grid,

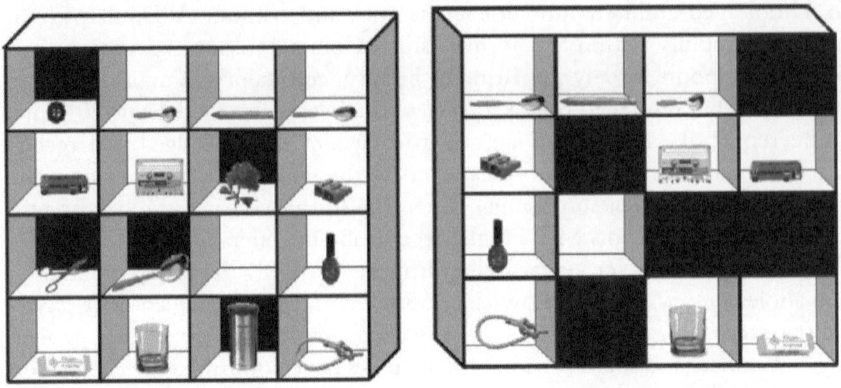

Figure 9.2 The Director task (Begeer et al., 2010).

including open slots (some of which were closed from one side, see Figure 9.2). During this task, referred to as the Director task, the addressee (with or without autism) was instructed to pick up objects based on the instructions of the director (who was unable to see the objects behind the occluded slots). In order to select the correct objects, the addressees needed to take the perspective of the director (e.g., when asked to pick up the largest spoon, the addressee should realize that what the largest spoon is depends on where you are standing). First, it is important to note that typically developing adults, with normal intelligence, made a surprisingly high rate of errors around 30% (Keysar et al., 2003). This is already an interesting finding in itself. While these adults presumably have advanced theory of mind, this knowledge does not directly translate into other-oriented behavior. When we used this paradigm in adolescents with ASD, their perspective-taking skills were similar compared to their non-autistic peers (Begeer et al., 2010; Santiesteban et al., 2015). Both groups (34 participants with ASD, 34 without ASD) performed equally well (or equally poorly) at taking the director's perspective in order to interpret the instructions correctly. Thus, even during dynamic interactions, elementary skills related to theory of mind can be present in autistic adolescents. As nicely stated by (Zwickel et al., 2011): Autistic individuals are 'neither other-blind nor viewpoint-blind' (p. 570). Importantly, also in typically developing participants, the performance on this task keeps improving from adolescence to adulthood (Dumontheil et al., 2010), showing that theory of mind skills can be seen as a capacity that keeps developing long after the early childhood years (see Chapter 1 and Chapter 2 of this volume).

Still, we have also observed subtle atypicality in spontaneous theory of mind use in adolescents with ASD. Our participants with and without ASD read a story about two individuals. This story included no references to mental states (e.g., he *felt*, she *thought*) but mental states were implied by describing behavioral interactions (e.g., 'his hand trembled', 'she stormed out of the room'). After a brief distracting task, participants were asked to retell the story. Adolescents with ASD were less inclined to use mental state terms (e.g., he *felt*, she *thought*), and refrained from spontaneously representing interactions in mentalistic terms. This may be a crucial aspect of theory of mind that is different in autism: The spontaneous orientation towards others' internal states. Importantly, these outcomes do not suggest that autistic participants are 'mind blind', rather they are less oriented towards mindreading if they are not cued or motivated to do so. In various other studies, we showed that rewarding autistic children and adolescents for using their theory of mind can effectively increase their performance (Begeer et al., 2003). Similar patterns were found in a study where children and early adolescents had to present themselves to others either spontaneously or with the instruction to make a certain impression on their audience. Providing a simple instruction for self-promotion strongly increased the strategic self-presentation in autistic participants, showing adequate ability to impact others' perspectives of them (Scheeren et al., 2016).

If anything, the findings above suggest that theory of mind capacities may be dormant in autistic adolescents rather than absent. A limited spontaneous orientation towards others' mental states, also termed 'social attribution' or 'mind-mindedness', could be a problematic capacity for autistic individuals (Klin, 2000). This spontaneous orientation can be seen as an implicit, dynamic skill, and might be especially important during everyday social interactions.

The real difference in theory of mind in autism: Implicit dynamic skills

Due to the immense popularity of the false belief test, the construct and the measurement of theory of mind have become seemingly synonymous (see Chapter 3). However, theory of mind is a much more complex and dynamic ability than passing a false belief test. A simple variation on the false belief task can be used to illustrate this point. In the classic task, the participant has to infer the beliefs of a deceived protagonist. Without the protagonist's knowledge, a marble has been relocated to another location. The participant has witnessed the relocation and has to predict where the protagonist will look for the marble: In the new location (where the marble really is) or the old location (where the naïve protagonist thinks it is). A critique of the task is that the dichotomous outcome simplifies the task. To solve this issue, we used a continuous false belief task, where objects were relocated to a continuous location (e.g., by burying and re-burying them in a garden). This enabled us to measure theory of mind and egocentric bias in a more subtle way. Indeed, we were able to find limitations in the performance of autistic children and adolescents (N = 62) and a control group (N = 62), small to medium effect size (Begeer et al., 2012), but were unable to replicate our findings in a follow-up study in 7- to

13-year-olds with ASD (N = 76) or typical development (N = 113) (Begeer et al., 2016). An important conclusion of the study was related to the responses of the neurotypical children, who, like their autistic counterparts in the study, showed egocentric biases as well. This highlights that theory of mind skills in neurotypical children may be overestimated.

Children and adolescents, with and without ASD, continue to develop a more sophisticated understanding of social and inner worlds. There is an increasing consensus that theory of mind consists of explicit (social cognitive) and implicit (socio-perceptual) components (Achim et al., 2013; Low & Perner, 2012) though some reservations have been put forward (Carruthers, 2018). Implicit theory of mind abilities are used during fast, everyday social exchanges. These can be measured in various ways, for instance by tracking participants' spontaneous attention or attribution to mental phenomena (Low & Perner, 2012). In an elegant experiment, Senju et al. (2009) showed differences between adults with and without ASD while they were watching a video of a false belief task. Even though they performed equally well on the false belief task (unsurprising given their adult age) those with ASD showed different eye gaze patterns compared with the controls. However, the reliability of measures of implicit ToM has recently been questioned (Kulke et al., 2019). Related to these implicit skills is the more or less automatic inclination to attribute mental states, even to non-living entities. When asked to describe animations of two moving triangles, participants with ASD either showed a reduced tendency to anthropomorphize the 'behavior' of the triangles compared with those without autism (Klin, 2000), or they used mental state descriptions that were inconsistent with the animations (Abell et al., 2000; Salter et al., 2008). Of course, two moving triangles hardly capture the full complexity of everyday human interaction.

Another potential way to measure theory of mind in a more ecologically valid way is to ask people to interpret video clips of naturally occurring (or acted) social interactions. This is exactly what is done during an empathic accuracy test. Two informants are asked to report on the mental states of people in a video: (1) The people ('actors') themselves, and (2) the audience. If the reports of the audience and the actors show a great degree of overlap, it is taken as evidence that the audience has strong theory of mind abilities. Several small-scaled studies reveal reduced accuracy in mental state attributions in small groups of autistic adolescents (N = 13 to 24) (Demurie et al., 2011; Roeyers et al., 2001). These patterns were also found in adolescents and adults with ASD (Murray et al., 2017; Ponnet et al., 2008). However, the validity of the empathic accuracy test is based on the premise that people (without ASD) are able to retrospectively and correctly reflect on their flow of mental states. This remains open for debate, as retrospective awareness may be prone to bias. In addition, mental states are fleeting dynamic entities (thoughts can change). Someone may attribute a mental state to me that I may or may not have had, or may not have been aware of, begging the question who is to judge the correctness of a mental state.

Why and when is theory of mind applied during real-life interactions?

Despite some of the (at the time unexpected) adequate perspective-taking skills we and other researchers have found, adolescents with ASD may still be limited in putting their theoretical knowledge into everyday practice (Peterson & Wellman, 2019). It is surprising that the actual *use* of theory of mind in the dynamics of daily interactions has received so little attention (Schilbach et al., 2013). After all, the main function of theory of mind is to navigate and master real-life social interactions with other people. Being able to reflect on such situations using vignette tasks may be a related capacity, but in a way similar to how knowledge of football relates to playing football. If anything, the real-life behavioral capacity may drive the conceptual understanding rather than the other way around.

Besides conceptual and real-life features, a range of different sources of information can be relied on when people use their theory of mind. A very useful framework for disentangling these facets is presented by Achim et al. (2013). For instance, when you are talking to a friend, you may listen to what she says and look at her facial expression and her behavior. Thus, you have access to perceptual, linguistic, and behavioral information. But you also are aware of the specific and wider context, and remember previous behavior of your friend. Information can be directly available, but can also be stored. These sources of information all affect how easy or successful it is to mentalize. This framework helps to provide a comprehensive account of neurotypical theory of mind, which is required before we can start to conceptualize atypicality in autistic theory of mind.

The discrepancy between conceptual and practical theory of mind skills in ASD specifically suggests that other factors may impact whether theory of mind skills are applied. There is a wide variety of individual, contextual, and cultural/conventional differences that may affect to what extent theory of mind is used in daily life situations (Achim et al., 2013). For instance, social attention and motivation may be required to activate theory of mind (Chevallier et al., 2012). In addition, sensory overload in ASD might have a negative impact on the application of theory of mind in daily life. It is imaginable that being overwhelmed by sensory stimuli may impair the ability to interpret social cues correctly. In particular, the integration of incoming sensory information with inferences from context and prior experiences may provide problems for autistic individuals. Social interactions require the fast and dynamic integration of these streams of information at a highly abstract level, demanding strong central coherence (Baum et al., 2015; Thye et al., 2018). Limited abilities of autistic individuals to integrate and switch between these processes may be an impairing mechanism for real-life theory of mind use (Pellicano, 2010). Again, these findings nuance the theory of mind limitations of autistic individuals by directing us to possible underlying factors, presenting a limited theory of mind as the *consequence* rather than the *cause* of their behavioral symptoms.

A recent study operationalized two ToM-related constructs in a sample of autistic adolescents, disentangling the mentalizing skills (using the Triangles task) and making observations of real-life social behavior (using the Autism Diagnostic Observation Scale – in the absence of more specific measures). The distinction between conceptual and practical capacities might indicate that some individuals may have poor ToM skills, but are able to show relatively adequate social behavior (Livingston et al., 2019). Yet, these adolescents also showed higher levels of anxiety, possibly due to the prolonged effort to 'keep up appearances'. The camouflaging activities of individuals with ASD highlight the complexity of distinguishing between the core ability of theory of mind, the motivation to use, practice, and develop these skills, or the ability to disguise limitations.

We had the fortune to welcome a retired clinician to our team that developed a test that could become very useful for measuring the dynamic, real-life functioning related to theory of mind. Building on her 40-year experience as a clinician working with autistic children, Tineke Backer van Ommeren decided to do a PhD after her retirement. She wanted to validate empirically a test of reciprocity she developed during her years as a clinician, treating and assessing children with ASD. Her test is called the 'Interactive Drawing test'. It includes a brief dynamic interaction between a participant and an experimenter while making a mutual drawing. Importantly, the participant only receives the instruction 'we are going to draw together'. No other specification is given. This prevents participants from acting according to any top-down scripts or rules and allows for the study of spontaneous reciprocal behavior. During the creation of the drawing, reciprocal behavior is coded based on the contribution of the participant to mutual objects (e.g., adding

(a) (b)

Figure 9.3 Interactive drawing test (Backer van Ommeren, 2015). Examples of two drawings made by six-year-old boys with (right) and without (left) autism. The children draw in red. The experimenter always starts with the horizontal line of the house. The boy on the left clearly engages in finishing the house, taking turns in adding elements. The boy on the right engages in his own topics (racetracks), ignoring the initiatives of the experimenter.

apples to a tree). While the inclination to join another person in a drawing is no direct measure of theory of mind, it does reflect the intuitive orientation to and the engagement with another person's goals (i.e., drawing a tree). This basic tendency is difficult to compensate for or to camouflage, as it is unclear what is expected during the making of the drawing, and participants are free to draw whatever they want. Using a range of independent studies, including a total number of 392 children and adolescents with autism and 109 without autism (aged 6 to 20 years), we were able to show that autistic adolescents were less inclined to show spontaneous reciprocal interactions, with consistent large effect sizes (see Figure 9.3). Findings were stable across normally intelligent-, intellectually impaired-, and all-female samples (Backer van Ommeren et al., 2015, 2017a, 2017b).

Stigma and double empathy

The assumption that autism is related to 'mindblindness' or the absence of empathy has been experienced as stigmatizing by many autistic individuals (Milton, 2012). Moreover, as shown by some of our own experiments as well as many other studies, perspective-taking problems are not unique for individuals with ASD. In fact, research has repeatedly shown that most people find it difficult to ignore their own egocentric perspective to consider those of others (Begeer et al., 2016). Interestingly, neurotypical adults find it even more difficult to read the minds of individuals with autism than the minds of other neurotypicals (Alkhaldi et al., 2019). It is known that people usually find it easier to empathize with others who are 'like me' (Preston & de Waal, 2002). Apparently, neurotypical people view people with ASD as 'not like me', adding to a 'double empathy problem'. Both parties, with and without ASD, find it difficult to take the other's perspective (Milton, 2012). This sheds an interesting new light on the theory of mind problems of autistic individuals. Perspective-taking during an everyday social interaction is a two-way street where one is simultaneously trying to figure out the other's intentions and emotions. If one social agent experiences difficulties reading the other's mind, this may in turn affect the readability of the agent's mind and behavior. This way, the social realm becomes even more difficult to navigate.

Autistic adolescence

During typical adolescence, peer relations become increasingly important and complex (Carter et al., 2014). Like typically developing youth, adolescents with ASD want to become independent adults and form relations with peers. Normally intelligent adolescents and adults with ASD (N = 406, aged 10 to 52 years) have shown increased independence and friendship relations with peers over time (Smith et al., 2012). However, the 'two-hit model' of autism describes that the increased demand on complex social skills during adolescence may be particularly challenging for individuals with ASD, hindering their development into young adulthood (Picci & Scherf, 2015). Although strong scientific evidence is still lacking, it is plausible that social expectations and demands exceed the development of adolescent social skills (Rosenthal et al., 2013).

Longitudinal studies are needed to reflect on the change in social relationships, social expectations, and theory of mind within and around autistic adolescence. Not only does the capacity for theory of mind change, but also the expectations of adolescents' theory of mind change as they grow older. The onset of neurotypical 'adult' theory of mind in adolescence has hardly been studied. Much is still unknown, let alone regarding the autistic divergence in this development (Brizio et al., 2015). While the general symptoms of ASD remain during adolescence, the social involvement with the adolescent peer group has potential beneficial effects on theory of mind, in particular in normally intelligent autistic adolescents (McGovern & Sigman, 2005).

Conclusion and future directions

Most researchers now agree that theory of mind impairments do not offer a sufficient explanation for ASD and its symptoms. In fact, attempts to provide one explanation for autism have currently been largely abandoned (Happé et al., 2006). Although atypicality in (spontaneous) theory of mind use has been found in adolescents with ASD and normal intelligence, these adolescents have also shown a (sometimes more than) basic and theoretical understanding of their own and others' minds. While research on autistic individuals beyond school age offers new perspectives on theory of mind, the development of more subtle and ecologically valid measures of theory of mind in adolescence and adulthood remains a challenge (Peterson & Wellman, 2019). New and more sensitive measures may further demonstrate the full range of both capacities and limitations of autistic adolescents. Advances in this field were recently reviewed (Livingston et al., 2019). Digital, online, and virtual reality techniques may solve some of the methodological limitations. To date, the more ecologically valid interactive measures are generally time-consuming, as they involve the coding of verbal responses. Online abbreviated material and categoric scoring may offer more pragmatic tools. Another benefit of online measures is the ability to measure response time in detail. It is known that autistic individuals use strategies to compensate for their limitations, causing them to show delayed, yet accurate responses (Brosnan et al., 2014). An additional benefit of online tests is the ease of recruitment and the opportunity to upscale data collection.

Examining theory of mind in adolescents with ASD also brings us to the fundamental question of how *neurotypical* adolescents are able to understand other minds, if not in a theoretical way. Presumably, neurotypical adolescents rely more on implicit intuitive skills, and less so on theoretical, explicit knowledge to guide them through social interactions. Following this line of reasoning, one could argue that a *theory of mind*, that is, a theoretical approach to other minds, might be a more appropriate term to describe autistic functioning, while an *intuition* of mind may be a more accurate description of neurotypical functioning.

References

Abell, F., Happé, F., & Frith, U. (2000). Do triangles play tricks? Attribution of mental states to animated shapes in normal and abnormal development. *Cognitive Development, 15*(1), 1–16. doi:10.1016/S0885-2014(00)00014-9

Achim, A.M., Guitton, M., Jackson, P.L., Boutin, A., & Monetta, L. (2013). On what ground do we mentalize? Characteristics of current tasks and sources of information that contribute to mentalizing judgments. *Psychological Assessment, 25*(1), 117–126. doi:10.1037/a0029137

Alkhaldi, R.S., Sheppard, E., & Mitchell, P. (2019). Is there a link between autistic people being perceived unfavorably and having a mind that is difficult to read? *Journal of Autism and Developmental Disorders, 49*(10), 3973–3982. doi:10.1007/s10803-019-04101-1

Backer van Ommeren, T., Koot, H.M., & Begeer, S. (2017). Reciprocity in autistic and typically developing children and adolescents with and without mild intellectual disabilities. *Journal of Intellectual Disability Research: JIDR, 61*(8), 810–817. doi:10.1111/jir.12395

Backer van Ommeren, T., Koot, H., Scheeren, A., & Begeer, S. (2015). Reliability and validity of the interactive drawing test: A measure of reciprocity for children and adolescents with autism spectrum disorder. *Journal of Autism and Developmental Disorders*, 1–11. doi:10.1007/s10803-014-2353-x

Backer van Ommeren, T., Koot, H.M., Scheeren, A.M., & Begeer, S. (2017). Sex differences in the reciprocal behaviour of children with autism. *Autism: The International Journal of Research and Practice, 21*(6), 795–803. doi:10.1177/1362361316669622

Baron-Cohen, S., Leslie, A.M., & Frith, U. (1985). Does the autistic child have a "theory of mind" ? *Cognition, 21*(1), 37–46. doi:10.1016/0010-0277(85)90022-8

Baum, S.H., Stevenson, R.A., & Wallace, M.T. (2015). Behavioral, perceptual, and neural alterations in sensory and multisensory function in autism spectrum disorder. *Progress in Neurobiology, 134*, 140–160. doi:10.1016/j.pneurobio.2015.09.007

Begeer, S., Bernstein, D.M., Aßfalg, A., Azdad, H., Glasbergen, T., Wierda, M., & Koot, H.M. (2016). Equal egocentric bias in school-aged children with and without autism spectrum disorders. *Journal of Experimental Child Psychology, 144*, 15–26. doi:10.1016/j.jecp.2015.10.018

Begeer, S., Bernstein, D.M., van Wijhe, J., Scheeren, A.M., & Koot, H.M. (2012). A continuous false belief task reveals egocentric biases in children and adolescents with autism Spectrum Disorders. *Autism: The International Journal of Research and Practice, 16*(4), 357–366. doi:10.1177/1362361311434545

Begeer, S., Malle, B.F., Nieuwland, M.S., & Keysar, B. (2010). Using theory of mind to represent and take part in social interactions: Comparing individuals with high-functioning autism and typically developing controls. *European Journal of Developmental Psychology*, 7(1), 104–122. doi:10.1080/17405620903024263

Begeer, S., Rieffe, C., Terwogt, M.M., & Stockmann, L. (2003). Theory of mind—based action in children from the autism spectrum. *Journal of Autism and Developmental Disorders, 33*(5), 479–487. doi:10.1023/a:1025875311062

Bowler, D.M. (1992). "Theory of mind" in Asperger's syndrome. *Journal of Child Psychology and Psychiatry, and Allied Disciplines, 33*(5), 877–893. doi:10.1111/j.1469-7610.1992.tb01962.x

Brizio, A., Gabbatore, I., Tirassa, M., & Bosco, F.M. (2015). "No more a child, not yet an adult": Studying social cognition in adolescence. *Frontiers in Psychology, 6*, 1011. doi:10.3389/fpsyg.2015.01011

Brosnan, M., Chapman, E., & Ashwin, C. (2014). Adolescents with autism spectrum disorder show a circumspect reasoning bias rather than 'jumping-to-conclusions'. *Journal of Autism and Developmental Disorders*, *44*(3), 513–520. doi:10.1007/s10803-013-1897-5

Buitelaar, J.K., van der Wees, M., Swaab-Barneveld, H., & van der Gaag, R.J. (1999). Verbal memory and performance IQ predict theory of mind and emotion recognition ability in children with autistic spectrum disorders and in psychiatric control children. *Journal of Child Psychology and Psychiatry, and Allied Disciplines*, *40*(6), 869–881. doi:10.1111/1469-7610.00505

Carruthers, P. (2018). Implicit versus explicit attitudes: Differing manifestations of the same representational structures? *Review of Philosophy and Psychology*, *9*(1), 51–72. https://doi.org/10.1007/s13164-017-0354-3

Carter, E.W., Common, E.A., Sreckovic, M.A., Huber, H.B., Bottema-Beutel, K., Gustafson, J.R., Dykstra, J., & Hume, K. (2014). Promoting social competence and peer relationships for adolescents With autism spectrum disorders. *Remedial and Special Education*, *35*(2), 91–101. doi:10.1177/0741932513514618

Chevallier, C., Kohls, G., Troiani, V., Brodkin, E.S., & Schultz, R.T. (2012). The social motivation theory of autism. *Trends in Cognitive Sciences*, *16*(4), 231–239. doi:10.1016/j.tics.2012.02.007

Demurie, E., De Corel, M., & Roeyers, H. (2011). Empathic accuracy in adolescents with autism spectrum disorders and adolescents with attention-deficit/hyperactivity disorder. *Research in Autism Spectrum Disorders*, *5*(1), 126–134. doi:10.1016/j.rasd.2010.03.002

Dennett, D.C. (1978). Cognition and consciousness in nonhuman species—comment. *Behavioral and Brain Sciences*, *1*(4), 568–570. doi:10.1017/S0140525X00076664

Dumontheil, I., Apperly, I.A., & Blakemore, S.J. (2010). Online usage of theory of mind continues to develop in late adolescence. *Developmental Science*, *13*(2), 331–338. doi:10.1111/j.1467-7687.2009.00888.x

Frith, U., & Happé, F. (1994). Autism: Beyond 'theory of mind'. *Cognition*, *50*(1–3), 115–132

Happé, F.G.E. (1994). An advanced test of theory of mind: Understanding of story characters' thoughts and feelings by able autistic, mentally handicapped, and normal children and adults. *Journal of Autism and Developmental Disorders*, *24*(2), 129–154. doi:10.1007/BF02172093

Happé, F., Ronald, A., & Plomin, R. (2006). Time to give up on a single explanation for autism. *Nature Neuroscience*, *9*(10), 1218–1220. doi:10.1038/nn1770

Hughes, C., Adlam, A., Happé, F., Jackson, J., Taylor, A., & Caspi, A. (2000). Good test–retest reliability for standard and advanced false-belief tasks across a wide range of abilities. *Journal of Child Psychology and Psychiatry, and Allied Disciplines*, *41*(4), 483–490. doi:10.1017/s0021963099005533

Hughes, C., & Devine, R.T. (2015). Individual differences in theory of mind From preschool to adolescence: Achievements and directions. *Child Development Perspectives*, *9*(3), 149–153. doi:10.1111/cdep.12124

Hughes, C., & Russell, J. (1993). Autistic children's difficulty with mental disengagement from an object: Its implications for theories of autism. *Developmental Psychology*, *29*(3), 498–510

Jones, C.R.G., Simonoff, E., Baird, G., Pickles, A., Marsden, A.J.S., Tregay, J., Happé, F., & Charman, T. (2018). The association between theory of mind, executive function, and the symptoms of autism spectrum disorder. *Autism Research: Official Journal of the International Society for Autism Research*, *11*(1), 95–109. doi:10.1002/aur.1873

Kaland, N., Møller-Nielsen, A., Callesen, K., Mortensen, E.L., Gottlieb, D., & Smith, L. (2002). A new 'advanced' test of theory of mind: Evidence from children and adolescents with Asperger syndrome. *Journal of Child Psychology and Psychiatry, and Allied Disciplines, 43*(4), 517–528. doi:10.1111/1469-7610.00042

Kanner, L. (1944). Early infantile autism. *Journal of Pediatrics, 25*, 212–217

Kenny, L., Hattersley, C., Molins, B., Buckley, C., Povey, C., & Pellicano, E. (2016). Which terms should be used to describe autism? Perspectives from the UK autism community. *Autism: The International Journal of Research and Practice, 20*(4), 442–462. doi:10.1177/1362361315588200

Keysar, B., Lin, S.H., & Barr, D.J. (2003). Limits on theory of mind use in adults. *Cognition, 89*(1), 25–41. doi:10.1016/s0010-0277(03)00064-7

Klin, A. (2000). Attributing social meaning to ambiguous visual stimuli in higher-functioning autism and Asperger syndrome: The social attribution task. *Journal of Child Psychology and Psychiatry, and Allied Disciplines, 41*(7), 831–846. doi:10.1017/s0021963099006101

Kulke, L., Johannsen, J., & Rakoczy, H. (2019). Why can some implicit theory of mind tasks be replicated and others cannot? A test of mentalizing versus submentalizing accounts. *PLOS ONE, 14*(3). doi:10.1371/journal.pone.0213772

Livingston, L.A., Colvert, E., Bolton, P., Happe, F., & Social Relationships Study Team (2019). Good social skills despite poor theory of mind: Exploring compensation in autism spectrum disorder. *Journal of Child Psychology and Psychiatry, and Allied Disciplines, 60*(1), 102–110. doi:10.1111/jcpp.12886

Livingston, L.A., Shah, P., & Happé, F. (2019). Compensatory strategies below the behavioural surface in autism: A qualitative study. *Lancet Psychiatry, 6*(9), 766–777. doi:10.1016/S2215-0366(19)30224-X

Loomes, R., Hull, L., & Mandy, W.P.L. (2017). What is the male-to-female ratio in autism spectrum disorder? A systematic review and meta-analysis. *Journal of the American Academy of Child and Adolescent Psychiatry, 56*(6), 466–474. doi:10.1016/j.jaac.2017.03.013

Lord, C., Brugha, T.S., Charman, T., Cusack, J., Dumas, G., Frazier, T., Jones, E.J.H., Jones, R.M., Pickles, A., State, M.W., Taylor, J.L., & Veenstra-VanderWeele, J. (2020). Autism spectrum disorder. *Nature Reviews. Disease Primers, 6*(1). doi:10.1038/s41572-019-0138-4

Low, J., & Perner, J. (2012). Implicit and explicit theory of mind: State of the art. *British Journal of Developmental Psychology, 30*(1), 1–13. doi:10.1111/j.2044-835X.2011.02074.x

McGovern, C.W., & Sigman, M. (2005). Continuity and change from early childhood to adolescence in autism. *Journal of Child Psychology and Psychiatry, and Allied Disciplines, 46*(4), 401–408. doi:10.1111/j.1469-7610.2004.00361.x

Milton, D.E.M. (2012). On the ontological status of autism: The 'double empathy problem'. *Disability and Society, 27*(6), 883–887. doi:10.1080/09687599.2012.710008

Murray, K., Johnston, K., Cunnane, H., Kerr, C., Spain, D., Gillan, N., Hammond, N., Murphy, D., & Happé, F. (2017). A new test of advanced theory of mind: The "Strange Stories Film Task" captures social processing differences in adults with autism spectrum disorders. *Autism Research: Official Journal of the International Society for Autism Research, 10*(6), 1120–1132. doi:10.1002/aur.1744

Nolen-Hoeksema, S., Fredrickson, B.L., Loftus, G.R., & Lutz, C. (2014). *Hilgard's Introduction to Psychology* (16th ed.). New York: Harcourt College Publishers.

Pellicano, E. (2010). Individual differences in executive function and central coherence predict developmental changes in theory of mind in autism. *Developmental Psychology, 46*(2), 530–544. doi:10.1037/a0018287

Peterson, C.C., & Wellman, H.M. (2019). Longitudinal theory of mind (ToM) development from preschool to adolescence with and without ToM delay. *Child Development, 90*(6), 1917–1934. doi:10.1111/cdev.13064

Picci, G., & Scherf, K.S. (2015). A two-hit model of autism: Adolescence as the second hit. *Clinical Psychological Science: A Journal of the Association for Psychological Science, 3*(3), 349–371. doi:10.1177/2167702614540646

Ponnet, K., Buysse, A., Roeyers, H., & De Clercq, A. (2008). Mind-reading in young adults with ASD: Does structure matter? *Journal of Autism and Developmental Disorders, 38*(5), 905–918. doi:10.1007/s10803-007-0462-5

Premack, D., & Woodruff, G. (1978). Does the chimpanzee have a theory of mind? *Behavioral and Brain Sciences, 1*(4), 515–526. doi:10.1017/S0140525X00076512

Preston, S.D., & de Waal, F.B.M. (2002). Empathy: Its ultimate and proximate bases. *Behavioral and Brain Sciences, 25*(1), 1. doi:10.1017/s0140525x02000018

Roeyers, H., Buysse, A., Ponnet, K., & Pichal, B. (2001). Advancing advanced mind-reading tests: Empathic accuracy in adults with a pervasive developmental disorder. *Journal of Child Psychology and Psychiatry, and Allied Disciplines, 42*(2), 271–278. doi:10.1111/1469-7610.00718

Rosenthal, M., Wallace, G.L., Lawson, R., Wills, M.C., Dixon, E., Yerys, B.E., & Kenworthy, L. (2013). Impairments in real-world executive function increase From childhood to adolescence in autism spectrum disorders. *Neuropsychology, 27*(1), 13–18. doi:10.1037/a0031299

Salter, G., Seigal, A., Claxton, M., Lawrence, K., & Skuse, D. (2008). Can autistic children read the mind of an animated triangle? *Autism: The International Journal of Research and Practice, 12*(4), 349–371. doi:10.1177/1362361308091654

Santiesteban, I., Shah, P., White, S., Bird, G., & Heyes, C. (2015). Mentalizing or submentalizing in a communication task? Evidence from autism and a camera control. *Psychonomic Bulletin and Review, 22*(3), 844–849. doi:10.3758/s13423-014-0716-0

Scheeren, A.M., Banerjee, R., Koot, H.M., & Begeer, S. (2016). Self-presentation and the role of perspective taking and social motivation in autism spectrum disorder. *Journal of Autism and Developmental Disorders, 46*, 649–657. DOI: 10.1007/s10803-015-2610-7

Scheeren, A.M., de Rosnay, M., Koot, H.M., & Begeer, S. (2013). Rethinking theory of mind in high-functioning autism spectrum disorder. *Journal of Child Psychology and Psychiatry, and Allied Disciplines, 54*(6), 628–635. doi:10.1111/jcpp.12007

Schilbach, L., Timmermans, B., Reddy, V., Costall, A., Bente, G., Schlicht, T., & Vogeley, K. (2013). Toward a second-person neuroscience. *Behavioral and Brain Sciences, 36*(4), 393–414. doi:10.1017/S0140525X12000660

Senju, A., Southgate, V., White, S., & Frith, U. (2009). Mindblind eyes: An absence of spontaneous theory of mind in Asperger syndrome. *Science, 325*(5942), 883–885. doi:10.1126/science.1176170

Smith, L.E., Maenner, M.J., & Seltzer, M.M. (2012). Developmental trajectories in adolescents and adults With autism: The case of daily living skills. *Journal of the American Academy of Child and Adolescent Psychiatry, 51*(6), 622–631. doi:10.1016/j.jaac.2012.03.001

Steele, S., Joseph, R.M., & Tager-Flusberg, H. (2003). Brief report: Developmental change in theory of mind abilities in children with autism. *Journal of Autism and Developmental Disorders, 33*(4), 461–467. doi:10.1023/a:1025075115100

Thye, M.D., Bednarz, H.M., Herringshaw, A.J., Sartin, E.B., & Kana, R.K. (2018). The impact of atypical sensory processing on social impairments in autism spectrum disorder. *Developmental Cognitive Neuroscience, 29*, 151–167. doi:10.1016/j.dcn.2017.04.010

White, S., Hill, E., Happé, F., & Frith, U. (2009). Revisiting the strange stories: Revealing mentalizing impairments in autism. *Child Development, 80*(4), 1097–1117. doi:10.1111/j.1467-8624.2009.01319.x

Wimmer, H., & Perner, J. (1983). Beliefs about beliefs: Representation and constraining function of wrong beliefs in young children's understanding of deception. *Cognition, 13*(1), 103–128. doi:10.1016/0010-0277(83)90004-5

Yirmiya, N., Erel, O., Shaked, M., & Solomonica-Levi, D. (1998). Meta-analyses comparing theory of mind abilities of individuals with autism, individuals with mental retardation, and normally developing individuals. *Psychological Bulletin, 124*(3), 283–307. doi:10.1037/0033-2909.124.3.283

Zwickel, J., White, S.J., Coniston, D., Senju, A., & Frith, U. (2011). Exploring the building blocks of social cognition: Spontaneous agency perception and visual perspective taking in autism. *Social Cognitive and Affective Neuroscience, 6*(5), 564–571. doi:10.1093/scan/nsq088

10 Deafness as a window into theory of mind in middle childhood and adolescence

Candida C. Peterson

Theory of mind (ToM), or the representational understanding of how thoughts and feelings shape human behavior, is so fundamental to so many aspects of cognitive and social life as to be dubbed the 'quintessential ability that makes us human' (Baron-Cohen, 2001, p. 174). Mastery of ToM is prototypically assessed with standard explicit false belief tests that require children to predict or explain the behavior of people whose beliefs (not shared by the child being tested) are at odds with objective reality. Most three-year-olds fail these tests. Yet, by five to six years of age, the vast majority of hearing children without disabilities pass them. Thus, at the start of middle childhood, ToM development (as traditionally indexed via success on false belief tests) is likely to be close to ceiling for the average hearing child.

However, for most deaf children with severe-to-profound prelingual hearing losses, the developmental journey towards ToM is not nearly so rapid or uncomplicated. In fact, apart from the small minority (5% to 10%) of deaf children who have at least one signing deaf parent, deaf children whose only disability is hearing loss routinely continue to fail false belief tests not just throughout the preschool years but also throughout much of middle childhood (for reviews see: Peterson & Siegal, 2000; Peterson, 2009; Siegal & Peterson, 2008; Wellman & Peterson, 2013a). Indeed, even in high school at mean ages of 15 to 17 years, two studies of deaf children of hearing parents (known as DoH children) in the UK (Edmondson, 2006; Russell et al., 1998) revealed widespread failure of the simple false belief tasks that the vast majority of hearing children pass by age five. Similarly, Meristo et al. (2007) found that 50% of Swedish and 75% of Estonian DoH 12-year-olds failed at least one of a pair of standard (unexpected contents plus misleading container) false belief tasks.

Direct comparisons with children who have autism (see Chapter 9 of this volume) (another group prone to extremely protracted ToM delays; Baron-Cohen, 2001) typically show that, on average, deaf children of hearing parents fare no better (e.g., Peterson & Siegal, 2000; Peterson & Wellman, 2019). Yet, in contrast to autism, the deaf child's underlying developmental atypicality is not neurocognitive but instead is merely a difference with peripheral sense organs. An autism diagnosis entails numerous neurobiological differences and abnormalities that might in themselves delay ToM mastery (e.g., Baron-Cohen,

1995). Frith (2002, p. 182) wrote: 'The evidence that autism is a disorder of the brain is overwhelming'. This complicates the interpretation of findings of ToM delay in autistic children since they also often experience conversational and other experiential problems that can be difficult to tease apart from congenital neurocognitive ones when seeking a theoretical explanation for their ToM delay. This can therefore limit the relevance of data on ToM development in autism to non-autistic groups. By contrast, deaf children's evidence is often easier to interpret and hence of greater direct relevance to theories about ToM development for children generally.

Because deaf children's hearing losses are only sensory and peripheral, not neurocognitive, their ToM delays are more readily interpretable than autistic children's are in terms of experiential factors. When children are severely to profoundly deaf, they cannot easily perceive the sounds that occupy the normal range of speech. However, hearing loss per se does not inherently entail a neurocognitive or socio-cognitive abnormality. Thus a research focus on deaf children overcomes many of the methodological complexities bound up with studies of autism and other clinical groups with congenital cognitive impairments. Thus research into deaf children's ToM development and delay can make comparisons between deaf children and their age-matched hearing peers uniquely informative in terms of contextual, social, and environmental influences on ToM.

Capitalizing on this, a wealth of research evidence has accumulated over the past 25 years since Peterson and Siegal's (1995) study about how severely and profoundly deaf children develop ToM. From a review of such studies that had been published between 1995 to 2013, Wellman and Peterson (2013a, p. 59) concluded:

> Studies of more than 700 severely or profoundly deaf offspring of hearing parents from several different countries (and hence different signed and spoken languages, and approaches to deaf education) consistently reveal predominant failure on false belief tasks throughout primary school (ages 6–12). This is in clear contrast to hearing preschoolers' predominant success by age 4 or 5…These serious delays apply just as much to deaf children who sign vs. communicate orally and, within the latter group, to those who use cochlear implants vs. external hearing aids (see Peterson, 2004, for a review).

Deaf native signers

The variable of whether or not the family that a deaf child is born into happens to contain anyone else who is deaf might not at first seem especially significant. After all, family members vary on many dimensions (e.g., curly or straight hair; left- or right-handed; talented at music versus visual art) that exert no direct bearing on their development of a ToM-based understanding of others' minds. However, having at least one deaf family member who is a deaf signer does turn out to matter crucially for a deaf child's ToM growth. By definition, DoH (deaf-of-hearing [parents]) children are born with severe-to-profound hearing losses but no signing family members. By contrast, DoD (deaf-of-deaf) children, dubbed 'native signers', have signing deaf parent(s) with sign language as their fluent native language.

Decades of ToM research comparing ToM development in DoD children with that of DoH children have revealed striking differences. So much so that, arguably, if only one fact could be known about a particular deaf child, perhaps the most important one for ToM would be whether he/she is DoH or DoD. Because 90 to 95% of children born deaf are DoH, DoD children constitute a numerically tiny minority of the child population as a whole. Yet the theoretical contributions made possible by their participation in ToM research have been disproportionately large and very special. Comparisons between DoD children and their DoH peers as well as between each of these deaf subgroups and their hearing peers have advanced scientific understanding of ToM development for children generally in uniquely significant ways. As new questions about ToM and its social, cultural, and neurobiological underpinnings continue to arise for developmental psychology generally, this line of research continues to offer a unique important avenue for fresh insight.

Deaf native signers resemble hearing children in terms of conversational access and development. From birth, hearing children (in speech) and DoD children (in sign) both enjoy unfettered access to spontaneous family conversation in a natural language, including opportunities to converse at home with parents and siblings about topics like mental states such as thoughts, feelings, beliefs, memories, and pretend play that do not lend themselves to being communicated about through gesturing, pointing, or in any other way except via language. Thus the DoD child's pace of ToM mastery provides a natural test of the relevance of such mentalistic conversation to ToM growth. If DoD children master ToM understanding on the same early timetable as a hearing child, while outperforming DoH peers with whom they are closely matched on other variables like general intelligence, executive functioning, and language ability at the time of being tested (Woolfe et al., 2002), then their ready access to fluent mentalistic conversation at home will be clearly implicated as a contributor to timely ToM development.

These hypotheses were initially tested during the late 1990s, first by Peterson and Siegal in Australia (1997, 1998, 1999) and very shortly thereafter by an independent team in France (Courtin, 1999; Courtin & Melot, 1998, 2005). All these pioneering studies produced remarkably consistent (and highly theoretically provocative) results. Peterson and Siegal (1997) studied 35 Australian children who were all prelingually severely-to-profoundly deaf. Twenty-six of them were DoH and nine were DoD. Forty-eight hearing preschoolers also took part. Using standard false belief tests plus tests of folk physics (false photographic representation) and folk biology, results showed that the deaf native signers significantly outperformed their DoH peers. In fact, 89% of native signers earned perfect ToM scores compared with only 46% of DoH children.

(The latter were dubbed 'late signers' because, while now using sign language fluently, they had only begun learning it at preschool entry when aged three to four). By contrast, on the biology and physics tasks, DoH and DoD children did not differ from one another. Thus the striking advantage that native signers displayed over their DoH peers was specific to ToM-based understanding of false belief, rather than signifying more a general difference in domains not requiring mentalistic understanding.

Courtin and Melot (1998) similarly compared 13 French DoD native-signers aged five to seven years with 22 DoH late-signers of the same age on false belief tests and found, like Peterson and Siegal (1997), that the native signers scored significantly higher. Courtin (1999) did not include any DoH children in his sample but instead compared 19 French native signers aged five and six years to 24 age-matched French hearing children on a three-item false belief test battery. The DoD children not only mostly passed false belief (90% passed at age six, 78% at age five) but they also earned a significantly higher mean ToM score (mean = approx. 2.30/3) than their hearing peers (mean = 1.50/3 or only 50% correct). In the same year in Australia, Peterson and Siegal (1999) found even higher absolute levels of ToM performance by deaf native signers than Courtin (1999) did on a similar three-item false belief test battery. The 11 native signers in Peterson and Siegal's (1999) sample ranged in age from 5 to 13 years, as did their 34 late-signing DoH peers (means for each group were 9.42 years). Perhaps because of this, the native signers were essentially at ceiling on all three of the false belief tests (100%, 91%, and 82% perfect scores) and they significantly outperformed the late-signers (59%, 47%, and 38% success, respectively). This remained true even after controlling statistically for group differences in language ability.

Following on from these pioneering studies, dozens of additional ToM comparisons between deaf native signers, DoH children (oral-communicators as well as late signers), and hearing children have been published. The samples have included deaf children from all around the world, and with few exceptions, their results closely replicate the original studies' main findings (see reviews in Peterson, 2009; Peterson & Wellman, 2019; Siegal & Peterson, 2008; Wellman & Peterson, 2013a). In particular, the overall body of findings about ToM development in DoD native signers coincides with the earlier studies' conclusions that these children (1) outperform their DoH peers on false belief and other standard ToM tests and (2) often display levels of ToM test performance that are at least equal to those of the hearing comparison groups with whom they have been matched in various respects (e.g., age, language ability, nonverbal IQ, etc.).

Among these more recent false belief studies comparing DoD native signers with DoH children from hearing-only households, two studies (both published in 2007) are noteworthy for having substantially larger samples of native signers than most of the rest, thus further clarifying and reinforcing evidence both that (1) DoD deaf native signers develop ToM on the same early timetable as hearing children and (2) DoH children are significantly and substantially delayed behind DoD children as well as behind hearing peers. In particular, Schick et al. (2007) studied 49 DoD children aged four to seven years (mean: Six years seven months) in the USA who used American Sign Language (ASL) as their native language and attended schools teaching in ASL and written English only, not spoken English. Forty-one late-signing DoH children from the same signing-only schools were also included (mean age: 6 years 11 months) along with 86 orally communicating DoH children (mean age: 6.50 years). This oral-only deaf group attended different schools that were ordinary mainstream schools in the community and did not use any sign language. A hearing comparison group (mean age: 5.33 years) was also included.

Results showed that DoD children equaled the hearing group on a battery of seven standard false belief tasks and significantly outperformed the DoH children in both the signing and the orally communicating groups. The late-signing and oral-only DoH children did not differ significantly from each other. However, individual differences among DoH children were wide and interconnected both with general linguistic ability and with specific linguistic skill with the syntax of embedded sentential complements.

Likewise, in Europe, Meristo et al. (2007) studied false belief–based understanding in another impressively large sample of DoD deaf native signers (a total of 80) who were either Italian, Estonian, or Swedish and whose ages ranged from 4 through 15 years. They came from signing deaf families and used sign language at home as their main means of conversing with their parents and siblings. As expected, they significantly outperformed DoH peers, just as in past research. Interestingly, besides its unusually large DoD sample size, another unique feature of this study was its inclusion of a subgroup of DoD children who were attending 'oralist' mainstream schools using only spoken language and offering no conversational access at school to fluently signing peers or teachers. Indeed, in these schools, even if sign language was not actively discouraged, it was 'avoided as much as possible (p. 1161). Thus for these 43 orally educated deaf native signers (20 from Italy and 23 from Estonia), signed conversation was the norm at home but unavailable during school hours. The remaining 37 DoD children attended Total Communication (sign + speech) schools where they had full school-based conversational access to signing peers and teachers. Thus if daily dialogue with fluent signers both at home and at school exerts a cumulative influence on natively signing deaf children's pace of ToM mastery, then the bilingually educated DoD children would be expected to outperform their orally schooled DoD counterparts. On the other hand, if access to unfettered conversation (including mentalistic conversation) at home is sufficient in itself to promote timely ToM growth, then the DoD children attending oral-only schools would be predicted to score equally to hearing children and to bilingually schooled DoD groups.

Results on different sets of false belief tests in Italy and Scandinavia replicated one another and were compelling. They showed that DoH late-signers and oral DoH children equaled one another in ToM understanding and were significantly outperformed by age-matched hearing children. However, the most interesting result was the contrast in the DoD native-signer group between those who attended bilingual schools where sign language and speech were jointly used versus those in mainstream oral-only schools. Only those DoD native signers who used sign language at school as well as at home equaled their age-matched hearing peers in ToM understanding. By contrast, the orally schooled DoD children scored significantly lower than the hearing group. That is, even though both natively signing deaf groups had had access to fluent conversational exchanges in sign language at home since birth (and still did), their communicative situations at school made a difference to ToM mastery. Presumably, the opportunity to exchange fluently signed conversations with natively signing family members at home was not enough to outweigh the lack of these at school. In bilingual schools, mentalistic conversations in sign language with signing deaf peers during pretend play, peer gossip, school subjects, and so on would have been readily accessible on a daily basis at school, possibly contributing to the ToM contrast between the DoD groups attending the two different types of schooling.

In addition to these studies of false belief understanding, another important body of recent work on ToM in DoD native signers as compared with DoH late signers has explored their relative performance in other ToM domains besides false belief. Studies have explored ToM tasks requiring abilities like desire reasoning, visual and affective perspective-taking, understanding how knowledge is acquired, deliberate emotion concealment, and nonliteral language (e.g., O'Reilly et al., 2014; Peterson, 2003; Peterson et al., 2005, 2012). In each of these domains, DoD native signers are found to (1) significantly outperform their DoH deaf peers from hearing-only families and (2) usually perform on a par with hearing children their age.

DoH children with cochlear implants

Cochlear implants (CIs) are surgically installed electronic prosthetic devices that can, over time, help to provide a substitute for the sense of sound in the case of certain forms of deafness. The CI does not amplify the volume of sound the way a conventional hearing aid would. Instead, it creates an electronic alternative to sound by converting sound waves into electronic signals that enable auditory information to bypass damaged parts of the ear and directly stimulate the brain's auditory nerve. New-generation cochlear implants (CIs) can now be installed in infancy. However, extensive post-installation training, fine-tuning of the device, and rehabilitation therapy are needed for a child to master the use of a CI to the point of being able to hear sounds. Once sound perception is established, the learning of spoken language can begin. But then it may take numerous more years after that for spoken language to be mastered to the point of enabling reception and production of even very basic spoken communication (e.g., Bavin et al., 2018). For example, consider a recently reported longitudinal study of spoken language development in a sample of 33 Australian deaf infants and children of hearing parents (DoH children). A majority had received their first CI when aged between six and ten months. Children were tested first at the time of implantation and then followed up for further language tests at three-month intervals through 15 months after receiving the implant. Consistent with other evidence from older children implanted at older ages, the CI children's language development remained seriously delayed behind that of hearing children throughout the longitudinal period. Other evidence (e.g., Duchesne et al., 2009) indicates that even with early and successful cochlear implantation, most prelingually severely and profoundly deaf children with CIs require a minimum of at least five to six years post-implantation before their language skills come up to the range for hearing children on published language test norms.

Therefore, given that DoH children's opportunities for mentalistic conversations at home with family members depend on them all being able to share a common language fluently, irrespective of whether it is a spoken language or a signed one, this evidence on the timing of spoken language mastery following CI implantation implies that access to early family conversation at home is likely to be just as incomplete for DoH children who use CIs as for those who ultimately become late-signers. Little or no exposure to fluent mentalistic conversational input is likely to be available to either group during the preschool years.

But what happens once DoH children with CIs do master their use and gain fluency in spoken language once they begin to participate in informal conversational exchange of views and start to gain exposure to conversational mental-state input? Does having a CI make a difference to ToM development? Empirically, a number of studies have explored this question, asking whether DoH CI-users are ahead of (or perhaps behind) other DoH children in their pace of ToM mastery. In one of the first of these, Peterson (2004) found no significant differences on a comprehensive false belief test battery between two subgroups of orally communicating Australian DoH children born with severe-to-profound deafness. Group 1 were those who used CIs (N = 13) whereas Group 2 were matched DoH children who relied on conventional external amplifying hearing aids (HA: n = 13) for speech perception and communication. In addition to the aid-versus-implant dichotomy, the children were roughly evenly divided between bilingual schooling (using sign plus speech) and oralist (speech-only) mainstream schools. Like the CI variable, the schooling variable displayed no significant links with ToM scores. But there was a significant effect of hearing status. Even in middle childhood (ages seven to nine years), the DoH children scored significantly below hearing four-year-olds (71% ToM success) regardless of whether they attended mainstream or signing schools and irrespective of whether they used CIs (8% ToM success) or not (38% success).

In the USA, Moeller and Schick (2006) found essentially the same thing. At a mean age of seven years, the ten late-signing DoH children with CIs they studied performed equally to their sample of 12 DoH hearing-aid users on a standard battery of ToM tests. However, both DoH groups were significantly outperformed by hearing preschoolers some three years younger. In the UK, MacCauley and Ford (2006) studied ten deaf children with CIs (mean age 8.42 years) and found their 'performance was impaired' (p. 9) relative to hearing preschoolers. Only two deaf CI users (20%) consistently passed false belief tests and they were eight and ten years old, respectively. Remmel and Peters (2009) tested 30 American orally communicating DoH children with CIs (mean age 7.50 years) on a single forced-choice false belief test and found no clear evidence of above-chance performance. However, in a subsequent study, the same CI children (who again performed at chance on a standard false belief prediction test) were mostly able to use mental-state terms for perception (but not cognition) in their spontaneous story-telling.

Sundqvist et al. (2014) investigated ToM in 16 profoundly DoH Swedish children aged four to nine years, all of whom used CIs. All families had established some sign language communication with them prior to the implant. On the single false belief test used, the eight CI children who had received their first implant early (mean age: 17.6 months) did not differ from those implanted later (mean: 40 months). But their ToM understanding was poor overall. Pass rates were only 42% and 21%, respectively, for early- and late-implant DoH children, whereas an age-matched hearing comparison group scored 96% correct.

In another early-implant CI study with an impressively large sample, Ketelaar et al. (2012) compared 51 DoH children in the Netherlands (aged 2.58 to 5.00 years) with a TD hearing group of similar age. The deaf children all had CIs and most had received their first implant before the age of three years. The mean implant age was 17 months. Children took a standard false belief test and a test of a ToM concept that develops before false belief, namely diverse desires. This concept requires the recognition that different people can want different things. None of the deaf children (0%) managed to pass false belief, compared with significantly more (31%) in the hearing group. Even the simple desire test was failed by 80% of the deaf children, compared with only 38% of the age-matched hearing children. Thus, despite their early age at gaining a CI, widespread ToM delays were clearly evident in this impressively large young DoH sample.

CI users often encounter difficulties with aspects of ToM understanding even in adulthood. For example, using a battery of advanced ToM tests, Marschark et al. (2019) tested 46 deaf university students who used cochlear implants (and had done so since early childhood: Their mean age at receiving their first implant was 6.61 years). Two closely matched comparison groups were also included. The first consisted of 48 DoH students at the same university who were non-users of CIs. They either used external amplifying hearing aids or no auditory prosthetic devices. There was also a second comparison group consisting of 41 hearing university classmates of the deaf students. The advanced ToM concepts that were tested included second-order false belief (recursive understanding of Person A's true or false belief about Person B's belief), ToM-based understanding of sarcasm (e.g., O'Reilly et al., 2014), and double-bluffing. Compared with the hearing students, the deaf CI users and the deaf non-users both scored poorly on all the ToM measures, well below the hearing group. This suggests that even long-term CI use had not been fully sufficient for enabling the unimpaired development of a mature representational understanding of others' minds.

However, as CI technology itself continues to improve, along with commensurate advances in educational, psychological, and speech-therapeutic interventions for younger and older DoH children and greater involvement of parents from ever earlier ages in facilitating their DoH children's uptake and reliable usage of CIs (Bavin et al., 2018), the situation may well change. Teaching deaf children with CIs how to optimize the benefits (including conversational ones) to be gained from the device could conceivably lead to better ToM outcomes in future. Therefore, continuing research into new questions about ToM development in the context of CI prosthesis is clearly warranted.

Parental conversational input and deaf children's ToM development

For hearing children, frequent parental talk about mental states like beliefs and intentions is a significant predictor of rapid ToM mastery (see Chapter 5). Is the same true for deaf children? With a sample of late-signing DoH children, Moeller and Schick (2006) examined this in two ways. First, they gave the hearing mothers a sign language mental-state vocabulary test, reasoning that the more signs for cognitive states the mother knew (e.g., 'think', 'guess', 'remember', 'imagine'), the richer her conversational input of mental-state information to the deaf child would be. Second, they recorded mothers' actual mentions of mental states during conversations with these late-signing deaf children. They discovered wide individual differences among mothers on both measures. Some knew only one or two mental-state signs while others knew 18 to 25. Their actual signed conversations were similarly varied. Some almost never produced mentalistic utterances whereas others produced signed conversational input that was as rich and varied as in hearing mothers' spoken conversations with their hearing children. When links with DoH children's false belief test scores with these maternal variables were examined, they were each found to be statistically significant ToM predictors. In other words, late-signing DoH children's pace of ToM mastery, as assessed on laboratory false belief tests, showed clear links with the richness and variety of their mothers' talk about the mind. Though further research is clearly needed, this pattern for ToM-delayed DoH children is closely in keeping with that seen and repeatedly confirmed for hearing children (e.g., Devine & Hughes, 2018).

Longitudinal studies, critical periods, and widespread ToM progress

The varied studies of ToM development in deaf children that have been considered so far in this chapter have all used cross-sectional methodologies. An alternative method for examining developmental change is a longitudinal design. Despite costs, complexities, and the lengthier data-collection time they require, longitudinal studies have several unique and important advantages over cross-sectional ones. A longitudinal study follows the same individual children as they themselves grow up and develop, rather than relying on the often problematic inference entailed by cross-sectionally equating different children from different age groups on the assumption that the only relevant difference among them is chronological age. By contrast, a longitudinal design can pinpoint actual developmental change in individual children precisely. Since each child's own earlier performance (e.g., on a ToM test) is the yardstick against which later performance is compared, actual developmental change is directly visible. Longitudinal studies therefore enable key theoretical questions to be answered in ways not possible with other methods. However, only a few past longitudinal studies of ToM development among severely-to-profoundly deaf children have been reported. Specifically, these include Falkman et al. (2007), Peterson (2009), and Wellman et al. (2011). Furthermore, none of these three included age-matched hearing children or ToM tasks suitable for hearing children of middle-childhood age.

By contrast, numerous longitudinal studies of TD hearing children's ToM during middle and late childhood have clearly demonstrated the method's unique potential when applied to these age groups, as well as the theoretical value of going beyond the preschool period to continue the longitudinal tracking of ToM during the school years when new social, academic, and cognitive experiences create fresh ToM challenges. Useful new observations and theoretical ideas about ToM development in general have emerged from this growing body of longitudinal work. Findings are important for developmental theory as well as for practical application both inside and outside the classroom (e.g., Devine & Hughes, 2013; Lecce et al., 2014).

Arguably, studying the growth of ToM in DoH children longitudinally spanning middle childhood and beyond could hold even greater theoretical and practical promise, especially when combined with comparative examination of age-matched hearing children's developmental ToM trajectories over the same extended timeframes on exactly the same advanced (school age–appropriate) ToM tasks. Between the ages of 6 and 12 years, deaf children face many of the same challenges as hearing children do over peer popularity, friendships, and everyday social relations and social functioning within the classroom peer group (e.g., Fink et al., 2015; Peterson et al., 2018, 2016). But when it comes to peer interaction, DoH children face additional challenges as well. For some of them, school entry immerses them for the first time in the sign language that will soon become their fluent sole or predominant communication medium (Power & Carty, 1990). For others, entry into mainstream oral-only schooling can bring its own special challenges of potential relevance for ToM.

Longitudinal data comparing ToM in deaf and hearing school-aged children can shed new light on practical issues like these. It also holds theoretical promise for contributing new insights into longstanding theoretical debates in psychology over issues such as critical-period hypotheses, individual differences, and long-term outcomes and correlates of early versus late ToM mastery. For example, despite their preschool ToM delays, do most DoH children eventually master ToM and learn to 'read' minds during their school years just as they will eventually learn to read print while being schooled in literacy at the same age (Heyes & Frith, 2014)? Or, as Siegal and Varley (2002) proposed, is there a critical period for ToM acquisition? Tierney and Nelson (2009) noted that in neurobiological development, 'experiences in the early years of development can affect the development of the brain in ways that later experiences do not' (p. 11) and saw this as evidence for an 'experience-expectant sensitive period'. Early in development, there is believed to be a critical time when the human brain is biologically primed to be optimally ready for certain developmentally significant experiences. Deprivation during this time will have lasting adverse consequences, according to this theory, that belated exposure to the same experiences outside the critical time frame can never fully make up for.

For ToM, the preschool years have been proposed as one such critical (or 'sensitive') period. For example, as Siegal and Varley (2002, p.469) explained:

> Findings point to a critical period in ToM. Just as children seem to be irreparably impaired in their later language learning when not exposed at all to an early language environment, children require at least some minimal access to conversation about mental states to show ToM reasoning.

An alternative to this 'experience-expectant sensitive period' model, according to Tierney and Nelson (2009), is 'experience-dependent plasticity'. This hypothesis proposes that even though certain formative experiences (e.g., 'access to conversation' as proposed by Siegal & Varley [2002]) may well be necessary to trigger ToM, there is no particular time constraint on when such experiences must occur. Thus, according to the plasticity view, even though many DoH children (unlike their natively signing deaf peers) miss out on access to fluent mentalistic conversational exchanges at home as preschoolers, they can still develop ToM understanding fully (and without any lingering delays or limitations) once they do eventually gain such access at school or later on.

Longitudinal data are optimal for exploring questions like these. Studying an unusual group of deaf adults, Pyers and Senghas (2009) conducted a two-year longitudinal study of false belief understanding. The small sample (18 deaf adults) had grown up in Nicaragua in an unusual era for deaf education and access to Nicaraguan sign language (NSL) in that country. When the longitudinal study began, the oldest cohort (n = 8; mean age: 26.8 years) had grown up without any access to NSL. When they came together with other deaf children for the first time with entry into a special deaf primary school, neither they nor any of their deaf classmates or teachers used any form of sign language fluently. These members of Cohort 1 had therefore only communicated initially by means of a few simple iconic gestures (e.g., miming and pointing). Over their time together at the deaf school, in interaction with their deaf classmates, they had gradually developed a limited form of NSL gesturing that was not yet a true language. It lacked the necessary vocabulary and syntax for communicating about mental states. Thus, at the start of the study, Cohort 1 could neither converse informally about mental states nor pass standard false belief tests. The second cohort (n = 10) attended the same deaf school some 10 to 15 years later. Building on the efforts of the first cohort, this fresh generation of DoH pupils managed to expand NSL beyond the primitive gestures and iconic signs used by the first cohort so that it became 'a complete language' (p. 805) with all the lexical and syntactic capacity needed to converse about mental states.

Despite lacking a ToM throughout their growing up, Cohort 1 members enjoyed an active social life, including frequent interaction with other deaf Cohort 1 members of an adult-deaf social club. Serendipitously, between the first and the second longitudinal ToM tests, some members of Cohort 2 reached adulthood and joined the same club. There, they conversed with the older Cohort 1 members and taught them new signs and syntax. Thus, in their mid-twenties, Cohort 1 gained access to a richer sign language 'that included the new mental state words produced by their younger [second cohort] peers' (p. 810). Now equipped with 'the linguistic tools needed to support a mature ToM' (p. 810), their false belief scores improved significantly. From a mean at Time 1 of only 0.50/4.00 tasks correct, two years later (at mean age 28.6) their mean had risen to 1.50/3.00 (or 50% correct). Now they no longer differed significantly from Cohort 2. Still, while ruling out an extreme version of the critical period hypothesis (such that no ToM gain at all is possible after early childhood), these results are silent on the contrast between 'sensitive periods' and 'experience-dependent plasticity' (Tierney & Nelson, 2009). Irrespective of cohort membership, none of these unusual Nicaraguan deaf adults did well enough at the end of the study on any ToM measures to clearly inform a decision between these models.

Further longitudinal research, ideally sampling DoH *children* across a broad age range is therefore clearly needed. Between 2002 and 2011, three longitudinal studies of ToM development in late-signing DoH children who were severely-to-profoundly prelingually deaf were published (Falkman et al., 2007; Peterson, 2009; Wellman et al., 2011). Their pioneering results made valuable contributions, both theoretical and applied. However, because (1) none of these three studies included any age-matched hearing children and (2) measures used in all of them were limited to preschool ToM tasks that hearing children normally master by age five, results of these studies do not fully explore the contrast between the sensitive period hypothesis that ToM growth slows or stops after preschool versus the experience-dependent plasticity hypothesis that genuine development of new ToM concepts can continue indefinitely. Nor do results of these studies allow comprehensive examination of comparative trajectories of ToM growth by DoH children versus age-matched hearing peers not only during the preschool period but through the middle and late childhood years and into pre-adolescence.

In light of these considerations, an ambitious longitudinal study that was reported recently (Peterson & Wellman, 2019) deserves special attention. Its sample of 107 Australian children ranged in age from 3 to 11 years at the start of the study and from 4.50 to 13 years at its end. There were 27 DoH children and 37 closely age-matched TD hearing children plus an additional comparison group of 36 age-matched ToM-delayed children with autism. The longitudinal interval between the first and last test was lengthy (one to two years) for research of this kind and the ToM assessment was a comprehensive eight-task ToM measure. The 27 DoH children (mean Time 1 age: 7.33 years) all had severe-to-profound prelingual hearing losses and no fluently signing family members. Recruited from bilingual (sign and speech) primary schools and preschools that used Australian sign language (Auslan) bilingually along with spoken English for classroom communication, they all currently preferred (and fluently used) sign as their primary language. All had extensive daily opportunities at school to converse with other fluent signers (deaf peers and teachers).

Another key methodological innovation of the study was its use of a developmentally sensitive six-step ToM Scale (Peterson et al., 2012) as well as a standard false belief battery in the composite eight-task ToM measure. This six-step developmental ToM Scale contains two post–false belief sequential steps (Sarcasm and Hidden Emotion) that are often failed even by TD hearing children aged 9 to 12 years (e.g., Peterson et al., 2016). Past research with the scale (e.g., Peterson et al., 2012) has shown, via Guttman and Rasch scaling techniques, that the sequence of six increasingly difficult ToM concepts that it incorporates comprises a reliably sequentially developing series of ToM concepts of increasing difficulty that emerge in a significantly similar order from one child to the next. Furthermore, these past studies have shown, as did Peterson and Wellman's (2019) longitudinal data, that the sequence of ToM Scale steps is the same for deaf and hearing alike, despite DoH children's slower progress through it. Thus the developmentally sequenced ToM Scale is optimally sensitive both to ToM growth as a continuing step-by-step process and also to the emergence of further conceptual advances beyond the one-off mastery of the concept of false belief. Furthermore, this applies to TD hearing children, as well as the deaf, even during middle and late childhood.

Results of group comparisons using the composite ToM total score (eight items subsuming the six-step ToM Scale plus a false belief battery) showed that even though the DoH children were outperformed by their age-matched hearing peers at both the beginning of the study and at its end, evidence of genuine developmental gain over the longitudinal interval was as strikingly apparent for the DoH children as for their TD peers. In fact, 70% of DoH children displayed genuine ToM progress by scoring higher on the composite measure at Time 2 than they had at Time 1. This widespread frequency of longitudinal gain did not differ significantly from TD hearing children. This was true both for the full TD sample of 37 and also for the 28 TD children who had room to display gain at the start of the study on the ToM composite score because they had not yet reached ceiling on it before the study began. That is, despite their initially slow start, once these DoH children gained fluent conversational access to signing peers and teachers in school, their comprehensive ToM progress was no less impressive than hearing peers' progress.

Using the six-step developmental ToM Scale, the picture was similar. Excluding the eight TD ceiling performers, 15 of 28 hearing (54%) and 14 of 27 deaf children (52%) progressed impressively by passing at least one more sequential ToM Scale concept at Time 2 than they did at Time 1. That is, an equal majority in both groups progressed upwards by at least one full scale step over the study's one- to two-year period. Furthermore, even the minority who did not progress remained stable over time, not losing any developmental ground they had previously covered. In fact, only one child in the total sample went backward between Times 2 and 1 (and this was actually a hearing child, not a deaf one).

As a further examination of age effects in relation to the hypothesis of a preschool critical period, subgroups of children aged three to six years at Time 1 were compared with those 7.08 years and over on the ToM composite and the ToM Scale. No significant differences emerged either for the sample as a whole, for the deaf group separately, or for the hearing group separately on either measure. Thus even TD hearing children appear just as capable of genuine conceptual mastery of new sequentially ordered ToM concepts in middle as in early childhood and, despite their slower initial start, the same is true for the deaf. Thus these data do not clearly support the notion of either a critical or a sensitive period for ToM (assuming the period in question coincides with the preschool years). Conversely, findings for both groups are fully consistent with the 'experience-dependent plasticity' model of ToM, the formative experience in this case being access to fluent mentalistic conversation exchange with peers as well as adults.

Social consequences of ToM development for deaf children

For hearing children, the transition into false belief understanding coincides with a number of positive developmental outcomes in their everyday social lives and social relationships. Is the same true for deaf children? In a recent study, Peterson et al. (2016) tested 36 school-aged late-signing deaf children (mean age: 9.76 years; range 5 to 14 years) and 21 age-matched hearing children (mean age: 8.87 years; range 7 to 13 years) on a five-step developmental ToM Scale (Peterson et al., 2005; Wellman & Liu, 2004). Each child was likewise described and rated by a teacher who knew him/her well in terms of their everyday social behavior and their social situation in the peer group on dimensions of (1) popularity versus unpopularity, (2) friendship versus friendlessness and social isolation, (3) leadership in the peer group, and (4) positive skills for, and dispositions to engage in, cooperative peer interaction.

Results for deaf children showed statistically significant positive correlations between ToM and each of these everyday skill dimensions apart from leadership (which was positive but non-significant). In other words, when facing the special peer-group challenges posed by school entry and the new world of classroom peer groups that this opens up, ToM skills can prove to be important assets in negotiating successful and satisfying social relationships with peers, and this is no less true for deaf children than for hearing children.

ToM training interventions for deaf children

Could intervention strategies involving teaching or training DoH children with ToM delays to understand specific ToM concepts prove effective? If so, would these boost deaf children's understanding of ToM generally beyond the specific concepts trained in a manner that persists over time? If so, this could suggest strategies that parents, teachers, and others working with DoH children might, in future, be able to apply in the context of assisting these children to cope with peer-group problems and challenges (like unpopularity) and with new peer-group opportunities (like leadership)?

In fact, though the body of past research exploring the teaching of ToM understanding and mindreading skills to ToM-delayed deaf children from hearing families is still very small, the success of a few carefully controlled and evaluated published studies does in fact indicate DoH children's ability to profit from certain kinds of ToM training. Two of these, in particular, stand out for their relevance to themes and concepts discussed throughout this chapter. Wellman and Peterson (2013b) developed a six-stage progressively ordered program of training deaf children in the use of pictorial thought bubbles to represent thinking. They discovered it to be highly successful in producing improved levels of success not only on the specific ToM tasks used in training (changed-location false belief tasks) but also in yielding generalization to novel false belief tasks (e.g., misleading container, misleading appearance). Furthermore, there was even wider generalization to other ToM concepts besides false belief (e.g., knowledge access) and success persisted to a delayed post-test.

More recently, Peterson and Wellman (2019) devised and validated a successful ToM training procedure for deaf children that required children to generate their own spontaneous explanations for the paradoxical actions of storybook and puppet-play protagonists whose false beliefs had led them astray. The children were simply asked to answer 'why' questions about false belief–driven behaviors. Over a series of multiple training sessions per week spread over a three-week period, a sample of school-age late-signing DoH children who took part gained extensive practice thinking about, and generating explanations for, actions inspired by false beliefs. Compared with a control group, these DoH children's mindreading skills improved substantially as a result of training. This was seen in increased post-test success on standard false belief–prediction tasks as compared with pre-test levels and in a significant contrast at post-test between the trained group's performance and that of an untrained control group that had performed equally before the training began. Furthermore, ToM gains persisted for several months to a delayed post-test. Strikingly, the simple activity of being required to explain why actors with false beliefs did what they did boosted the trained group's ToM understanding even though the training procedures themselves included no coaching or feedback to the children during training about whether their explanations were correct or wrong.

Conclusions

This chapter has explored a broad range of theoretically and practically significant research themes in deaf children's ToM development and has highlighted the fresh insights about ToM understanding in deaf and hearing children alike that such research can supply. Findings of striking differences in the pace of ToM growth between deaf children who, as native signers, resemble hearing children in having unfettered access to conversation with family members in a fluently shared language from birth versus deaf children of hearing parents (DoH children) who lack this have key theoretical importance. The serious setbacks and ToM delays that DoH children typically encounter in early childhood when no one else in their family can sign fluently highlight how important early access to family conversation is for timely ToM mastery. New evidence about conversation as well as about a variety of related questions concerning the ToM development of deaf children from hearing-only families (including about parental mental state input, use of cochlear implants, oralist versus bilingual schooling, critical periods, interventions via ToM training, and consequences of ToM mastery for deaf children's peer-group social relationships) were all explored. Overall, the collective evidence reviewed here (including that from longitudinal studies and novel developmental ToM Scales) optimistically highlights deaf children's widespread potential for ToM gains during middle childhood and beyond, while also raising a rich array of provocative further questions to inspire future research.

References

Baron-Cohen, S. (1995). *Mindblindness: An Essay on Autism and Theory of Mind*. Cambridge, MA: MIT Press.

Baron-Cohen, S. (2001). Theory of mind in normal development and autism. *Prisme, 34*, 174–183.

Bavin, E.L., Sarant, J., Leigh, G., Prendergast, L., Busby, P., & Peterson, C. (2018). Children with cochlear implants in infancy: Predictors of early vocabulary. *International Journal of Language and Communication Disorders, 53*(4), 788–798.

Courtin, C. (1999). Theories of mind in deaf children: The impact of sign language. *Enfance, 3*, 248–257.

Courtin, C., & Melot, A. (1998). Development of theories of mind in deaf children. In M. Marschark & M.D. Clark (Eds.), *Psychological Perspectives on Deafness* (pp. 79–102). Malwah, NJ: Erlbaum.

Courtin, C. & Melot, A.M. Metacognitive development of deaf children: lessons from the appearance-reality and false belief tasks. *Developmental Science, 8*, 16–25.

Devine, R.T., & Hughes, C. (2013). Silent films and strange stories: Theory of mind, gender, and social experiences in middle childhood. *Child Development, 84*(3), 989–1003. doi: 10.1111/cdev.12017

Devine, R.T. & Hughes, C. (2018). Family correlates of false belief understanding in early childhood: A meta-analysis. *Child Development*, *89*, 971–987.

Duschesne, L. Sutton, A. & Bergeron, F. (2009). Language achievement in children who received cochlear implants between 1 and 2 years of age: Group trends and individual patterns. *Journal of Deaf Studies and Deaf Education*, *14*, 465–485.

Edmondson, P. (2006). Deaf children's understanding of other people's thought processes. *Educational Psychology in Practice*, *22*(2), 159–169.

Falkman, K., Roos, C., & Hjelmquist, E. (2007). Mentalizing skills of non-native, early signers: A longitudinal perspective. *European Journal of Developmental Psychology*, *4*(2), 178–197.

Figueras-Costa, B., & Harris, P. (2001). Theory of mind development in deaf children: A nonverbal test of false-belief understanding. *Journal of Deaf Studies and Deaf Education*, *6*(2), 92–102.

Fink, E., Begeer, S., Peterson, C., Slaughter, V. & De Rosnay, M. (2015). Friendlessness and theory of mind: A prospective longitudinal study. *Developmental Psychology*, *33*, 1–17.

Frith, U. (2002). *Autism: Explaining the Enigma*. Oxford, UK: Blackwell.

Harris, P.L. (2005). Conversation, pretense and theory of mind. In J.W. Astington & J. Baird (Eds.), *Why Language Matters for Theory of Mind* (pp. 70–83). New York, NY: Oxford University Press.

Harris, P.L. (2006). Social cognition. In W. Damon (Ed.), *Handbook of Child Psychology* (pp. 811–857). New York: Wiley.

Heyes, C. & Frith, C.D. (2014). The cultural evolution of mind reading. *Science*, *344*, 1243091

Ketelaar, L., Rieffe, C., Wiefferink, C.H., & Frijns, J.H. (2012). Does hearing lead to understanding? Theory of mind in toddlers and preschoolers with cochlear implants. *Journal of Pediatric Psychology*, *37*(9), 1041–1050.

Lecce, S., Caputi, M., & Pagnin, A. (2014). Long-term effect of theory of mind on school achievement: The role of sensitivity to criticism. *European Journal of Developmental Psychology*, *11*(3), 305–318.

Macaulay, C.E., & Ford, R.M. (2006). Language and theory-of-mind development in prelingually deafened children with cochlear implants: A preliminary investigation. *Cochlear Implants International*, 7(1), 1–14. doi: 10.1179/cim.2006.7.1.1

Marschark, M., Edwards, L., Peterson, C., Crowe, K., & Walton, D. (2019). Understanding theory of mind in deaf and hearing college students. *Journal of Deaf Studies and Deaf Education*, *24*, 104–118.

Meristo, M., Falkman, K., Hjelmquist, E., Tedoldi, M., Surian, L., & Siegal, M. (2007). Language access and theory of mind reasoning: Evidence from deaf children in bilingual and oralist environments. *Developmental Psychology*, *43*(5), 1156–1169. doi: 10.1037/0012-1649.43.5.1156

Moeller, M.P. & Schick, B. (2006). Relations between maternal input and theory of mind understanding in deaf children. *Child Development*, *77*, 751–766.

O'Reilly, K., Peterson, C.C., & Wellman, H.M. (2014). Sarcasm and advanced theory of mind understanding in children and adults with prelingual deafness. *Developmental Psychology*, *50*(7), 1862–1877. doi: 10.1037/a0036654

Peterson, C.C. (2003). The social face of theory of mind. In B. Repacholi & V. Slaughter (Eds.), *Individual Differences in Theory of Mind Development* (pp. 171–196). New York: Psychology Press.

Peterson, C.C. (2004). Theory of mind development in oral deaf children with cochlear implants or conventional hearing aids. *Journal of Child Psychology and Psychiatry*, *45*, 1096–1106.

Peterson, C.C. (2009). Development of social-cognitive and communication skills in children born deaf. *Scandinavian Journal of Psychology, 50*(5), 475–483. doi: 10.1111/j.1467-9450.2009.00750.x

Peterson, C.C. & Siegal, M. (1995). Deafness, conversation and theory of mind. *Journal of Child Psychology and Psychiatry, 36*, 459–474.

Peterson, C. & Siegal, M. (2000). Insights into theory of mind from deafness and autism. *Mind & Language, 15*, 123–145.

Peterson, C.C., O'Reilly, K., & Wellman, H.M. (2016). Deaf and hearing children's development of theory of mind, peer popularity, and leadership during middle childhood. *Journal of Experimental Child Psychology, 149*, 146–158.

Peterson, C.C., & Siegal, M. (1997). Domain specificity and everyday biological, physical and psychological thinking in normal, autistic and deaf children. In H.M. Wellman & K. Inagaki (Eds.), *The Emergence of Core Domains of Thought* (pp. 55–70). San Francisco: Jossey-Bass.

Peterson, C.C., & Siegal, M. (1999). Representing inner worlds: Theory of mind in autistic, deaf, and normal hearing children. *Psychological Science, 10*(2), 126–129. doi: 10.1111/1467-9280.00119

Peterson, C.C., Wellman, H.M., & Liu, D. (2005). Steps in theory-of-mind development for children with deafness or autism. *Child Development, 76*(2), 502–517. doi: 10.1111/j.1467-8624.2005.00859.x

Peterson, C.C., Wellman, H.M., & Slaughter, V. (2012). The mind behind the message: Advancing theory-of-mind scales for typically developing children, and those with deafness, autism, or Asperger syndrome. *Child Development, 83*(2), 469–485. doi: 10.1111/j.1467-8624.2011.01728.x

Peterson, C.C., Slaughter, V., & Wellman, H.M. (2018). Nimble negotiators: How theory of mind (ToM) interconnects with persuasion skills in children with and without ToM delay. *Developmental Psychology, 54*(3), 494–509.

Peterson, C.C., & Wellman, H.M. (2019). Longitudinal Theory of Mind (ToM) Development From Preschool to Adolescence With and Without ToM Delay. *Child Development, 90*, 1917–1934.

Power, D., & Carty, B. (1990). Cross-cultural communication and the Deaf community in Australia. In C. Hendrick & R. Holton (Eds.), *Cross-Cultural Communication and Professional Education* (pp. 233–236). Adelaide, Australia: Flinders University.

Pyers, J.E., & Senghas, A. (2009). Language promotes false-belief understanding: Evidence from learners of a new sign language. *Psychological Science, 20*(7), 805–812.

Remmel, E., & Peters, K. (2009). Theory of mind and language in children with cochlear implants. *Journal of Deaf Studies and Deaf Education, 14*(2), 218–236.

Russell, P.A., Hosie, A., Gray, C.D., Scott, C., Hunter, N., Banks, J.S., & Macaulay, M.C. (1998). The development of theory of mind in deaf children. *Journal of Child Psychology and Psychiatry, and Allied Disciplines, 39*(6), 903–910.

Schick, B., de Villiers, P., de Villiers, J., & Hoffmeister, R. (2007). Language and theory of mind: A study of deaf children. *Child Development, 78*(2), 376–396. doi: 10.1111/j.1467-8624.2007.01004.x

Siegal, M., & Peterson, C.C. (2008). Language and theory of mind in atypically developing children: Evidence from deafness, blindness and autism. In C. Sharp, P. Fonagy & I. Goodyear (Eds.), *Social Cognition and Developmental Psychopathology* (pp. 81–112). Oxford: Oxford University Press.

Siegal, M., & Varley, R. (2002). Neural systems involved in 'theory of mind'. *Nature Reviews. Neuroscience, 3*(6), 463–471.

Sundqvist, A., Lyxell, B., Jönsson, R., & Heimann, M. (2014). Understanding minds: Early cochlear implantation and the development of theory of mind in children with profound hearing impairment. *International Journal of Pediatric Otorhinolaryngology*, *78*(3), 537–543.

Tierney, A.L. & Nelson, C.A. (2009). Brain development and the role of experience in the early years. *Zero Three*, *30*, 9–13.

Wellman, H.M., Fang, F., & Peterson, C.C. (2011). Sequential progressions in a theory-of-mind scale: Longitudinal perspectives. *Child Development*, *82*(3), 780–792. doi: 10.1111/j.1467-8624.2011.01583.x

Wellman, H.M., & Liu, D. (2004). Scaling of theory-of-mind tasks. *Child Development*, *75*(2), 523–541.doi: 10.1111/j.1467-8624.2004.00691.x

Wellman, H.M., & Peterson, C.C. (2013a). Theory of mind, development, and deafness. In S. Baron-Cohen, H. Tager-Flusberg & M. Lombardo (Eds.), *Understanding Other Minds* (pp. 51–71). Oxford, UK: Oxford University Press.

Wellman, H.M., & Peterson, C.C. (2013b). Deafness, thought bubbles, and theory-of-mind development. *Developmental Psychology*, *49*(12), 2357–2367. doi: 10.1037/a0032419

Woolfe, T., Want, S., & Siegal, M. (2002). Signposts to development: Theory of mind in deaf children. *Child Development*, *73*(3), 768–778.

11 Mindreading and psychopathology in middle childhood and adolescence

Carla Sharp and Jessica Hernandez

The human capacity to understand other people's thoughts, intentions, emotions, and desires – in short, 'theory of mind' (ToM) (also known as mindreading or mentalizing) not only ensures the survival of our species but facilitates the two most important functions associated with psychological health: In Freud's words, love and work (cf. Freud as quoted in Erikson, 1950). The ability to get along, while also getting ahead, relies on the capacity for making sense of our social and interpersonal world in terms of mental states. As intentional beings, we understand that we do not simply behave randomly, but that our behaviors can be explained by and are causally linked to mental states. We also understand that just because we think something, truth is not automatically implied and that the truth we hold dear may differ markedly from the truth another holds dear. We understand that we can change our minds, which may or may not reflect a change in reality. In short, we understand that the mind constructs a *representation* of the world around us – that the mind and reality are decoupled from each other. Our knowledge and awareness of these facts and the flexibility by which we can adapt to varying viewpoints and perspectives as we change, mature, and develop over time ultimately determines our success in negotiating love and work. Mindreading self and others, therefore, has a profound impact on our ability to love and work, and it is not surprising that impairments in this capacity derail optimal developmental trajectories in psychological health. Indeed, since the 1980s when Baron-Cohen et al. (1985) first began to apply a theory of mind framework to understanding child psychopathology, we have seen an impressive expansion of our knowledge base regarding the reciprocal influences between the development of theory of mind and psychopathology.

The goal of this chapter is to provide an up-to-date review of the state of the science on the relation between mindreading and psychopathology in middle childhood and adolescence. We begin the chapter by highlighting two important reasons why we need to pay special attention to theory of mind development and psychopathology in middle childhood and adolescence. We then provide an update to previous reviews (Sharp, 2006; Sharp et al., 2008; Sharp & Venta, 2012) on the link between mindreading and psychopathology in middle childhood and adolescence. To organize the update, we make use of a framework for managing the multidimensional nature of mindreading in relation to basic dimensions underlying psychopathology, whereby mindreading capacity is organized according to four dimensions, including 'accurate ToM', 'no ToM' (no mentalizing), 'under ToM' (under-mentalizing), and 'excessive ToM' (hyper-mentalizing) (Badcock, 2011; Dziobek et al., 2006; Gambin et al., 2015; Sharp & Venta, 2012). We then reflect on emerging data in support of the existence of a psychopathology factor ('p-factor') that may turn out to be a more important correlate of mentalizing capacity than any individual form of psychopathology.

Before we begin, a brief note on definitions. Thus far, we have used the terms theory of mind (ToM), mindreading, and mentalizing interchangeably. The term ToM was coined by Premack and Woodruff (1978) in the context of their seminal work as primatologists. It was picked up in the developmental literature in the 1980s (e.g., Baron Cohen et al., 1985; Perner & Wimmer, 1985) and used interchangeably with the term 'mindreading' (Baron-Cohen, 1995). Soon thereafter, the terms ToM and mindreading entered into the developmental psychopathology and clinical psychology and psychiatry literature (Fonagy, 1989, 1991), as well as social neuroscience literature (Frith & Frith, 1999). By the 1990s, many researchers began using the term mentalizing and mindreading to refer to ToM for several reasons.

First, compared with 'ToM', the broader terms 'mentalizing' and 'mindreading' seemed to be more nimble in accommodating different psychopathologies beyond autism and different measurement approaches beyond the false belief task (O'Connor & Hirsch, 1999). Second, these also allowed the acknowledgment that thinking about minds include both the mind of others (associated with the original ToM concept) and our own minds (Fonagy, 2006), and, third, opened the door for the assessment of mindreading through the concept of reflective function (RF) (Ensink, Target, & Oandasan, 2013; Fonagy et al., 1997). Like mentalizing, RF is considered to be an attachment-related capacity that is typically assessed through coding transcripts from the Adult Attachment Interview (George et al., 1984) or Child Attachment Interview (Shmueli-Goetz et al., 2008). Research provides some evidence for a relationship between measures of RF and general mentalizing. In a study of 330 inpatient adolescents using the Movie for the Assessment of Social Cognition (MASC) and the Child Reflective Function Scale (CRFS), correlations were found between mentalizing and RF of the self ($r = 0.18$) and mentalizing and RF of attachment figures ($r = 0.13$) (Vanwoerden et al., 2019). Additionally, regression analyses revealed that RF of the self had a moderate effect ($\eta 2 = 0.067$) on the prediction of ToM after controlling for age and verbal comprehension. Another study of 146 adolescents found correlations between mentalizing, as measured by the MASC, and RF, as measured by the CRFS ($r = 0.35$) and the Reflective Function Questionnaire for Youths (RFQ-Y) ($r = 0.28$) (Ha et al., 2013). However, this same study found no association between measures of RF and the Child's Reading the Mind in the Eyes Test (CET) in which children are asked to identify emotions depicted in photographs of eyes. This is corroborated by other research that has also failed to find associations between similar measures of ToM (e.g., the Reading the Mind in the Eyes Test) and RF in adolescent and adult samples (Morandotti et al., 2018; Rothschild-Yakar et al., 2019). One hypothesis for this lack of association is that measures such as the CET and RMET focus on a person's ability to make inferences based on external cues, while RF focuses on inferring mental states based on other cues. Generally, research on mind-mindedness, a similar construct to RF, but operationalized behaviorally rather than through attachment-based representations, however, has not found associations with traditional measures of mindreading (Barreto et al., 2016; Devine & Hughes, 2019; Meins et al., 2006). One exception is a study in which parental embodied mentalizing was associated with appropriate mind-related comments (r = 0.28) in a sample of 206 mothers (Shai & Meins, 2018). Additionally, there is some evidence for an association between parental mind-mindedness and RF as demonstrated by moderate correlations between RF and general attuned (r = 0.39), positive (r = 0.32), and neutral (r = 0.38) mind-minded comments (Riva Crugnola et al., 2018; Rosenblum et al., 2008).

Fourth, the terms mindreading, mentalizing, and RF furthermore allow for consideration of assessing distorted or biased mindreading, or 'interpretative ToM'. In contrast to early research on mentalizing (which addressed the question of whether children *are able* to understand others' thoughts), studies have examined whether children *misperceive* others' thoughts, feelings, and intentions (O'Connor & Hirsch, 1999). In such studies, new methods of testing distortions, misperceptions, or biases in mentalizing were developed (Sharp et al., 2006). Researchers that have pursued this line of research have argued for a distinction between understanding that beliefs depend on having access to information (e.g., false belief comprehension) and the more complex understanding that, even with access to the same information, people may interpret situations differently and thus end up with different beliefs, an insight achieved around middle childhood (Carpendale & Chandler, 1996; Chandler & Carpendale, 1998). Finally, another advantage of the broader terms of mentalizing and mindreading relates to the fact that traditional ToM tasks show developmental ceiling effects. Therefore, most of the research in ToM has been carried out in infancy, pre-schoolers, and elementary school-age children with fewer studies conducted in adolescence. While major developmental shifts also occur in pre-adolescence, it is important that mindreading capacity be studied beyond elementary school age, because of the social reorientation that takes place in adolescence (see below). Terms such as mindreading and mentalizing are not as closely aligned to ToM methodology and are therefore developmentally more adaptable and more readily applicable to studying adolescent populations. In this chapter, we will use mindreading to include both ToM and mentalizing capacity, and we will refer to ToM and mentalizing if measurement approaches were specifically designed to assess one or the other.

Two important reasons for paying attention to mindreading and psychopathology in middle childhood and adolescence

A first and obvious reason for paying special attention to mindreading and psychopathology in middle childhood and adolescence is because the onset of most adult disorders can be traced back to childhood or adolescence (Kessler et al., 2005). Adolescence, specifically, appears to be a particularly vulnerable period for the development of psychiatric problems (Merikangas et al., 2010) with prevalence rates for anxiety disorders at 31.9%, followed by behavior disorders (19.1%), mood disorders (14.3%), and substance use disorders (11.4%), with approximately 40% of participants with one class of disorder also meeting criteria for another class of lifetime disorder. Between 10% and 50% of youths are likely to meet diagnostic criteria for a mental health disorder at any one time (Collins et al., 2011). The median age of onset for disorder classes appears to be earliest for anxiety disorders (six years), followed by 11 years for behavior disorders, 13 years for mood disorders, 15 years for substance use disorders, and late adolescence/early adulthood for psychotic spectrum disorders. Recent research also confirms the onset of personality disorder in adolescence, with an approximate prevalence rate of 3% (Chanen et al., 2017). Moreover, adolescents are 90% more likely than children to use mental health services, and total mental health costs are estimated at $10.9 billion in the United States (Davis, 2014). Mental health problems are the leading cause of disability in middle childhood and adolescence and are associated with numerous social difficulties, including peer rejection and poor adjustment at school (Erskine et al., 2015; Gore et al., 2011).

The challenge of adolescence and the reason for the heightened vulnerability for psychopathology has been explained by the qualitative maturational shift induced by puberty (Dahl et al., 2018). These authors liken this period to 'starting the engines with an unskilled driver', and describe it as characterized by intense motivational and emotional changes against a backdrop of limited cognitive control to manage them (Dahl, 2004, p. 17). Which brings us to the second important reason for why we need to pay special attention to mindreading and psychopathology in young people, especially adolescence. Two decades of research in adolescent humans and animals point to adolescence as a distinct developmental period for social learning (Dahl et al., 2018), that is, learning from the social environment. Dahl and colleagues (2018) point out that across development, the capacity for learning does not only increase gradually, but may change in nonlinear ways, such that certain developmental periods are better for certain kinds of learning to take place. It turns out that early to mid-adolescence constitutes a period of increased plasticity (flexibility) for social learning (Gopnik et al., 2017). During this period, young people show increases in exploration, sensation seeking, and sensitivity to novelty, especially of a social kind. In addition, adolescents experience an increased capacity for probabilistic feedback learning (Davidow et al., 2016; Hauser et al., 2015; van den Bos et al., 2012). Probabilistic feedback learning refers to the process by which we learn from predicted and unpredicted rewards through prediction error-related activation in dopaminergic midbrain structures, and is an important tool to manage the complex, unpredictable, and stochastic nature of interpersonal interactions. Research also shows that the peer environment confers a particularly important context for positive and negative feedback learning (Crone & Dahl, 2012). The increased receptiveness for social learning during adolescence is naturally predicated on mindreading ability, which similarly, and probably in tandem, shows exponential expansion during adolescence. For instance, studies have demonstrated that adolescence is associated with increased perspective-taking ability (Choudhury et al., 2006; Dumontheil et al., 2010), which in turn, appears to associate with increased cooperation and trust (Fett et al., 2014). Using a broad-based assessment tool, the ToM Assessment Scale, Bosco et al. (2014) demonstrated increases in ToM capacities over the course of pre-adolescence into adolescence. While these studies assessed cognitive mentalizing capacity, studies of affective ToM have shown similar increases in capacity, coinciding with increases in executive functions (Vetter et al., 2013) and metacognitive ability over the course of adolescence (Weil et al., 2013).

Taken together, adolescence is associated with a neural-level social reorientation (Nelson et al., 2005), and constitutes a major second window of opportunity for social learning (with preschool being the first). This window of opportunity is naturally also associated with increased risk if development does not take a typical course. Indeed, as we will show below, psychopathology may disrupt the normative increase in mentalizing capacity over the course of adolescence into adulthood. This, in turn, may disrupt the normative increased capacity for social learning associated with adolescence, impeding adult social role adoption. Conversely, maladaptive development in mindreading capacity may derail healthy psychosocial development, resulting in mental illness. In short, consistent with a developmental psychopathology approach to understanding risk, resilience, and psychopathology, we propose a reciprocal and bidirectional relationship between mindreading and psychopathology in terms of onset and maintenance of mental illness over the life course.

Mindreading and psychopathology: A dimensional approach

The limitations of a categorically defined nosological system for classifying psychiatric disorders are well-known. A dimensional alternative to the DSM-based categorical system for understanding and assessing psychopathology in children and adolescents was recommended in the 1960s (Achenbach, 1966), but has only recently been accepted as a more empirically informed and potentially clinically useful way of understanding and assessing psychopathology in young people and adults. The dimensional model of psychopathology converges on the idea that covariation among common psychiatric syndromes and symptoms is best explained by a correlated two-factor model of internalizing (e.g., anxiety, depression, and traumatic symptoms) and externalizing (e.g., substance use problems, conduct problems, and oppositional defiance) dimensions, in addition to a third dimension of psychoticism. Below, we use these dimensions to organize the literature on mindreading impairment associated with psychopathology, also keeping in mind the scheme referred to earlier for parsing different kinds of mindreading capacity (i.e., accurate mentalizing, no mentalizing, under-mentalizing, and hyper-mentalizing). We do so intentionally because, as we will show, the internalizing–externalizing spectrum, with psychoticism, and combined with the proposed mindreading scheme, lays the foundation for understanding the role of mindreading as a resilience factor in thinking about overall psychiatric severity (the p-factor) which will introduce in the last section of the chapter. At this juncture, it is helpful to point out that we exclude Autism Spectrum Disorders from this review because autism is not included in the internalizing–externalizing spectrum model of psychopathology. Links between mindreading and autism are examined in Chapter 9.

Externalizing problems

Externalizing problems are problem behaviors under the umbrella of the diagnostic category of Disruptive, Impulse-Control, and Conduct Disorders in the DSM-5. Disorders such as Conduct Disorder and Oppositional Defiant Disorder are placed into this category based on criteria characteristic of the violation of the rights of others and potential conflicts with societal norms (American Psychiatric Association, 2013). Behaviors common to these disorders are aggression, impulsivity, and conduct problems. Social difficulties are characteristic of children with externalizing problems, as evidenced by poor peer and familial relationships. Given the social basis and implications of externalizing behavior problems, mindreading capacity is of particular interest in understanding these problems and their respective disorders. Indeed, a substantive amount of literature has been dedicated to understanding externalizing behaviors and disorders from a social-cognitive perspective.

A well-known approach in researching this relationship is the social information processing (SIP) approach (Dodge et al., 2002). Through this approach, research has shown children with externalizing problems have difficulties across various social information processing domains such as encoding, attribution, intention-cue deficits, and response access. While the SIP model goes beyond mindreading ability *per se* to also include response selection, the inclusion of hostile attribution bias is very consistent with the idea of biased or distorted mindreading that has been shown to be a hallmark feature of children with conduct problems (Sharp, 2000). For instance, earlier work by Happé and Frith (1996) showed that children in middle childhood can read minds, but do so inaccurately by demonstrating a theory of 'nasty' minds, assuming negative intentions in others. Moving beyond vignette-based mindreading tasks, Sharp et al. (2011) adapted a trust game to investigate the relations between externalizing behavior problems, trust, trustworthiness, and social-cognitive reasoning. Trust games offer ecologically valid interaction paradigms where research participants get the opportunity to 'invest' in a relationship through trusting their partner's reciprocity. Mindreading underlies these social decisions. In our study, a total of 171 (79 age-matched pairs) boys aged 8 through 18 years (mean age = 12.84 years, SD = 1.80) were recruited from community groups where social networks and relationships among peers had been established. A trust game was played under two conditions: An anonymous version where the identity of the trust game partner was not known and a known identity version where identities were revealed. Results supported the conclusion that boys with externalizing behavior problems were generally less trustworthy, but not less trusting, and that this was true especially for the known identity version of the game as demonstrated by a moderate effect size of an interaction between experiment condition and group status ($\eta^2 = 0.07$). Moreover, and specifically relevant for the current chapter, anomalies in trust behavior were associated with hostile intentions, but not reflective of a general ToM deficit, thereby emphasizing the context-specific nature of mindreading deficits associated with externalizing problems, as well as the value of a biased mindreading or distorted mentalizing construct (a theory of nasty minds). In a follow-up study of the effect of reputation on reward-related social decision-making, neural correlates in the form of insula activation were established for atypical social decision-making in the context of externalizing problems (Sharp et al., 2011). More recently, in the context of a multi-round trust game, we have shown that anomalies in trust behavior associated with externalizing behavior are specific to reward-related *social* decision-making in particular, and not reward-related decision-making in general (Mellick et al., 2019), suggesting that dopaminergic pathways underlying social decision-making must relate to mindreading pathways in the brain (Blakemore, 2008) to produce such an effect. This study conducted with a sample of 263 adolescents between the ages of 12 and 17 years (mean age = 14.75 years, SD = 1.50; 68% female) found that those with externalizing disorders invested less in the trust game than the lottery condition as compared with other psychiatric controls, although the effect size was small ($\eta^2 = 0.01$).

Other distorted forms of mindreading have also been demonstrated for children with externalizing disorders. Using the Distorted Mentalizing task, Sharp et al. (2007) demonstrated higher levels of conduct problems in 7- to 11-year-old children (N = 659; mean age = 9 years, 3 months, SD = 1 year, 2 months; 52% female) with overly positive mindreading styles. Overly positive mindreading styles were also associated with age and IQ, such that younger children and those with a lower IQ were more likely to have an overly positive mindreading style. These unrealistic, overly positive biases were interpreted as a defense in evaluating social situations that might be potentially threatening to young people; a self-protective bias that prevents them from processing negative feedback from others. These biases in mindreading have, more recently, been referred to as hyper-mentalizing (Sharp, 2015; Sharp & Vanwoerden, 2015), a construct we will return to later when we discuss personality pathology in adolescents.

Researchers have also turned their attention to studying attachment-based mentalizing (RF) in the context of externalizing problems. In a sample of 131 children aged from 8 to 15 years, Bizzi et al. (2019) evaluated RF scores based on the Child Attachment Interview between three groups: A healthy control group (N = 46; mean age = 10.86 years, SD = 21.69; 63% male), children with disruptive behavior disorders (N = 40; mean age = 10.84 years, SD = 2.12; 77% male), and children with somatic symptom disorders (N = 45; mean age = 11.50 years, SD = 1.83; 47% male). Children with disruptive behavior disorders and somatic symptoms scored lower in RF compared with healthy controls (d = 0.80), and children with disruptive behavior disorders scored lower than those with somatic complaints (internalizing problems) (d = 0.82). Importantly, and consistent with theoretical models of attachment-based mentalizing (Sharp & Fonagy, 2008a; Sharp et al., 2006), RF was associated with attachment security, evidencing a medium effect size (η^2 = 0.054). Covariates were not included in this study. Using a similar measure for RF, Taubner and colleagues (2013) found that, in a sample of 104 adolescents ages 15 to 24 years (mean age = 16.4 years, SD = 1.8; 57% male) recruited from the community, deficits in RF were significantly associated with both psychopathic traits (r = –0.22) and proactive aggression (r = –0.36). Other correlates of RF included immigration status (r = –0.32), general intelligence (r = 0.25), and reactive aggression (r = –0.22). Additionally, psychopathic traits were related to proactive (r = 0.59) and reactive (r = 0.40) aggression and gender (r = 0.28). After controlling for potential confounding variables, RF was found to play a moderating role in the relationship between proactive aggression and psychopathic traits (ß = –0.35), such that individuals with increased psychopathic tendencies did not display increased proactive aggression when they had higher mentalizing capacities. When controlling for proactive aggression, this same effect was nullified in the relationship between reactive aggression and psychopathic traits (Taubner et al., 2013).

Another line of research has focused on affective ToM as assessed, for instance, through the Child's Eyes Task (Baron Cohen et al., 1997). Early research on this topic showed a generalized impairment in affective ToM in children with conduct problems (Sharp, 2008), as indicated by a significant relation between poor Eyes Test performance and conduct problems (ß = –0.33), even when IQ, sex, and age were controlled for in a community sample of 79 children ages 9 to 13 years (mean age = 11 years, SD = 11 months; 56% female). More recently, other research has confirmed these findings. In a study conducted with 36 adolescent girls ages 15 to 17 years, those with conduct disorder did poorly in comparison with healthy controls on a measure of affective ToM (d = 0.78) but passed the Faux Pas task, which is a measure of cognitive ToM (Arango Tobón et al., 2018). Consistent with these findings, researchers have also found seemingly intact and even advanced cognitive mindreading abilities in groups of children with severe externalizing problems. Early research in this regard includes the works of Sutton et al. (1999) who demonstrated advanced cognitive mentalizing skills in bullies in a sample of children in middle childhood. Recent research continues to support these findings (Caravita et al., 2010; Stellwagen & Kerig, 2013). One framework for understanding this kind of pseudo-mentalizing in children and adolescents with psychopathic tendencies suggests that, while these individuals may effectively engage in perspective-taking, they lack the ability to have an affective empathic response to another's state (Blair, 2010).

Taken together, mindreading appears to be affected in externalizing disorders in three different ways. First, those with externalizing disorders appear to evidence hyper-mentalizing (in this case, a theory of nasty minds), expecting others to be hostile and malevolent towards them, sometimes in the absence of data to suggest such attitudes. Second, while children and adolescents with externalizing problems appear to not show problems in cognitive mindreading, they do appear to have deficits related to affective mindreading. Third, children and adolescents with externalizing problems appear to struggle with attachment-related mindreading (RF).

Internalizing problems

Research investigating the association between mentalizing and internalizing problems in children and adolescents is relatively scarce, but important, given the known socio-cognitive impairment associated with internalizing problems. A socio-cognitive framework developed for child anxiety suggests that childhood anxiety problems are marked by hypervigilance in relation to threat and negative evaluations of past events and encounters (Banerjee, 2008). Furthermore, Banerjee suggests deficits in mentalization are what underlie the hypervigilance presented by anxious children. Consistent with this model, in a study examining symptoms of panic disorder, depression, and separation anxiety in relation to ToM, as assessed by the Strange Stories task in a healthy community sample of 318 children (51% female) with a mean age of 11 years and 3 months (SD = 1 year and 9 months), results indicated that reduced mentalizing was related to higher symptoms of depression ($r = -0.24$), separation anxiety ($r = -0.19$), and panic disorder ($r = -0.11$) (Caputi & Schoenborn, 2018). After controlling for covariates of verbal ability and socioeconomic status, depressive symptoms and separation anxiety remained associated with mentalizing (partial $r \geq 0.14$). Girls were more likely to report separation anxiety symptoms than boys ($d = -0.54$). Attachment-related anxiety has also been found to be related to reduced mentalizing in adolescents in a study using the Reading the Mind in the Eyes Test in a sample of 402 adolescents (58% male) ages 14 to 19 years (mean age = 16.7 years, SD = 1.0) (Hünefeldt et al., 2013), although our work suggests the opposite pattern for boys (Mellick & Sharp, 2016). Sex and age had effects on mentalization such that girls had higher mentalization scores than boys ($\eta_p^2 = 0.11$) and the group of 17- to 19-year-olds had higher mentalization scores than the group of 14- to 16-year-olds ($\eta_p^2 = 0.01$). Anxiety with a mother was related to mentalization for both the group of 14- to 16-year-olds ($\beta = -0.51$) and that of 17- to 19-year-olds (ß = –0.15), even after controlling for sex. In a study of 63 children ages 8 to 9 years (N = 33; mean age = 8 years 9 months; 61% male) and 6 to 11 years (N = 30; mean age = 8 years 6 months; 57% male), Banerjee and Henderson (2001) found that social anxiety was more strongly related to deficits in social cognition for children with high shy negative affect (partial *r*[25] = –.044) than for those with low shy negative affect (partial *r*[26] = –.14). Although nationality and age were associated with social cognition, this effect remained for the subgroups based on nationality. Additionally, this study did not find correlations between social anxiety and second-order false belief. Another study examining mentalizing and social anxiety in a sample of children of ages 8 to 12 years (N = 105; mean age = 9.50 years, SD = 1.18; 56% female) found a quadratic relationship between mentalizing and social anxiety (ß = 0.33) such that children low and high in mentalizing had higher social anxiety (Nikolić et al., 2019). However, children with low mentalizing reached higher levels of social anxiety than children with advanced mentalizing, suggesting that children with lower mentalizing may be more likely to reach clinical levels of social anxiety. Sex and age were not found to be related to mentalizing or social anxiety. Additionally, Belvederi Murri and colleagues (2017) found that in a community (N = 145; mean age = 16.9 years, SD = 1.9; 68% female) and a clinical (N = 83; mean age = 16.8 years, SD = 2.0; 86% female) sample of adolescents, reduced mentalizing was associated with severe depressive symptomology (*r* = –0.68) as well as childhood trauma (*r* = –0.30) even after adjusting for gender. There was a higher prevalence of females in the low mentalization group. Similarly, another study using the Reflective Functioning Coding of the Child Attachment Interview found that depressive symptoms were associated with reduced mentalizing in children (N = 168) ages 7 to 12 years with and without a history of abuse, although children with a history of abuse had worse mentalizing (*d* = 0.75) and more severe depressive symptoms (*d* = 0.71) than children without abuse history (Ensink et al., 2016). Age was also associated with mentalizing such that older children had better mentalizing abilities (*r* = 0.44). We have also shown reduced capacity for mentalizing self to be associated with depression in adolescent girls (Mellick et al., 2017).

In conclusion, research appears to support a pattern of reduced mindreading capacity in children and adolescents with internalizing problems for both mindreading of self and others. However, there is still work to be done in evaluating Banerjee's (2008) model of social cognition in anxious children, which is simultaneously associated with under- and hyper-mentalizing, and to resolve mixed findings.

Schizophrenia/psychoticism

Lagndon (2005) suggested a link between schizophrenic-spectrum disorders or psychoticism and what she termed hyper-mentalizing, the idea being that over-attribution of mental states occurs as a function of deficiencies in accurate mindreading. Put differently, due to challenges in under-mentalizing (not understanding minds), individuals with schizophrenia imagine or make up, or hyper-mentalize, what might be going on in the mind of another person. Research has supported this combination of under- and hyper-mentalizing in individuals with schizophrenia and psychotic experiences also in adolescence. In a study of 1,630 preadolescent children, Clemmensen et al. (2016) used a ToM Storybook task to assess mindreading in 11- to 12-year-old children (48% male). This task is designed to assess mentalizing by reading a storybook aloud to participants while simultaneously presenting them with pictures and asking them questions about the story. The questions are meant to tap into the comprehension of second-order false belief, faux pas, irony, white lies, and double bluffs. The task itself consists of 24 questions and 16 pictures. The questions are divided into two categories: 16 tests and 8 justifications. Responses to test questions are coded based on whether they are correct or incorrect, while responses to the justification questions are coded based on a set of categories such as desire, fact, belief, and situation (Clemmensen et al., 2014). Results suggested that hyper-mentalizing was the only factor related to psychotic experiences after controlling for potential covariates including comorbid psychiatric problems such as depression and anxiety (OR 1.81). Hyper-mentalizing was also weakly associated with cognitive abilities (r = –0.07) as measured by performance on the Block Design subtest of the WISC-III. Barragan and colleagues (2011) conducted a study with adolescents (N = 72; 46% female) aged 13 to 16 years old (mean age = 14.51 years, SD = 0.63) in which results suggested first-rank psychotic-like experiences (B = –0.38) were related to reduced mentalizing according to the Strange Stories task. However, high levels of mentalization were associated with persecutory beliefs (B = 0.30). Other correlates for mentalizing included verbal ability (B = 0.12). These findings support Langdon and colleagues' (2010) suggestion that only certain positive symptoms related to schizophrenia are related to hyper-mentalizing, while other aspects of mindreading (under-mentalizing) relate to negative symptoms. Accordingly, a study exploring possible ToM deficits in adolescents aged 13 to 18 years with adolescent-onset schizophrenia (N = 35; mean age = 16.48 years, SD = 1.42; 57% male) as compared with healthy controls (N = 35; mean age = 16.31 years, SD =1.21; 57% male) found that those with adolescent-onset schizophrenia showed reduced mentalizing as measured by the Yoni Task and the Faux Pas Recognition Test (Li et al., 2017). This reduced mentalization was found for first-order cognitive (η^2 = 0.057) and affective (η^2 = 0.092) ToM as well as second-order cognitive (η^2 = 0.200) and affective (η^2 = 0.169) ToM. This was also found for faux pas recognition (η^2 = 0.060) and understanding (η^2 = 0.104). Within the adolescent-onset group, executive function was related to second-order cognitive (r = –0.44) and affective ToM (r = –0.59).

In summary, there is good evidence to suggest that psychotic symptoms in schizophrenia are associated with a tendency to overthink, overattribute, or hyper-mentalize the mind of self and others. To be clear, hyper-mentalizing is seen as a form of maladaptive mindreading where an individual goes beyond the available data in making attributions about the content of another's mind. As suggested earlier, the idea is that this tendency may occur as a result of a basic deficit in mindreading (under-mentalizing) resulting in over-imagining or over-believing the content of minds.

The p-factor and personality pathology

Thus far, we have discussed the so-called common mental disorders covering the internalizing–externalizing and psychoticism spectra. The location of personality pathology in the internalizing–externalizing and psychoticism spectra is a topic of hot debate. Recently, we proposed a model of psychopathology where Criterion A (maladaptive self and interpersonal function) of the new DSM-5 Section III description of personality disorder is located on the severity pathway (p-factor) previously identified in the work of Caspi et al. (2014) and others (e.g., Lahey et al., 2015) between the internalizing–externalizing spectra and psychoticism spectra. This model is presented in Figure 11.1 and has been presented elsewhere (Sharp et al., in press; Sharp & Wall, 2018).

The model attempts to explain the development of psychopathology along a severity dimension, called the psychopathology factor (or p-factor). The idea of the p-factor developed out of the observation of high covariation among symptoms of psychopathology. As mentioned earlier, comorbidity among discreet disorders is the rule rather than the exception, suggesting that covariance between different types of psychopathology is better explained by latent dimensional constructs (e.g., internalizing, externalizing, and psychoticism). It turns out, however, that correlations between internalizing and externalizing disorders are so high that it suggests a higher-order latent factor in the meta-structure of psychopathology. Accordingly, factor analytic studies have shown that this covariation among symptoms is best explained by a general factor (the p-factor) similar to the g-factor of intelligence, in addition to a set of specific factors that denote specific disorders or spectra (like the internalizing, externalizing, and psychotic spectra) (Caspi et al., 2014). While the exact nature of the p-factor is still being evaluated, it is reasonable to argue that the p-factor, at the very least, denotes overall severity in psychopathology. In this model, internalizing and externalizing pathology typically onset in pre-adolescence, personality pathology (maladaptive self and interpersonal dysfunction) onsets in adolescence, and psychotic disorders onset in late adolescence and young adulthood.

As reviewed earlier, a host of mentalizing deficits and anomalies are associated with internalizing, externalizing, and psychotic disorders in middle childhood and adolescence, cutting across hyper-mentalizing, under-mentalizing, and no mentalizing. Personality pathology, in particular Borderline Personality Disorder, has been shown to similarly be associated with a mindreading impairment (for reviews see, e.g., Fonagy & Luyten, 2016; Sharp & Vanwoerden, 2015). Mentalizing failures most reliably emerge in studies using experimental tasks with high task demands (e.g., multimodal tasks requiring the integration

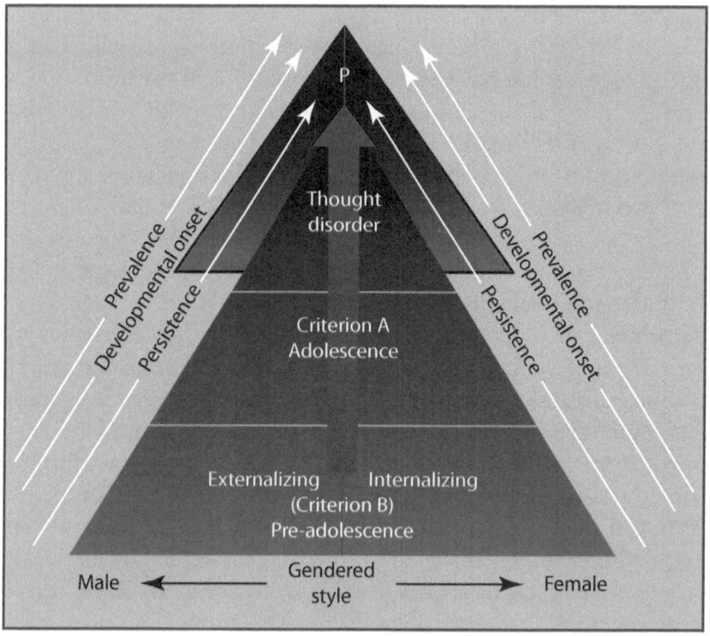

Figure 11.1 A developmental psychopathology model for personality pathology, adapted from Sharp & Wall (2018) and Sharp et al. (under review). Notes: Criterion A (or Level of Personality Function) in the DSM-5 Section III alternative model for personality disorder refers to the general features shared by all personality disorders and is defined as maladaptive self and interpersonal function. Specifically, Criterion A dysfunction refers to impairment in identity, self-direction, intimacy, and empathy. Criterion B in the DSM-5 Section III alternative model for personality disorder refers to maladaptive trait function which gives flavor to general personality disorder dysfunction. Five trait domains are included (i.e., negative affectivity, detachment, antagonism, disinhibition, and psychoticism) which show significant overlap with internalizing–externalizing and psychoticism spectra. 'P' refers to the psychopathology (or severity) factor as suggested by Caspi et al. (2014). It is suggested to capture vulnerability to mental disorder, comorbidity among disorders, persistence of disorders over time, severity of symptoms, and therapeutic response. Psychopathology is understood to be somewhat 'gendered' in that externalizing pathology is more often observed in males, and internalizing pathology is more often observed in females.

of information across modalities) and emotionally charged stimuli. This suggests that a task's complexity or ecological validity may require a certain threshold in order for a clear borderline-related deficit to emerge. In addition, our research has shown that adolescents with BPD are more likely to hyper-mentalize, or over-attribute extreme mental states to others, rather than under-mentalize (Sharp et al., 2011). Thus, when presented with mutually exclusive response options for no mentalizing, under-mentalizing, hyper-mentalizing, and accurate mentalizing, borderline features do not associate with deficits in mentalizing, but rather an altered style of mentalizing, in the form of hyper-mentalizing (Sharp et al., 2013, 2011), similar to the positive symptoms of psychotic spectrum disorders. Hyper-mentalizing, also referred to as excessive theory of mind (Dziobek et al., 2006), is defined as a social-cognitive process that involves making assumptions about other people's mental states that go so far beyond observable data that others may struggle to see how they are justified (Sharp et al., 2013). Similarly, Fonagy et al. (2015) described hyper-mentalizing as making groundless inferences about mental states. Elsewhere, we have provided rich clinical illustrations of hyper-mentalizing (Bo et al., 2017).

As with externalizing problems, the tendency for borderline adolescents to hyper-mentalize may be attributable to the attachment trauma histories associated with BPD (Zanarini, 2000; Zanarini et al., 1989). Animal research suggests that early attachment trauma may permanently affect the hypothalamic-pituitary-adrenal (HPA) axis (Oitzl et al., 2000). Increased stress responsiveness, in turn, affects mentalizing capacity. Smeets et al. (2009) used the MASC in a sample of 64 young adults (mean age = 25.89 years, SD = 4.33; 50% female) to show that high cortisol–responding women make more mentalizing errors, in particular due to a tendency to hyper-mentalize, after stress induction, thereby demonstrating that stress responsiveness modulates mentalizing. The correlation for cortisol stress-responding and mentalizing was positive in men ($r = 0.54$) as opposed to a negative correlation for the women ($r = -0.56$). It is also possible that hyper-mentalization may develop not only in the presence of abuse but in the absence of the protective factors that dampen the effects of stress, most notably secure attachment. In the developmental model of mentalization, attachment security provides the infant with the context to develop their own mentalizing capacity through the caregiver's capacity to treat them as a psychological agent (see Sharp & Fonagy, 2008b for a discussion). This brings us to consider how mentalizing factors in with the p-factor (Fonagy et al., 2017a, 2017b).

Fonagy and colleagues have argued that the p-factor should be understood not as some kind of general index of psychopathology, but rather as an index of poor resilience (Fonagy et al., 2017a, 2017b). Resilience, in turn, is best understood as a function of the relation between the social environment as a system on the one hand, and individual differences in mentalizing capacity on the other. Implied is the assumption that mindreading deficits alone cannot drive psychopathology, but that psychopathology must be the result of entrenched adaptation to stimuli from the social environment. Put differently, mindreading deficits or impairment are often desperate attempts of an individual to adapt to an impossible environment, 'a learned expectation about cultural context' (Fonagy et al., 2017a, p. 2). As such, psychopathology denotes an inflexibility in the human capacity for social communication and learning. Conversely, when protective factors afford an individual with adequate mindreading capacity, the individual is able to make use of social learning opportunities, thereby building resilience. Returning to adolescence as a sensitive period for social learning as discussed earlier, it is now easy to see how the transition from childhood to adolescence may be thwarted for individuals who, by virtue of low mindreading capacity, cannot make use of their expanding social learning opportunities to adapt to adult role-functioning – love and work.

Conclusions

The goal of this chapter was to provide an up-to-date review of the state of the science on the relation between mindreading and psychopathology in middle childhood and adolescence. We proposed adolescence to be a special period of increased plasticity for social learning and advances in mindreading capacity. We reviewed data supporting the links between mindreading impairment and internalizing–externalizing and psychotic spectrum disorders, but highlighted the importance of moving toward an understanding of mentalizing as resilience, the key ingredient protecting individuals from the negative effects of the environment while simultaneously facilitating learning from the social environment. We look forward to future work in this regard.

References

Achenbach, T.M. (1966). The classification of children's psychiatric symptoms: A factor-analytic study. *Psychological Monographs, 80*(7), 1–37. doi:10.1037/h0093906

American Psychiatric Association (2013). *Diagnostic and Statistical Manual of Mental Disorders* (5th edition). Washington, DC: American Psychiatric Association.

Arango Tobón, O.E., Olivera-La Rosa, A., Restrepo Tamayo, V., & Puerta Lopera, I.C. (2018). Empathic skills and theory of mind in female adolescents with conduct disorder. *Revista Brasileira de Psiquiatria, 40*(1), 78–82. doi:10.1590/1516-4446-2016-2092

Badcock, C. (2011). *The Imprinted Brain: How Genes Set the Balance between Autism and Psychosis*. London: Jessica Kingsley Publishers.

Banerjee, R. (2008). Social cognition and anxiety in children. In C. Sharp, P. Fonagy, & I. Goodyer (Eds.), *Social Cognition and Developmental Psychopathology* (pp. 239–269). Oxford: Oxford Univeristy Press.

Banerjee, R., & Henderson, L. (2001). Social-cognitive factors in childhood social anxiety: A preliminary investigation. *Social Development, 10*(4), 558–572.

Baron-Cohen, S. (1995). *Mindblindness: An Essay on Autism and Theory of Mind*. Cambridge, MA: MIT Press.

Baron-Cohen, S., Jolliffe, T., Mortimore, C., & Robertson, M. (1997). Another advanced test of theory of mind: Evidence from very high functioning adults with autism or Asperger syndrome. *Journal of Child Psychology and Psychiatry, and Allied Disciplines, 38*(7), 813–822.

Baron-Cohen, S., Leslie, A.M., & Frith, U. (1985). Does the autistic child have a "theory of mind"? *Cognition, 21*(1), 37–46.

Barragan, M., Laurens, K.R., Navarro, J.B., & Obiols, J.E. (2011). 'Theory of mind', psychotic-like experiences and psychometric schizotypy in adolescents from the general population. *Psychiatry Research, 186*(2–3), 225–231. doi:10.1016/j.psychres.2010.07.051

Barreto, A.L., Fearon, R.M., Osório, A., Meins, E., & Martins, C. (2016). Are adult mentalizing abilities associated with mind-mindedness? *International Journal of Behavioral Development, 40*(4), 296–301. doi:10.1177/0165025415616200

Belvederi Murri, M., Ferrigno, G., Penati, S., Muzio, C., Piccinini, G., Innamorati, M., ... & Amore, M. (2017). Mentalization and depressive symptoms in a clinical sample of adolescents and young adults. *Child and Adolescent Mental Health, 22*(2), 69–76.

Bizzi, F., Ensink, K., Borelli, J.L., Mora, S.C., & Cavanna, D. (2019). Attachment and reflective functioning in children with somatic symptom disorders and disruptive behavior disorders. *European Child and Adolescent Psychiatry, 28*(5), 705–717. doi:10.1007/s00787-018-1238-5

Blair, R.J. (2010). Neuroimaging of psychopathy and antisocial behavior: A targeted review. *Current Psychiatry Reports, 12*(1), 76–82. doi:10.1007/s11920-009-0086-x

Blakemore, S.J. (2008). Development of the social brain during adolescence. *Quarterly Journal of Experimental Psychology, 61*(1), 40–49.

Bo, S., Sharp, C., Fonagy, P., & Kongerslev, M. (2017). Hypermentalizing, attachment, and epistemic trust in adolescent BPD: Clinical illustrations. *Personality Disorders, 8*(2), 172–182. doi:10.1037/per0000161

Bosco, F.M., Gabbatore, I., & Tirassa, M. (2014). A broad assessment of theory of mind in adolescence: The complexity of mindreading. *Consciousness and Cognition, 24*, 84–97. doi:10.1016/j.concog.2014.01.003

Caputi, M., Schoenborn, H., & Walla, P. (2018). Theory of mind and internalizing symptoms during middle childhood and early adolescence: The mediating role of coping strategies. *Cogent Psychology, 5*(1). doi:10.1080/23311908.2018.1487270. http://www.ncbi.nlm.nih.gov/pubmed/1487270

Caravita, S.C.S., Di Blasio, P., & Salmivalli, C. (2010). Early adolescents' participation in bullying: Is ToM involved? *Journal of Early Adolescence, 30*(1), 138–170. doi:10.1177/0272431609342983

Carpendale, J., & Chandler, M.J. (1996). On the distinction between false belief understanding and subscribing to an interpretive theory of mind. *Child Development, 67*(4), 1686–1706.

Caspi, A., Houts, R.M., Belsky, D.W., Goldman-Mellor, S.J., Harrington, H., Israel, S., ... & Moffitt, T.E. (2014). The p factor: One general psychopathology factor in the structure of psychiatric disorders? *Clinical Psychological Science, 2*(2), 119–137.

Chandler, M.J., & Carpendale, J. (1998). Inching toward a mature theory of mind. In M. Ferrari & R.J. Sternberg (Eds.), *Self-Awareness: Its Nature and Development* (pp. 148–190). New York: Guilford Press.

Chanen, A., Sharp, C., Hoffman, P., & Global Alliance for Prevention and Early Intervention for Borderline Personality (2017). Prevention and early intervention for borderline personality disorder: A novel public health priority. *World Psychiatry: Official Journal of the World Psychiatric Association, 16*(2), 215–216. doi:10.1002/wps.20429

Choudhury, S., Blakemore, S.J., & Charman, T. (2006). Social cognitive development during adolescence. *Social Cognitive and Affective Neuroscience, 1*(3), 165–174. doi:10.1093/scan/nsl024

Clemmensen, L., van Os, J., Drukker, M., Munkholm, A., Rimvall, M.K., Væver, M., ... & Jeppesen, P. (2016). Psychotic experiences and hyper-theory-of-mind in preadolescence—a birth cohort study. *Psychological Medicine, 46*(1), 87–101. doi:10.1017/S0033291715001567

Clemmensen, L., van Os, J., Skovgaard, A.M., Væver, M., Blijd-Hoogewys, E.M.A., Bartels-Velthuis, A.A., & Jeppesen, P. (2014). Hyper-theory-of-mind in children with psychotic experiences. *PLOS ONE, 9*(11), e113082.

Collins, P.Y., Patel, V., Joestl, S.S., March, D., Insel, T.R., Daar, A.S., ... & Stein, D.J. (2011). Grand challenges in global mental health. *Nature, 475*(7354), 27–30.

Crone, E.A., & Dahl, R.E. (2012). Understanding adolescence as a period of social-affective engagement and goal flexibility. *Nature Reviews Neuroscience, 13*(9), 636–650. doi:10.1038/Nrn3313

Dahl, R.E. (2004). Adolescent brain development: A period of vulnerabilities and opportunities. Keynote address. *Annals of the New York Academy of Sciences, 1021*(1), 1–22.

Dahl, R.E., Allen, N.B., Wilbrecht, L., & Suleiman, A.B. (2018). Importance of investing in adolescence from a developmental science perspective. *Nature, 554*(7693), 441–450. doi:10.1038/nature25770

Davidow, J.Y., Foerde, K., Galván, A., & Shohamy, D. (2016). An upside to reward sensitivity: The hippocampus supports enhanced reinforcement learning in adolescence. *Neuron, 92*(1), 93–99. doi:10.1016/j.neuron.2016.08.031

Davis, K.E. (2014). *Expenditures for Treatment of Mental Health Disorders among Children, Ages 5–17, 2009–2011: Estimates for the U.S. Civilian Noninstitutionalized Population.* Agency for Healthcare Research and Quality. https://meps.ahrq.gov/data_files/publications/st440/stat440.shtml

Devine, R.T., & Hughes, C. (2019). Let's talk: Parents' mental talk (not mind-mindedness or mindreading capacity) predicts children's false belief understanding. *Child Development, 90*(4), 1236–1253. doi:10.1111/cdev.12990

Dodge, K.A., Laird, R., Lochman, J.E., Zelli, A., & Conduct Problems Prevention Research Group (2002). Multidimensional latent-construct analysis of children's social information processing patterns: Correlations with aggressive behavior problems. *Psychological Assessment, 14*(1), 60–73. doi:10.1037//1040-3590.14.1.60

Dumontheil, I., Apperly, I.A., & Blakemore, S.J. (2010). Online usage of theory of mind continues to develop in late adolescence. *Developmental Science, 13*(2), 331–338. doi:10.1111/j.1467-7687.2009.00888.x

Dziobek, I., Fleck, S., Kalbe, E., Rogers, K., Hassenstab, J., Brand, M., ... & Convit, A. (2006). Introducing MASC: A movie for the assessment of social cognition. *Journal of Autism and Developmental Disorders, 36*(5), 623–636. doi:10.1007/s10803-006-0107-0

Ensink, K., Bégin, M., Normandin, L., & Fonagy, P. (2016). Maternal and child reflective functioning in the context of child sexual abuse: Pathways to depression and externalising difficulties. *European Journal of Psychotraumatology*, 7, 30611. doi:10.3402/ejpt.v7.30611

Ensink, K., Target, M., & Oandasan, C. (2013). *Child Reflective Functioning Scale Scoring Manual: For Application to the Child Attachment Interview.* London: Anna Freud Center—University College London.

Erikson, E. (1950). *Childhood in Society.* New York: Norton.

Erskine, H.E., Moffitt, T.E., Copeland, W.E., Costello, E.J., Ferrari, A.J., Patton, G., ... & Scott, J.G. (2015). A heavy burden on young minds: The global burden of mental and substance use disorders in children and youth. *Psychological Medicine, 45*(7), 1551–1563. doi:10.1017/S0033291714002888

Fett, A.K.J., Shergill, S.S., Gromann, P.M., Dumontheil, I., Blakemore, S.J., Yakub, F., & Krabbendam, L. (2014). Trust and social reciprocity in adolescence—A matter of perspective-taking. *Journal of Adolescence, 37*(2), 175–184. doi:10.1016/j.adolescence.2013.11.011

Fonagy, P. (1989). On tolerating mental states: Theory of mind in borderline personality. *Bulletin of the Anna Freud Centre, 12,* 91-115.

Fonagy, P. (1991). Thinking about thinking: Some clinical and theoretical considerations in the treatment of a borderline patient. *International Journal of Psycho-Analysis, 72*(4), 639–656.

Fonagy, P. (2006). The mentalization-focused approach to social development. In Allen, J.G. & Fonagy, P. (Eds). *Handbook of Mentalization-Based Treatment* (pp. 53–100). Hoboken, NJ: Wiley.

Fonagy, P., & Luyten, P. (2016). A multilevel perspective on the development of borderline personality disorder. In D. Cicchetti (Ed.), *Developmental Psychopathology. Vol. 3: Maladaptation and Psychopathology* (3rd ed., pp. 726–792). New York: John Wiley & Sons.

Fonagy, P., Luyten, P., Allison, E., & Campbell, C. (2017a). What we have changed our minds about: Part 1. Borderline personality disorder as a limitation of resilience. *Borderline Personality Disorder and Emotion Dysregulation, 4*, 11. doi:10.1186/s40479-017-0061-9

Fonagy, P., Luyten, P., Allison, E., & Campbell, C. (2017b). What we have changed our minds about: Part 2. Borderline personality disorder, epistemic trust and the developmental significance of social communication. *Borderline Personality Disorder and Emotion Dysregulation, 4*, 9. doi:10.1186/s40479-017-0062-8

Fonagy, P., Luyten, P., & Bateman, A. (2015). Translation: Mentalizing as treatment target in borderline personality disorder. *Personality Disorders, 6*(4), 380–392. doi:10.1037/per0000113

Fonagy, P., Steele, M., Steele, H., & Target, M. (1997). *Reflective-Functioning Manual* (*Version 4.1*). Unpublished Manual. London: University College London.

Frith, C.D., & Frith, U. (1999). Interacting minds—A biological basis. *Science, 286*(5445), 1692–1695.

Gambin, M., Gambin, T., & Sharp, C. (2015). Social cognition, psychopathological symptoms, and family functioning in a sample of inpatient adolescents using variable-centered and person-centered approaches. *Journal of Adolescence, 45*, 31–43. doi:10.1016/j.adolescence.2015.08.010

George, C., Kaplan, N., & Main, M. (1984). *The Adult Attachment Interview. Unpublished. Protocol* (3rd Edition). Berkeley, CA: Department of Psychology, University of California at Berkeley.

Gopnik, A., O'Grady, S., Lucas, C.G., Griffiths, T.L., Wente, A., Bridgers, S., ... & Dahl, R.E. (2017). Changes in cognitive flexibility and hypothesis search across human life history from childhood to adolescence to adulthood. *Proceedings of the National Academy of Sciences of the United States of America, 114*(30), 7892–7899. doi:10.1073/pnas.1700811114

Gore, F.M., Bloem, P.J.N., Patton, G.C., Ferguson, J., Joseph, V., Coffey, C., ... & Mathers, C.D. (2011). Global burden of disease in young people aged 10–24 years: A systematic analysis. *The Lancet, 377*(9783), 2093–2102. doi:10.1016/S0140-6736(11)60512-6

Ha, C., Sharp, C., Ensink, K., Fonagy, P., & Cirino, P. (2013). The measurement of reflective function in adolescents with and without borderline traits. *Journal of Adolescence, 36*(6), 1215–1223. doi:10.1016/j.adolescence.2013.09.008

Happé, F.G.E., & Frith, U. (1996). Theory of mind and social impairment in children with conduct disorder. *British Journal of Developmental Psychology, 14*(4), 385–398.

Hauser, T.U., Iannaccone, R., Walitza, S., Brandeis, D., & Brem, S. (2015). Cognitive flexibility in adolescence: Neural and behavioral mechanisms of reward prediction error processing in adaptive decision making during development. *NeuroImage, 104*, 347–354. doi:10.1016/j.neuroimage.2014.09.018

Hünefeldt, T., Laghi, F., Ortu, F., & Belardinelli, M.O. (2013). The relationship between 'theory of mind' and attachment-related anxiety and avoidance in Italian adolescents. *Journal of Adolescence, 36*(3), 613–621. doi:10.1016/j.adolescence.2013.03.012

Kessler, R.C., Demler, O., Frank, R.G., Olfson, M., Pincus, H.A., Walters, E.E., ... & Zaslavsky, A.M. (2005). Prevalence and treatment of mental disorders, 1990 to 2003. *New England Journal of Medicine, 352*(24), 2515–2523. doi:10.1056/NEJMsa043266

Langdon, R. (2005). Theory of mind in schizophrenia. In B.F. Malle & S.D. Hodges (Eds.), *Other Minds: How Humans Bridge the Divide between Self and Others* (pp. 333–342). London: Guilford Press.

Langdon, R., Ward, P.B., & Coltheart, M. (2010). Reasoning anomalies associated with delusions in schizophrenia. *Schizophrenia Bulletin, 26*, 321–330.

Lahey, B.B., Rathouz, P.J., Keenan, K., Stepp, S.D., Loeber, R., & Hipwell, A.E. (2015). Criterion validity of the general factor of psychopathology in a prospective study of girls. *Journal of Child Psychology and Psychiatry, and Allied Disciplines, 56*(4), 415–422.

Li, D., Li, X., Yu, F., Chen, X., Zhang, L., Li, D., ... & Wang, K. (2017). Comparing the ability of cognitive and affective theory of mind in adolescent onset schizophrenia. *Neuropsychiatric Disease and Treatment, 13*, 937–945. doi:10.2147/NDT.S128116

Meins, E., Fernyhough, C., Johnson, F., & Lidstone, J. (2006). Mind-mindedness in children: Individual differences in internal-state talk in middle childhood. *British Journal of Developmental Psychology, 24*(1), 181–196. doi:10.1348/026151005X80174

Mellick, W., & Sharp, C. (2016). Mental state decoding in adolescent boys with major depressive disorder versus sex-matched healthy controls. *Psychopathology, 49*(1), 53–59. doi:10.1159/000443989

Mellick, W., Sharp, C., & Sumlin, E. (2019). Trust and general risk-taking in externalizing adolescent inpatients versus non-externalizing psychiatric controls. *Scandinavian Journal of Child and Adolescent Psychiatry and Psychology*, 7, 92–96.

Mellick, W., Vanwoerden, S., & Sharp, C. (2017). Experiential avoidance in the vulnerability to depression among adolescent females. *Journal of Affective Disorders, 208*, 497–502. doi:10.1016/j.jad.2016.10.034

Merikangas, K.R., He, J.P., Burstein, M., Swanson, S.A., Avenevoli, S., Cui, L., ... & Swendsen, J. (2010). Lifetime prevalence of mental disorders in U.S. adolescents: Results from the National Comorbidity Survey Replication—Adolescent Supplement (NCS-A). *Journal of the American Academy of Child and Adolescent Psychiatry, 49*(10), 980–989.

Morandotti, N., Brondino, N., Merelli, A., Boldrini, A., De Vidovich, G.Z., Ricciardo, S., ... & Luyten, P. (2018). The Italian version of the reflective functioning questionnaire: Validity data for adults and its association with severity of borderline personality disorder. *PLOS ONE, 13*(11), e0206433. doi:10.1371/journal.pone.0206433

Nelson, E.E., Leibenluft, E., McClure, E.B., & Pine, D.S. (2005). The social re-orientation of adolescence: A neuroscience perspective on the process and its relation to psychopathology. *Psychological Medicine, 35*(2), 163–174. doi:10.1017/s0033291704003915

Nikolić, M., van der Storm, L., Colonnesi, C., Brummelman, E., Kan, K.J., & Bögels, S. (2019). Are socially anxious children poor or advanced mindreaders? *Child Development, 90*(4), 1424–1441. doi:10.1111/cdev.13248

O'Connor, T.G., & Hirsch, N. (1999). Intra-individual differences and relationship-specificity of mentalising in early adolescence. *Social Development, 8*(2), 256–274.

Oitzl, M.S., Workel, J.O., Fluttert, M., Frösch, F., & De Kloet, E.R. (2000). Maternal deprivation affects behaviour from youth to senescence: Amplification of individual differences in spatial learning and memory in senescent Brown Norway rats. *European Journal of Neuroscience, 12*(10), 3771–3780.

Perner, J., & Wimmer, H. (1985). "John thinks that Mary thinks that…" attribution of second-order beliefs by 5- to 10-year-old children. *Journal of Experimental Child Psychology, 39*(3), 437–471 http://www.academicpress com/jecp

Premack, D., & Woodruff, G. (1978). Does the chimpanzee have a theory of mind? *Behavioral and Brain Sciences*, 1(4), 515–526.

Riva Crugnola, C., Ierardi, E., & Canevini, M.P. (2018). Reflective functioning, maternal attachment, mind-mindedness, and emotional availability in adolescent and adult mothers at infant 3 months. *Attachment and Human Development, 20*(1), 84–106.

Rosenblum, K.L., McDonough, S.C., Sameroff, A.J., & Muzik, M. (2008). Reflection in thought and action: Maternal parenting reflectivity predicts mind-minded comments and interactive behavior. *Infant Mental Health Journal, 29*(4), 362–376. doi:10.1002/imhj.20184

Rothschild-Yakar, L., Stein, D., Goshen, D., Shoval, G., Yacobi, A., Eger, G., ... & Gur, E. (2019). Mentalizing self and other and affect regulation patterns in anorexia and depression. *Frontiers in Psychology, 10*, 2223. doi:10.3389/fpsyg.2019.02223

Shai, D., & Meins, E. (2018). Parental embodied mentalizing and its relation to mind-mindedness, sensitivity, and attachment security. *Infancy, 23*(6), 857–872. doi:10.1111/infa.12244

Sharp, C. (2000). *Biased Minds: Theory of Mind and Emotional-Behavior Disorders of Middle Childhood.* Unpublished Ph.D. University of Cambridge.

Sharp, C. (2006). Mentalizing problems in childhood disorders. In J.G. Allen & P. Fonagy (Eds.), *Handbook of Mentalization-Based Treatments* (pp. 101–121). Chichester: John Wiley & Sons.

Sharp, C. (2008). Theory of mind and conduct problems in children: Deficits in reading the "emotions of the eyes". *Cognition and Emotion, 22*(6), 1149–1158. doi:10.1080/02699930701667586

Sharp, C. (2015). *Hypermentalizing in adolescent BPD compared to psychiatry and healthy controls: Introducing a new measure.* Paper presented at the Annual Meeting of the American Psychiatric Association, Montreal.

Sharp, C., Burton, P.C., & Ha, C. (2011). "Better the devil you know": A preliminary study of the differential modulating effects of reputation on reward processing for boys with and without externalizing behaviour problems. *European Child and Adolescent Psychiatry, 20*(11–12), 581–592. doi:10.1007/s00787-011-0225-x

Sharp, C., Croudace, T.J., & Goodyer, I.M. (2007). Biased mentalising in children aged 7–11: Latent class confirmation of response styles to social scenarios and associations with psychopathology. *Social Development, 16*(1), 81–202.

Sharp, C., & Fonagy, P. (2008a). Social cognition and attachment-related disorders. In C. Sharp, P. Fonagy, & I.M. Goodyer (Eds.), *Social Cognition and Developmental Psychopathology* (pp. 271–304). Oxford: Oxford University Press.

Sharp, C., & Fonagy, P. (2008b). The parent's capacity to treat the child as a psychological agent: Constructs, measures and implications for developmental psychopathology. *Social Development, 17*(3), 737–754.

Sharp, C., Fonagy, P., & Goodyer, I.M. (2006). Imagining your child's mind: Psychosocial adjustment and mothers' ability to predict their children's attributional response styles. *British Journal of Developmental Psychology, 24*(1), 197–214.

Sharp, C., Fonagy, P., & Goodyer, I.M. (2008). *Social Cognition and Developmental Psychopathology*. Oxford: Oxford University Press.

Sharp, C., Ha, C., Carbone, C., Kim, S., Perry, K., Williams, L., & Fonagy, P. (2013). Hypermentalizing in adolescent inpatients: Treatment effects and association with borderline traits. *Journal of Personality Disorders*, *27*(1), 3–18. doi:10.1521/pedi.2013.27.1.3

Sharp, C., Ha, C., & Fonagy, P. (2011). Get them before they get you: Trust, trustworthiness, and social cognition in boys with and without externalizing behavior problems. *Development and Psychopathology*, *23*(2), 647–658. doi:10.1017/S0954579410000003

Sharp, C., Kerr, S., & Chanen, A. (under review). Prevention and early identification and prevention of personality pathology: An AMPD informed model of clinical staging. In *The American Psychiatric Publishing Textbook of Personality Disorders*. Washington: APA.

Sharp, C., Pane, H., Ha, C., Venta, A., Patel, A.B., Sturek, J., & Fonagy, P. (2011). Theory of mind and emotion regulation difficulties in adolescents with borderline traits. *Journal of the American Academy of Child and Adolescent Psychiatry*, *50*(6), 563–573.e1. doi:10.1016/j.jaac.2011.01.017

Sharp, C., & Vanwoerden, S. (2015). Hypermentalizing in borderline personality disorder: A model and data. *Journal of Infant, Child, and Adolescent Psychotherapy*, *14*(1), 33–45. doi:10.1080/15289168.2015.1004890

Sharp, C., & Venta, A. (2012). Mentalizing problems in children and adolescents. In N. Midgley & I. Vrouva (Eds.), *Minding the Child: Mentalization-Based Interventions with Children, Young People and Their Families* (pp. 35–53). London: Routledge.

Sharp, C., & Wall, K. (2018). Personality pathology grows up: Adolescence as a sensitive period. *Current Opinion in Psychology*, *21*, 111–116. doi:10.1016/j.copsyc.2017.11.010

Shmueli-Goetz, Y., Target, M., Fonagy, P., & Datta, A. (2008). The child attachment interview: A psychometric study of reliability and discriminant validity. *Developmental Psychology*, *44*(4), 939–956.

Smeets, T., Dziobek, I., & Wolf, O.T. (2009). Social cognition under stress: Differential effects of stress-induced cortisol elevations in healthy young men and women. *Hormones and Behavior*. doi:10.1016/j.yhbeh.2009.01.011

Stellwagen, K.K., & Kerig, P.K. (2013). Ringleader bullying: Association with psychopathic narcissism and theory of mind among child psychiatric inpatients. *Child Psychiatry and Human Development*, *44*(5), 612–620. doi:10.1007/s10578-012-0355-5

Sutton, J., Smith, P.K., & Swettenham, J. (1999). Social cognition and bullying: Social inadequacy or skilled manipulation? *British Journal of Developmental Psychology*, *17*(3), 435–450.

Taubner, S., White, L.O., Zimmermann, J., Fonagy, P., & Nolte, T. (2013). Attachment-related mentalization moderates the relationship between psychopathic traits and proactive aggression in adolescence. *Journal of Abnormal Child Psychology*, *41*(6), 929–938. doi:10.1007/s10802-013-9736-x

van den Bos, W., Cohen, M.X., Kahnt, T., & Crone, E.A. (2012). Striatum-medial prefrontal cortex connectivity predicts developmental changes in reinforcement learning. *Cerebral Cortex*, *22*(6), 1247–1255. doi:10.1093/cercor/bhr198

Vanwoerden, S., Greiner, I., Ensink, K., & Sharp, C. (2019). The relations between self- and caregiver- focused reflective function and theory of mind in the context of borderline pathology in adolescence. *Psychiatry Research*, *273*, 274–280. doi:10.1016/j.psychres.2019.01.042

Vetter, N.C., Altgassen, M., Phillips, L., Mahy, C.E., & Kliegel, M. (2013). Development of affective theory of mind across adolescence: Disentangling the role of executive functions. *Developmental Neuropsychology*, *38*(2), 114–125. doi:10.1080/87565641.2012.733786

Weil, L.G., Fleming, S.M., Dumontheil, I., Kilford, E.J., Weil, R.S., Rees, G., ... & Blakemore, S.J. (2013). The development of metacognitive ability in adolescence. *Consciousness and Cognition*, *22*(1), 264–271. doi:10.1016/j.concog.2013.01.004

Zanarini, M.C. (2000). Childhood experiences associated with the development of borderline personality disorder. *Psychiatric Clinics of North America*, *23*(1), 89–101.

Zanarini, M.C., Gunderson, J.G., Marino, M.F., Schwartz, E.O., & Frankenburg, F.R. (1989). Childhood experiences of borderline patients. *Comprehensive Psychiatry*, *30*(1), 18–25.

Conclusions and future directions

Integrating multiple perspectives

Serena Lecce and Rory T. Devine

The aim of the current volume was to examine how the neural, cognitive, psychological, and social changes of middle childhood and adolescence shape the ongoing development of theory of mind and how theory of mind, in turn, helps children to navigate life during this period of development. Furthermore, in extending the developmental scope of research on theory of mind beyond early childhood, the current volume provided an opportunity to scrutinize existing theoretical accounts of theory of mind and consider new alternatives. The preceding chapters highlight multiple perspectives on theory of mind in middle childhood and adolescence. Rather than recapitulating each contribution, we conclude this volume by attempting to integrate these perspectives by highlighting emerging themes and identifying new directions for future research.

Concepts and measurement

Overall, the studies cited in the preceding chapters provide considerable evidence for both age-related differences and developmental change on a range of theory of mind measures in middle childhood and adolescence (e.g., Apperly et al., 2011; Devine & Hughes, 2013; Dumontheil et al., 2010; Lagattuta et al., 2016; Osterhaus et al., 2016; Peterson & Wellman, 2019). These developmental changes appear to be, at least in part, independent of other variables such as family socioeconomic status, verbal ability, and executive functions. The preceding chapters highlight how ongoing development in theory of mind in middle childhood and adolescence has given rise to differing perspectives on how theory of mind development is conceptualized. One possibility is that ongoing theory of mind development signals the emergence of new insights about the nature of mental states, the links between them, and relations with future behaviors (Chapter 1; Chapter 10). This 'competence' account seeks to identify universal changes that occur in middle childhood and adolescence and expands on prior research on the developmental scaling of various theory of mind tasks (e.g., Wellman & Liu, 2004; Osterhaus et al., 2016). A second possibility is that developments in theory of mind in middle childhood and adolescence do not necessarily entail any new or advanced insights about the mind. Instead, theory of mind development represents an increasing capacity to use mindreading in a way that is flexible, rapid, and appropriate to the context (Chapter 2; Chapter 3; Chapter 9). According to this account, changes in middle childhood and adolescence reflect in part an increasing ability to inhibit egocentric biases (Chapter 2) and/or underlying neural changes in functional connectivity and selectivity (Chapter 4). These two perspectives on what develops are not incompatible and, arguably, tackle distinct but equally important questions about theory of mind. Understanding the emergence of new concepts or insights about others' minds can illuminate what is common across all children and provide a benchmark against which to evaluate children's development. Research focused on theory of mind use, on the other hand, can provide greater understanding of the role of individual differences in mindreading in children's lives.

In terms of measurement, the preceding chapters highlight a wide variety of measures used to investigate theory of mind in middle childhood and adolescence. These include carefully designed experimental tasks intended to isolate distinct processes involved in reasoning about others' minds (e.g., Chapter 1; Chapter 10) and more open-ended tasks designed to capture individual differences in the propensity to explain others' actions with reference to mental states (e.g., Chapter 8; Chapter 11). The measurement of mindreading in middle childhood and adolescence will inevitably draw on increasingly complex social scenarios where there may not be a straightforward 'correct' way to interpret others' minds (like in the class false belief task). It is possible that what becomes relevant during this period is not being correct but, rather, not being incorrect. This underscores the need for future work to consider the 'errors' that children make in mindreading beyond 'failing' to impute a mental state to another individual (Chapter 11). Although the wide range of measures available to study theory of mind in middle childhood and adolescence can create challenges for integrating research findings (e.g., Rice-Warnell et al., 2019), the diversity of measures can be viewed as an asset to the field if these measures are recognized as serving different purposes. The lack of a 'hegemonic' measure, equivalent in status to the false belief task in early childhood research, does not necessarily represent a shortcoming in the field. The standard version of the false belief task is unsuitable for capturing developmental change or individual differences in middle childhood and adolescence but can be modified to examine underlying cognitive and neural processes in belief reasoning in this developmental period (Chapter 2, Chapter 4). Problems may arise if tasks are used inappropriately (e.g., using a developmentally sensitive measure to study individual differences). Instead, different measures may be more or less suited to different research questions. Researchers must carefully consider the rationale for choosing a specific measure (e.g., is the aim to investigate development change or individual differences?) and the properties of that measure (e.g., is the measure sensitive to between-group differences or within-group individual differences?) (Chapter 3).

New opportunities and future directions

The extension of research on theory of mind into middle childhood and adolescence has given (and will continue to give) researchers the opportunity to address a variety of new issues and poses a set of new questions. Extending the scope of research on theory of mind beyond a limited age range in the preschool years into middle childhood and adolescence has already (and will continue to) provided researchers with new opportunities. The chapters in this collection highlight how research on theory of mind in middle childhood and adolescence provides three opportunities for future research: (1) To refine and extend theoretical accounts of mindreading; (2) to harness the social milieu of middle childhood and adolescence; and (3) to embrace diversity.

Refining and extending theoretical accounts

The focus on a narrow age range limits theoretical progress in at least three ways. First, it is clear that theory of mind development does not reach maturity with the attainment of false belief understanding (e.g., Apperly et al., 2009). Continued research in middle childhood and adolescence will provide the opportunity to examine the emergence of new concepts or insights about others' minds and the mastery of existing abilities bridging the gap between early childhood and adulthood (Chapter 1; Chapter 2). Second, focusing on a limited age range precludes the possibility of examining the cognitive and neural mechanisms underlying theory of mind after its initial emergence (Chapter 2; Chapter 4). Different strategies might be involved in solving basic and 'advanced' mindreading tasks and some factors might be important for the emergence of theory of mind in the preschool years but not its continued development or vice versa. For instance, it is not clear whether language continues to have the same role in the development of advanced forms of theory of mind that it has in the emergence of false belief understanding (Milligan et al., 2007). Studies investigating the relative contribution of executive function and language ability to the continued development and use of theory of mind in middle childhood and adolescence will provide a more complete understanding of mindreading that is not focused solely on the initial emergence of theory of mind. Third, studying theory of mind in a wider age range permits greater interrogation of apparent individual differences in theory of mind. Numerous studies demonstrate that among school-aged children and adolescents, there are striking individual differences in performance across a wide range of tasks purporting to measure theory of mind (Chapter 3; Chapter 9). Extending longitudinal studies, for example, will provide crucial insights into whether individual differences in theory of mind are stable and meaningful.

The social milieu of middle childhood and adolescence

In addition to ongoing research on the role of family life in children's development in theory of mind, extending research into middle childhood and adolescence provides exciting possibilities to examine peer and teacher influences on children's mindreading and the consequences of mindreading for children's social and academic success. Early family experiences play an important role in the emergence of children's understanding of others' minds (e.g., Devine & Hughes, 2018). Family life undoubtedly continues to influence children's mindreading development in middle childhood and adolescence but the nature and quality of family interactions change with progress into middle childhood and adolescence (Chapter 5). While early parent–child conversation about minds casts a long shadow (e.g., Ensor et al., 2014) it is unclear whether parent–child talk contributes to further growth in mindreading in middle childhood and adolescence. Future work will illuminate the ways in which the dynamics of family interactions contribute to theory of mind beyond early childhood.

Middle childhood and adolescence are associated with several key social milestones including the transition to school, a growing reliance on peers, and the gradual transition to the workplace (OECD, 2018; Larson & Richards, 1991; Larson et al., 1996). The chapters contained in this collection show the consequences of theory of mind for children's success at school both academically (Chapter 8) and socially (Chapter 6; Chapter 7) and lay a foundation for future work investigating both the influence of peers and teachers on the continued growth of theory of mind and the consequences of theory of mind for social and academic success in adolescence. The social milieu of middle childhood and adolescence provides a ripe opportunity to test the limits of social accounts of theory of mind. The chapters in this volume underscore the need to adopt complex models when looking at the academic and social correlates of theory of mind. Theory of mind is a skill that children and adolescents do not necessarily or immediately put into use. Instead, theory of mind is a 'tool' that can be used or not, depending on a number of factors: Motivational, emotional, contextual, and cognitive (Chapter 7; Chapter 8; Chapter 9). Theory of mind may also allow children and adolescents to benefit from learning experiences through developing more advanced forms of behavior (e.g., prosocial behaviors, communication) and of cognition (e.g., metacognition, beliefs about learning) that, in turn, have beneficial effects on children's social and cognitive outcomes (Chapter 8).

Embracing diversity

The preceding chapters highlight the continued importance of research involving diverse samples of children and adolescents. Studies conducted in the context of neurodiversity, disability, and youth mental health provide insights into the underlying nature of theory of mind in middle childhood and adolescence as well as the origins and social consequences of theory of mind (Chapter 9; Chapter 10; Chapter 11). For example, in reassessing longstanding accounts of autism (such as 'mindblindness' theory), work with school-aged children and adolescents with autism highlights how motivational factors may contribute to theory of mind use (Chapter 9). Research with deaf school-aged children and adolescents provides clues about both the long-term effect of early family interactions and the potential influence of the school context on children's theory of mind (Chapter 10). Likewise, research in middle childhood and adolescence indicates that mindreading difficulties cross-cut traditional mental health conditions and may explain the adverse social outcomes associated with psychopathology among school-aged children (Chapter 11).

Despite these obvious inroads, the chapters in this collection highlight one key shortcoming of the existing literature on theory of mind in middle childhood and adolescence. Research on theory of mind in early childhood has a long tradition of cross-cultural research (e.g., Perez-Zapata & Slaughter, 2014). With some exceptions (e.g., Dixson et al., 2018; Lim et al., 2020; Wang et al., 2016) much of the existing work on theory of mind in middle childhood and adolescence has originated from Europe, North America, and Australia. Cross-cultural work has been instrumental in testing the universality of theoretical accounts of theory of mind (e.g., Liu et al., 2008) and examining the social influences on and consequences of theory of mind (e.g., Hughes et al., 2018). There is an urgent need to examine mindreading in middle childhood and adolescence beyond so-called 'WEIRD' (Western, Educated, Industrialized, Rich, and Democratic) nations (Henrich et al., 2010).

The chapters in this volume attest to the emergence of a vibrant new line of inquiry in research on theory of mind. The field has made considerable progress in the past decade underscoring the importance of extending research on theory of mind beyond early childhood. Research on theory of mind in middle childhood and adolescence is providing a fresh perspective on long-standing theoretical accounts of theory of mind but, crucially, is generating new ideas about the development and use of theory of mind.

References

Apperly, I.A., Samson, D. & Humphreys, G. (2009). Studies of adults can inform accounts of theory of mind development. *Developmental Psychology*, 45, 190–201.

Apperly, I.A., Warren, F., Andrews, B.J., Grant, J., & Todd, S. (2011). Developmental continuity in theory of mind: Speed and accuracy of belief-desire reasoning in children and adults. *Child Development*, *82*(5), 1691–1703. https://doi.org/10.1111/j.1467-8624.2011.01635.x

Devine, R.T., & Hughes, C. (2013). Silent films and strange stories: Theory of mind, gender, and social experiences in middle childhood. *Child Development*, *84*(3), 989–1003. https://doi.org/10.1111/cdev.12017

Devine, R.T., & Hughes, C. (2018). Family correlates of false belief understanding in early childhood: A meta-analysis. *Child Development*, *89*(3), 971–987. https://doi.org/10.1111/cdev.12682

Dixson, H.G.W., Komugabe-Dixson, A.F., Dixson, B.J., & Low, J. (2018). Scaling theory of mind in a small-scale society: A case study from Vanuatu. *Child Development*, *89*(6), 2157–2175. https://doi.org/10.1111/cdev.12919

Dumontheil, I., Apperly, I.A., & Blakemore, S. (2010). Online usage of theory of mind continues to develop in late adolescence. *Developmental Science, 13*(2), 331–338

Ensor, R., Devine, R.T., Marks, A., & Hughes, C. (2014). Mothers' cognitive references to 2-year-olds predict theory of mind at ages 6 and 10. *Child Development, 85*(3), 1222–1235. https://doi.org/10.1111/cdev.12186

Henrich, J., Heine, S.J., & Norenzayan, A. (2010). The weirdest people in the world? *Behavioral and Brain Sciences, 33*(2–3), 61–83. https://doi.org/10.1017/S0140525X0999152X

Hughes, C., Devine, R.T., & Wang, Z. (2018). Does parental mind-mindedness account for cross-cultural differences in preschoolers' theory of mind? *Child Development, 89*(4), 1296–1310. https://doi.org/10.1111/cdev.12746

Lagattuta, K.H., Elrod, N.M., & Kramer, H.J. (2016). How do thoughts, emotions, and decisions align? A new way to examine theory of mind during middle childhood and beyond. *Journal of Experimental Child Psychology, 149*, 116–133. https://doi.org/10.1016/j.jecp.2016.01.013

Larson, R., & Richards, M.H. (1991). Daily companionship in late childhood and early adolescence: Changing developmental contexts. *Child Development, 62*(2), 284–300

Larson, R.W., Richards, M.H., Moneta, G., Holmbeck, G., & Duckett, E. (1996). Changes in adolescents' daily interactions with their families from ages 10 to 18: Disengagement and transformation. *Developmental Psychology, 32*(4), 744–754

Lim, J., Peterson, C.C., De Rosnay, M., & Slaughter, V. (2020).). Children's moral evaluations of prosocial and self-interested lying in relation to age, ToM, cognitive empathy and culture. *European Journal of Developmental Psychology, 17*(4), 504–526

Liu, D., Wellman, H.M., Tardif, T., & Sabbagh, M.A. (2008). Theory of mind development in Chinese children: A meta-analysis of false-belief understanding across cultures and languages. *Developmental Psychology, 44*(2), 523–531

Milligan, K., Astington, J.W., & Dack, L.A. (2007). Language and theory of mind: Meta-analysis of the relation between language ability and false-belief understanding. *Child Development, 78*(2), 622–646

OECD. (2018). *Education at a Glance: OECD Indicators*. Paris: OECD Publishing. https://doi.org/10.1787/eag-2018-en

Osterhaus, C., Koerber, S., & Sodian, B. (2016). Scaling of advanced theory-of-mind tasks. *Child Development, 87*(6), 1971–1991. https://doi.org/10.1111/cdev.12566

Peterson, C., & Wellman, H.M. (2019). Longitudinal theory of mind (ToM) development from preschool to adolescence with and without ToM delay. *Child Development, 90*(6), 1917–1934. https://doi.org/10.1111/cdev.13064

Slaughter, V., & Perez-Zapata, D. (2014). Cultural variations in the development of mind reading. *Child Development Perspectives, 8*(4), 237–241. https://doi.org/10.1111/cdep.12091

Warnell, K.R., & Redcay, E. (2019). Minimal coherence among varied theory of mind measures in childhood and adulthood. *Cognition, 191*. http://www.ncbi.nlm.nih.gov/pubmed/103997

Wang, Z., Devine, R.T., Wong, K.K., & Hughes, C. (2016). Theory of mind and executive function during middle childhood across cultures. *Journal of Experimental Child Psychology, 149*, 6–22

Wellman, H.M., & Liu, D. (2004). Scaling of theory-of-mind tasks. *Child Development, 75*(2), 523–541.

Index

Page numbers in **bold** denote tables, those in *italic* denote figures.